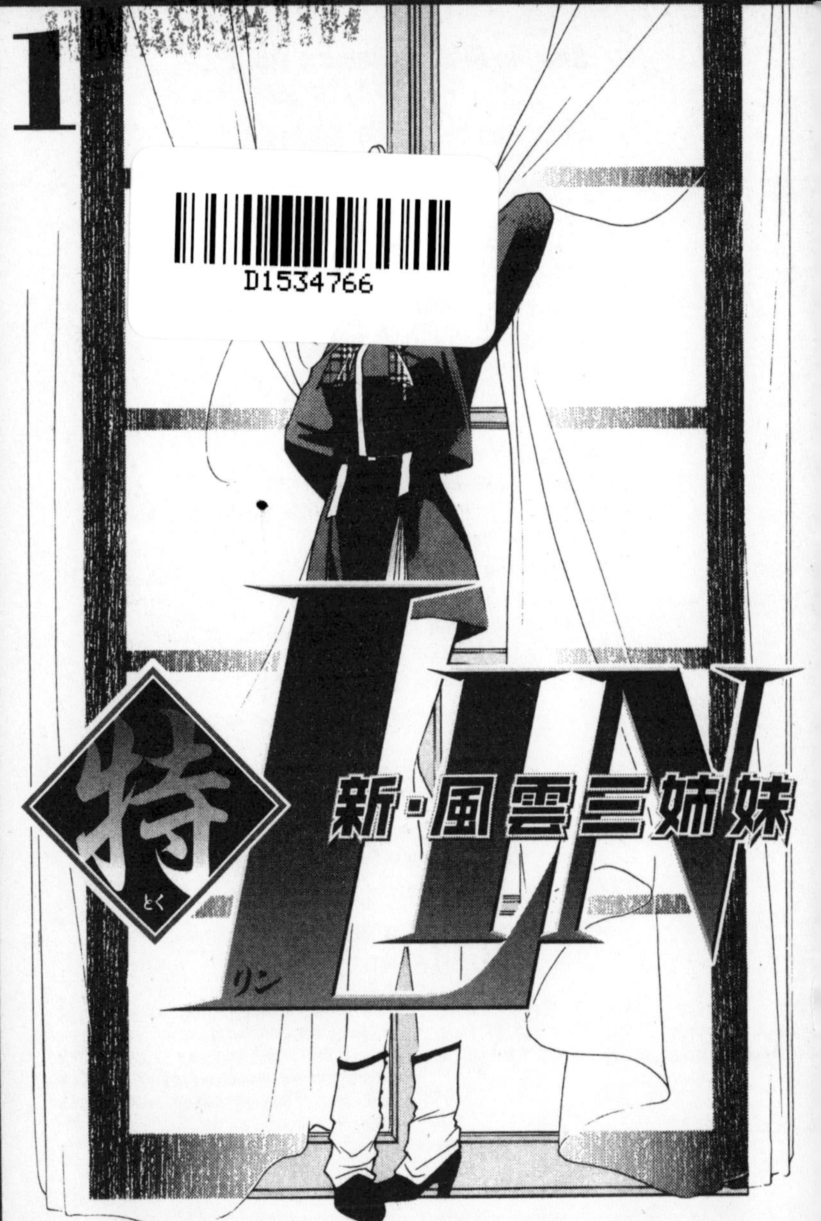
1
特
とく
LIN
リン
新·風雲三姉妹


垣野内成美　原作　平野俊貴

# Shaolin Sisters: Reborn Vol. 1
## Written by Toshiki Hirano
## Illustrated by Narumi Kakinouchi

Translation - Alethea Nibley
English Adaptation - Aaron Sparrow
Copy Editor - Suzanne Waldman
Retouch and Lettering - Benchcomix
Production Artist - Jason Milligan
Cover Design - S. R. Cable

Editor - Tim Beedle
Digital Imaging Manager - Chris Buford
Pre-Press Manager - Antonio DePietro
Production Managers - Jennifer Miller and Mutsumi Miyazaki
Art Director - Matt Alford
Managing Editor - Jill Freshney
Editor in Chief - Mike Kiley
VP of Production - Ron Klamert
President and C.O.O. - John Parker
Publisher and C.E.O. - Stuart Levy

A  Manga

TOKYOPOP Inc.
5900 Wilshire Blvd. Suite 2000
Los Angeles, CA 90036

E-mail: info@TOKYOPOP.com
Come visit us online at www.TOKYOPOP.com

ISBN: 1-59532-507-7

First TOKYOPOP printing: May 2005
10 9 8 7 6 5 4 3 2 1
Printed in Canada

# 鈴 SHAOLIN SISTERS REBORN

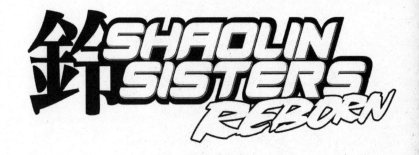

## Volume 1

by
Toshiki Hirano
&
Narumi Kakinouchi

TOKYOPOP®

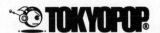

HAMBURG // LONDON // LOS ANGELES // TOKYO

# WHAT CAME BEFORE...

IT WAS AN AGE WHEN MARTIAL ARTISTS RULED THE LAND. JULIN KENGA, WHO LOST HER MASTER IN AN ATTACK BY THE WHITE QUEEN BAI WANG OF THE WHITE LOTUS CLAN, SET OUT ON A JOURNEY TO FIND HER TWO SISTERS, KNOWN ONLY TO POSSESS BELLS SUCH AS HERS, AND HER FATHER, WHOM SHE HAD NEVER MET. REPELLING FREQUENT ATTACKS FROM THE WHITE LOTUS CLAN, JULIN, AT LONG LAST, WAS REUNITED WITH HER TWO SISTERS: SEILIN, THE ELDEST, AND KALIN, THE MIDDLE CHILD. BUT WHEN THE SISTERS' THREE BELLS ARE BROUGHT TOGETHER, THE SOULS OF THE ANCIENTS, WHO HAD PLAGUED MANKIND IN ANCIENT TIMES, ARE REVIVED. A BLOODY BATTLE BETWEEN THE THREE SISTERS, THE WHITE LOTUS CLAN AND THE ANCIENTS AROSE OVER THE BELLS, DURING WHICH THE THREE SISTERS DISCOVERED THAT BAI WANG WAS ACTUALLY THEIR FATHER, RYU. MADE UNRECOGNIZABLE BY HIS TRANSFORMATION, BAI WANG OBTAINED THE POWER OF THE ANCIENTS, PUTTING ALL OF CREATION IN GRAVE DANGER. USING THE POWER OF THE BELLS, THE SISTERS MADE THEIR HEARTS AS ONE TO OPPOSE THEIR MISGUIDED FATHER. ENVELOPED IN A DAZZLING LIGHT, JULIN, KALIN, SEILIN, BAI WANG AND EVEN THE MASSIVE LI FENG PEAK ALL VANISHED. BUT WAS THEIR EPIC STRUGGLE OVER?

IT APPEARS THAT ETERNAL REST HAS NOT YET ARRIVED FOR OUR HEROINES. FOR NOW, MANY CENTURIES LATER, THE SISTERS' NEW BATTLE IS ABOUT TO BEGIN...

 **CONTENTS**

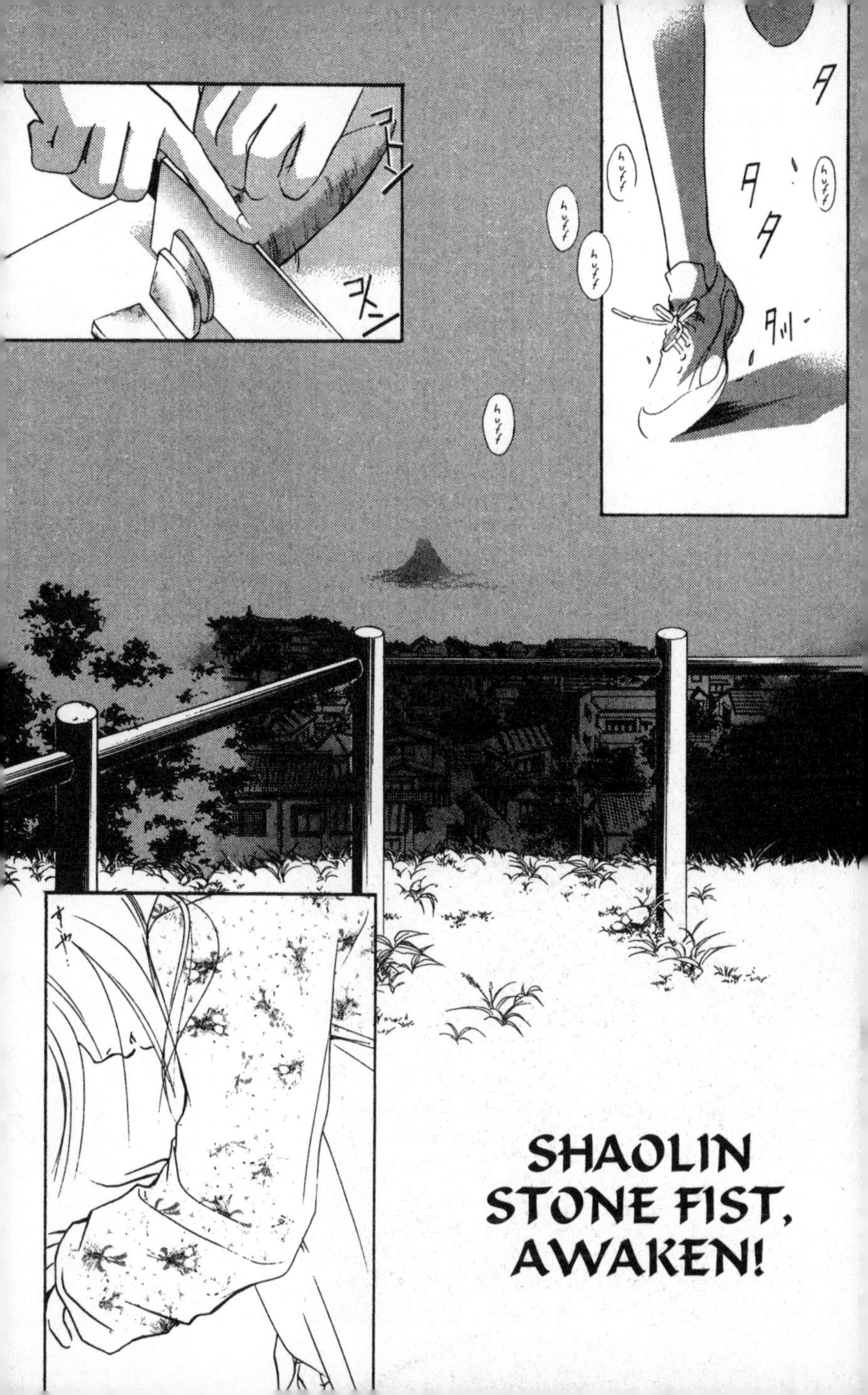

タ
タ
タ
タッ
コトン
コトン
SHAOLIN STONE FIST, AWAKEN!

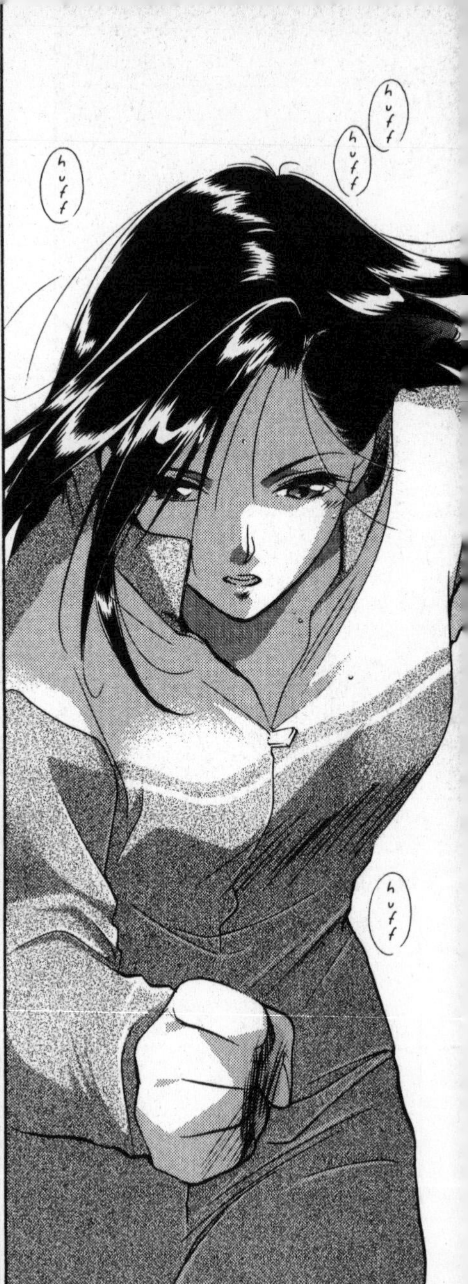
huff
huff
huff
huff
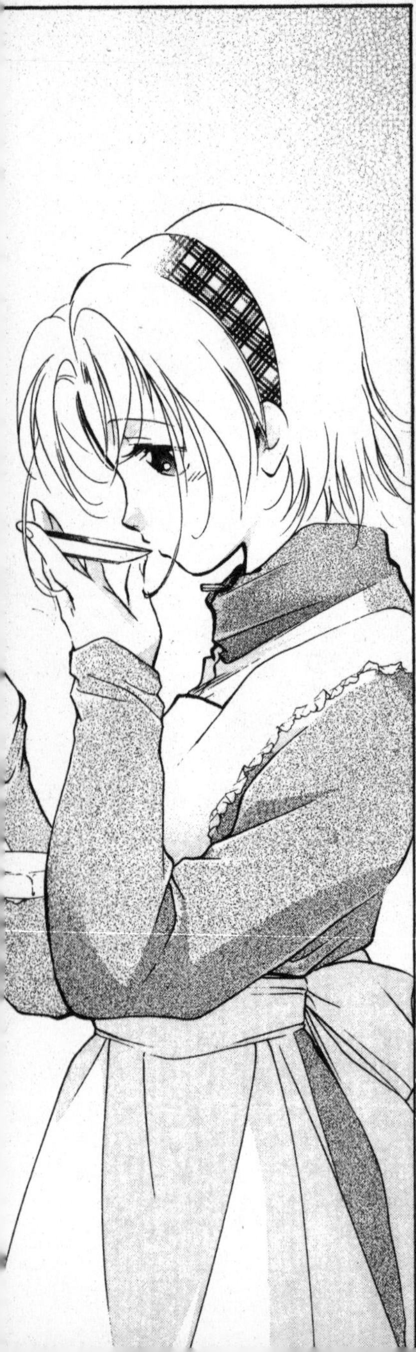

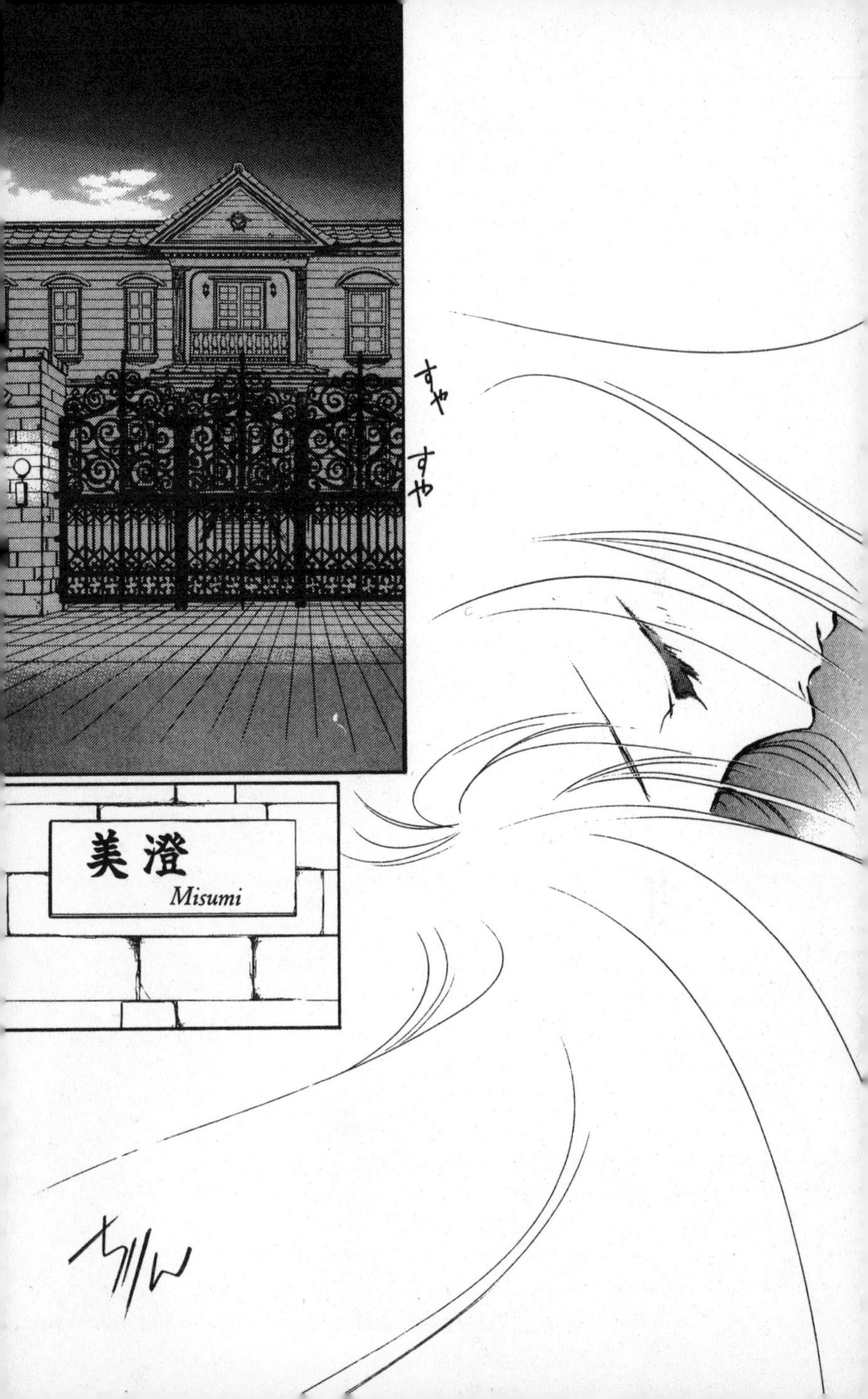
すや すや
美澄
Misumi
ちりん

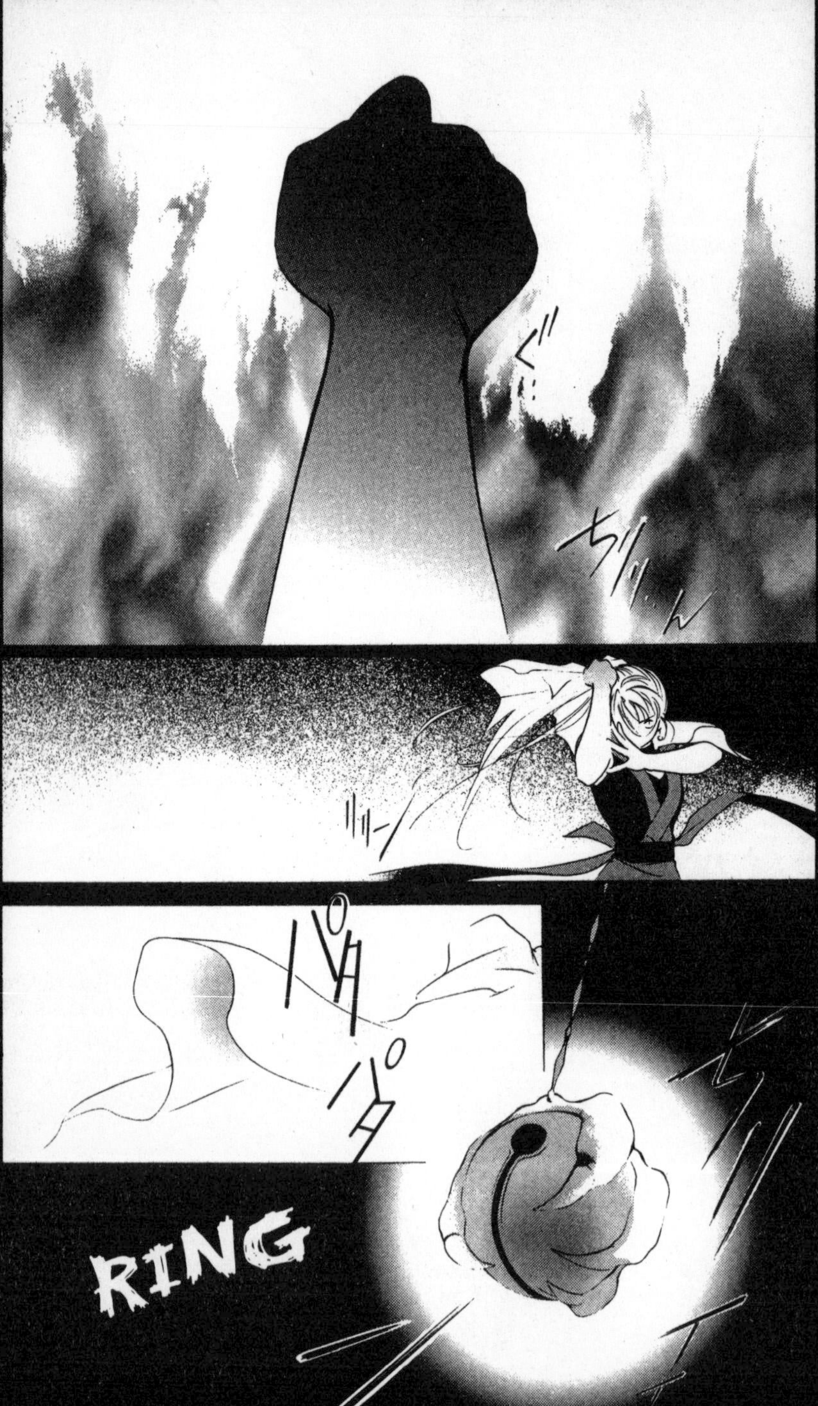
ぐ…
ちりりん
リィー
パタパタ
RING

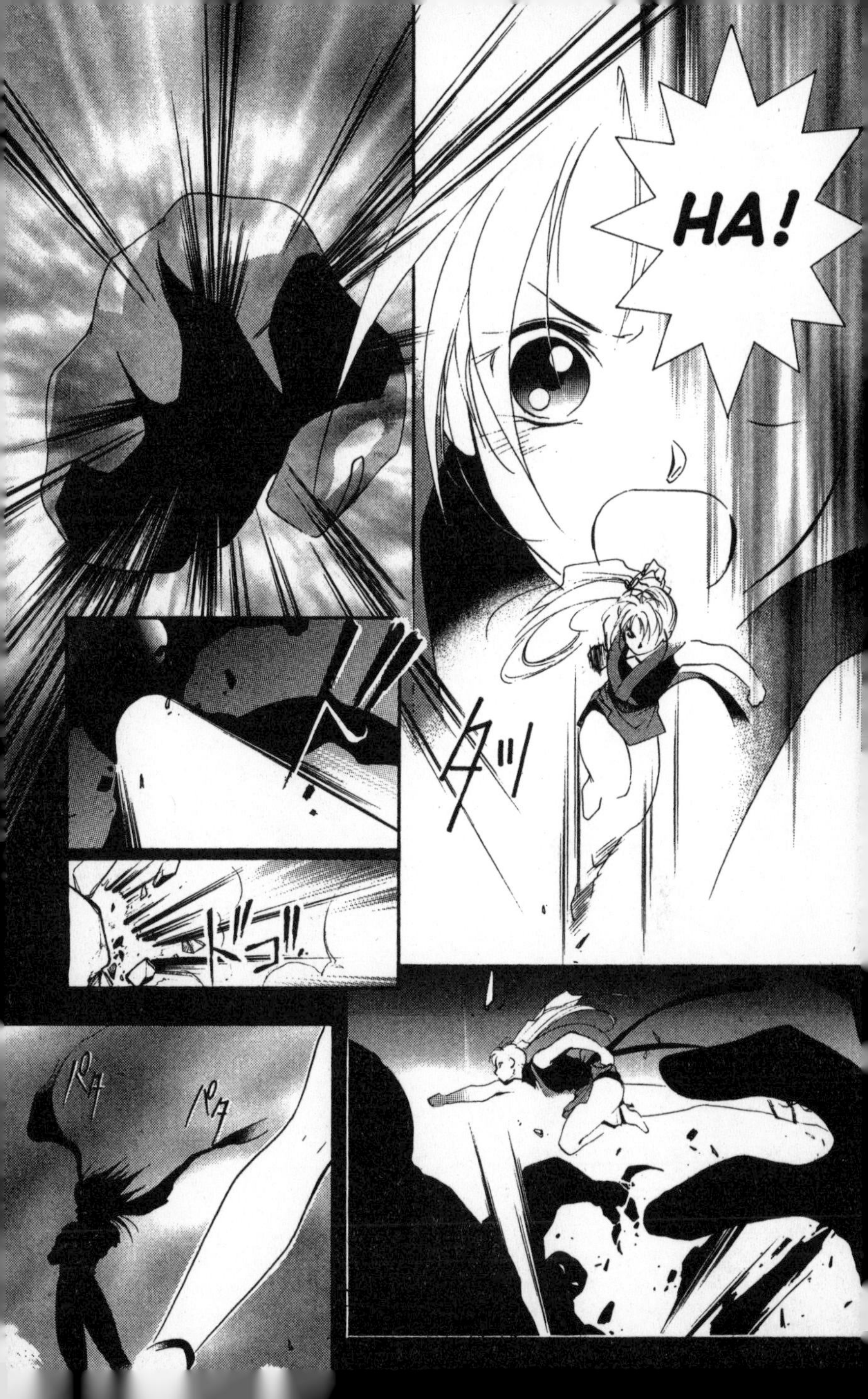
HA!
タッ
ドゴ!!
パタ
パタ

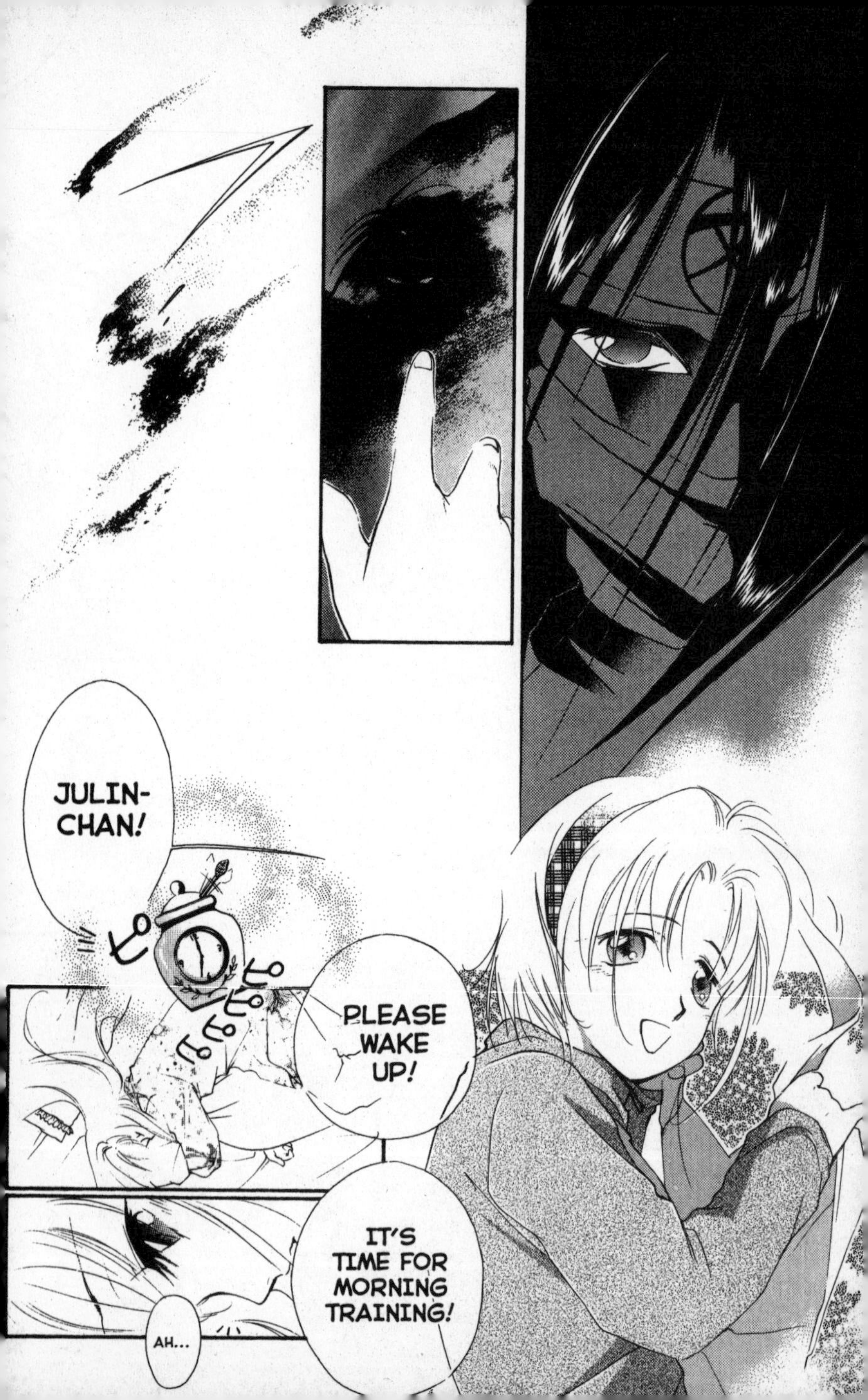
JULIN-CHAN!
ピ
ピピピピ
PLEASE WAKE UP!
IT'S TIME FOR MORNING TRAINING!
AH...

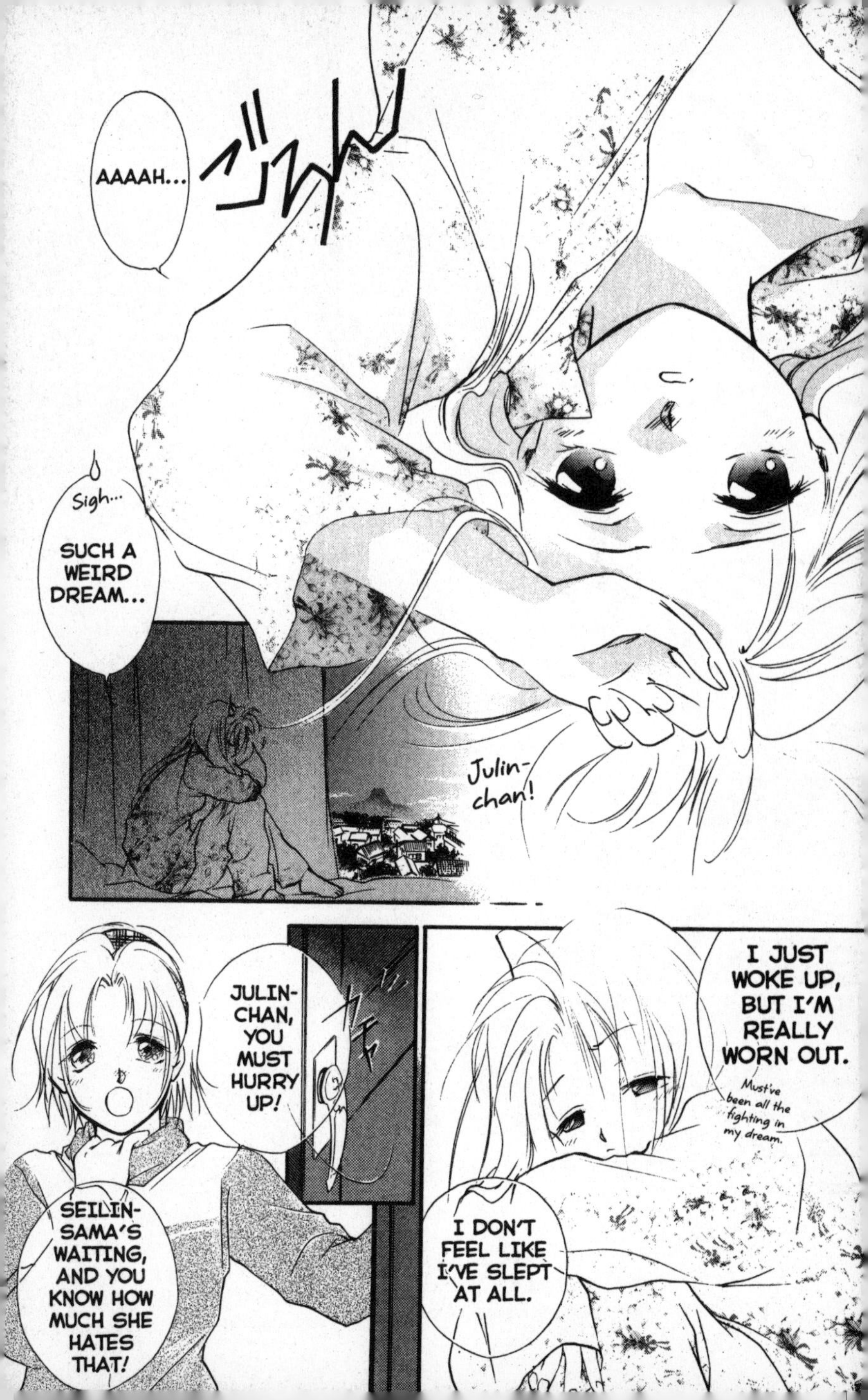
AAAAH...
Sigh... SUCH A WEIRD DREAM...
Julin-chan!
I JUST WOKE UP, BUT I'M REALLY WORN OUT.
Must've been all the fighting in my dream.
I DON'T FEEL LIKE I'VE SLEPT AT ALL.
JULIN-CHAN, YOU MUST HURRY UP!
SEILIN-SAMA'S WAITING, AND YOU KNOW HOW MUCH SHE HATES THAT!

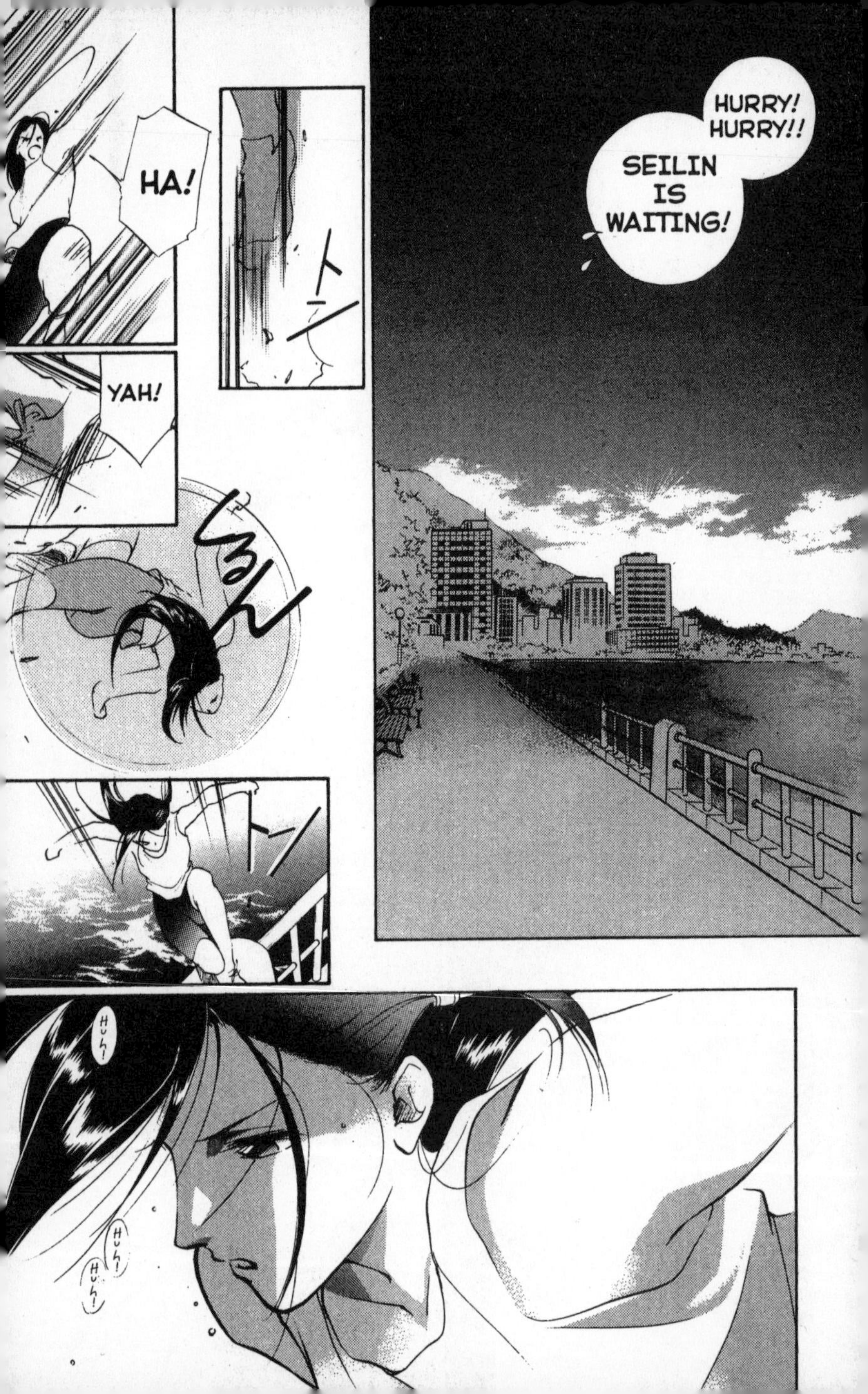
HURRY! HURRY!!
SEILIN IS WAITING!
HA!
YAH!
HUH!
HUH!
HUH!

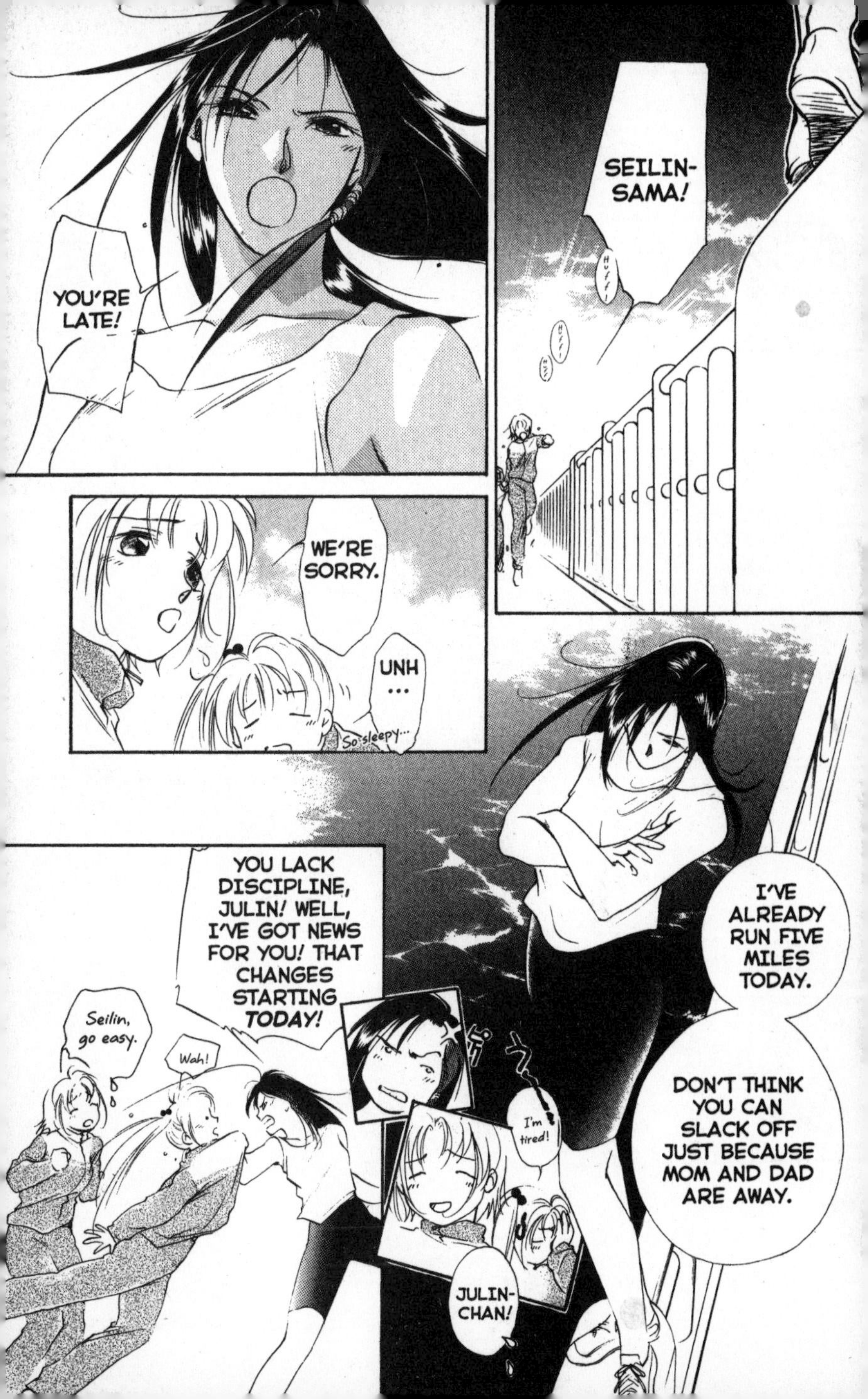
SEILIN-SAMA!
Huff!
Huff!
YOU'RE LATE!
WE'RE SORRY.
UNH...
So sleepy...
I'VE ALREADY RUN FIVE MILES TODAY.
DON'T THINK YOU CAN SLACK OFF JUST BECAUSE MOM AND DAD ARE AWAY.
YOU LACK DISCIPLINE, JULIN! WELL, I'VE GOT NEWS FOR YOU! THAT CHANGES STARTING *TODAY*!
I'm tired!
JULIN-CHAN!
Wah!
Seilin, go easy.

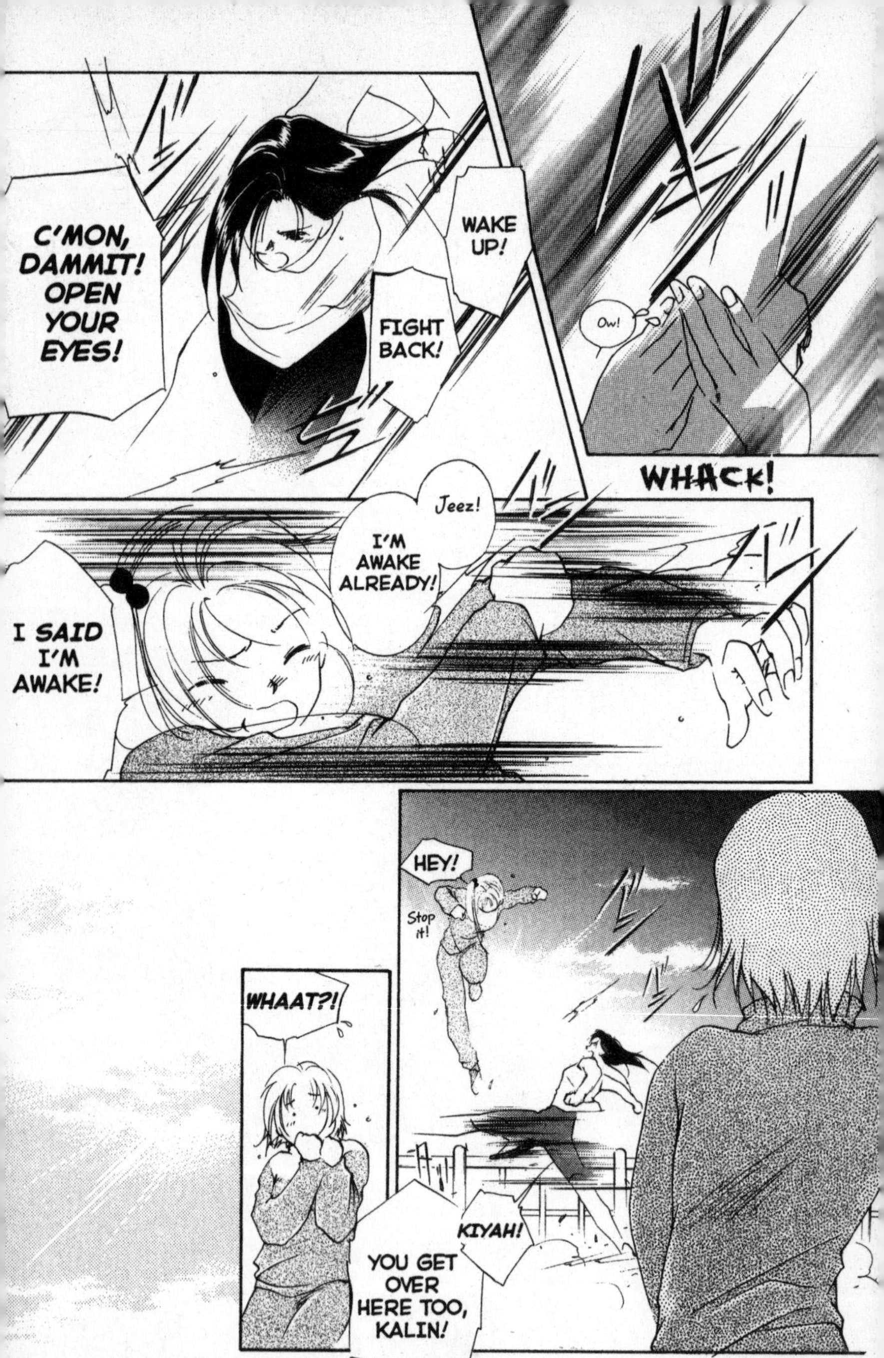

Ow!
WHACK!
WAKE UP!
FIGHT BACK!
C'MON, DAMMIT! OPEN YOUR EYES!
Jeez!
I'M AWAKE ALREADY!
I SAID I'M AWAKE!
HEY!
Stop it!
KIYAH!
YOU GET OVER HERE TOO, KALIN!
WHAAT?!

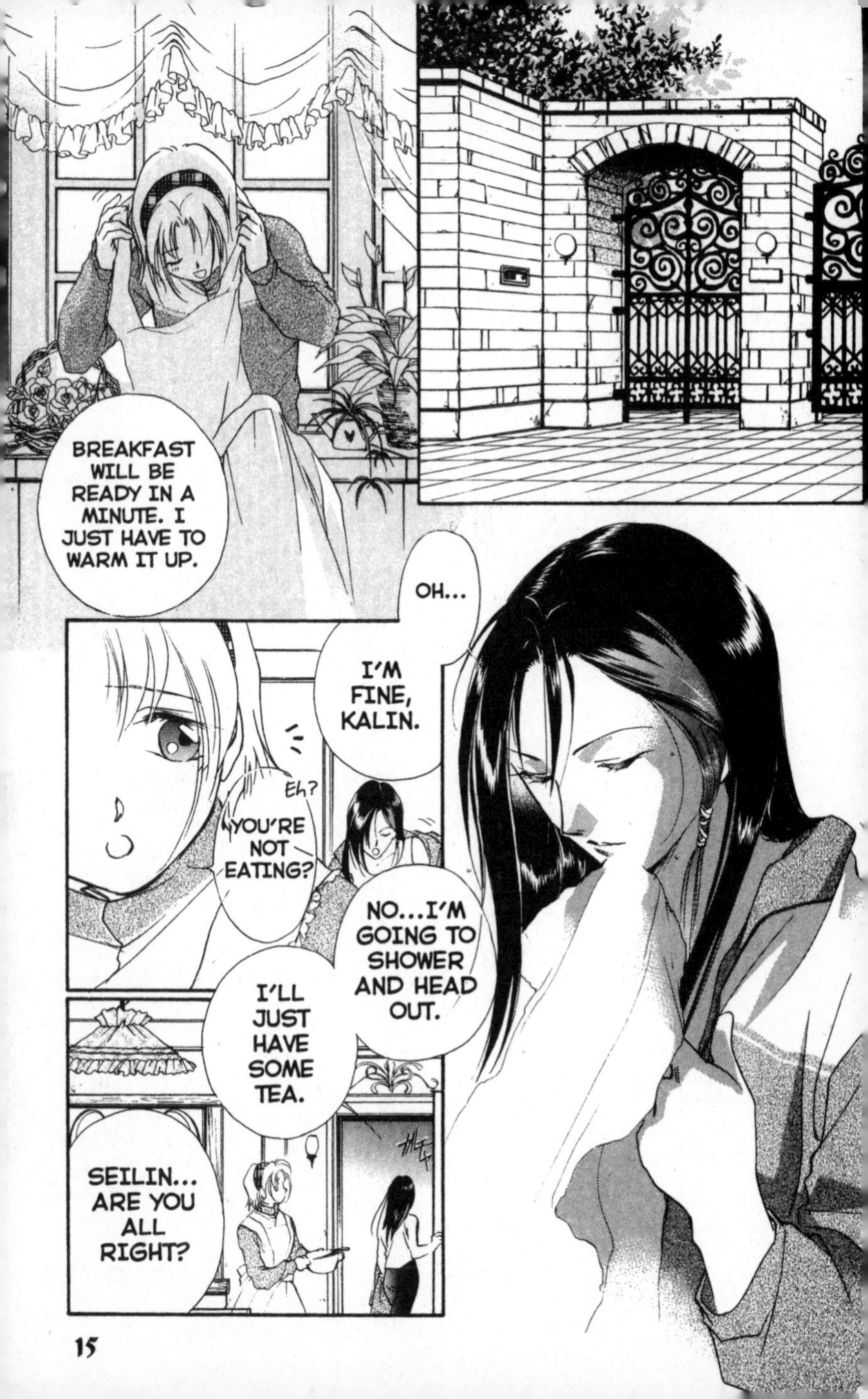
BREAKFAST WILL BE READY IN A MINUTE. I JUST HAVE TO WARM IT UP.
OH...
I'M FINE, KALIN.
Eh?
YOU'RE NOT EATING?
NO...I'M GOING TO SHOWER AND HEAD OUT.
I'LL JUST HAVE SOME TEA.
SEILIN... ARE YOU ALL RIGHT?

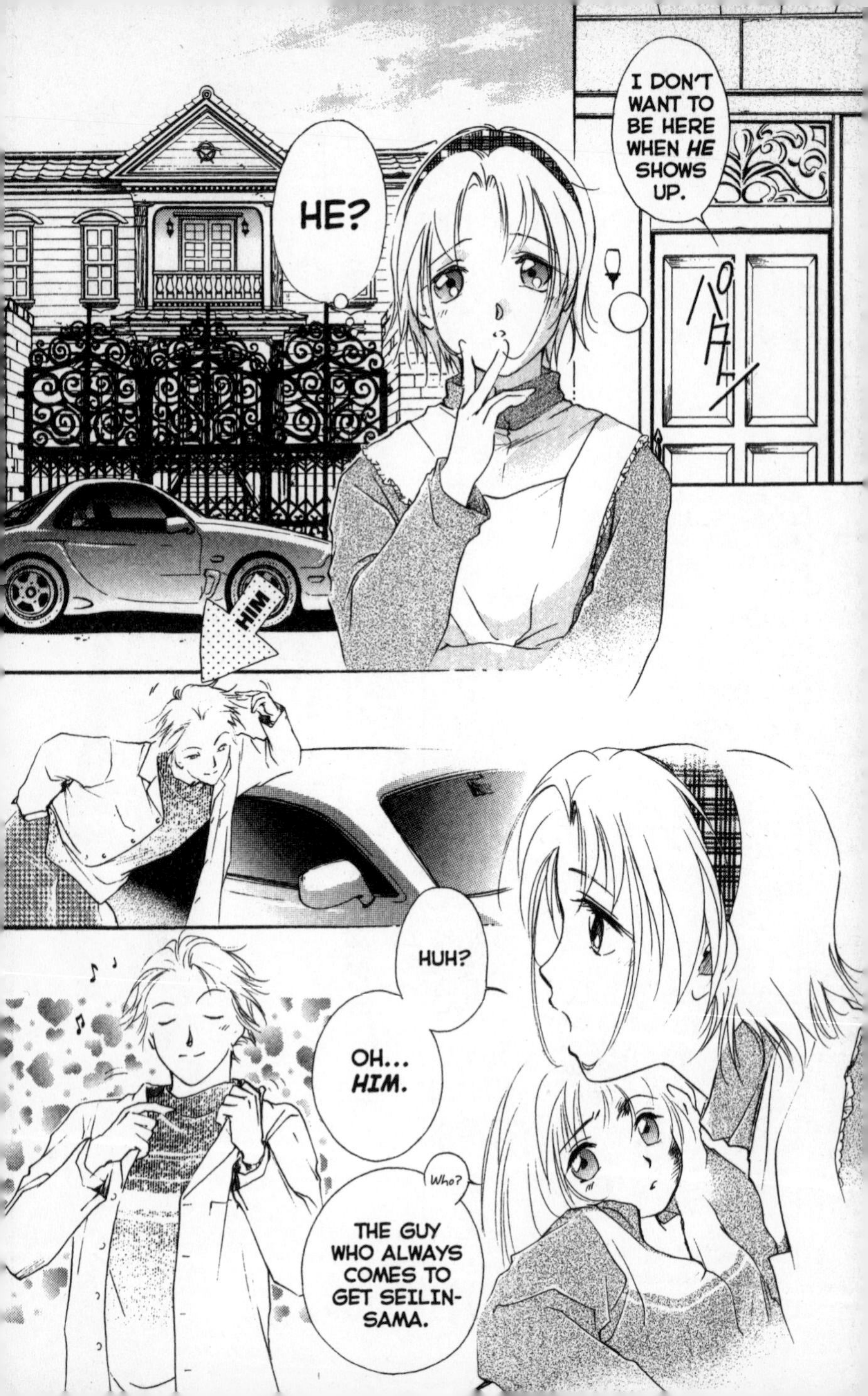
I DON'T WANT TO BE HERE WHEN *HE* SHOWS UP.
HE?
HIM
HUH?
OH... *HIM*.
Who?
THE GUY WHO ALWAYS COMES TO GET SEILIN-SAMA.

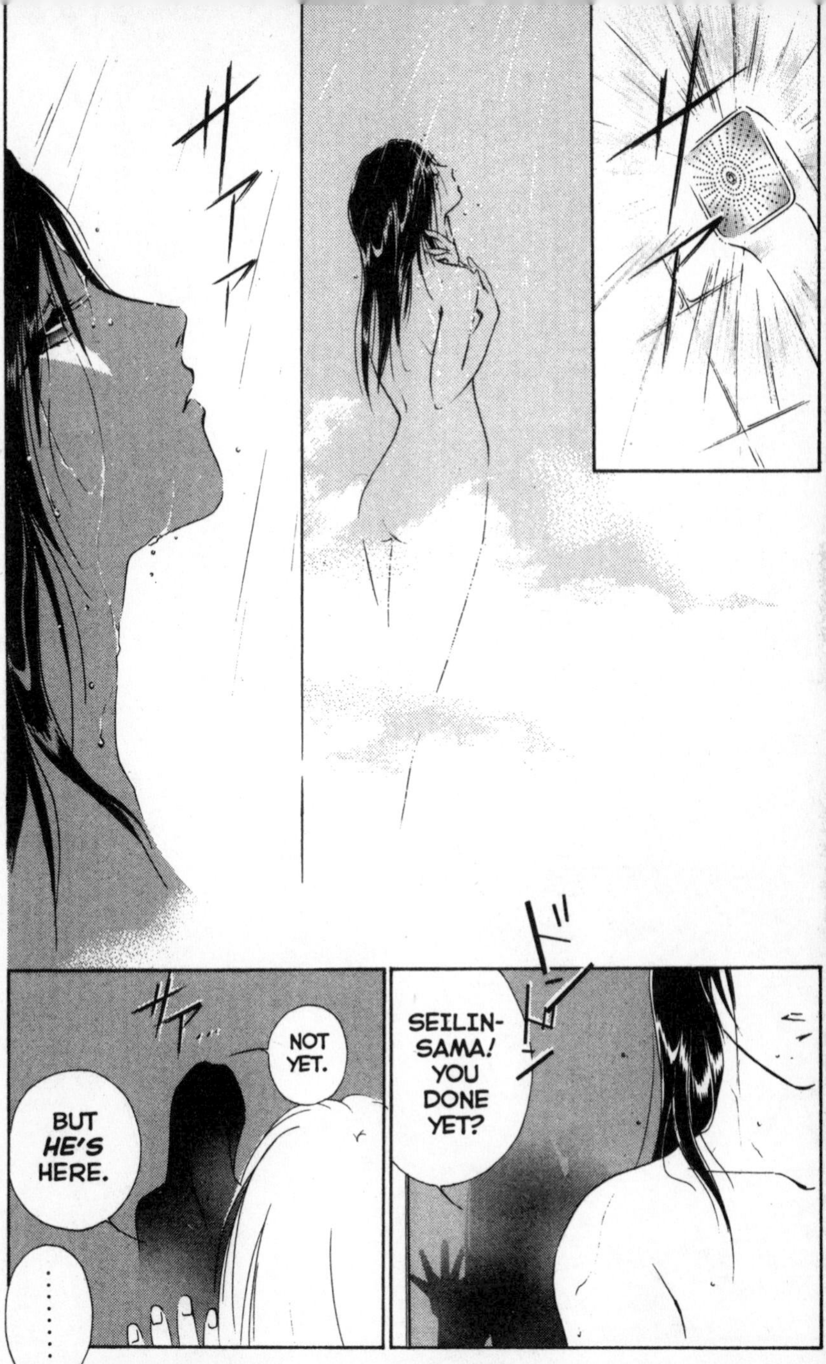
SEILIN-SAMA! YOU DONE YET?
NOT YET.
BUT *HE'S* HERE.
......

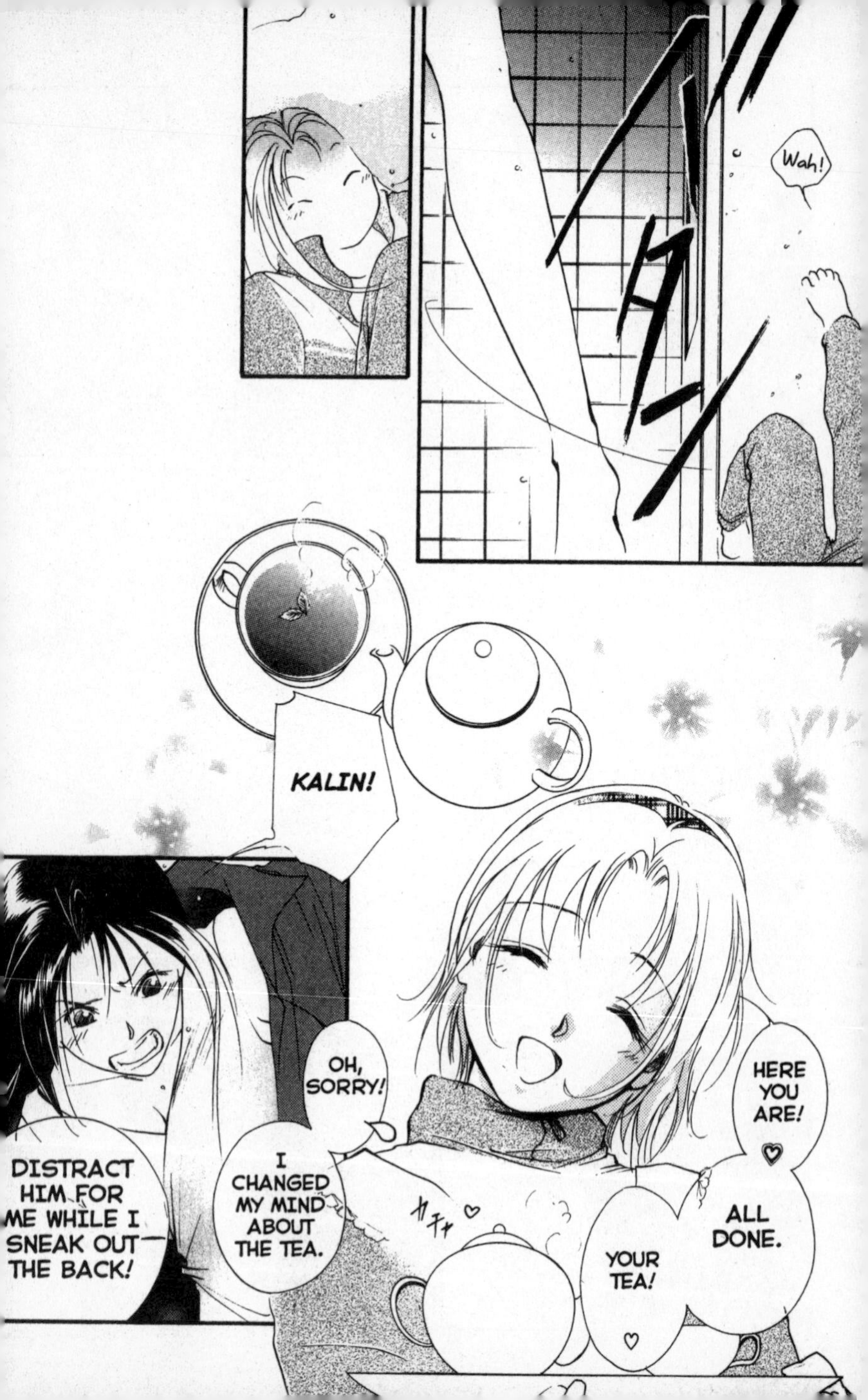
Wah!
HERE YOU ARE! ♥
ALL DONE.
YOUR TEA! ♥
カチャ ♥
KALIN!
OH, SORRY!
I CHANGED MY MIND ABOUT THE TEA.
DISTRACT HIM FOR ME WHILE I SNEAK OUT THE BACK!

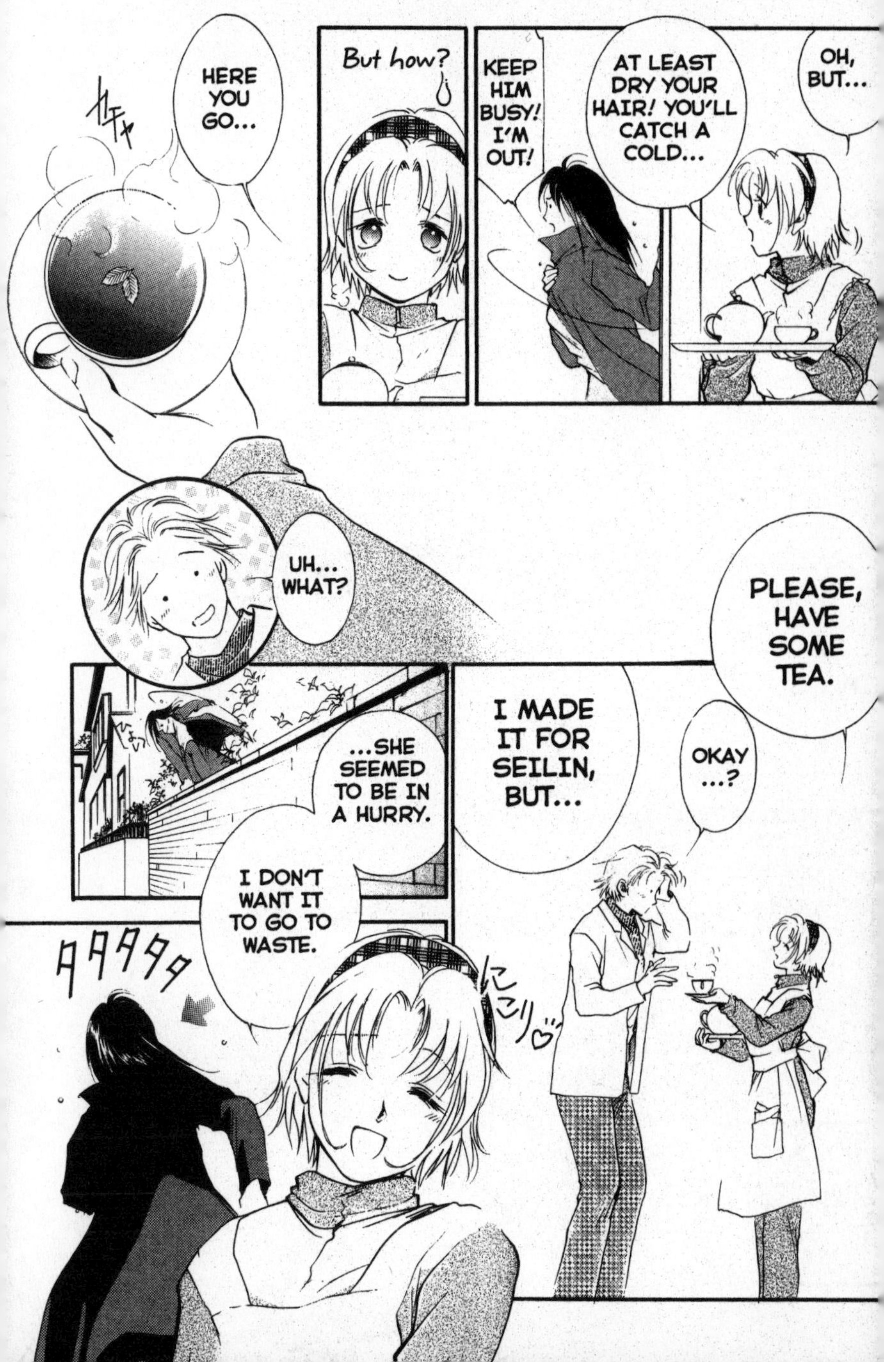
OH, BUT...
AT LEAST DRY YOUR HAIR! YOU'LL CATCH A COLD...
KEEP HIM BUSY! I'M OUT!
But how?
カチャ
HERE YOU GO...
UH... WHAT?
PLEASE, HAVE SOME TEA.
OKAY ...?
I MADE IT FOR SEILIN, BUT...
...SHE SEEMED TO BE IN A HURRY.
I DON'T WANT IT TO GO TO WASTE.
にこり
タタタタ

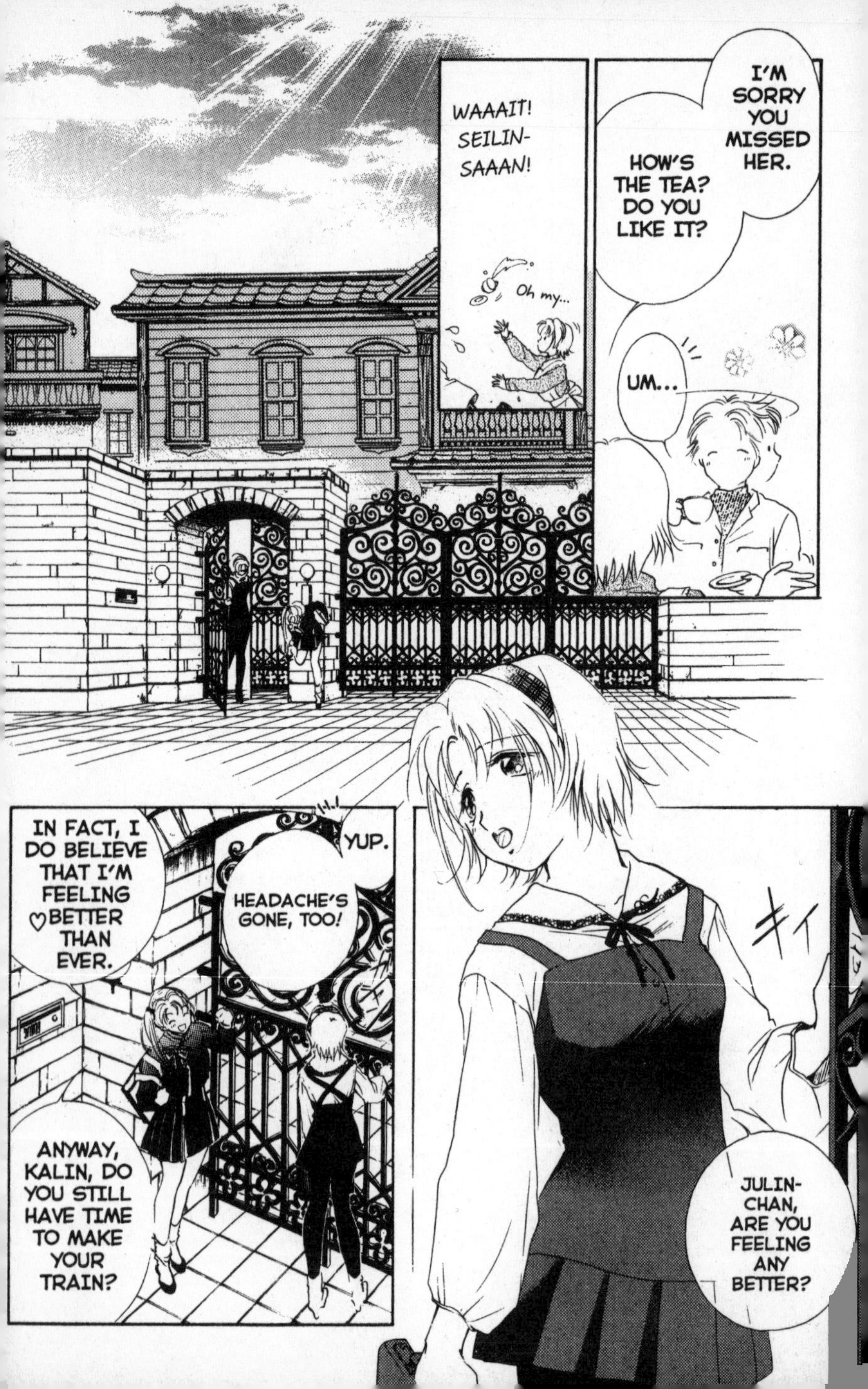
I'M SORRY YOU MISSED HER.
HOW'S THE TEA? DO YOU LIKE IT?
UM...
WAAAIT! SEILIN-SAAAN!
Oh my...
JULIN-CHAN, ARE YOU FEELING ANY BETTER?
キイ
YUP.
HEADACHE'S GONE, TOO!
IN FACT, I DO BELIEVE THAT I'M FEELING ♡BETTER THAN EVER.
ANYWAY, KALIN, DO YOU STILL HAVE TIME TO MAKE YOUR TRAIN?

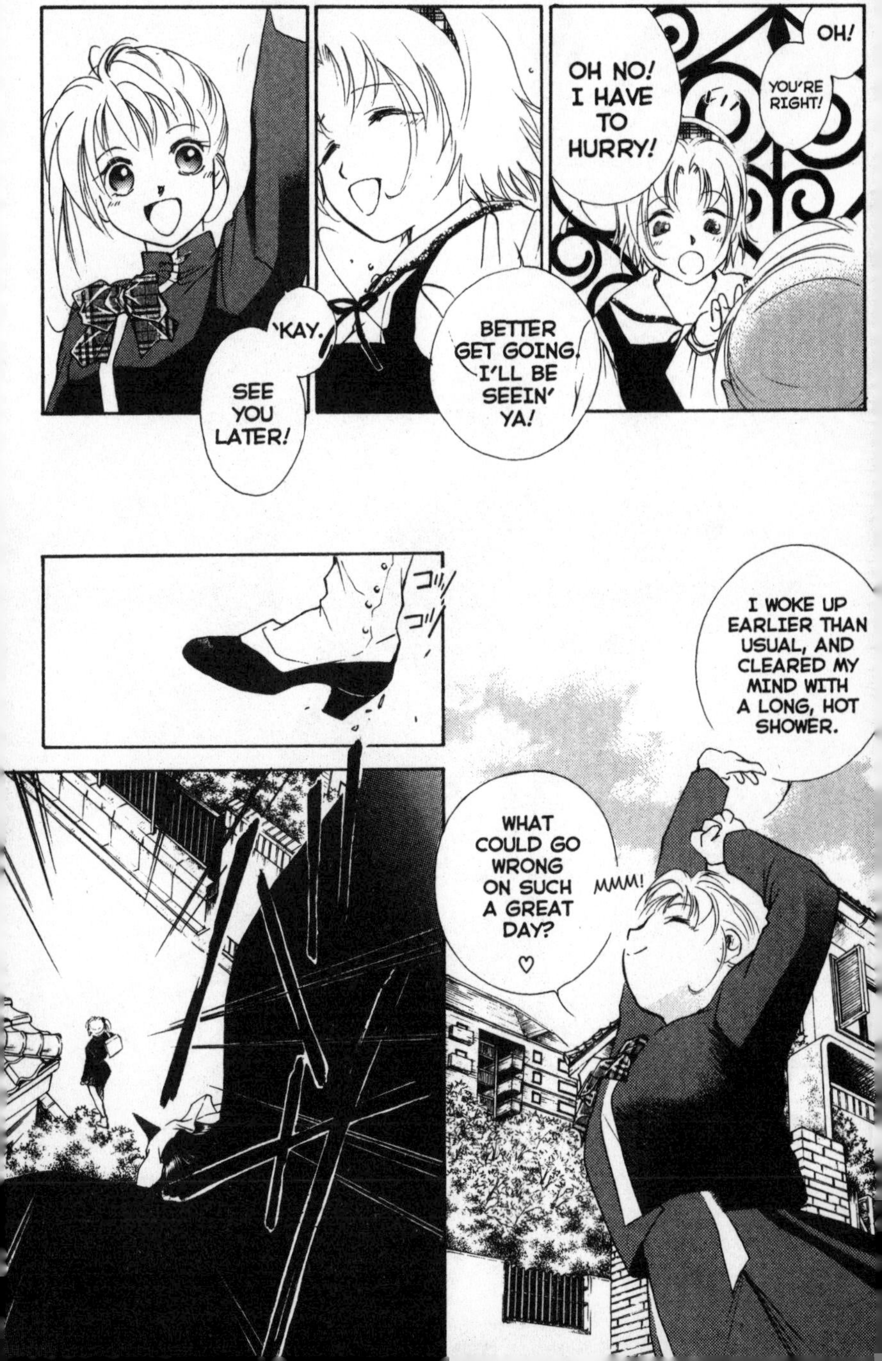
OH!
YOU'RE RIGHT!
OH NO! I HAVE TO HURRY!
BETTER GET GOING. I'LL BE SEEIN' YA!
'KAY.
SEE YOU LATER!
I WOKE UP EARLIER THAN USUAL, AND CLEARED MY MIND WITH A LONG, HOT SHOWER.
MMM!
WHAT COULD GO WRONG ON SUCH A GREAT DAY? ♡

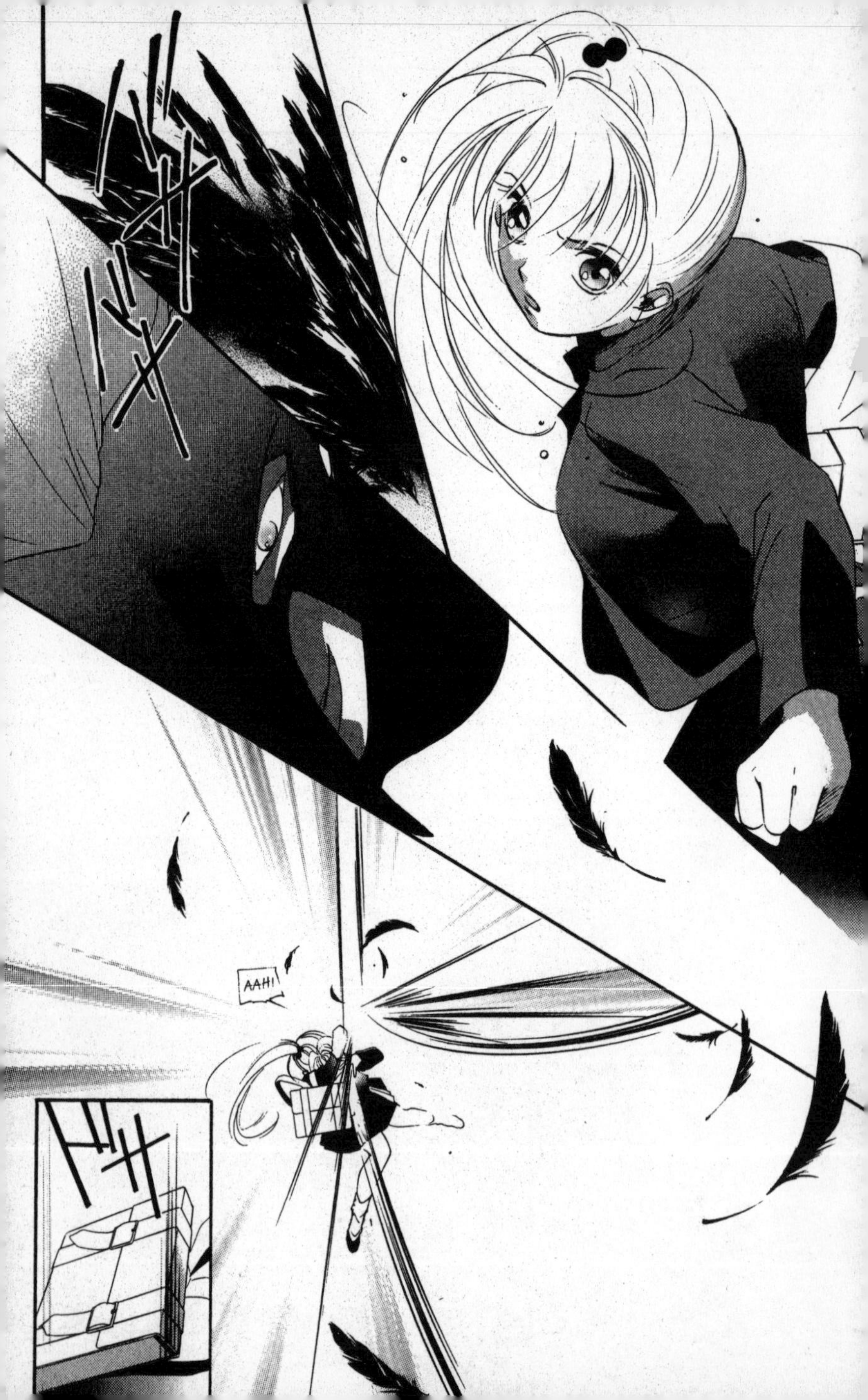
AAH!

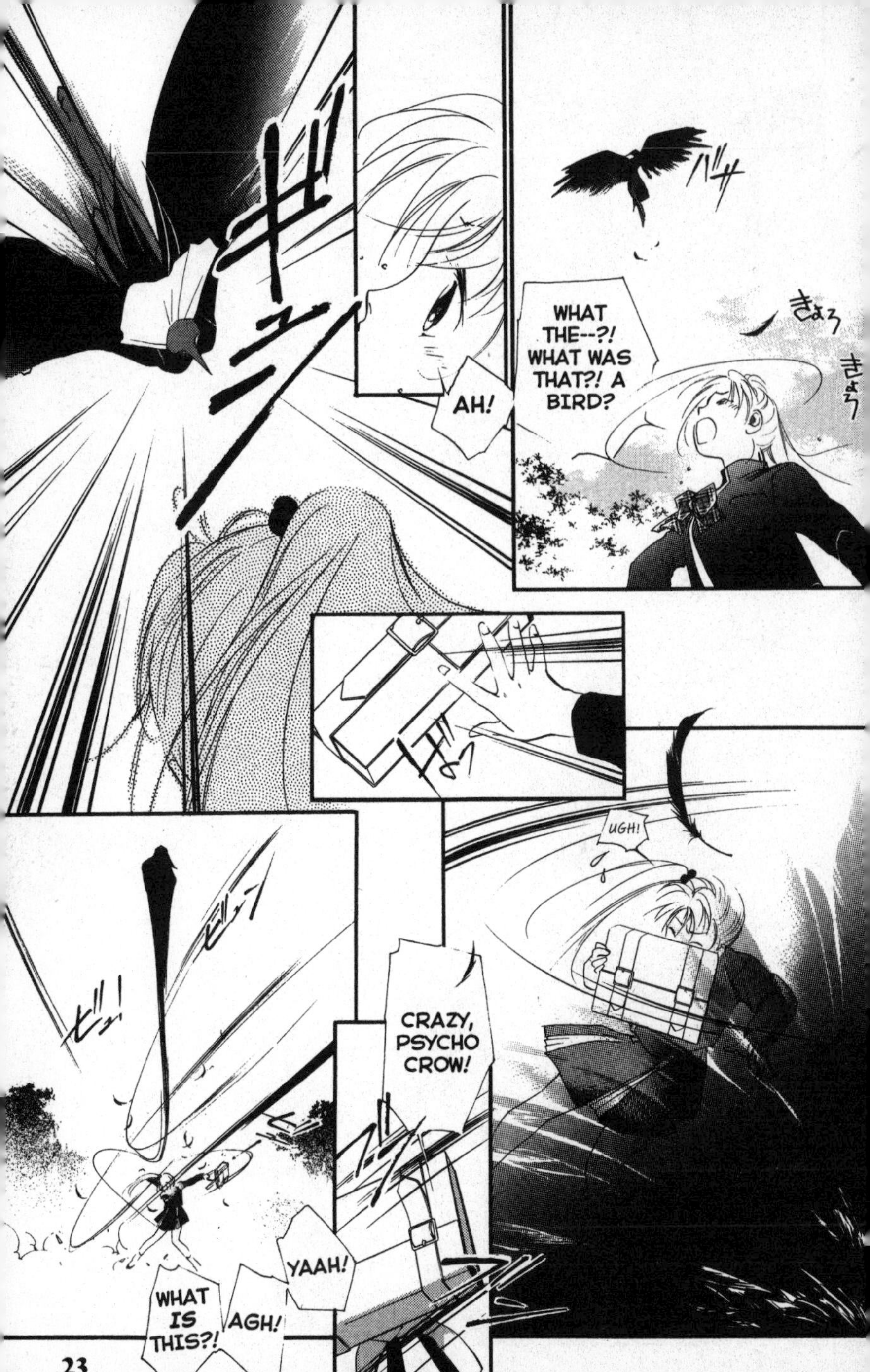
WHAT THE--?! WHAT WAS THAT?! A BIRD?
AH!
UGH!
CRAZY, PSYCHO CROW!
YAAH!
AGH!
WHAT IS THIS?!

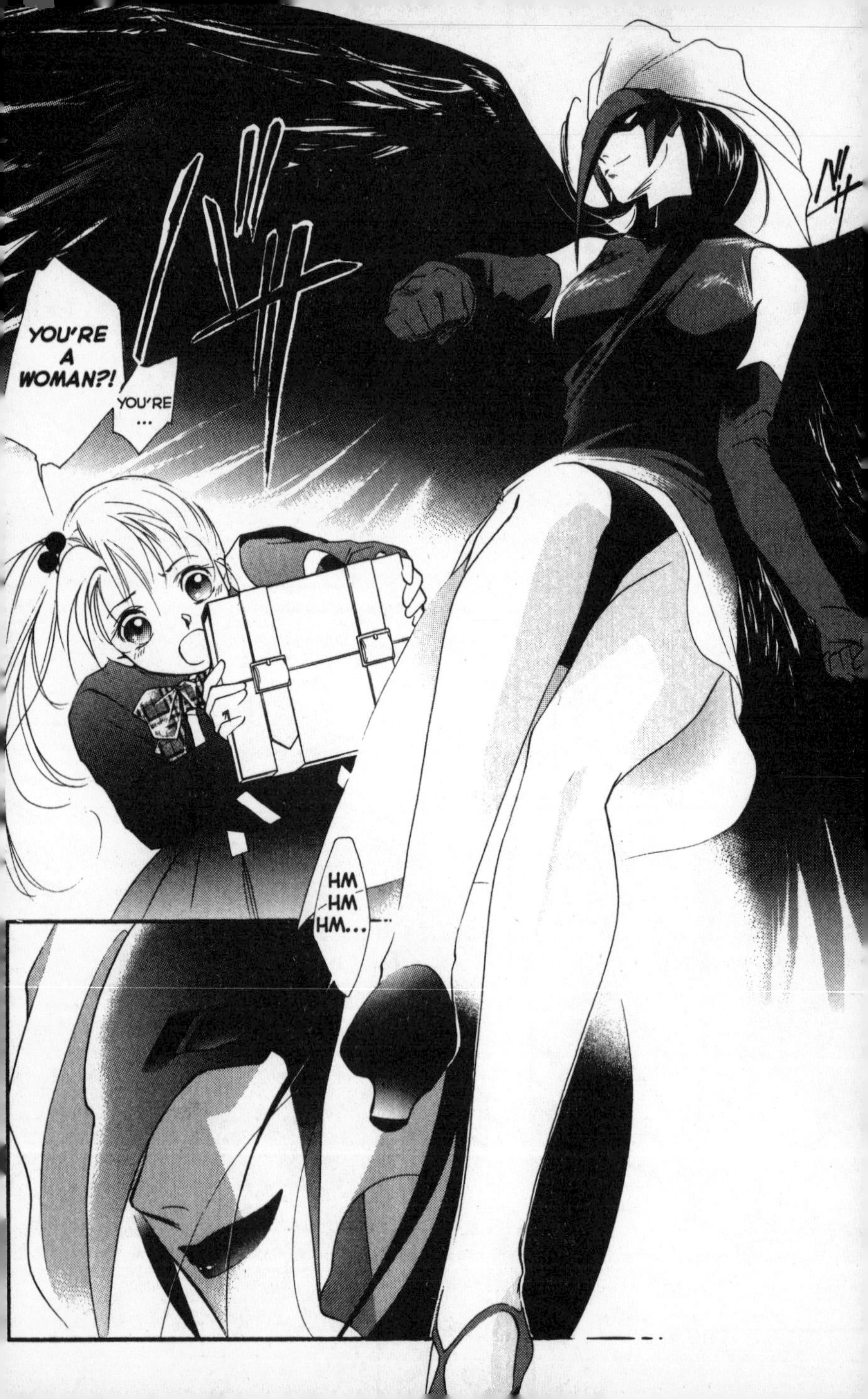
YOU'RE ...
YOU'RE A WOMAN?!
HM HM HM...

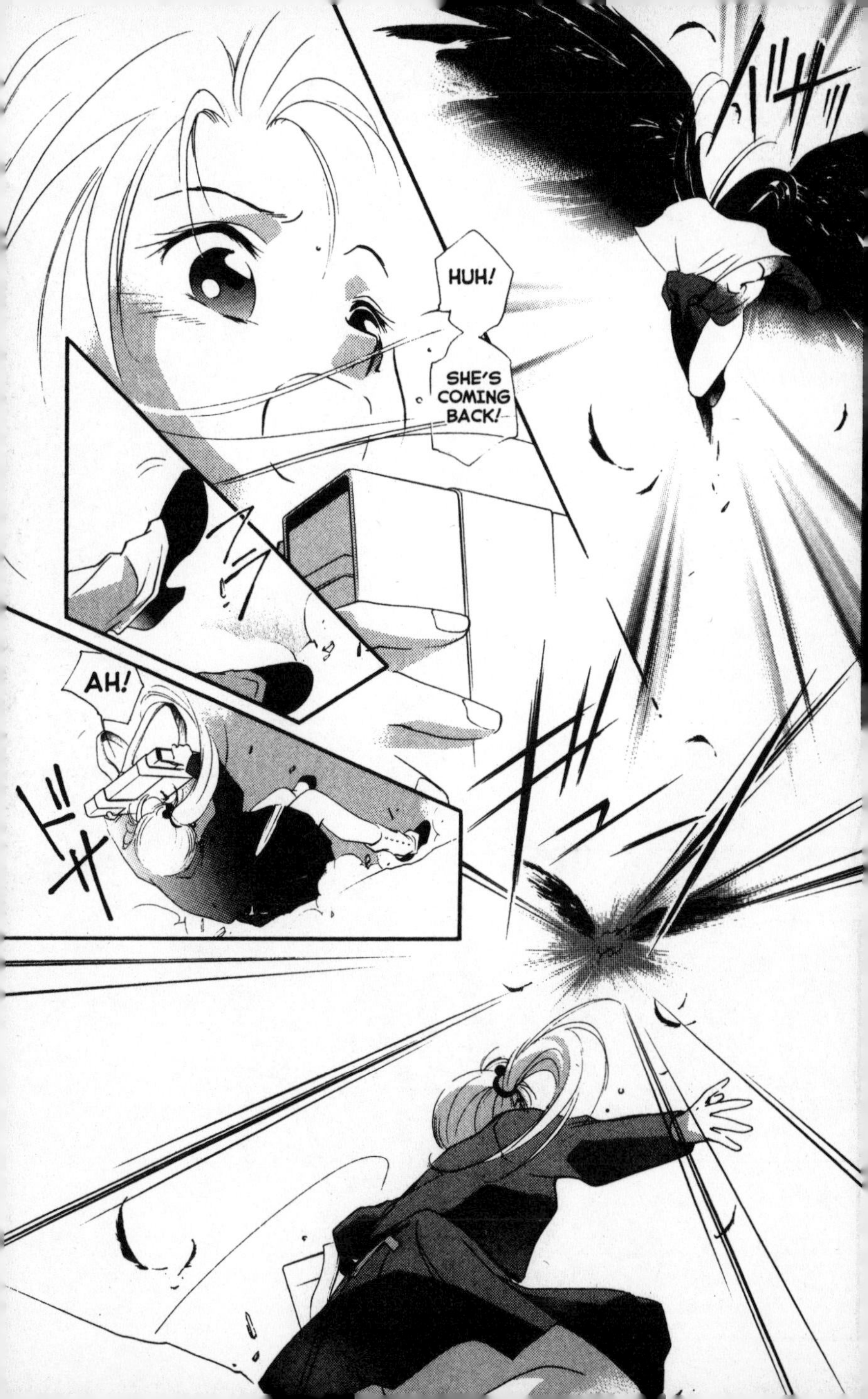
HUH!
SHE'S COMING BACK!
AH!

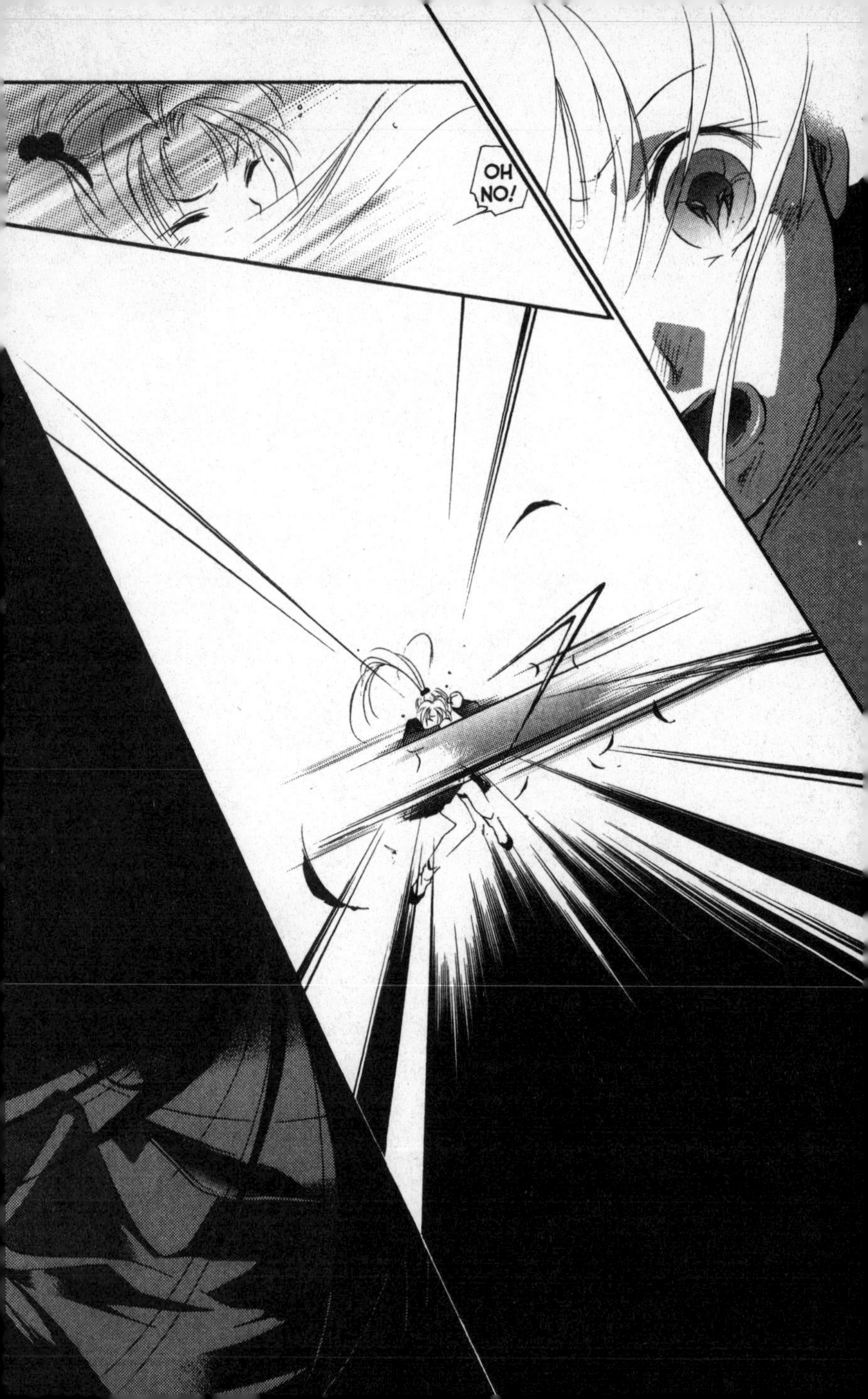
OH NO!

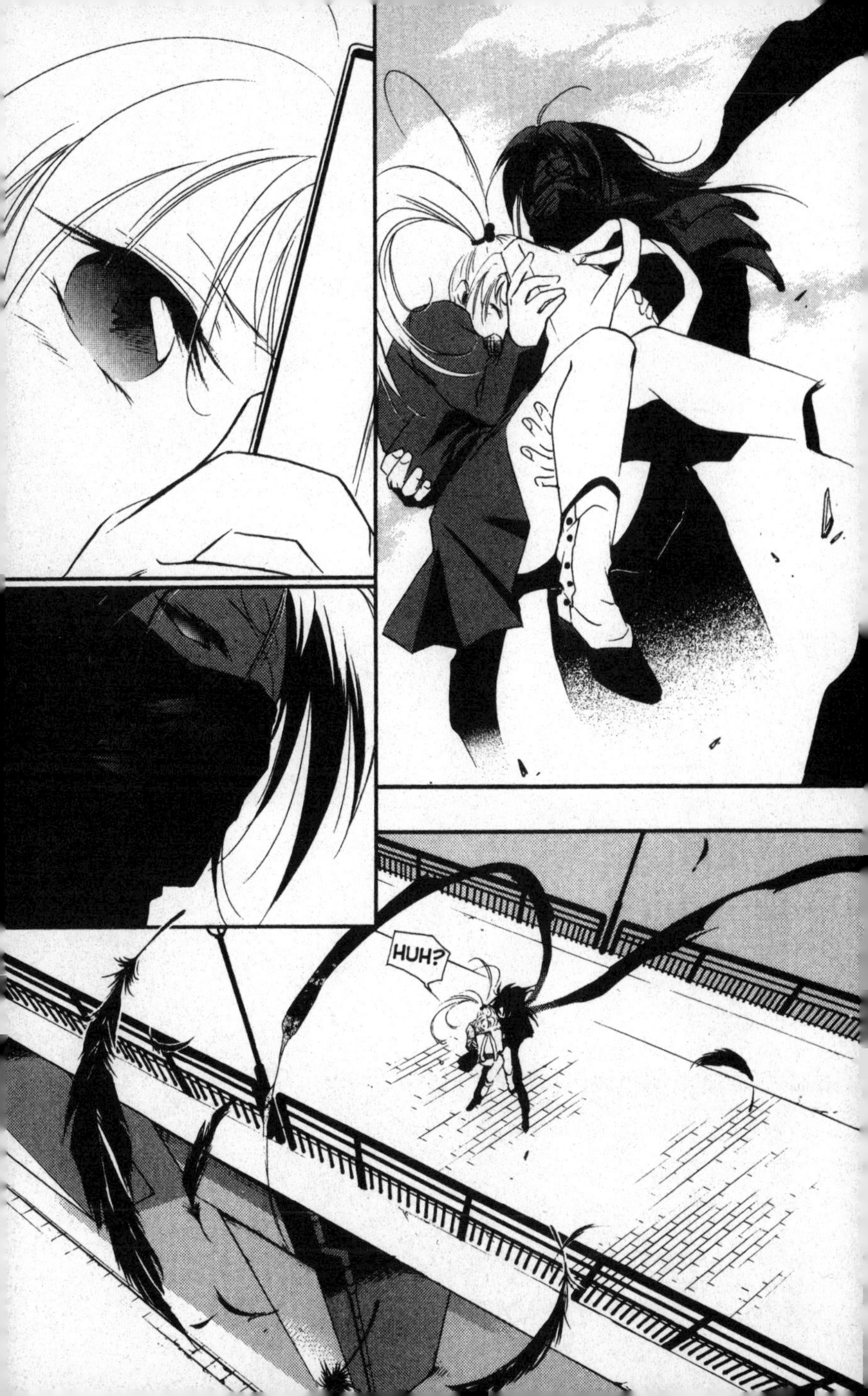
HUH?

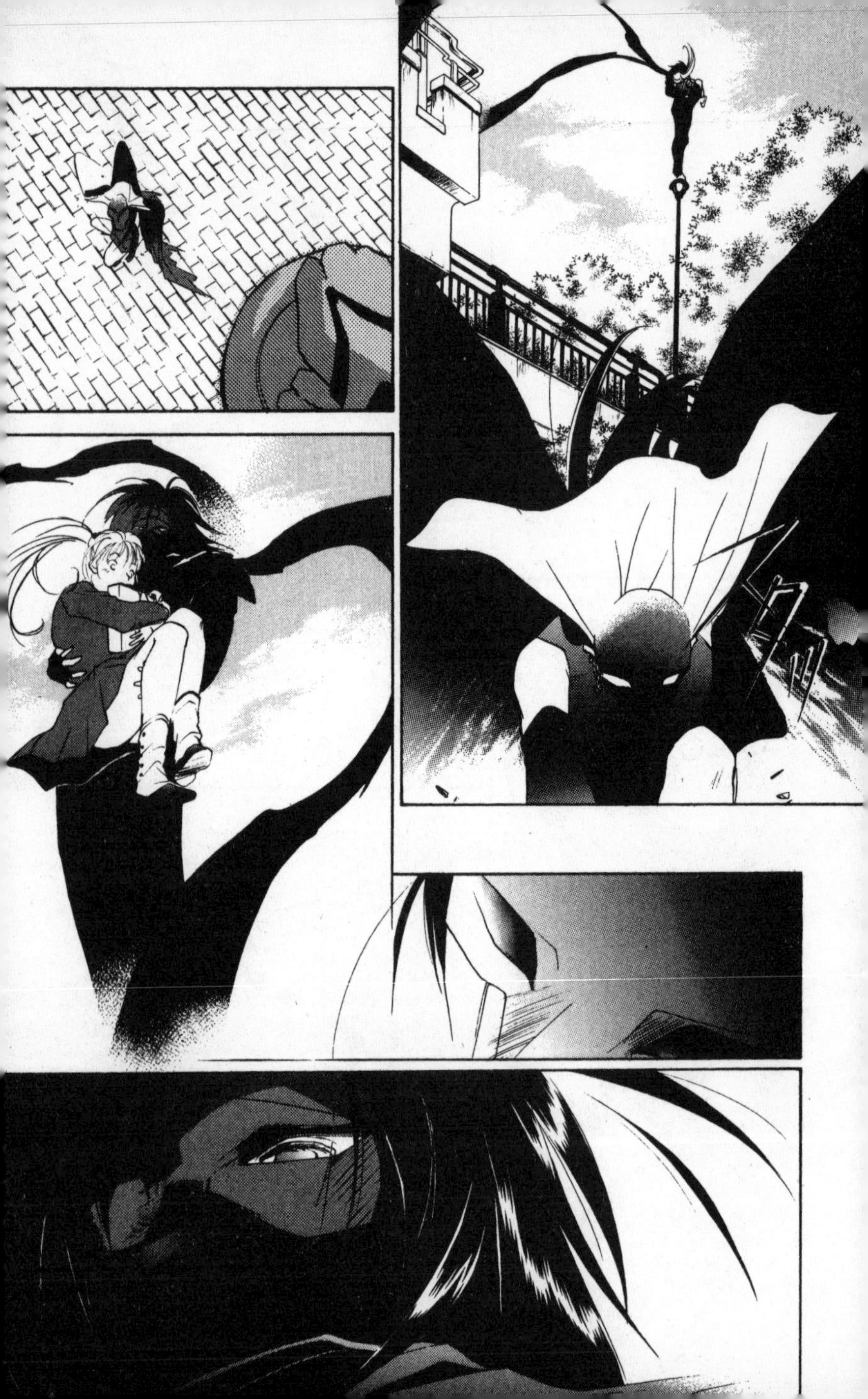

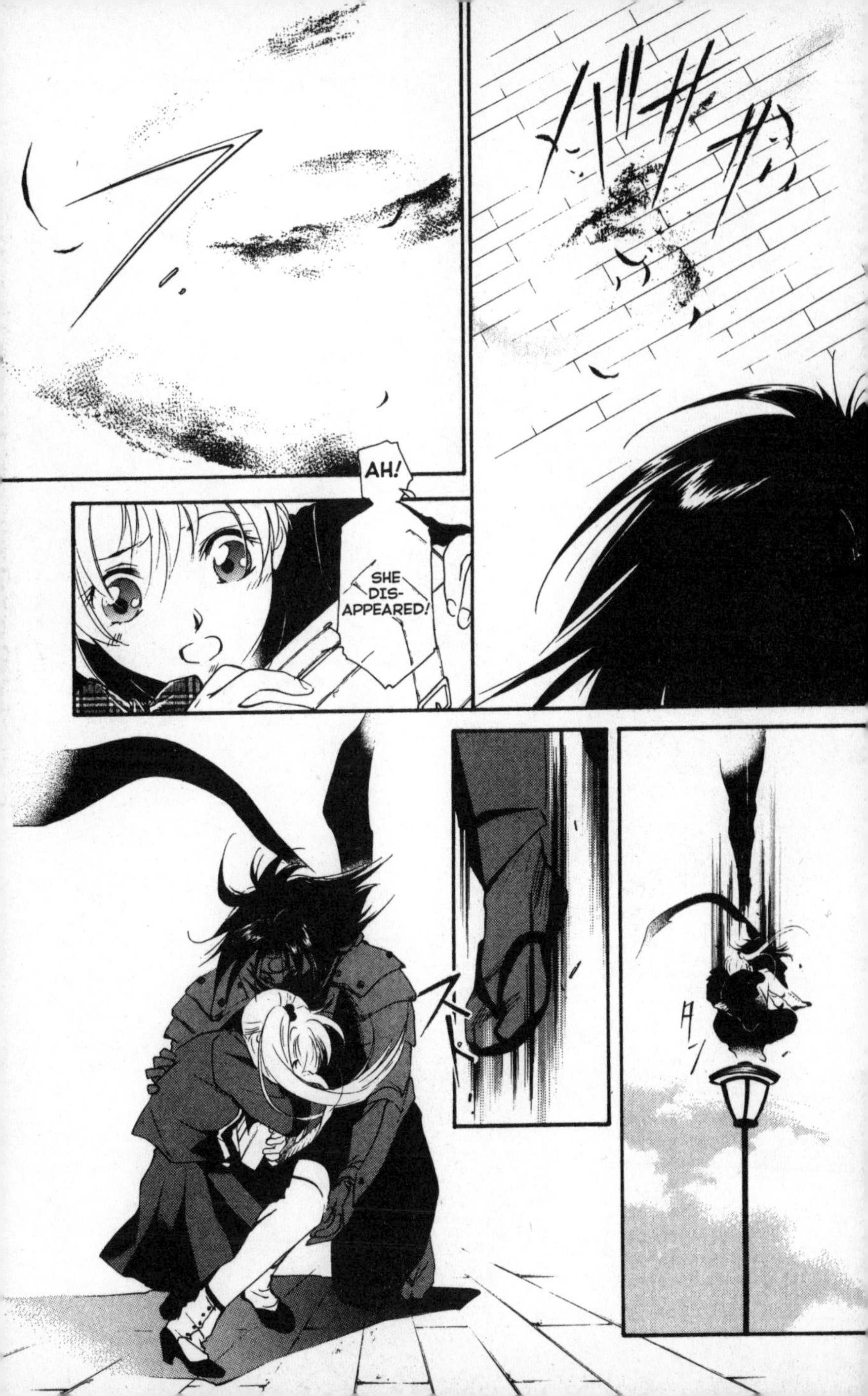
AH!
SHE DIS-APPEARED!

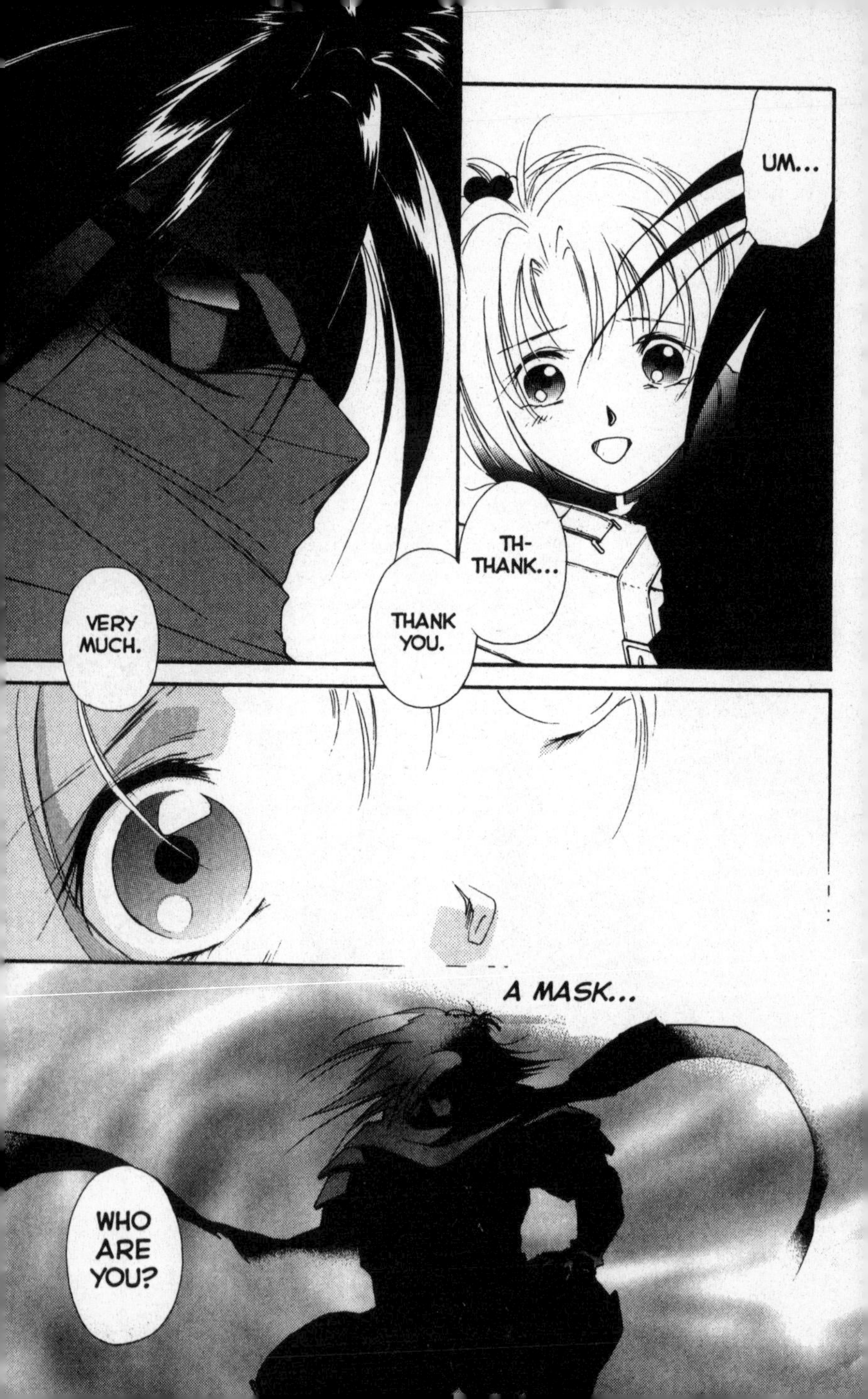
UM...
TH-THANK...
THANK YOU.
VERY MUCH.
A MASK...
WHO ARE YOU?

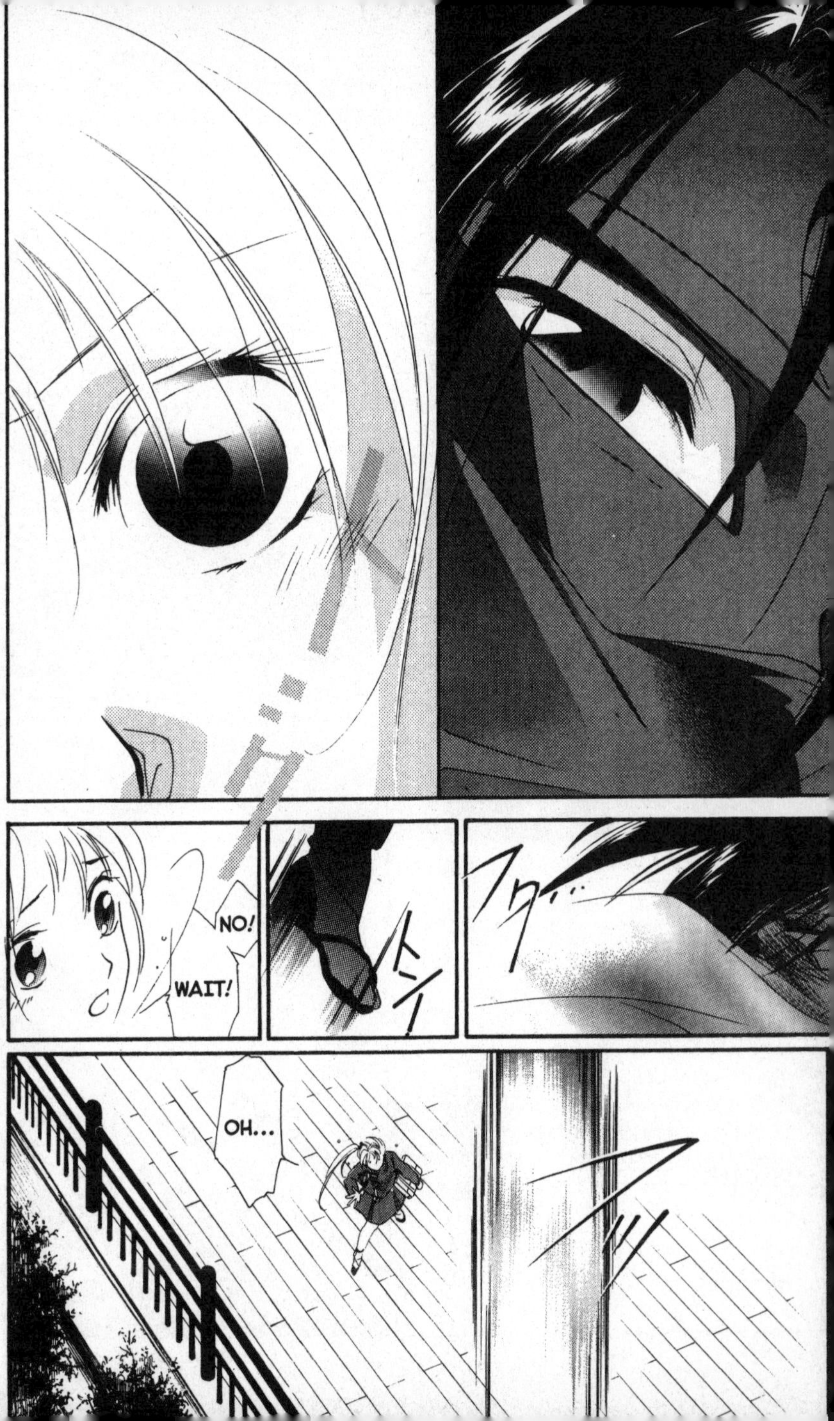
NO!
WAIT!
OH...

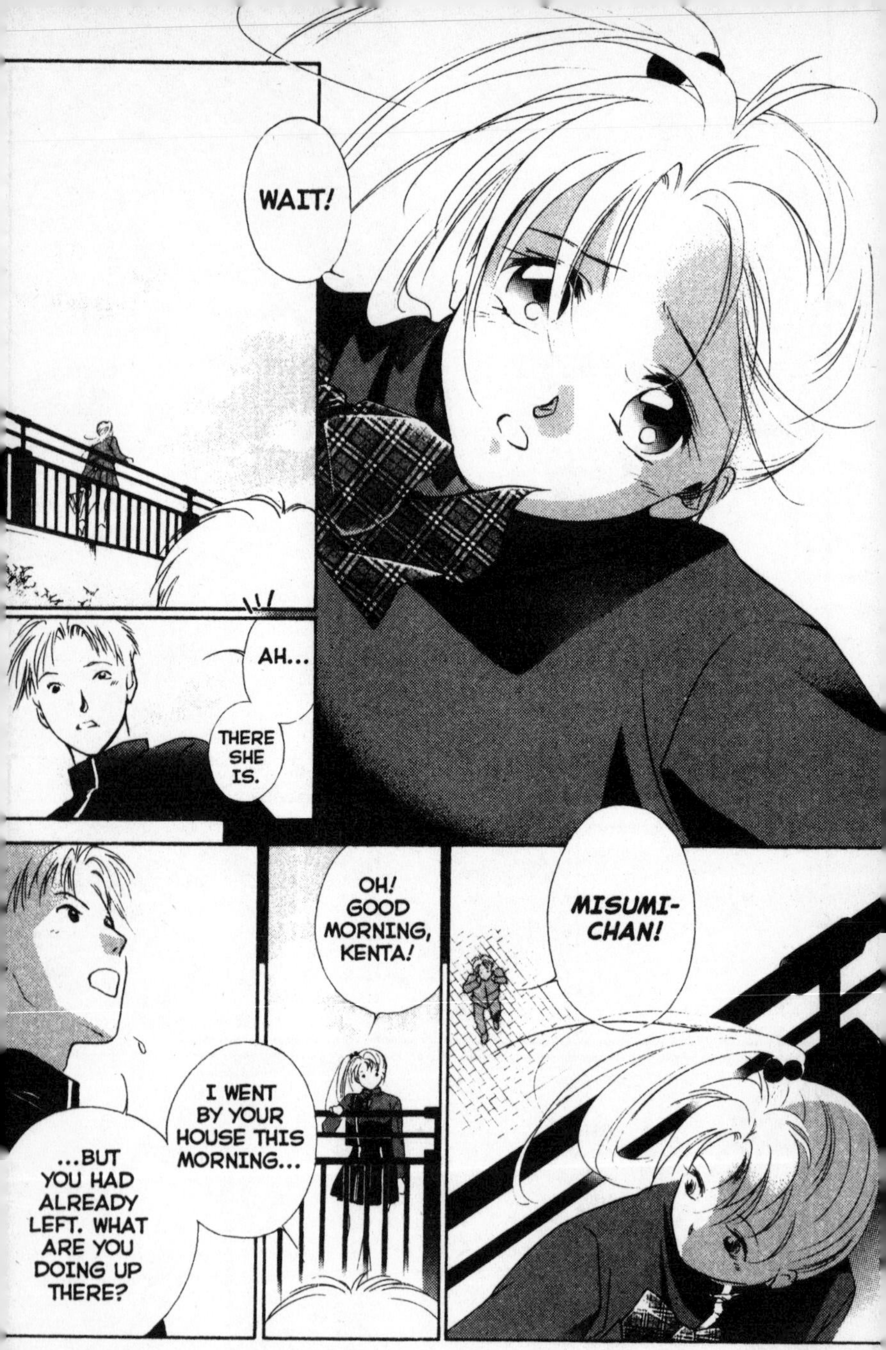
WAIT!
AH...
THERE SHE IS.
MISUMI-CHAN!
OH! GOOD MORNING, KENTA!
I WENT BY YOUR HOUSE THIS MORNING...
...BUT YOU HAD ALREADY LEFT. WHAT ARE YOU DOING UP THERE?

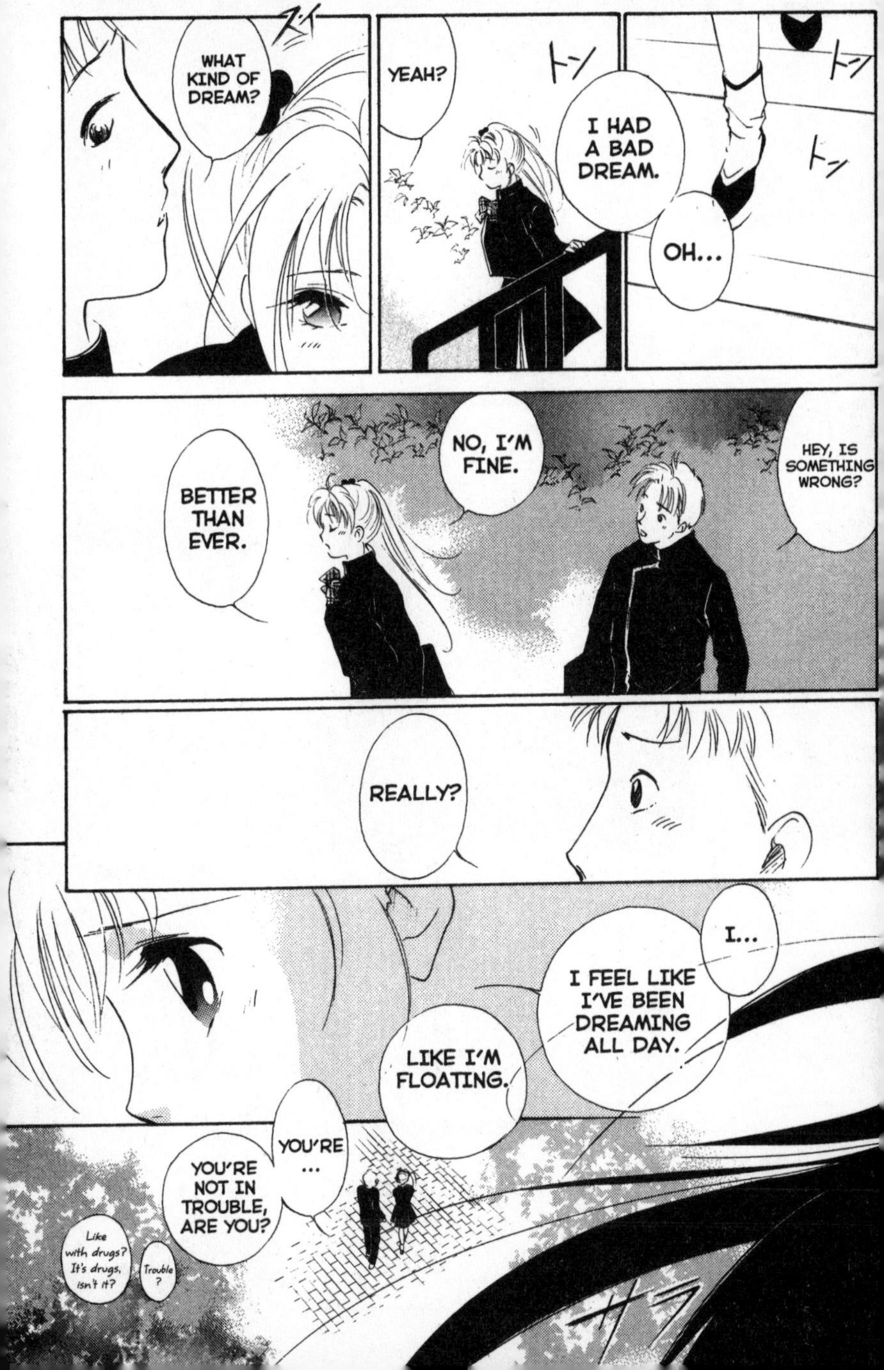
OH...
I HAD A BAD DREAM.
YEAH?
WHAT KIND OF DREAM?
HEY, IS SOMETHING WRONG?
NO, I'M FINE.
BETTER THAN EVER.
REALLY?
I...
I FEEL LIKE I'VE BEEN DREAMING ALL DAY.
LIKE I'M FLOATING.
YOU'RE...
YOU'RE NOT IN TROUBLE, ARE YOU?
Trouble?
Like with drugs? It's drugs, isn't it?

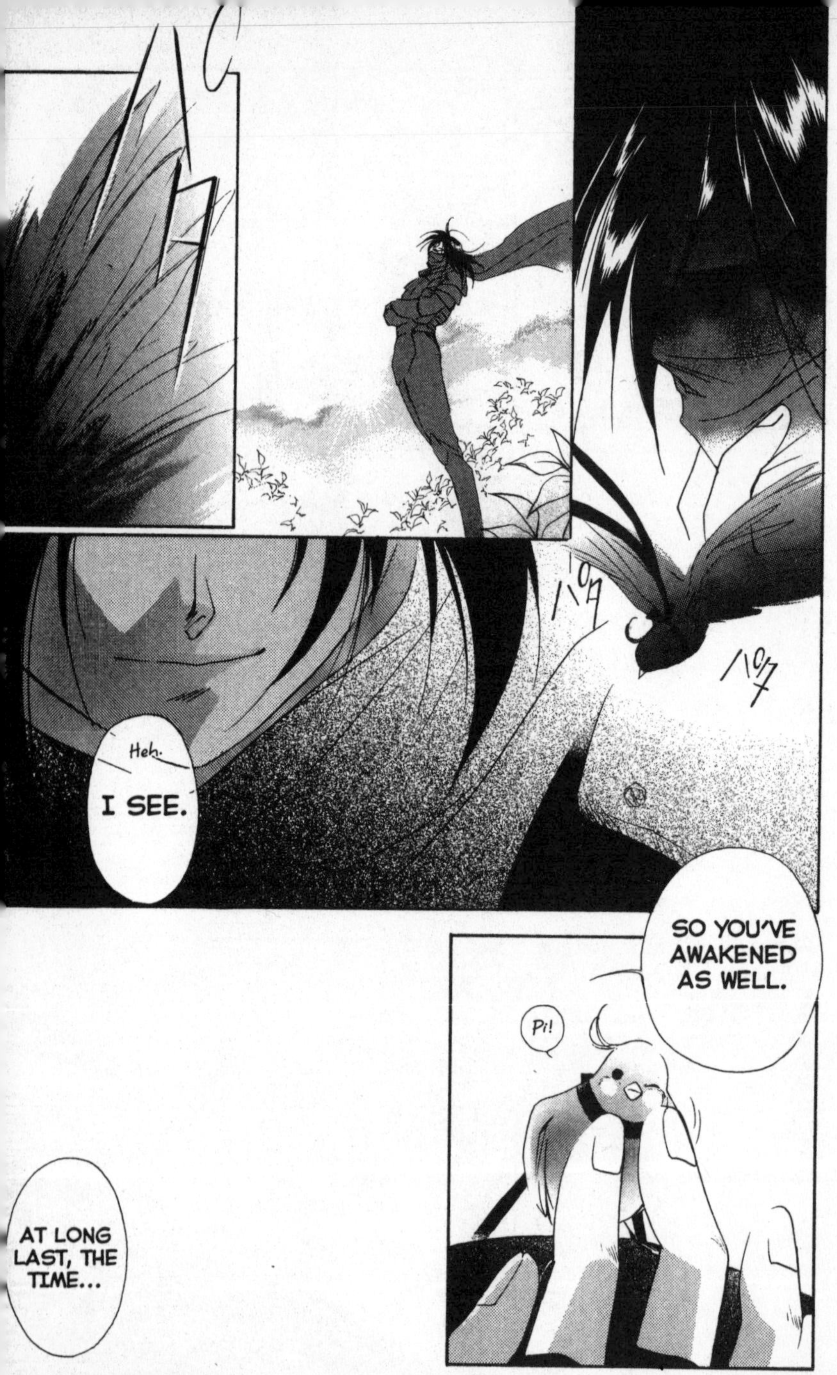

パタ
パタ
Heh.
I SEE.
SO YOU'VE AWAKENED AS WELL.
Pi!
AT LONG LAST, THE TIME...

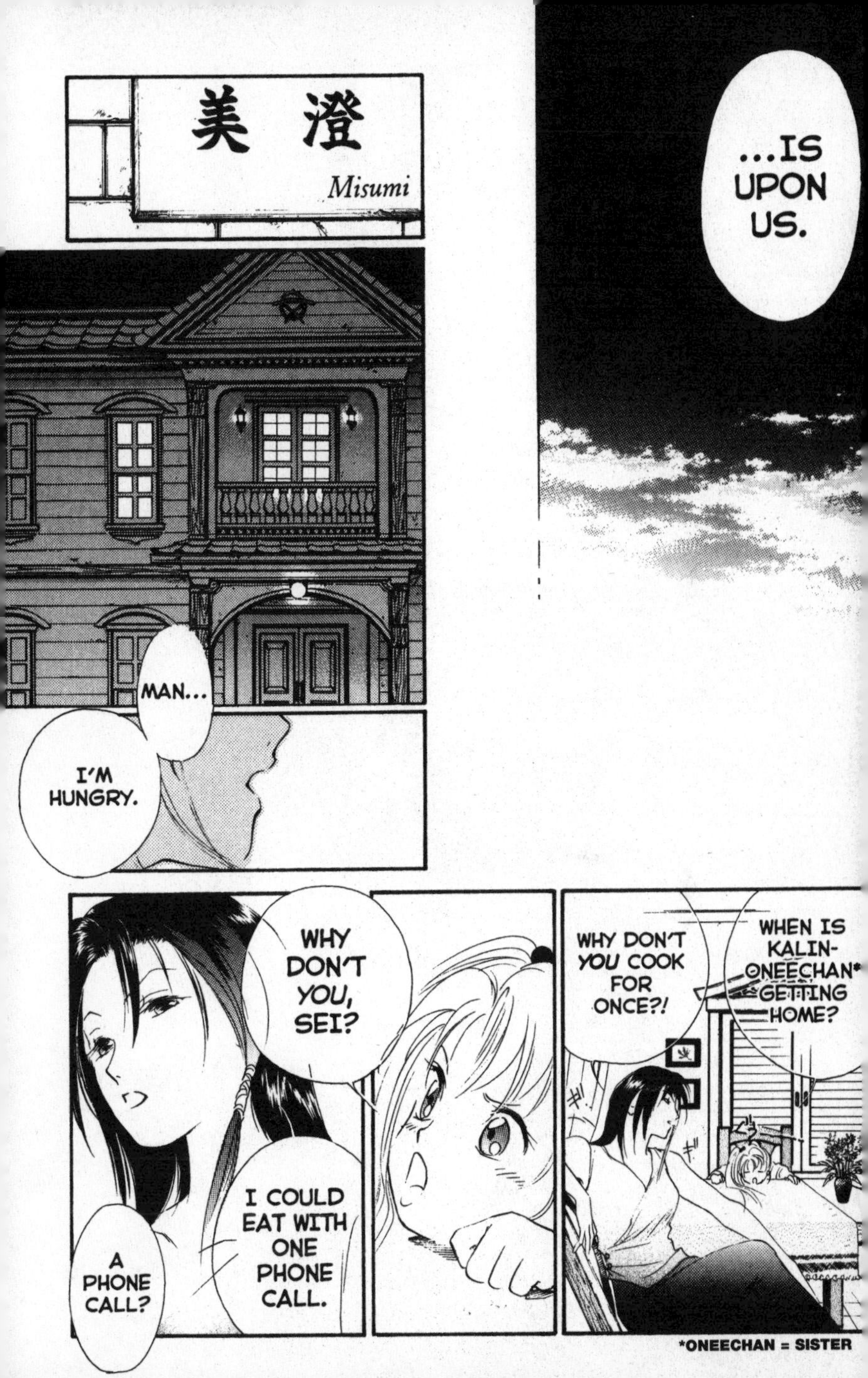
...IS UPON US.
美澄
Misumi
MAN...
I'M HUNGRY.
WHEN IS KALIN-ONEECHAN* GETTING HOME?
WHY DON'T YOU COOK FOR ONCE?!
WHY DON'T YOU, SEI?
I COULD EAT WITH ONE PHONE CALL.
A PHONE CALL?

*ONEECHAN = SISTER

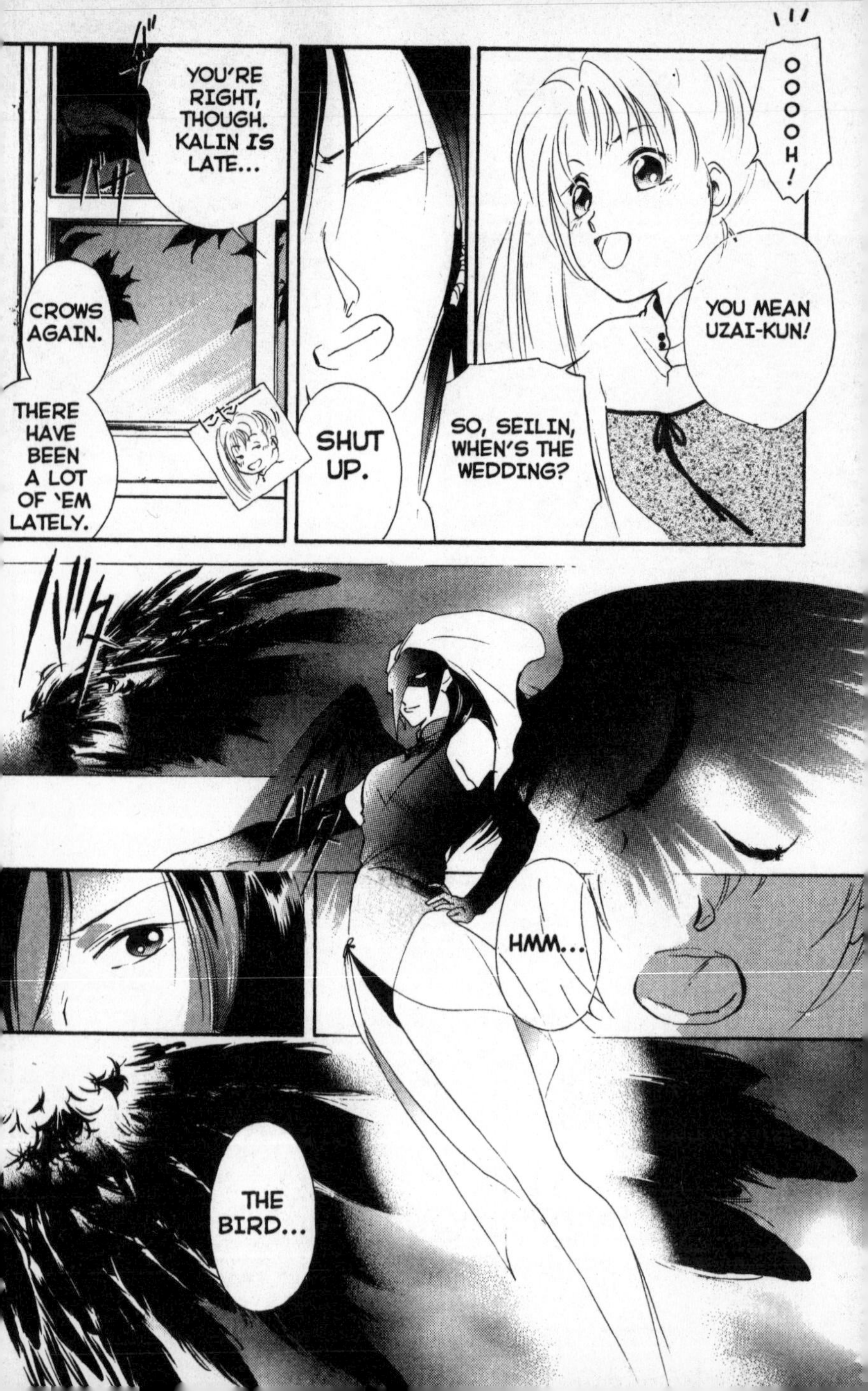
OOOOH!
YOU MEAN UZAI-KUN!
SO, SEILIN, WHEN'S THE WEDDING?
SHUT UP.
YOU'RE RIGHT, THOUGH. KALIN *IS* LATE...
CROWS AGAIN.
THERE HAVE BEEN A LOT OF 'EM LATELY.
HMM...
THE BIRD...

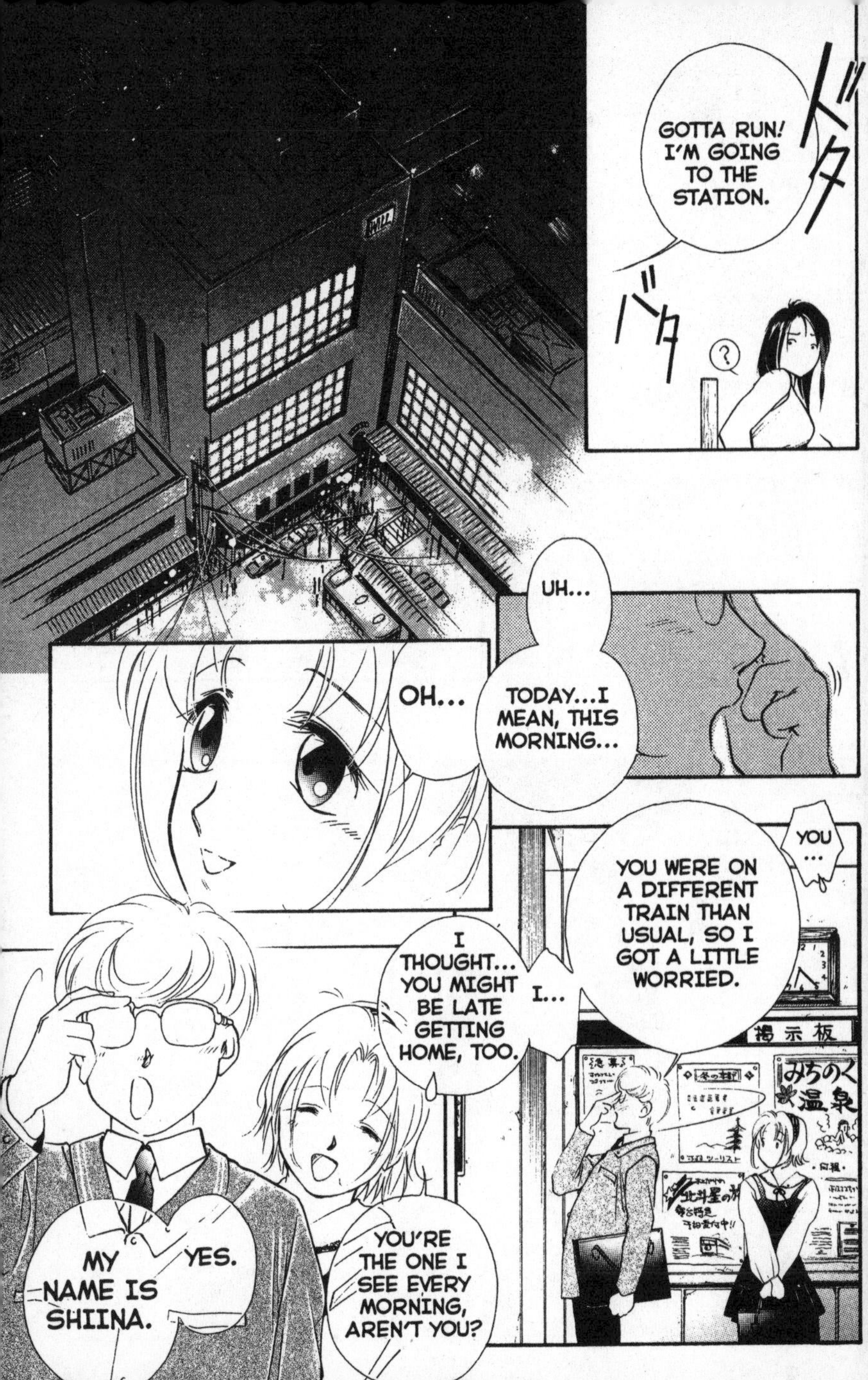
GOTTA RUN! I'M GOING TO THE STATION.
ドタ
バタ
?
UH...
TODAY...I MEAN, THIS MORNING...
OH...
YOU...
YOU WERE ON A DIFFERENT TRAIN THAN USUAL, SO I GOT A LITTLE WORRIED.
掲示板
みちのく温泉
I...
I THOUGHT... YOU MIGHT BE LATE GETTING HOME, TOO.
YOU'RE THE ONE I SEE EVERY MORNING, AREN'T YOU?
YES.
MY NAME IS SHIINA.

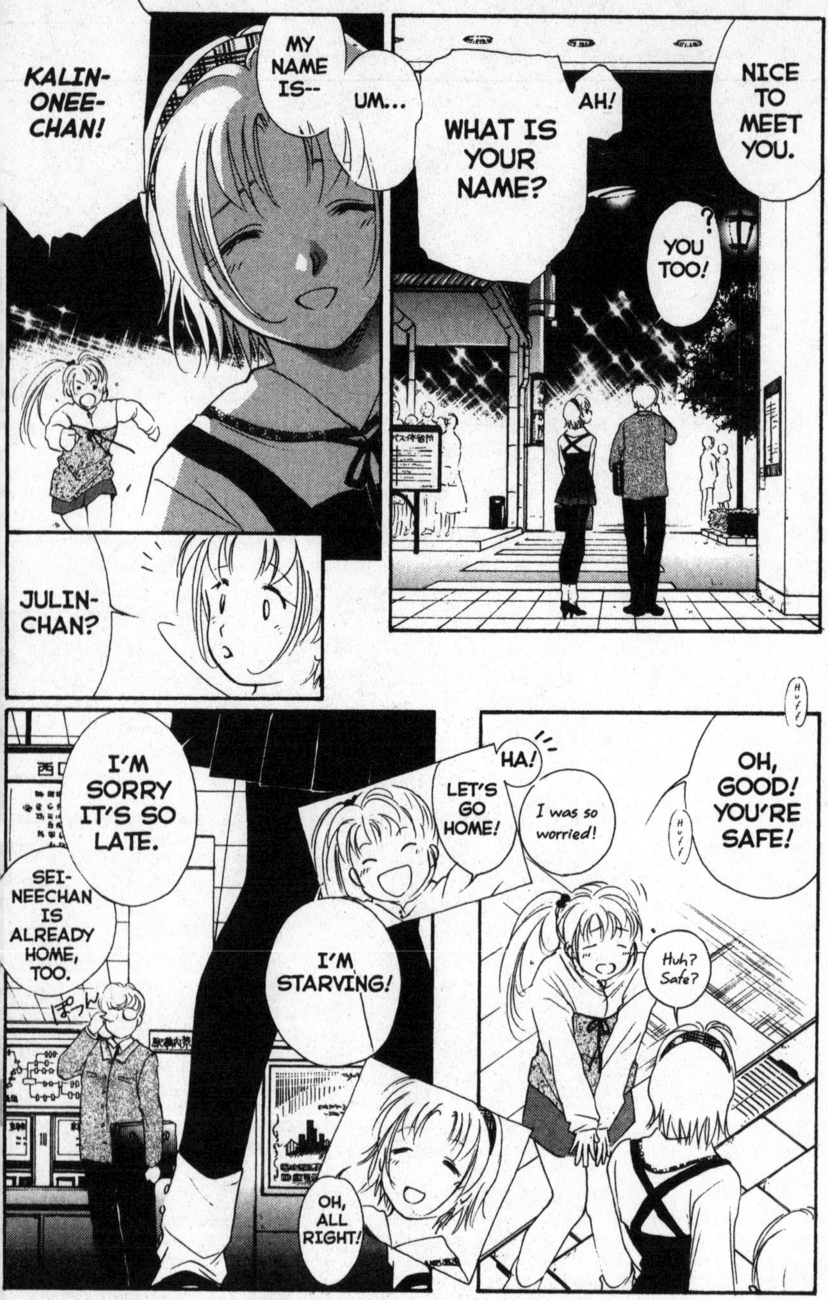
NICE TO MEET YOU.
YOU TOO!
AH!
WHAT IS YOUR NAME?
UM...
MY NAME IS--
KALIN-ONEE-CHAN!
JULIN-CHAN?
Huff
OH, GOOD! YOU'RE SAFE!
Huff
HA!
I was so worried!
Huh? Safe?
LET'S GO HOME!
I'M STARVING!
OH, ALL RIGHT!
I'M SORRY IT'S SO LATE.
SEI-NEECHAN IS ALREADY HOME, TOO.

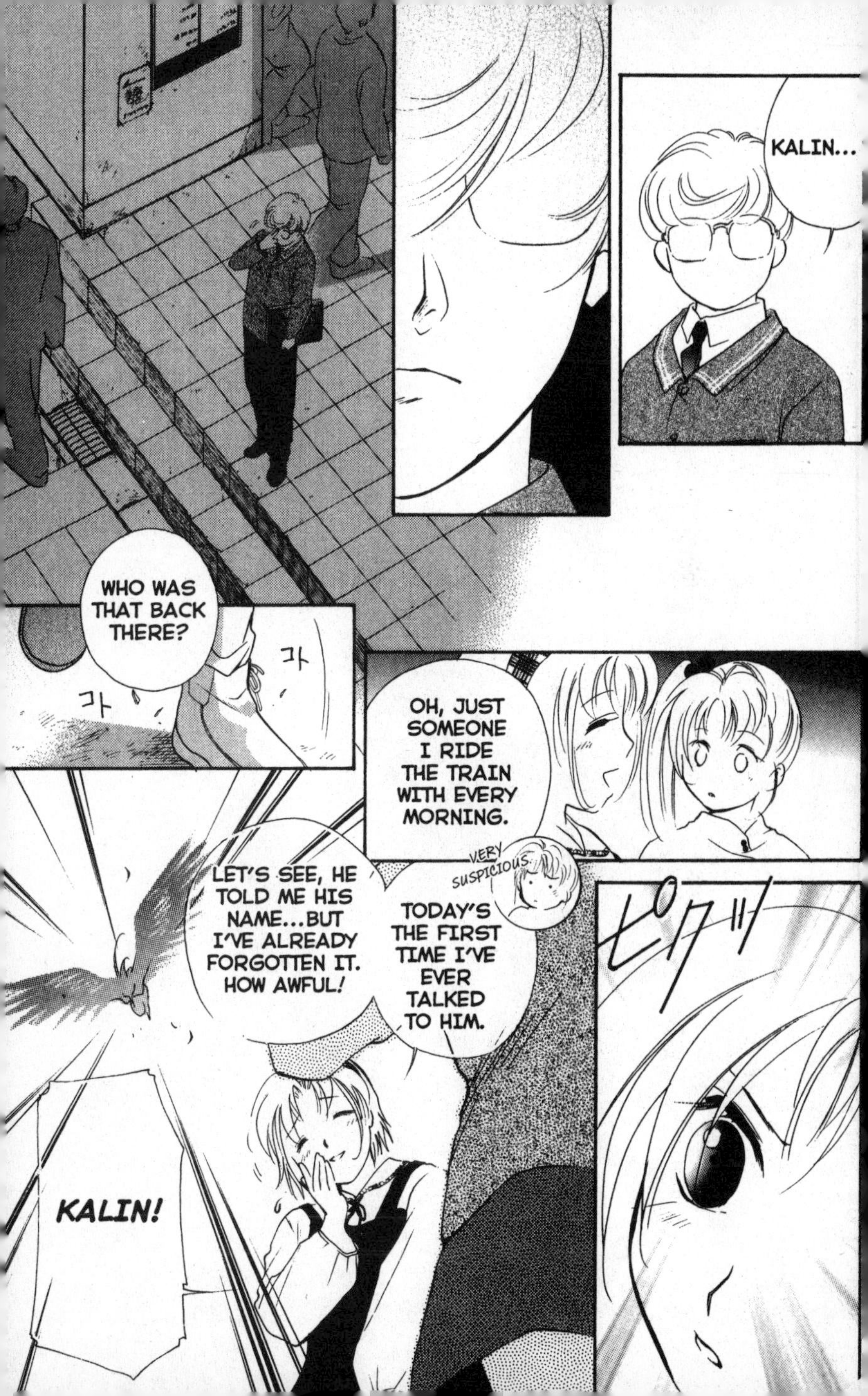
KALIN...
WHO WAS THAT BACK THERE?
OH, JUST SOMEONE I RIDE THE TRAIN WITH EVERY MORNING.
ピクッ
VERY SUSPICIOUS.
LET'S SEE, HE TOLD ME HIS NAME...BUT I'VE ALREADY FORGOTTEN IT. HOW AWFUL!
TODAY'S THE FIRST TIME I'VE EVER TALKED TO HIM.
KALIN!

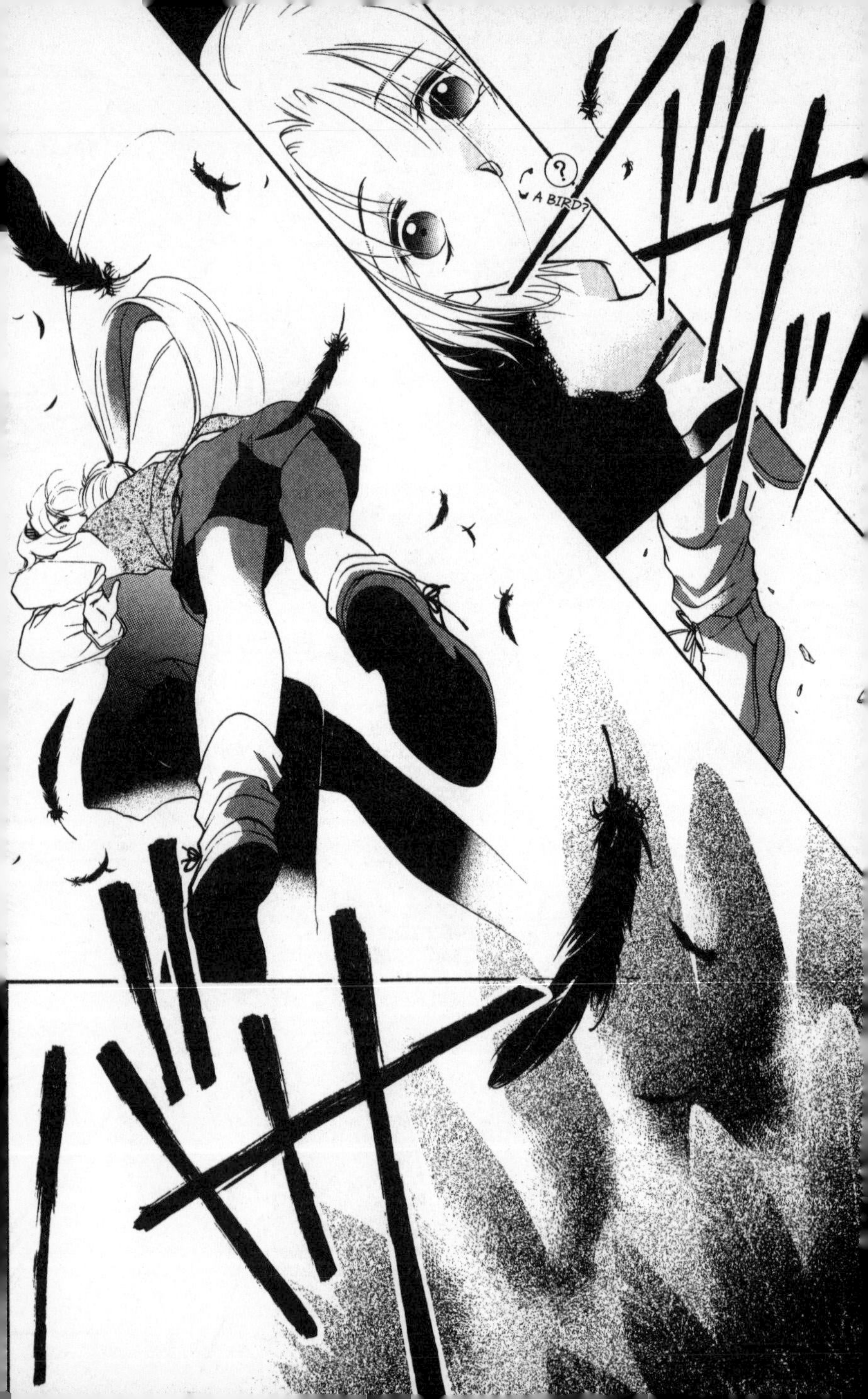
?
A BIRD?

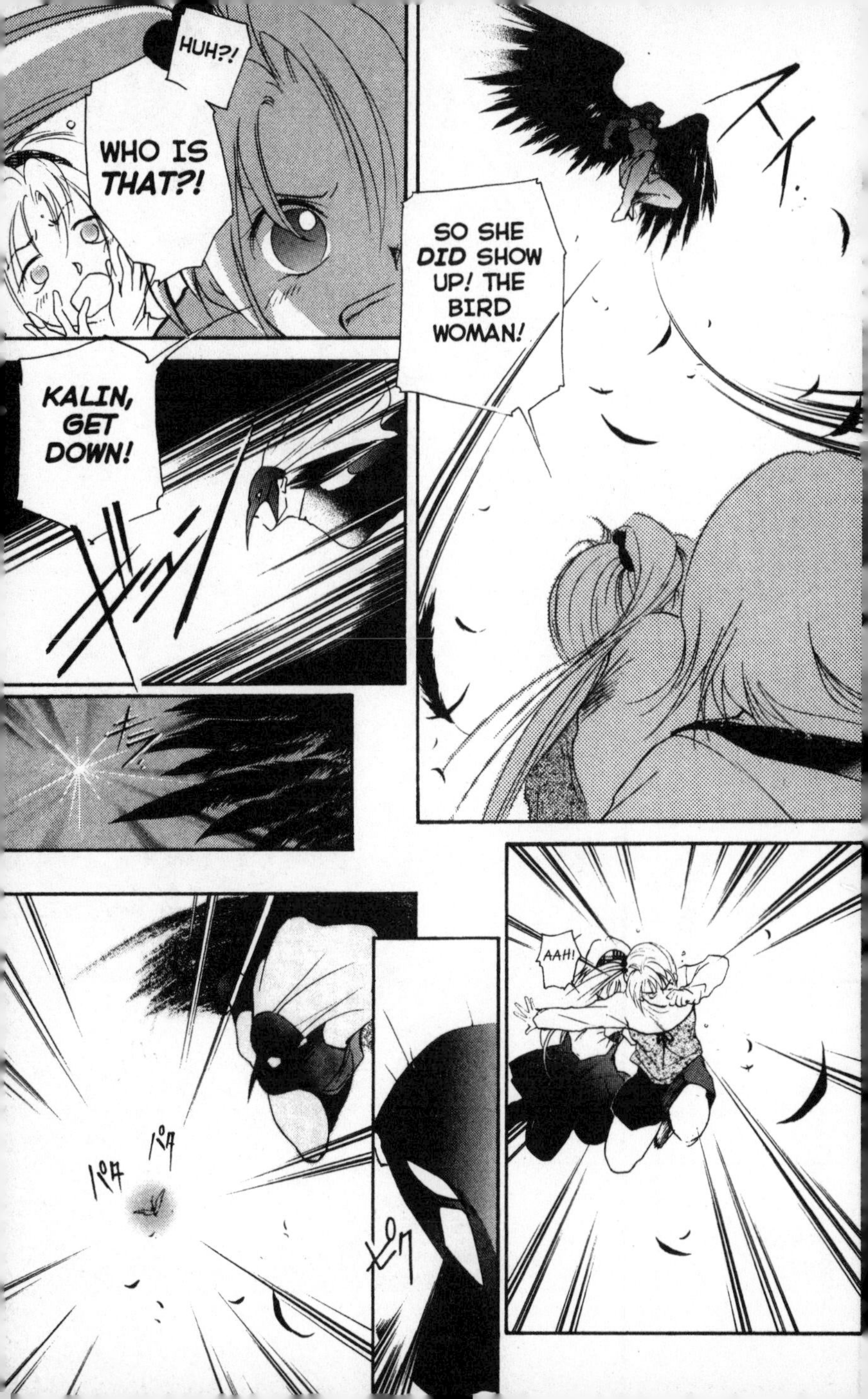
SO SHE DID SHOW UP! THE BIRD WOMAN!
HUH?!
WHO IS THAT?!
KALIN, GET DOWN!
AAH!

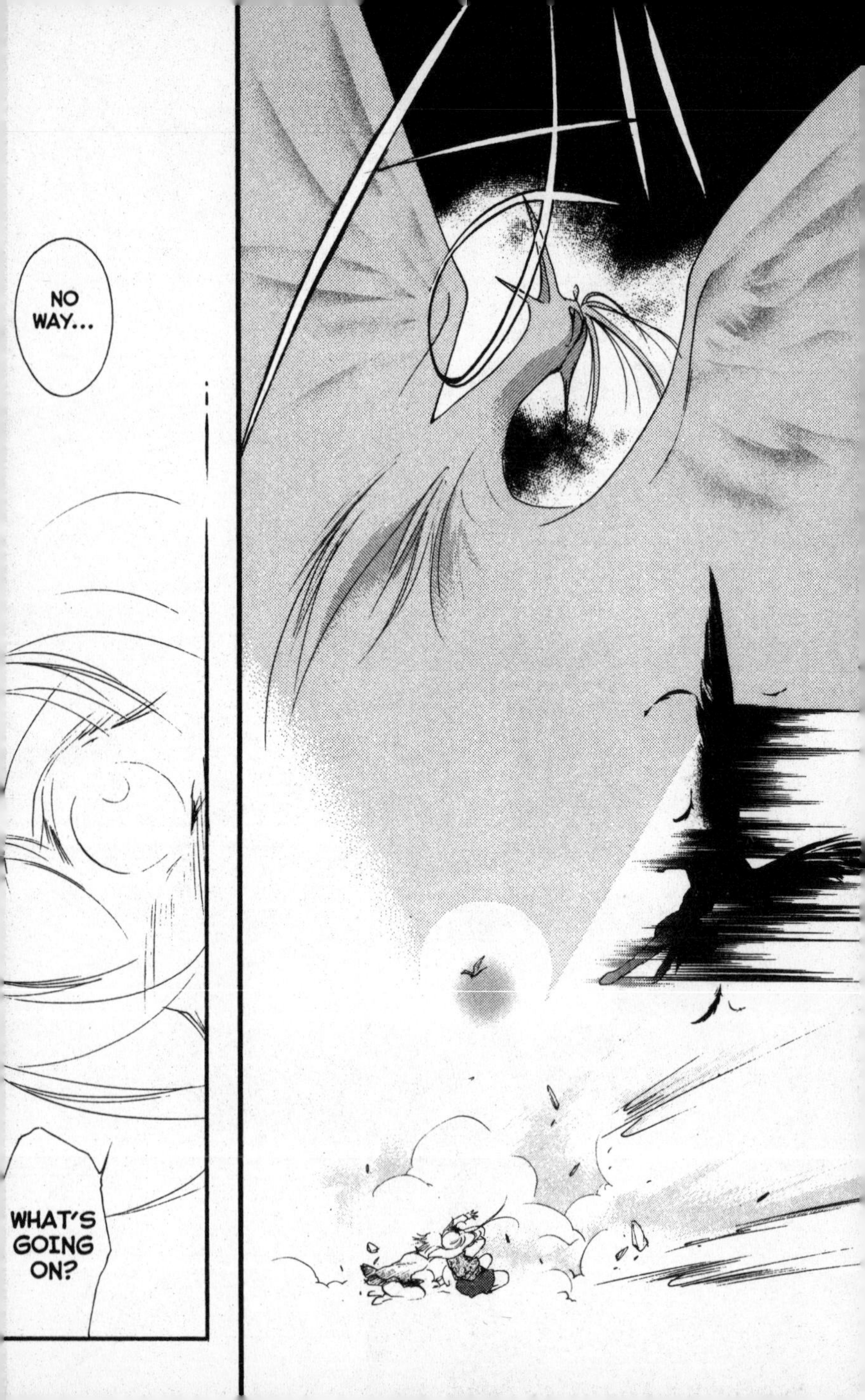
NO WAY...
WHAT'S GOING ON?

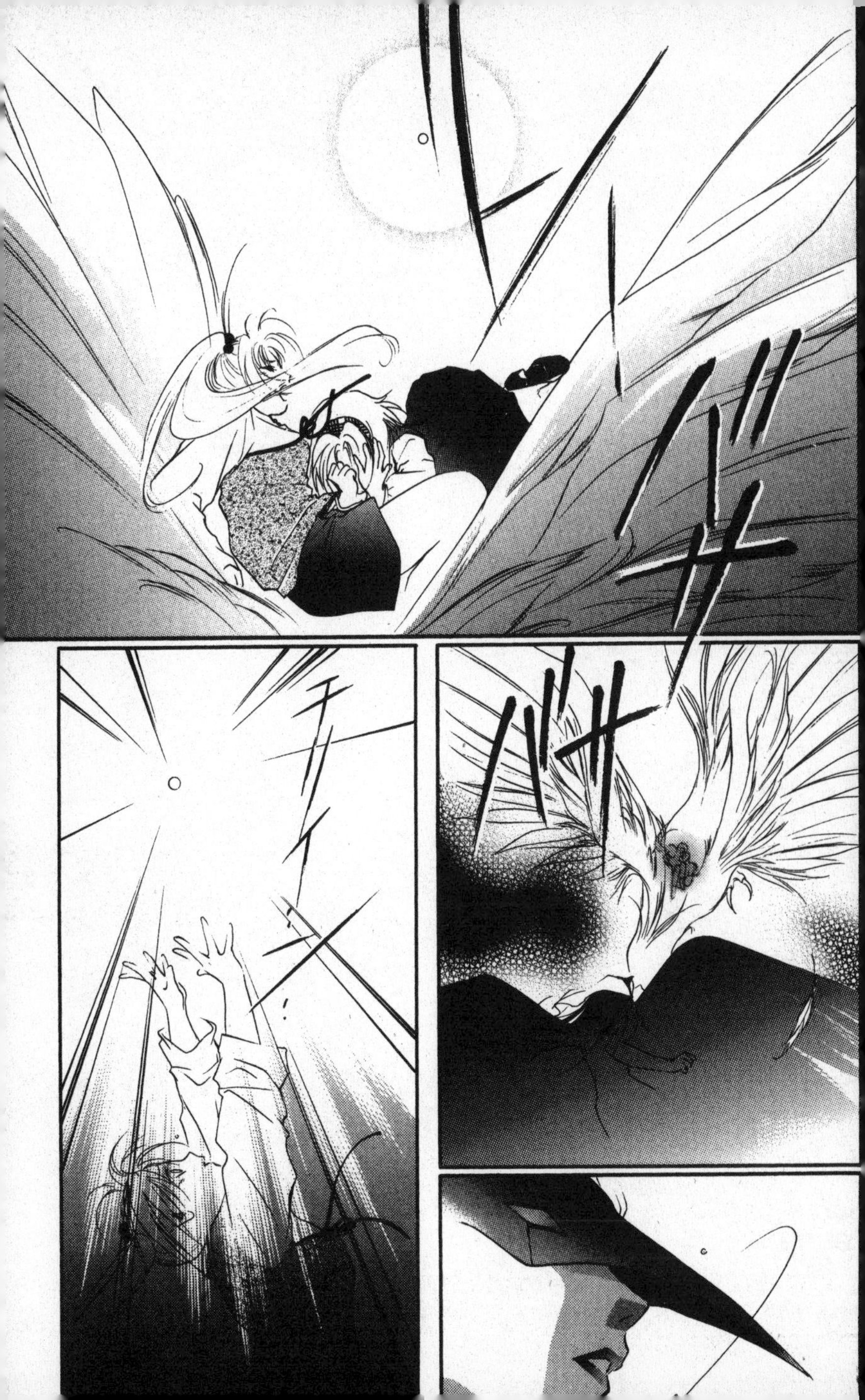
バサ
バサ
チイイン!

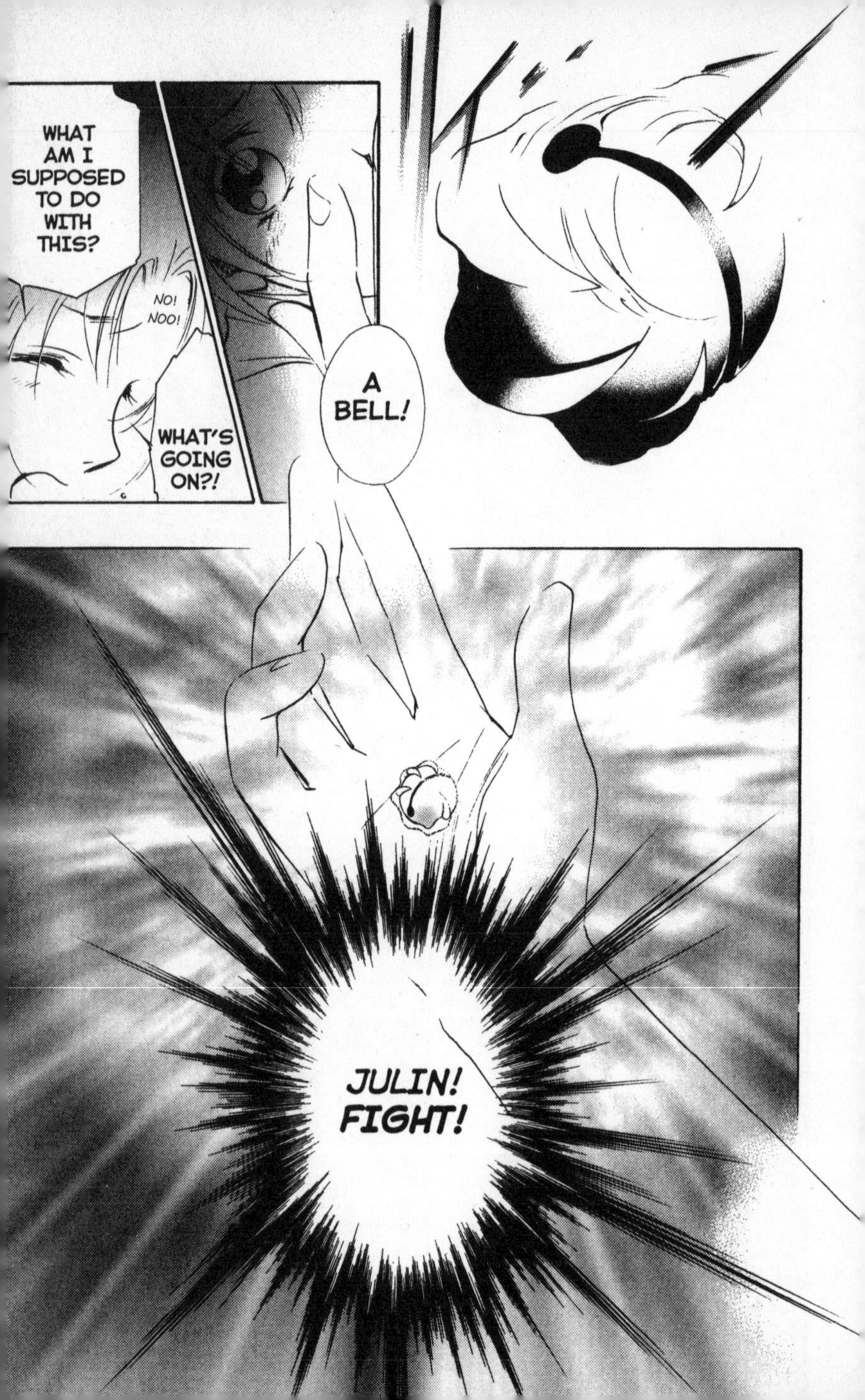
A BELL!
WHAT AM I SUPPOSED TO DO WITH THIS?
NO! NOO!
WHAT'S GOING ON?!
JULIN! FIGHT!

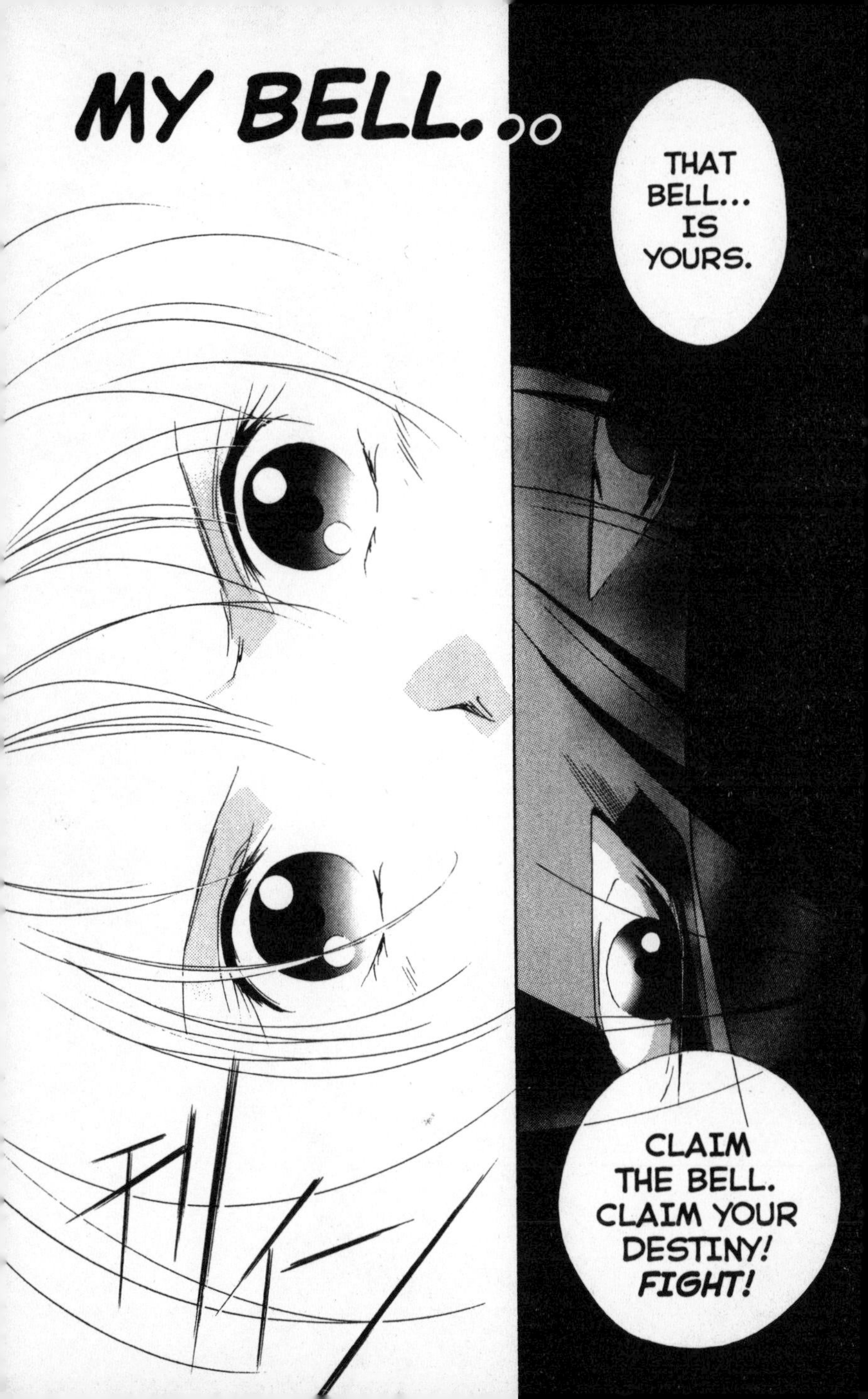
THAT BELL... IS YOURS.
CLAIM THE BELL. CLAIM YOUR DESTINY! *FIGHT!*
MY BELL...

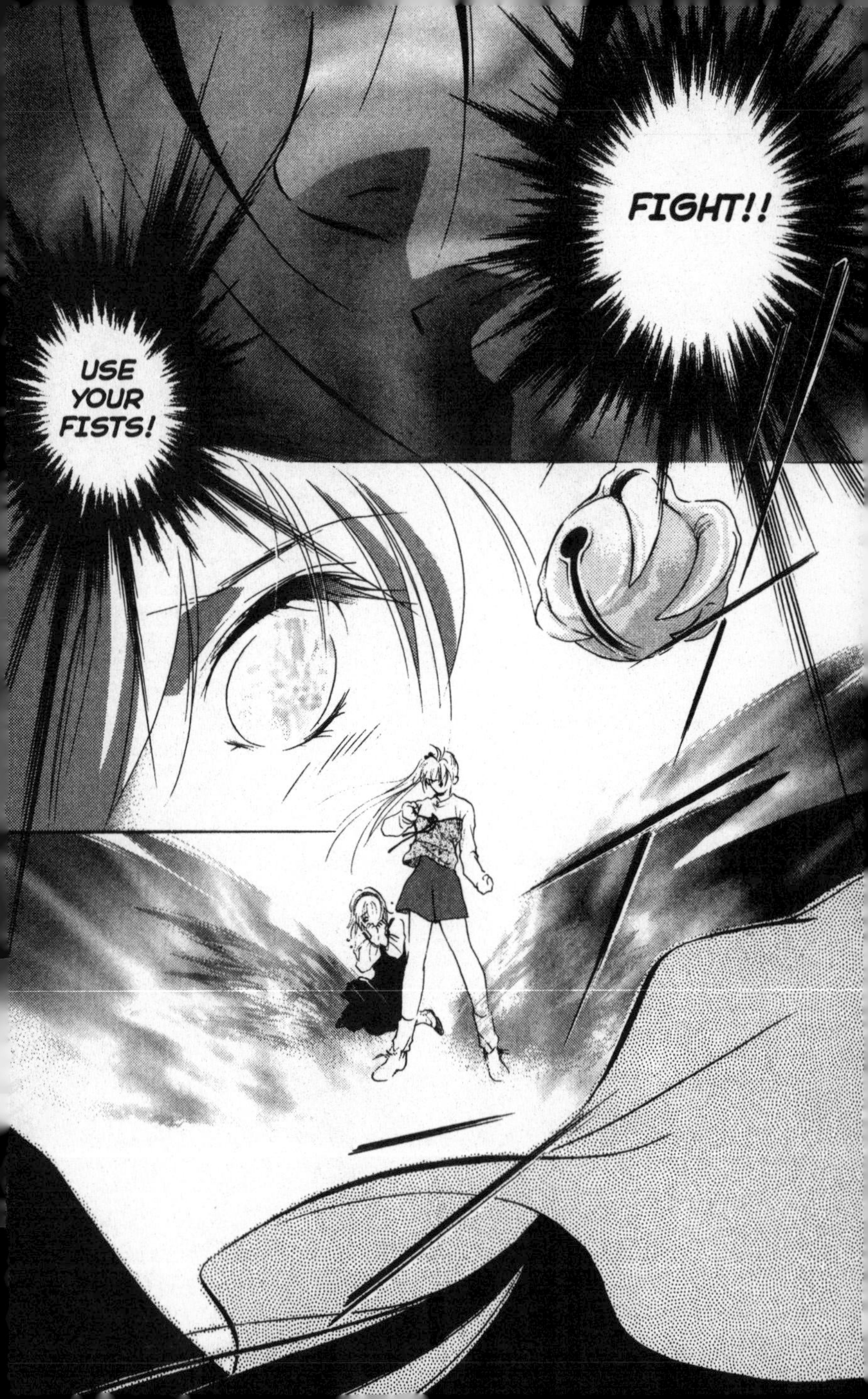
FIGHT!!
USE YOUR FISTS!

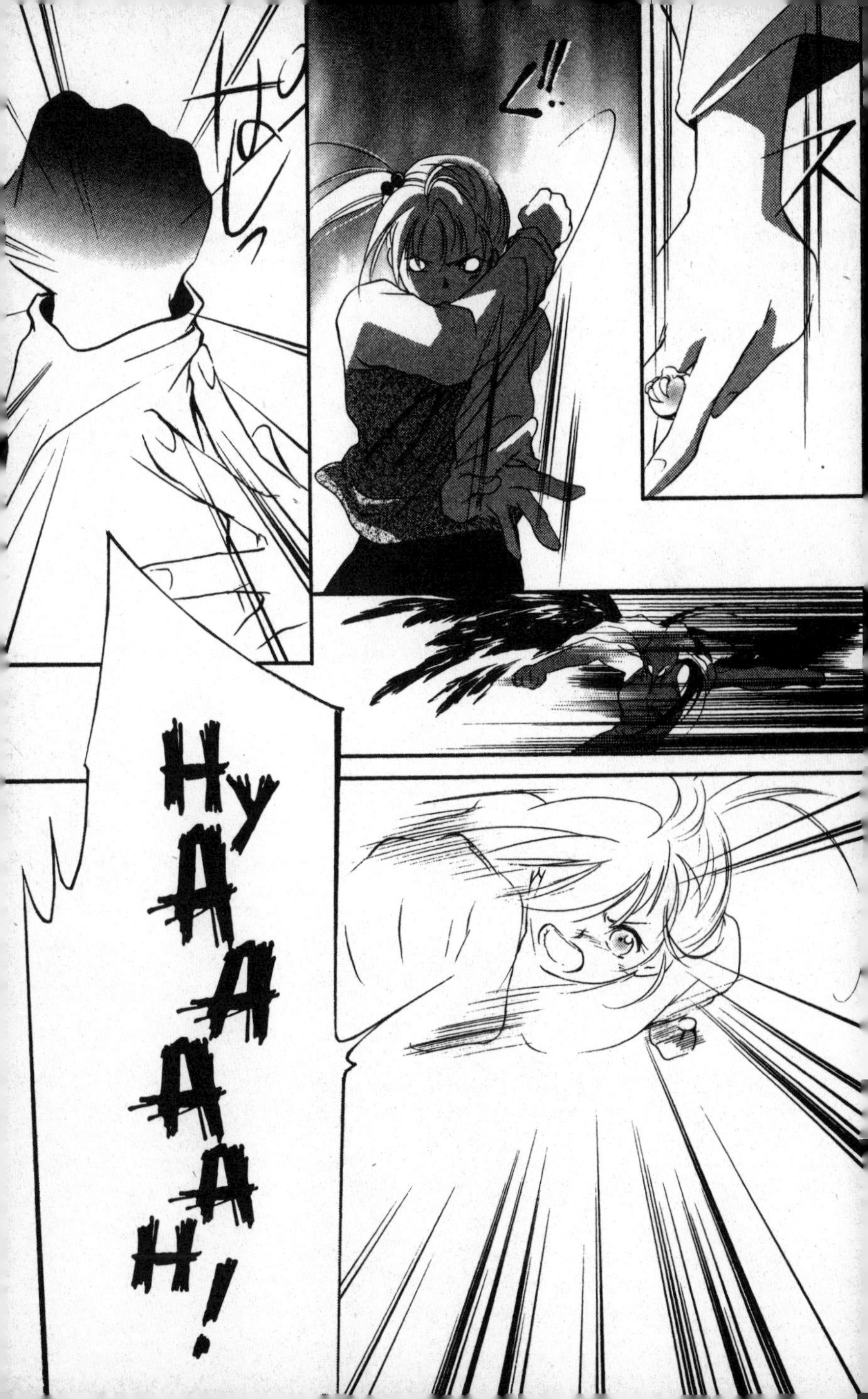
HyAAAAH!

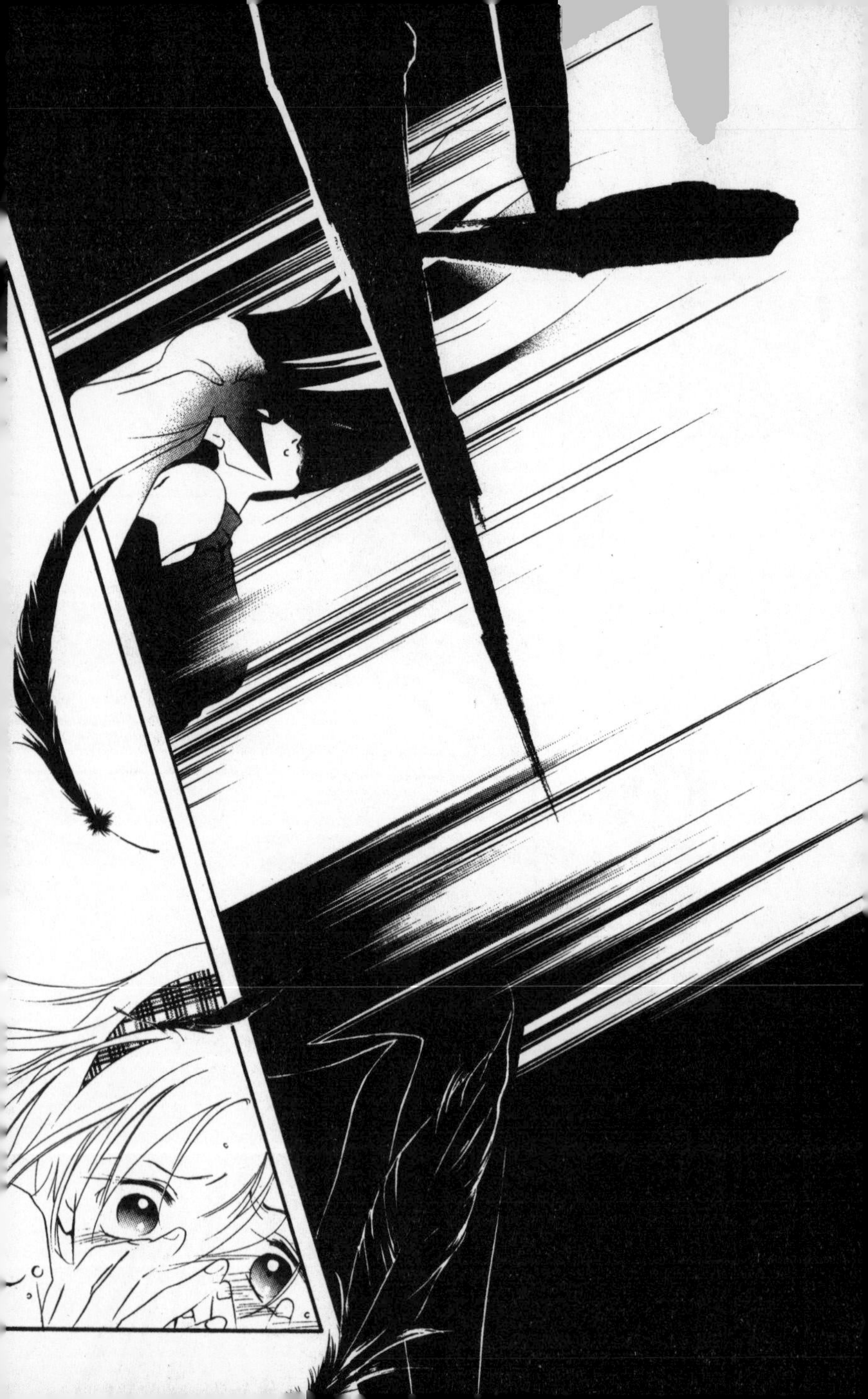

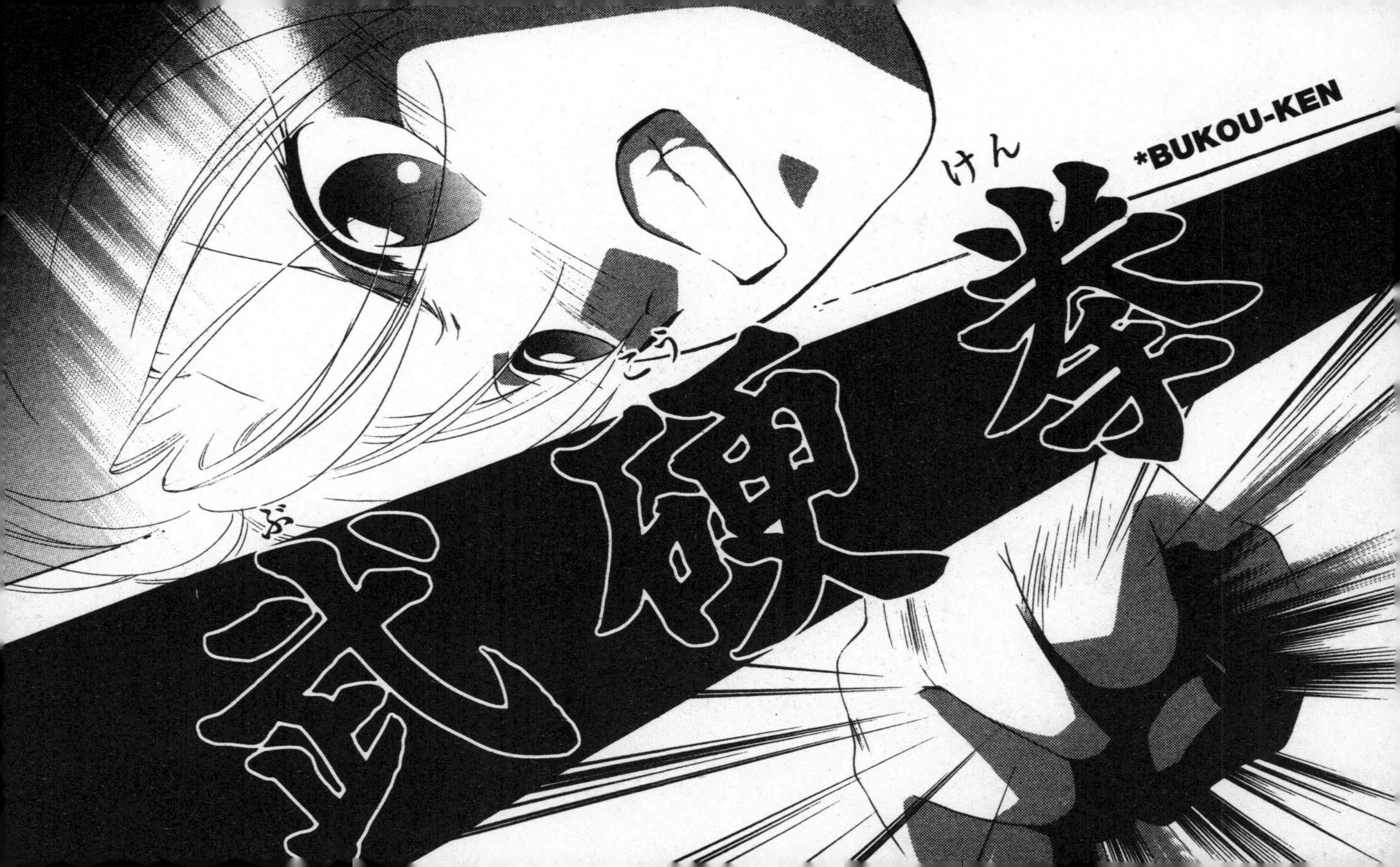
武硬拳
*BUKOU-KEN

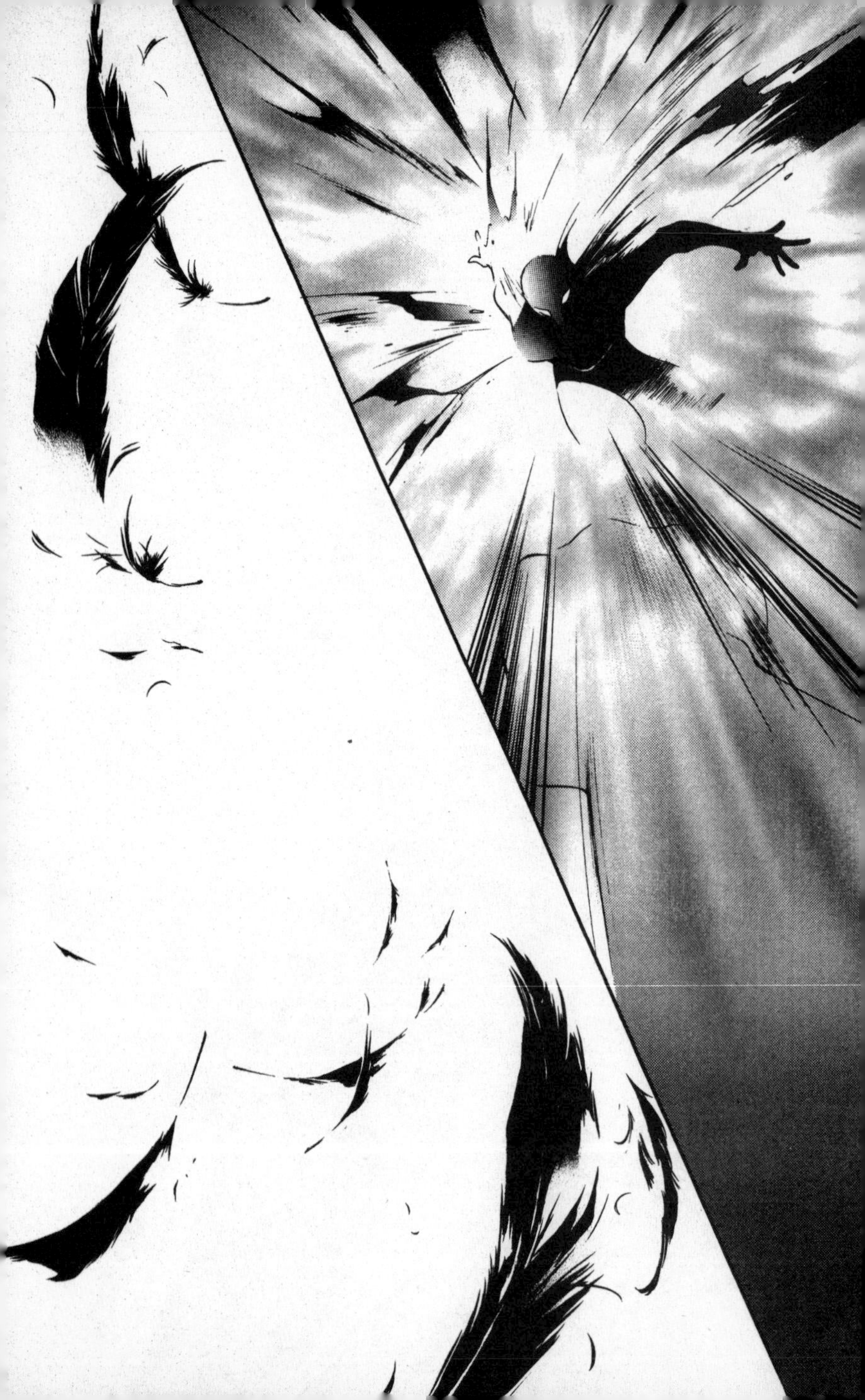

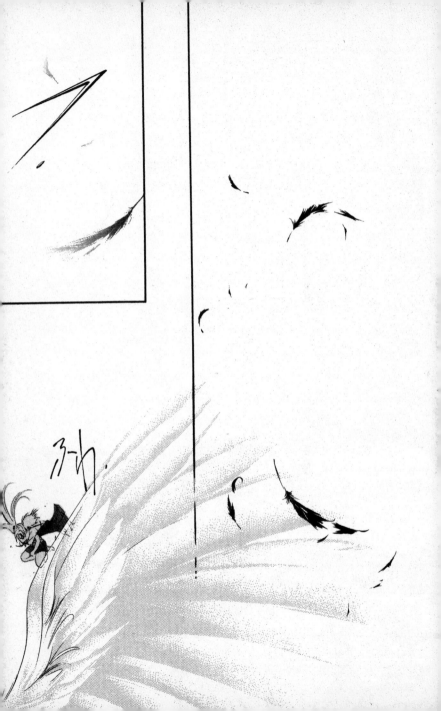

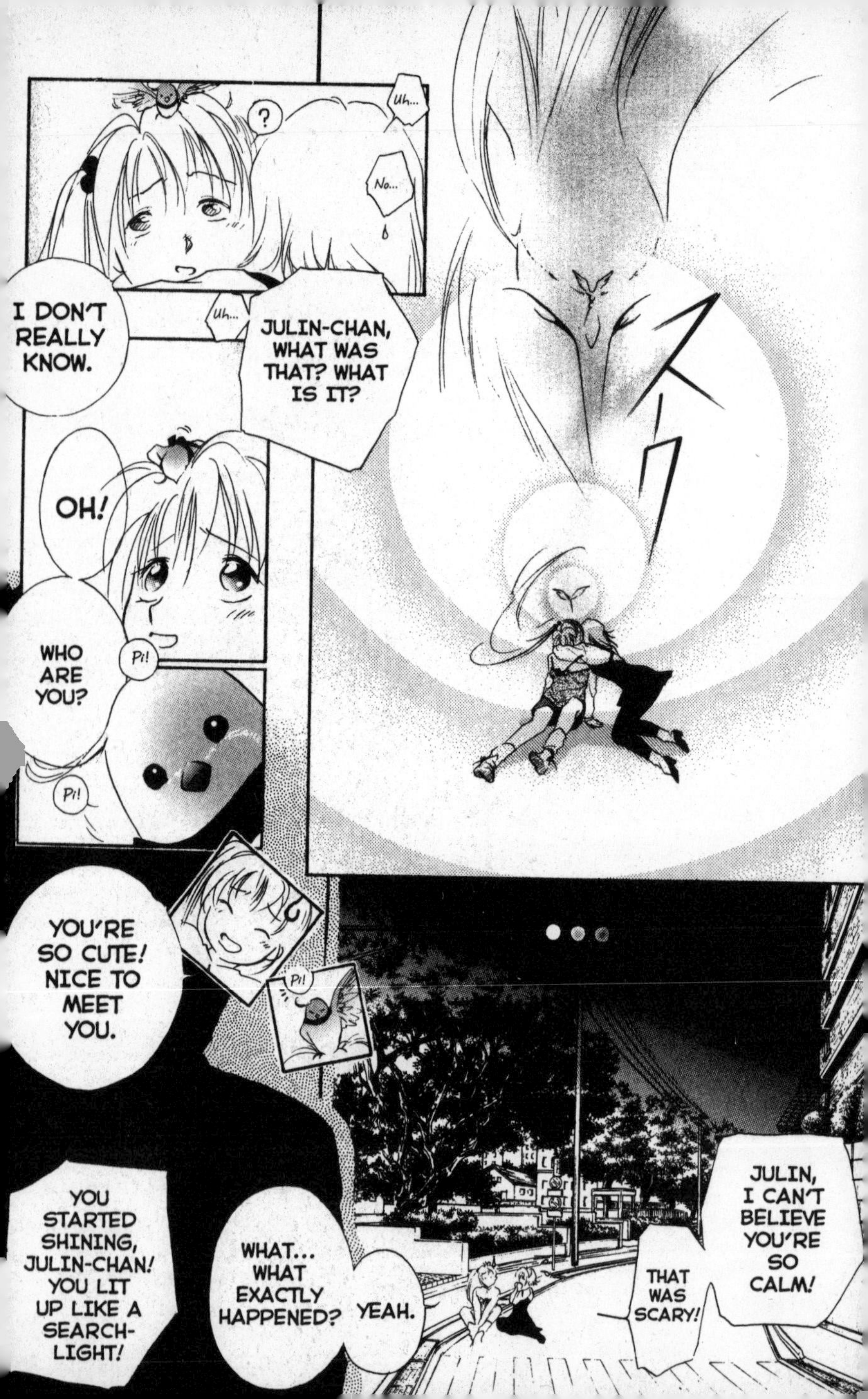
Uh...
?
No...
JULIN-CHAN, WHAT WAS THAT? WHAT IS IT?
Uh...
I DON'T REALLY KNOW.
OH!
WHO ARE YOU?
Pi!
Pi!
YOU'RE SO CUTE! NICE TO MEET YOU.
Pi!
JULIN, I CAN'T BELIEVE YOU'RE SO CALM!
THAT WAS SCARY!
YEAH.
WHAT... WHAT EXACTLY HAPPENED?
YOU STARTED SHINING, JULIN-CHAN! YOU LIT UP LIKE A SEARCH-LIGHT!

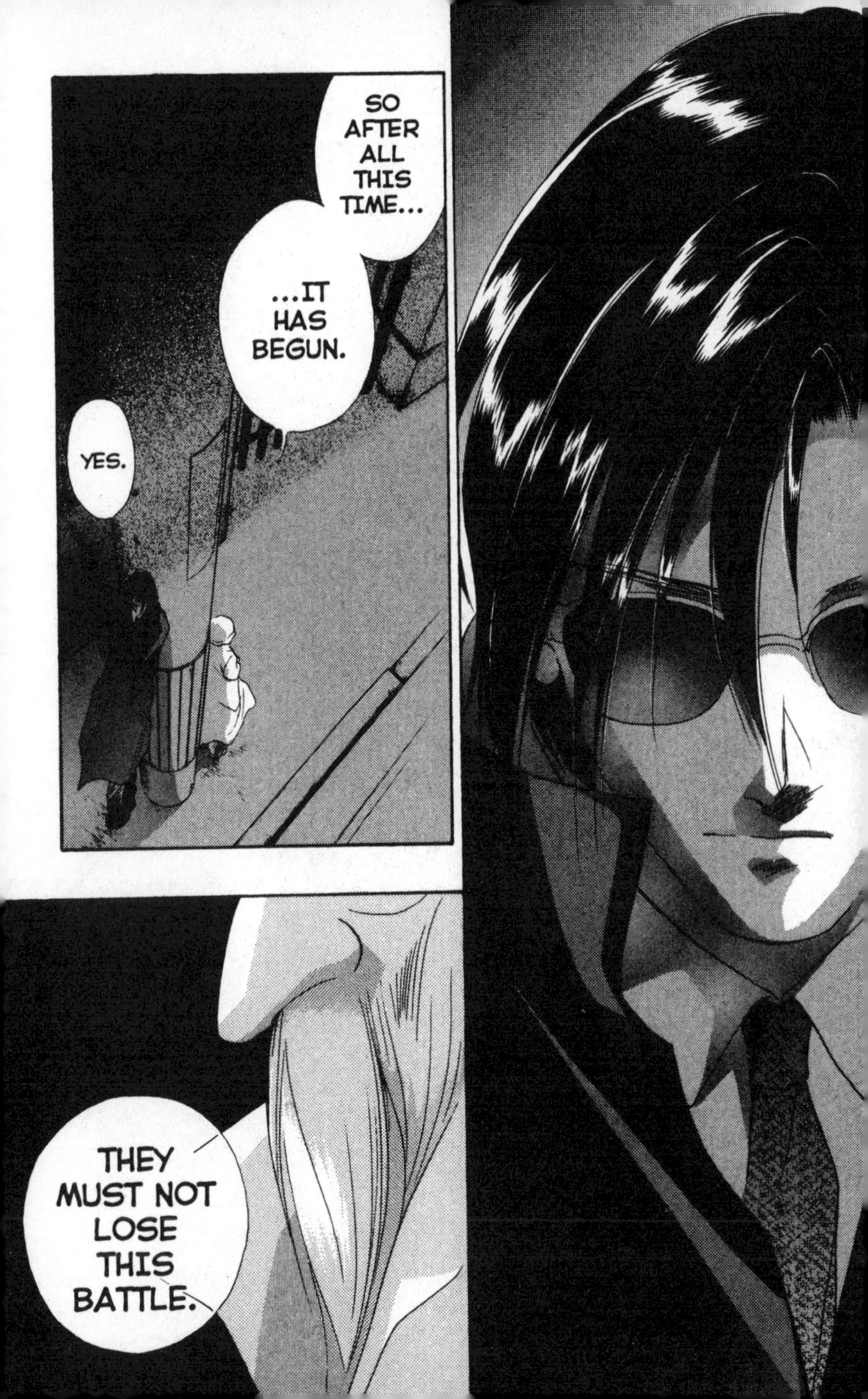
SO AFTER ALL THIS TIME...
...IT HAS BEGUN.
YES.
THEY MUST NOT LOSE THIS BATTLE.

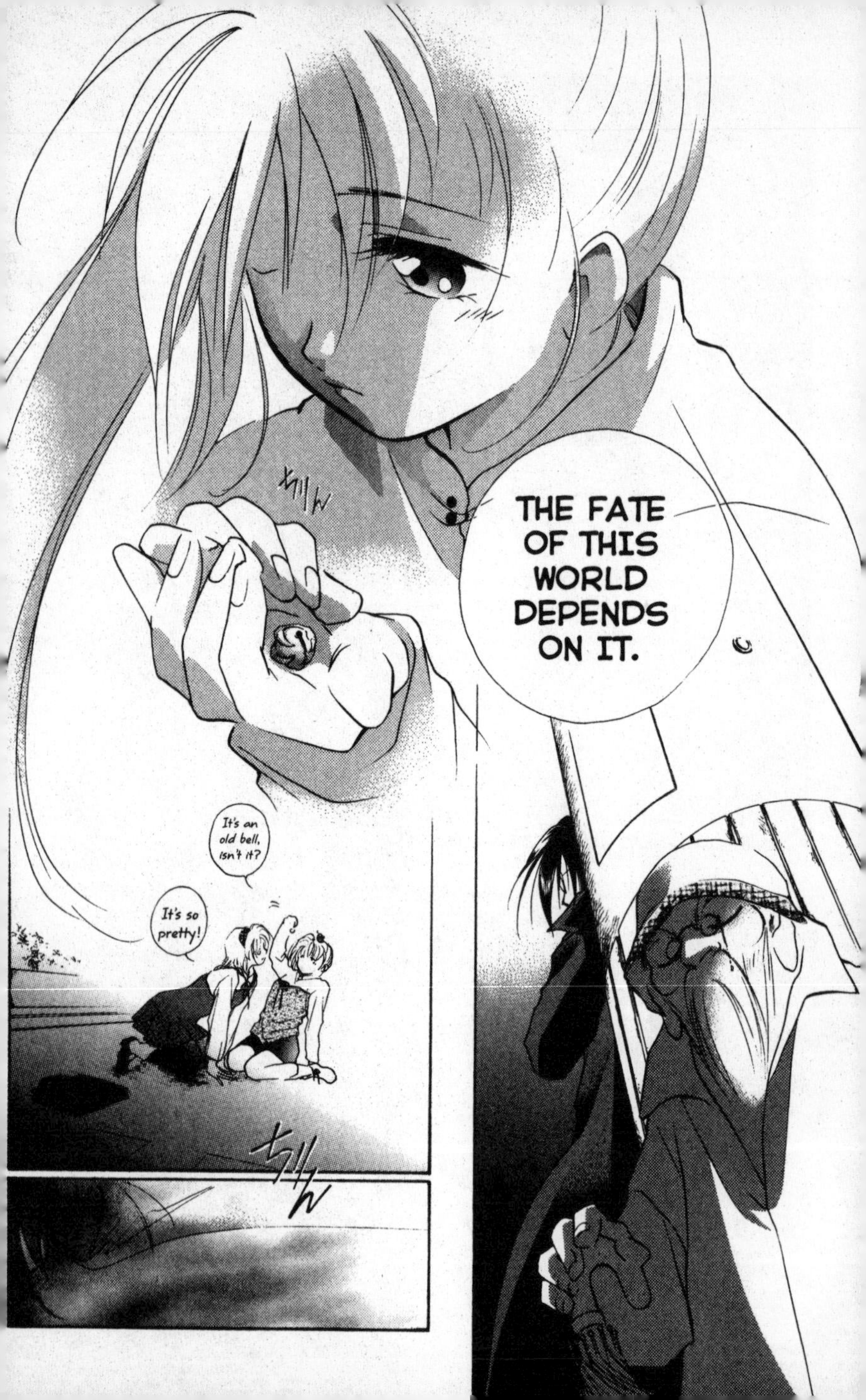
THE FATE OF THIS WORLD DEPENDS ON IT.
It's an old bell, isn't it?
It's so pretty!

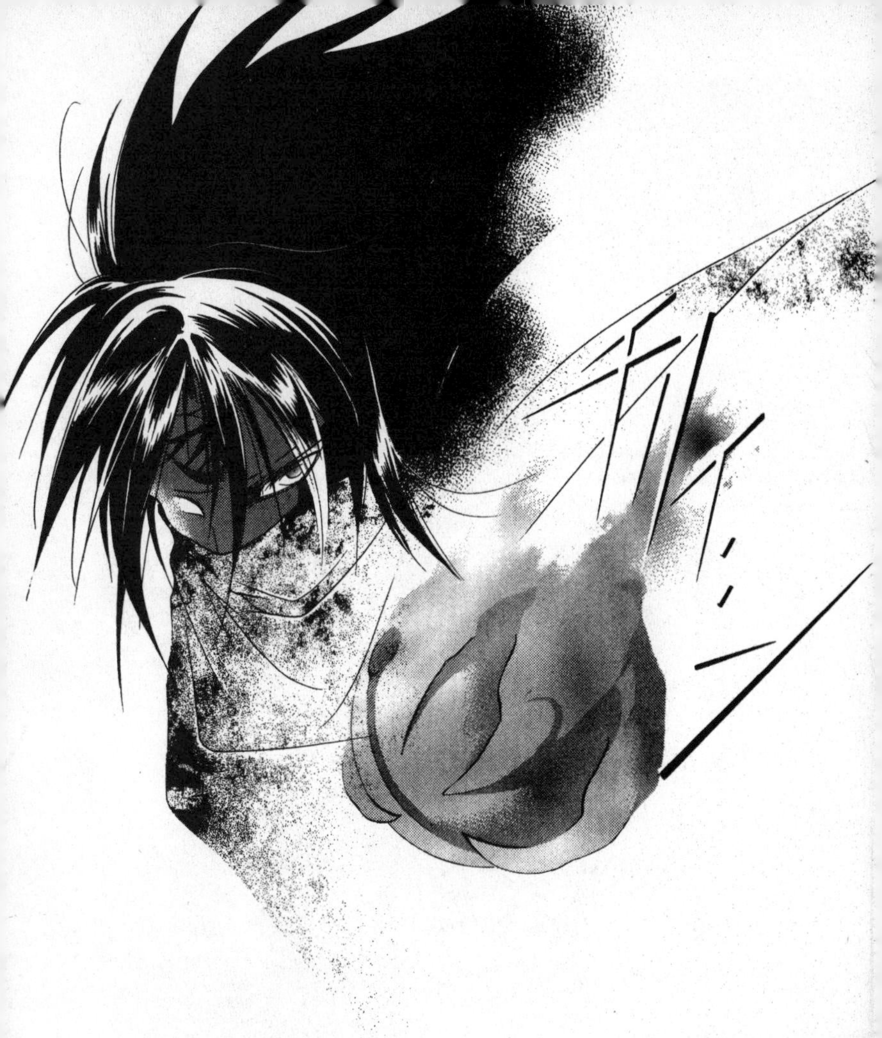

# TOKU-LIN

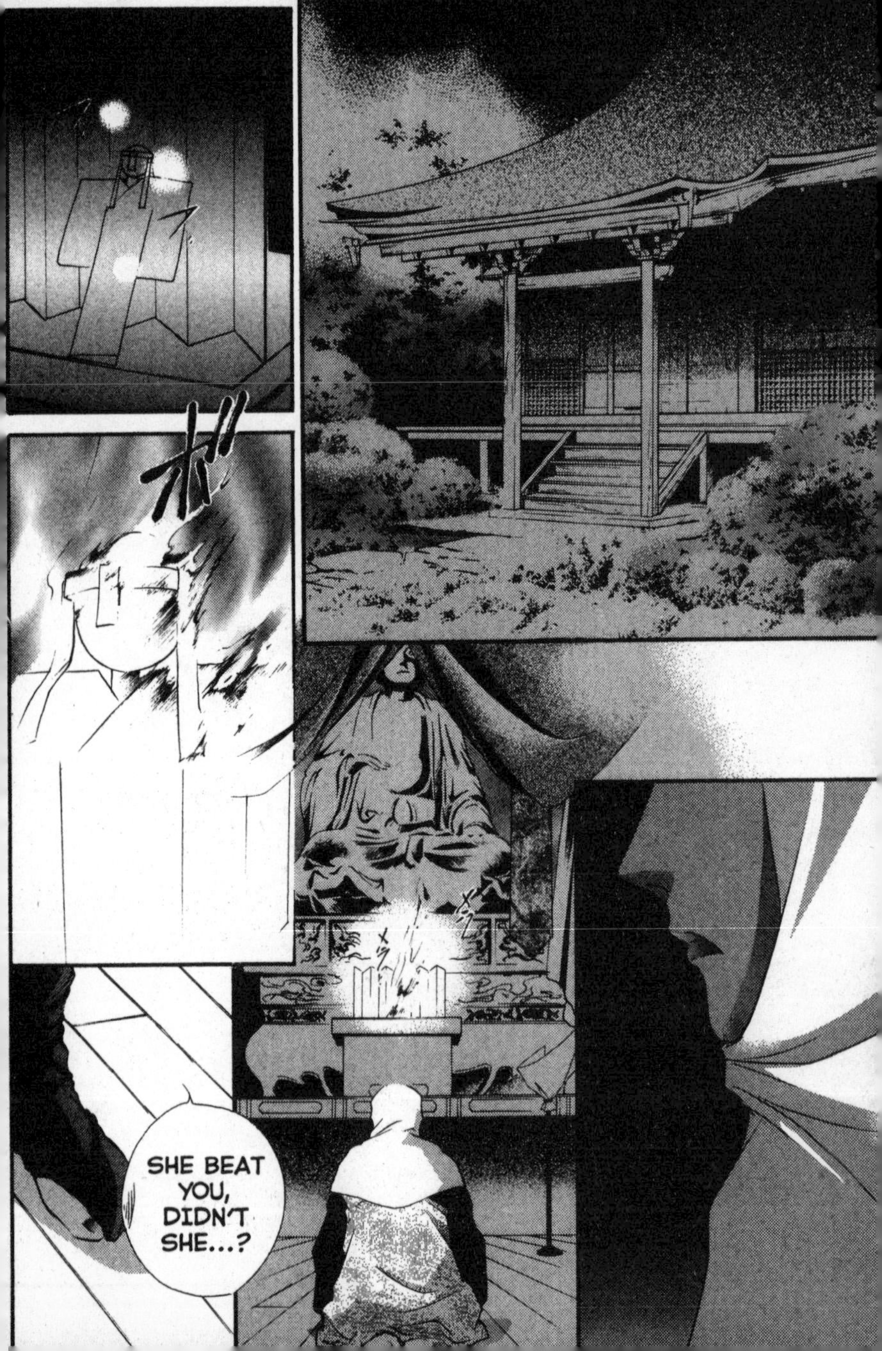
SHE BEAT YOU, DIDN'T SHE...?

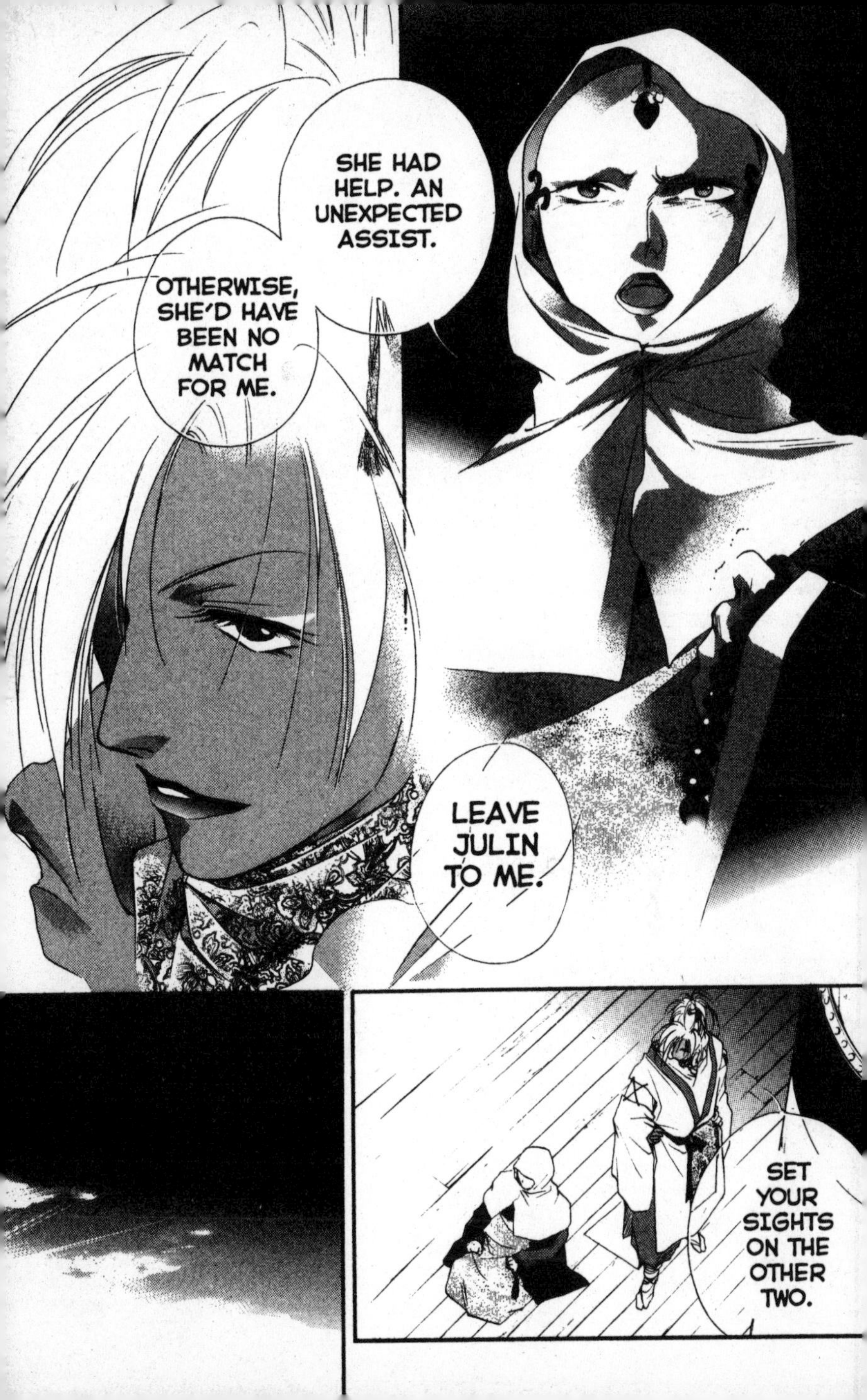
SHE HAD HELP. AN UNEXPECTED ASSIST.
OTHERWISE, SHE'D HAVE BEEN NO MATCH FOR ME.
LEAVE JULIN TO ME.
SET YOUR SIGHTS ON THE OTHER TWO.

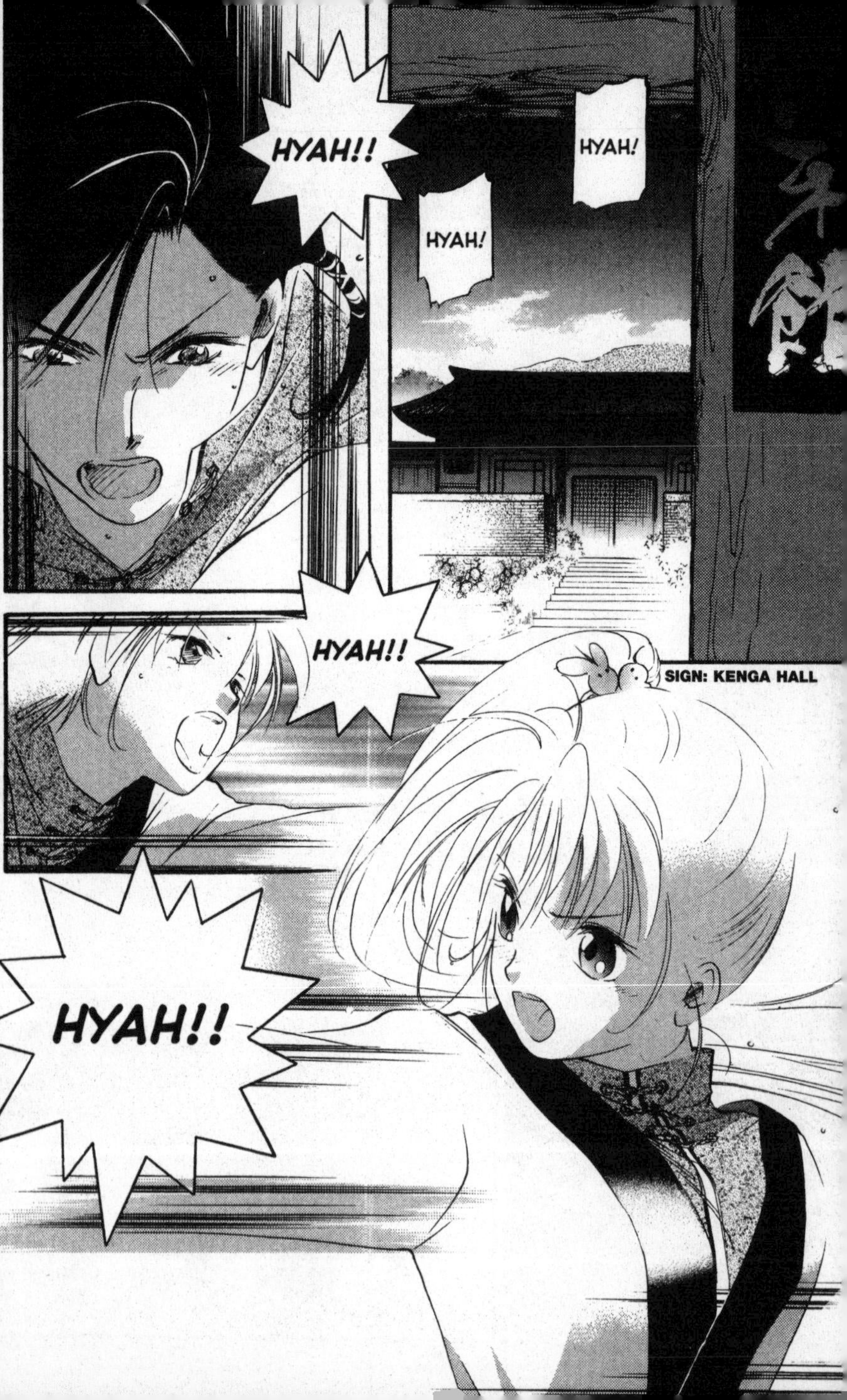
HYAH!
HYAH!
SIGN: KENGA HALL
HYAH!!
HYAH!!
HYAH!!

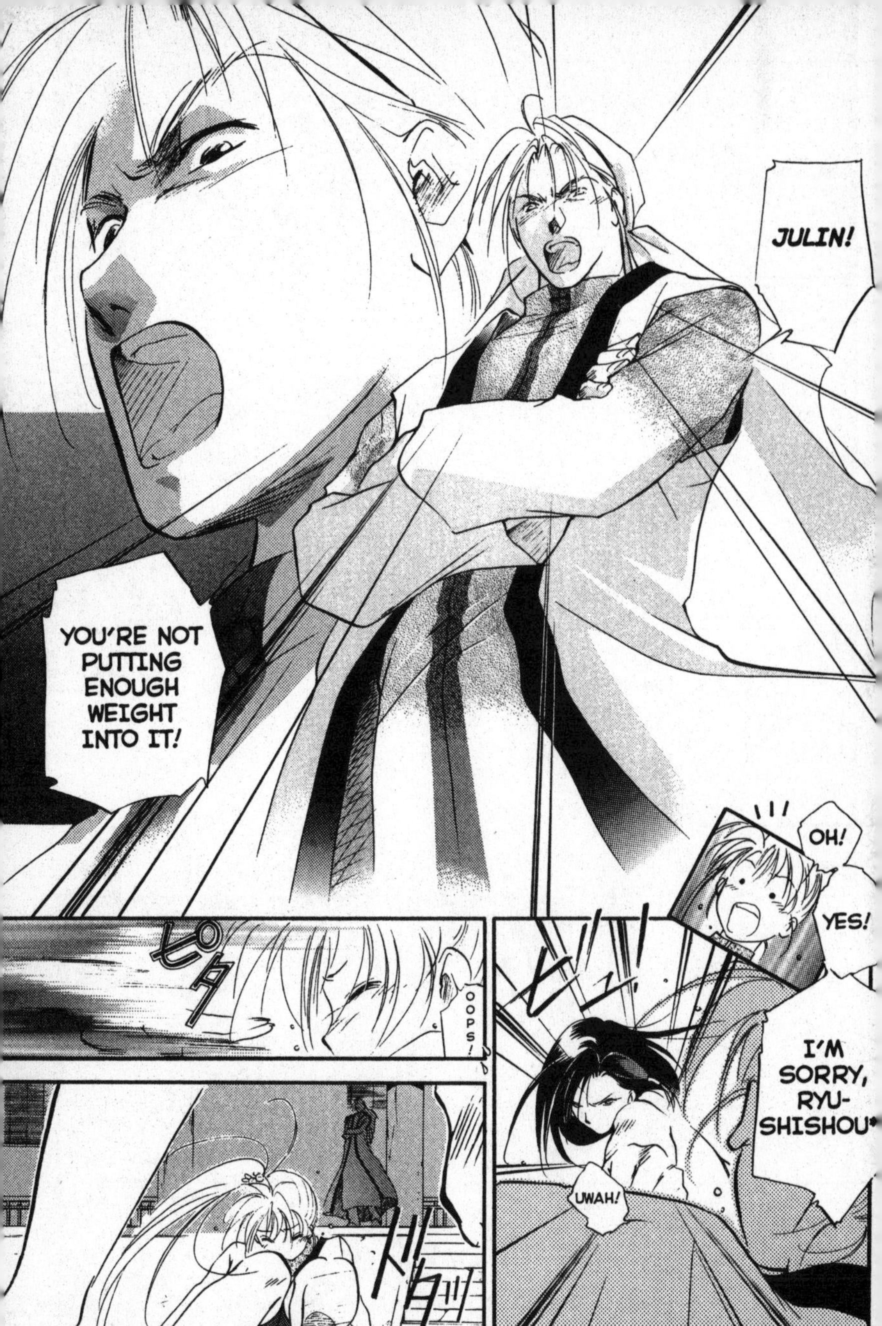
JULIN!
YOU'RE NOT PUTTING ENOUGH WEIGHT INTO IT!
OH!
YES!
I'M SORRY, RYU-SHISHOU*
UWAH!
OOPS!

*SHISHOU = MASTER

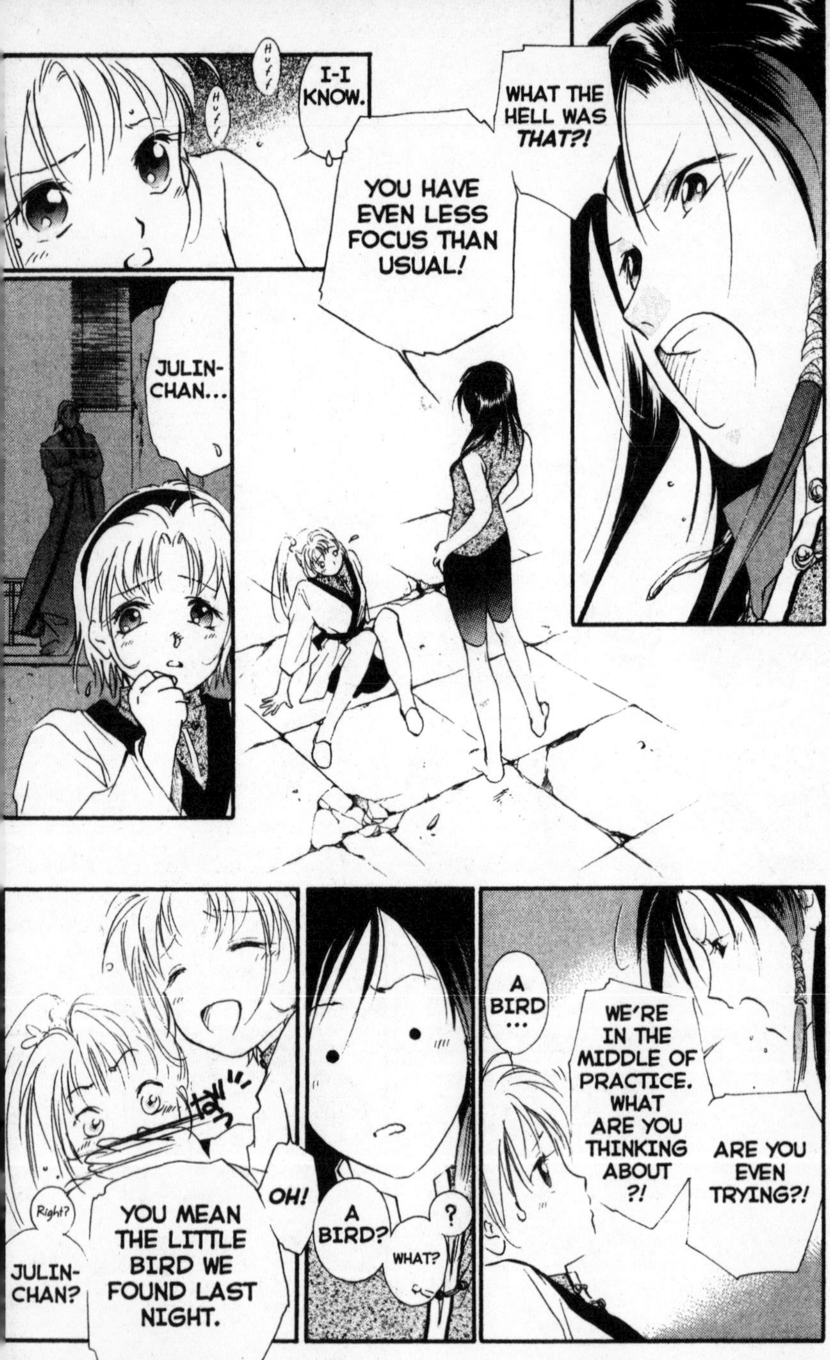
WHAT THE HELL WAS *THAT?!*
Huff
Huff
I-I KNOW.
YOU HAVE EVEN LESS FOCUS THAN USUAL!
JULIN-CHAN...
A BIRD...
WE'RE IN THE MIDDLE OF PRACTICE. WHAT ARE YOU THINKING ABOUT?!
ARE YOU EVEN TRYING?!
?
WHAT?
A BIRD?
OH!
YOU MEAN THE LITTLE BIRD WE FOUND LAST NIGHT.
Right?
JULIN-CHAN?

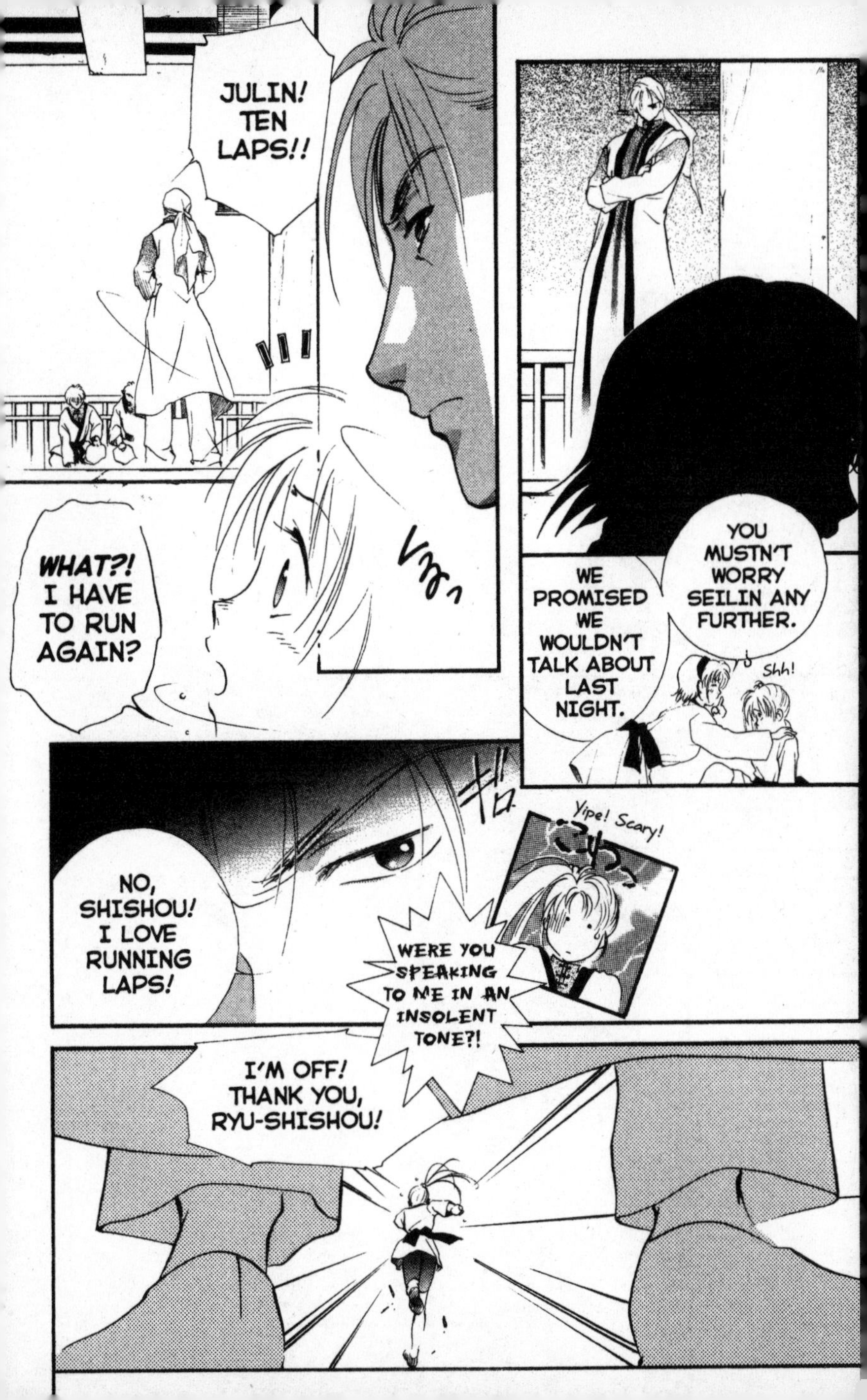

YOU MUSTN'T WORRY SEILIN ANY FURTHER.
WE PROMISED WE WOULDN'T TALK ABOUT LAST NIGHT.
Shh!
JULIN! TEN LAPS!!
WHAT?! I HAVE TO RUN AGAIN?
Yipe! Scary!
WERE YOU SPEAKING TO ME IN AN INSOLENT TONE?!
NO, SHISHOU! I LOVE RUNNING LAPS!
I'M OFF! THANK YOU, RYU-SHISHOU!

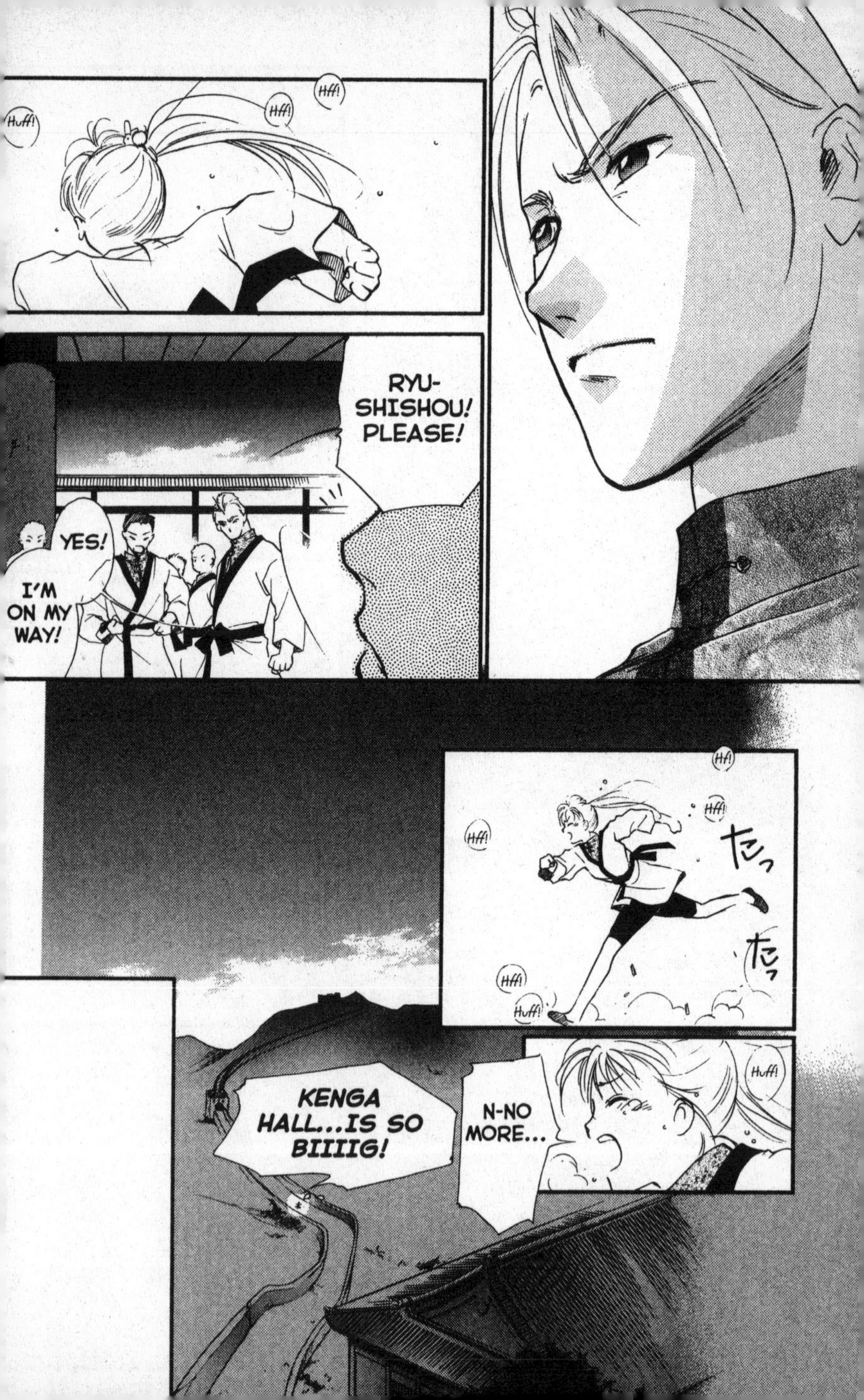
Hff!
Hff!
Huff!
RYU-SHISHOU! PLEASE!
YES!
I'M ON MY WAY!
Hff!
Hff!
たっ
Hff!
たっ
Hff!
Huff!
Huff!
N-NO MORE...
KENGA HALL...IS SO BIIIIG!

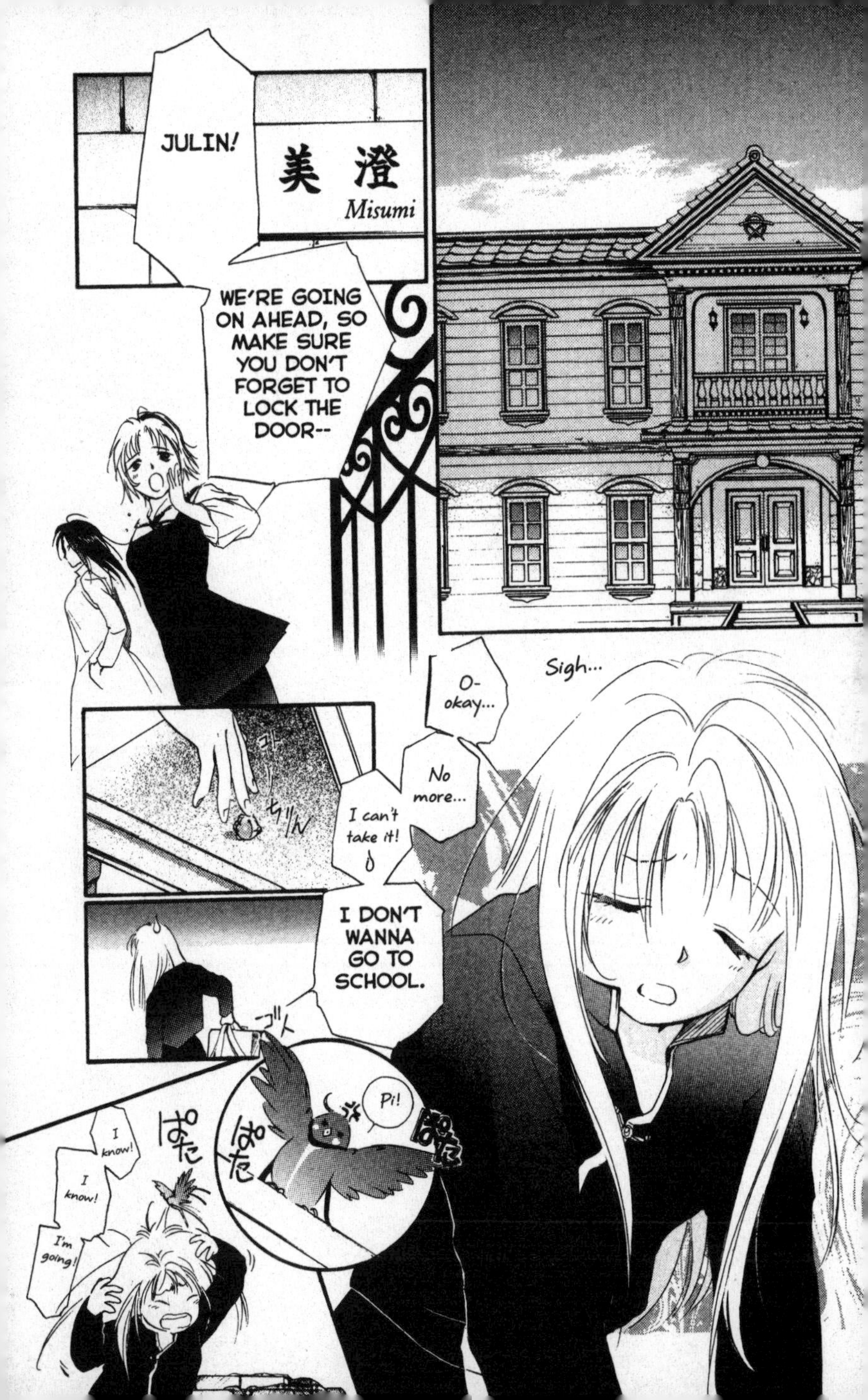
JULIN!
美澄
Misumi
WE'RE GOING ON AHEAD, SO MAKE SURE YOU DON'T FORGET TO LOCK THE DOOR--
Sigh...
O- okay...
No more...
I can't take it!
I DON'T WANNA GO TO SCHOOL.
Pi!
I know!
I know!
I'm going!

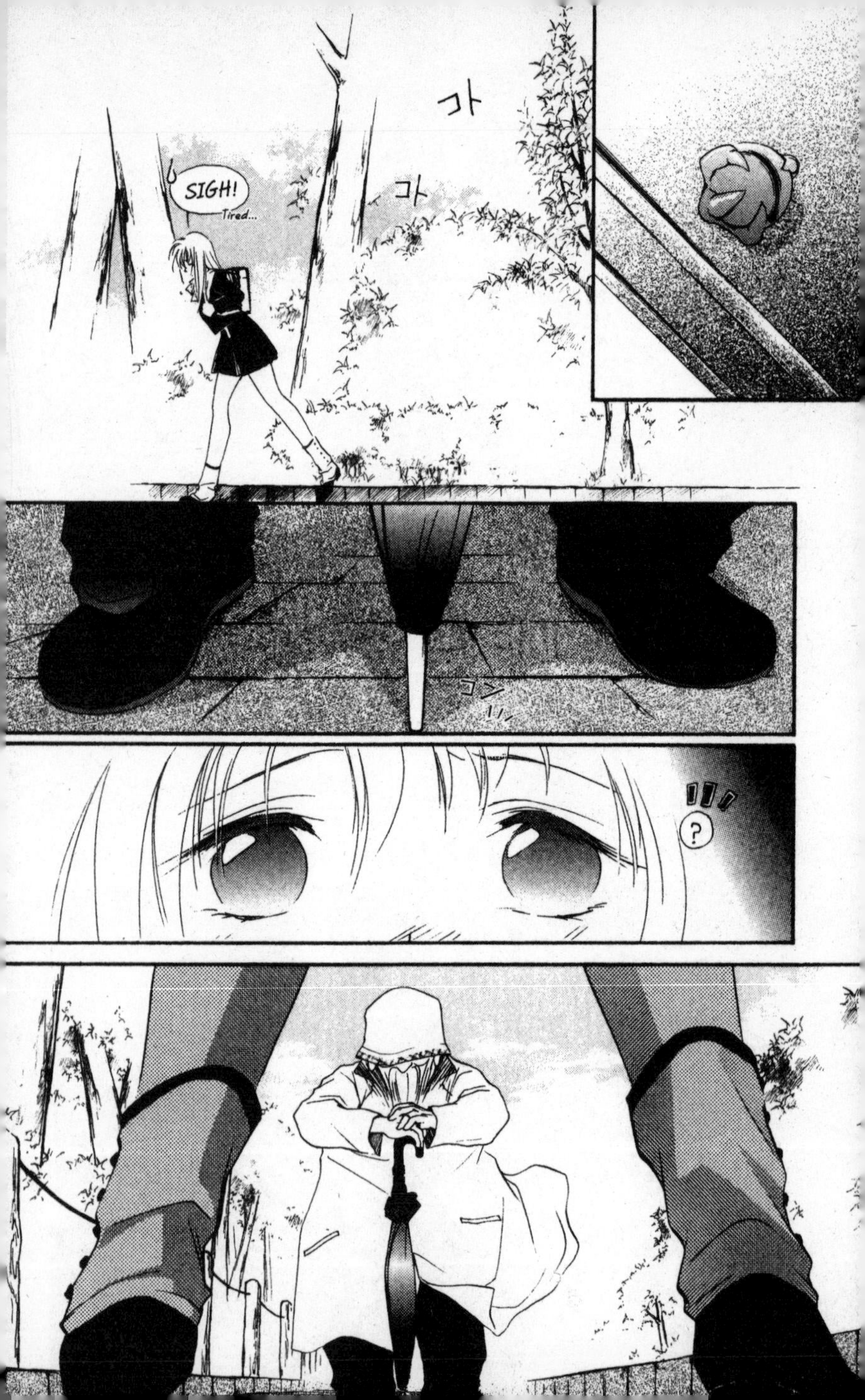
コト
コト
SIGH!
Tired...
コンッ
!!!
?

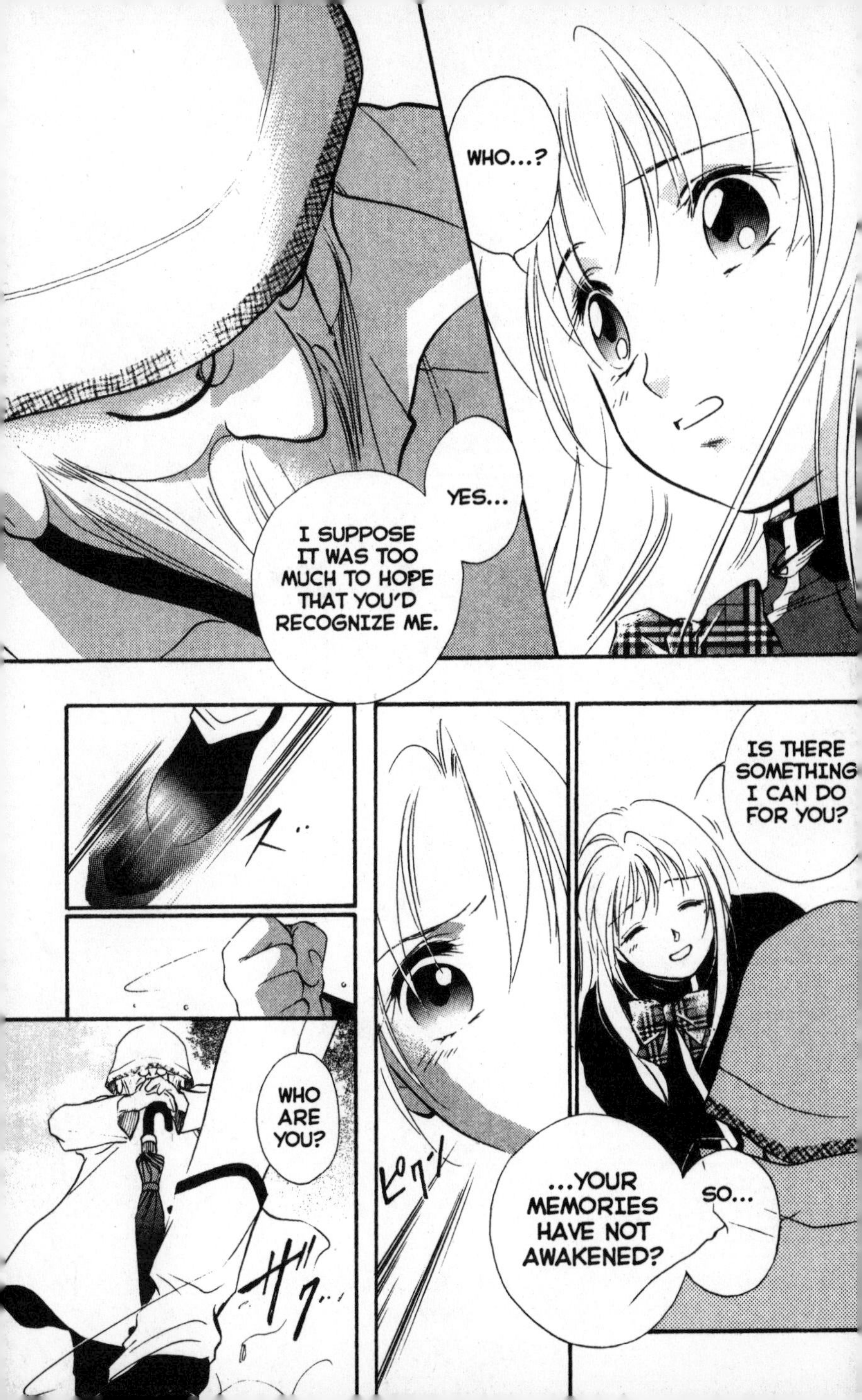
WHO...?
YES...
I SUPPOSE IT WAS TOO MUCH TO HOPE THAT YOU'D RECOGNIZE ME.
IS THERE SOMETHING I CAN DO FOR YOU?
SO...
...YOUR MEMORIES HAVE NOT AWAKENED?
WHO ARE YOU?

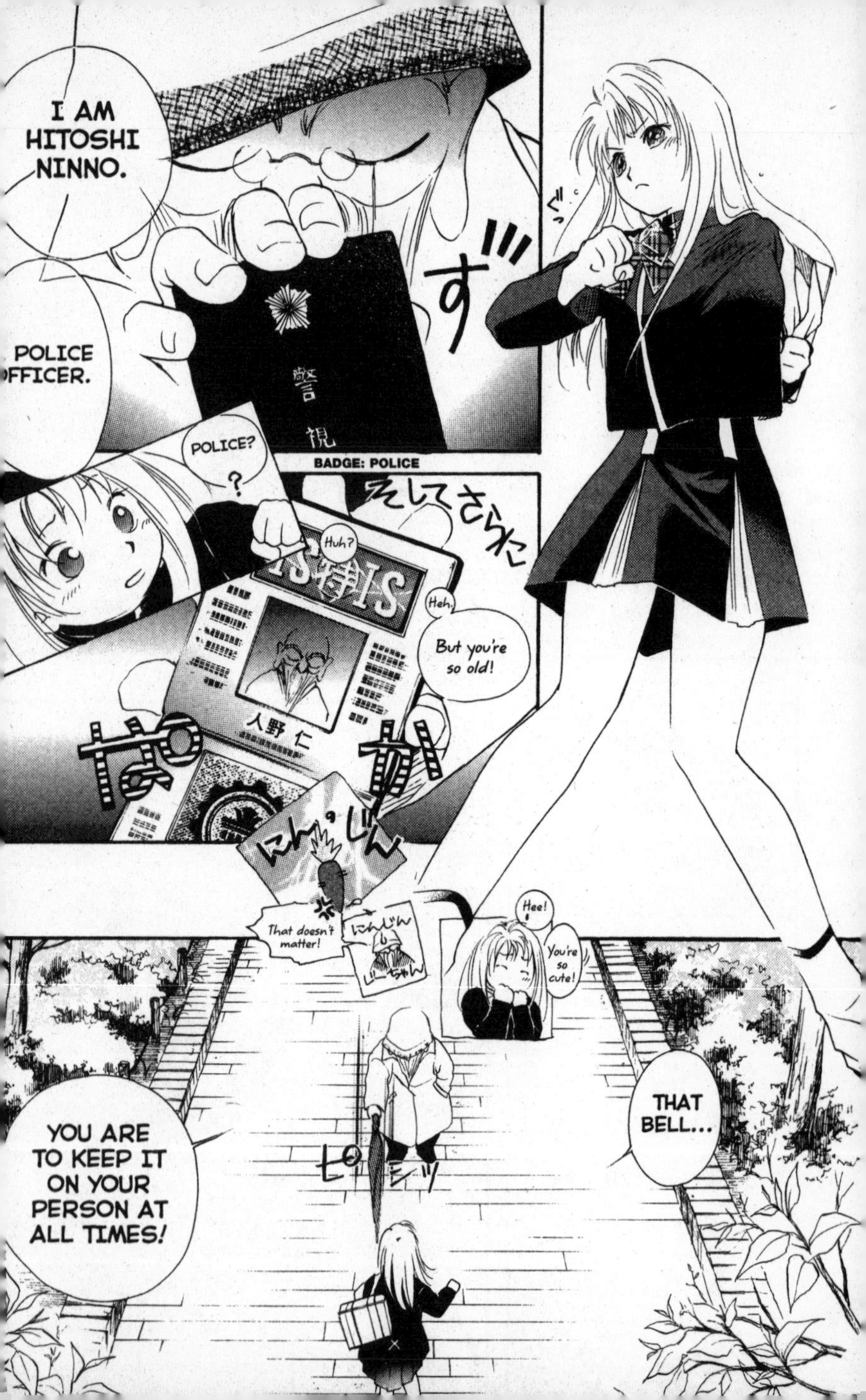
ぐっ
I AM HITOSHI NINNO.
POLICE OFFICER.
ず
BADGE: POLICE
そしてさらに
POLICE?
?
Huh?
Heh.
But you're so old!
人野 仁
にんじん
That doesn't matter!
にんじん じーちゃん
Hee!
You're so cute!
THAT BELL...
YOU ARE TO KEEP IT ON YOUR PERSON AT ALL TIMES!

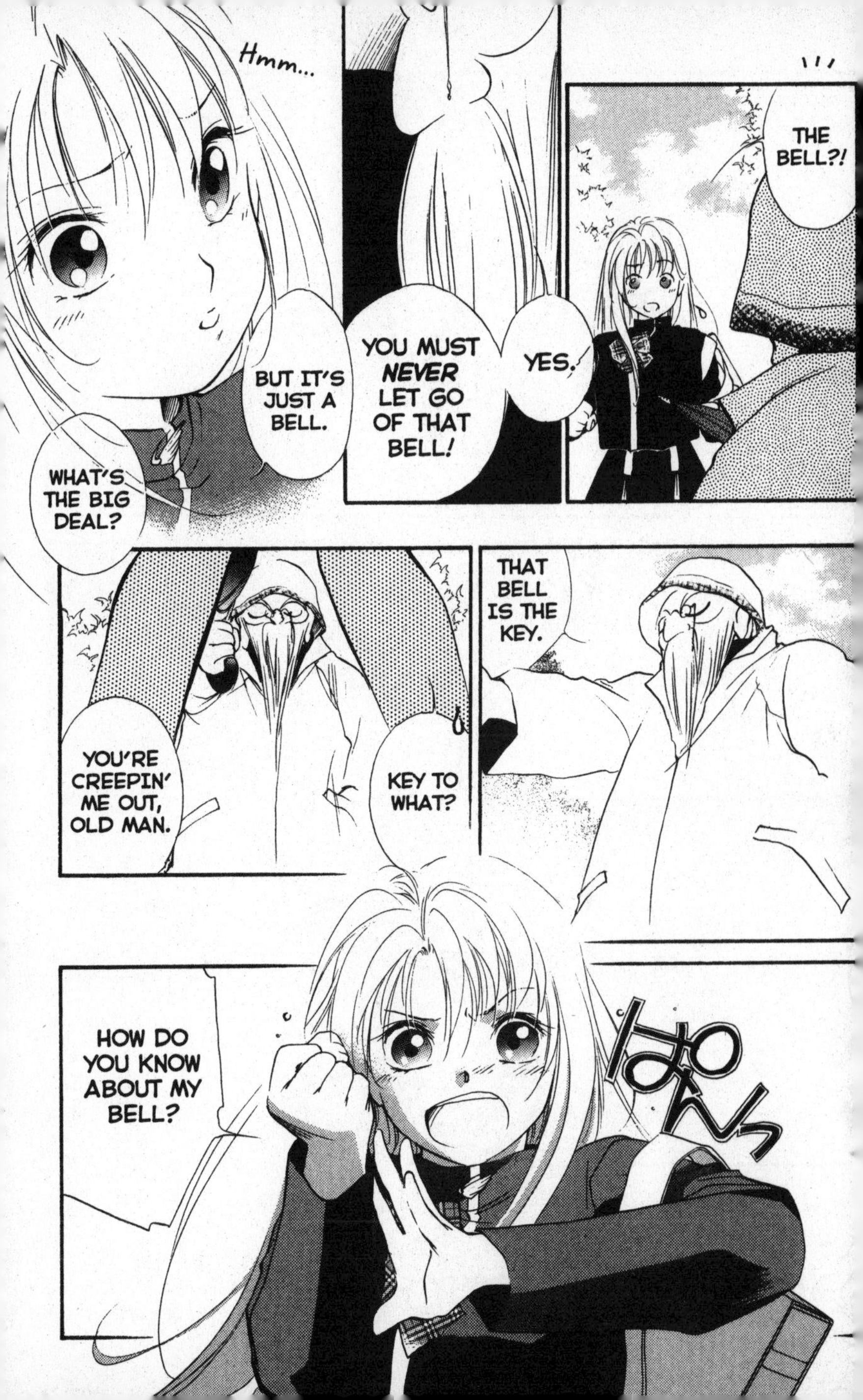

THE BELL?!
YES.
YOU MUST NEVER LET GO OF THAT BELL!
Hmm...
BUT IT'S JUST A BELL.
WHAT'S THE BIG DEAL?
THAT BELL IS THE KEY.
KEY TO WHAT?
YOU'RE CREEPIN' ME OUT, OLD MAN.
HOW DO YOU KNOW ABOUT MY BELL?

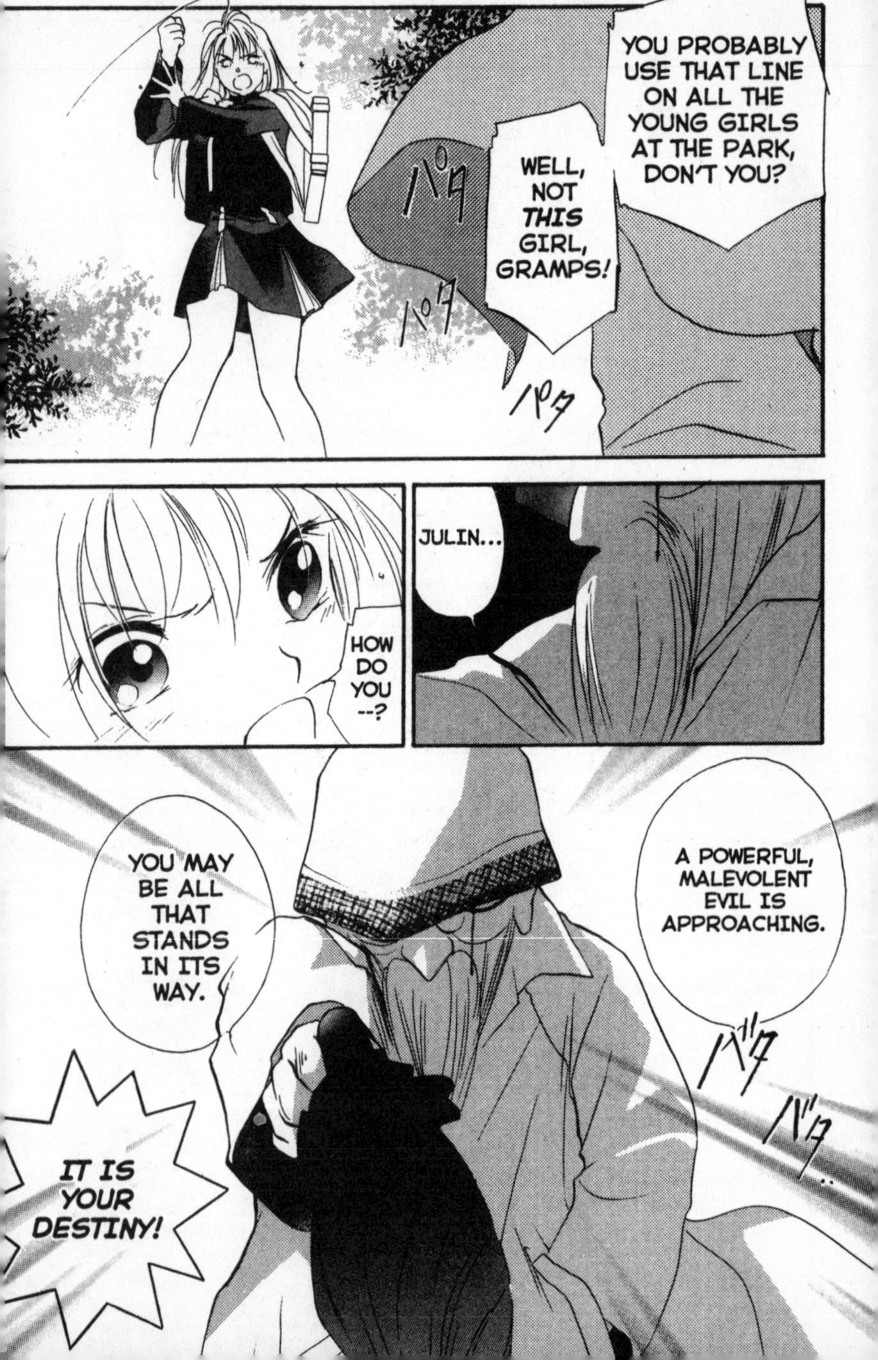
YOU PROBABLY USE THAT LINE ON ALL THE YOUNG GIRLS AT THE PARK, DON'T YOU?
WELL, NOT *THIS* GIRL, GRAMPS!
パタ
パタ
パタ
JULIN...
HOW DO YOU --?
A POWERFUL, MALEVOLENT EVIL IS APPROACHING.
YOU MAY BE ALL THAT STANDS IN ITS WAY.
バタ
バタ..
IT IS YOUR DESTINY!

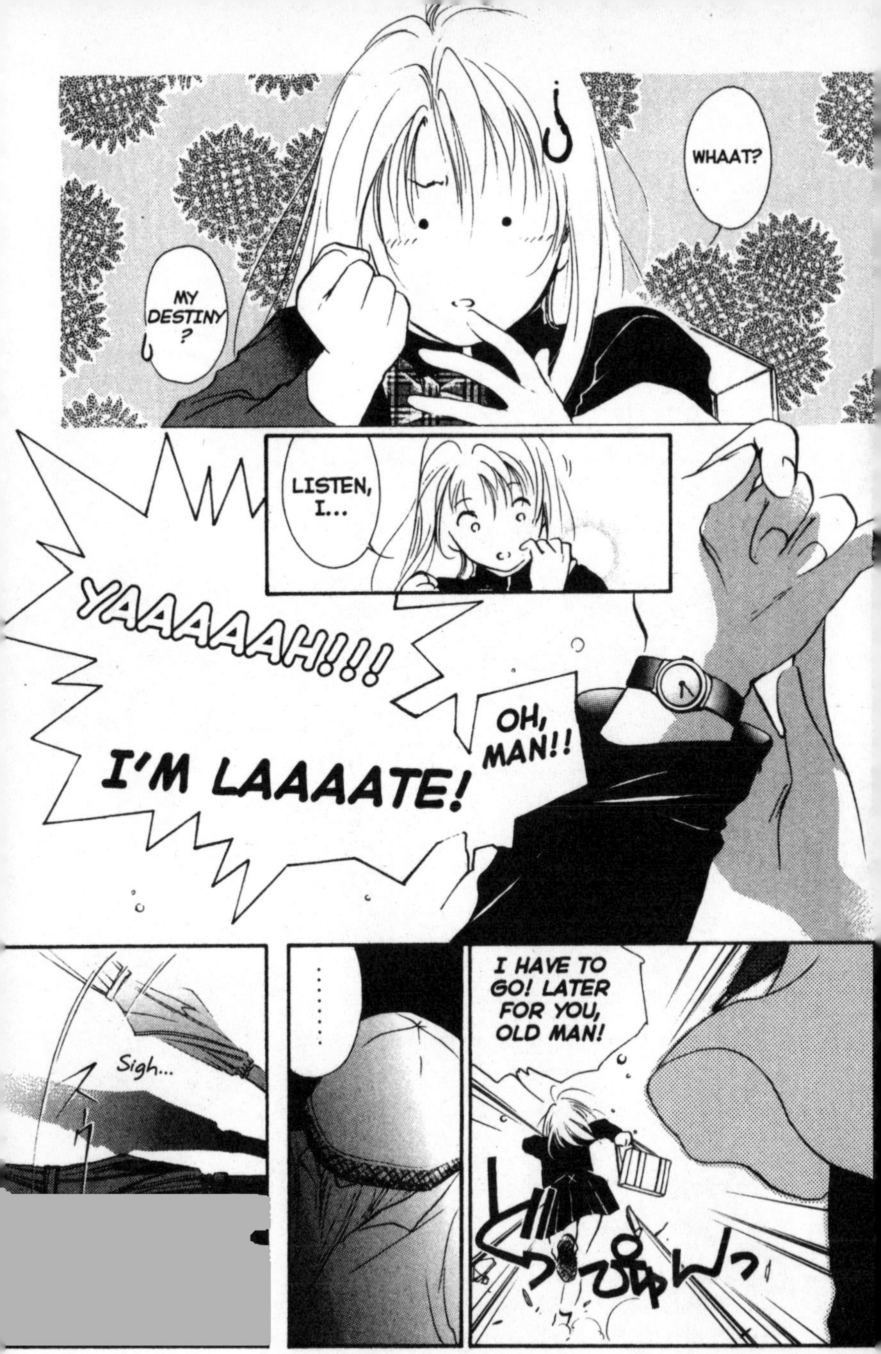
WHAAT?
MY DESTINY?
LISTEN, I...
YAAAAAAH!!!
I'M LAAAATE!
OH, MAN!!
I HAVE TO GO! LATER FOR YOU, OLD MAN!
.......
Sigh...

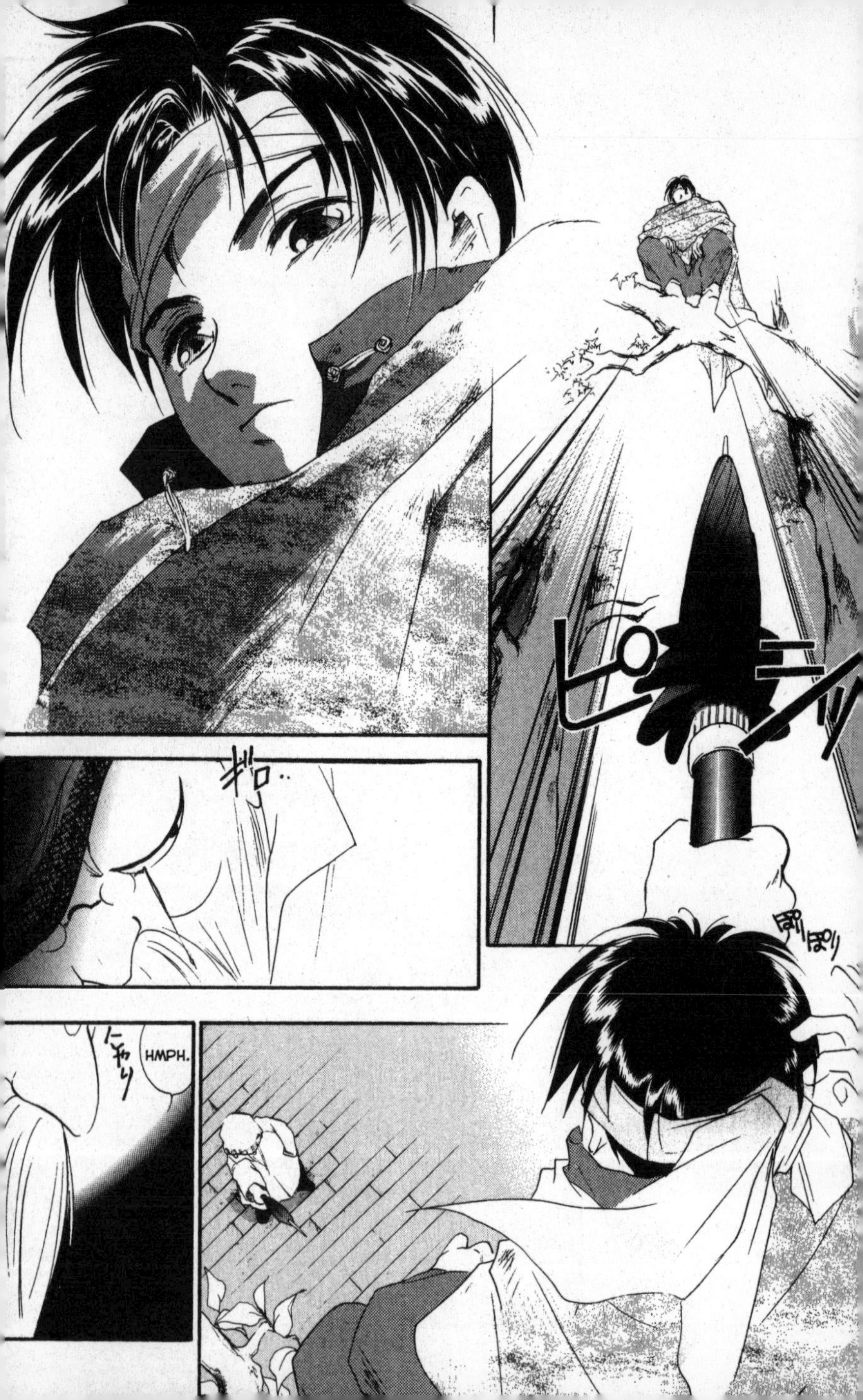
ギロ..
ぽりぽり
ニヤリ
HMPH.

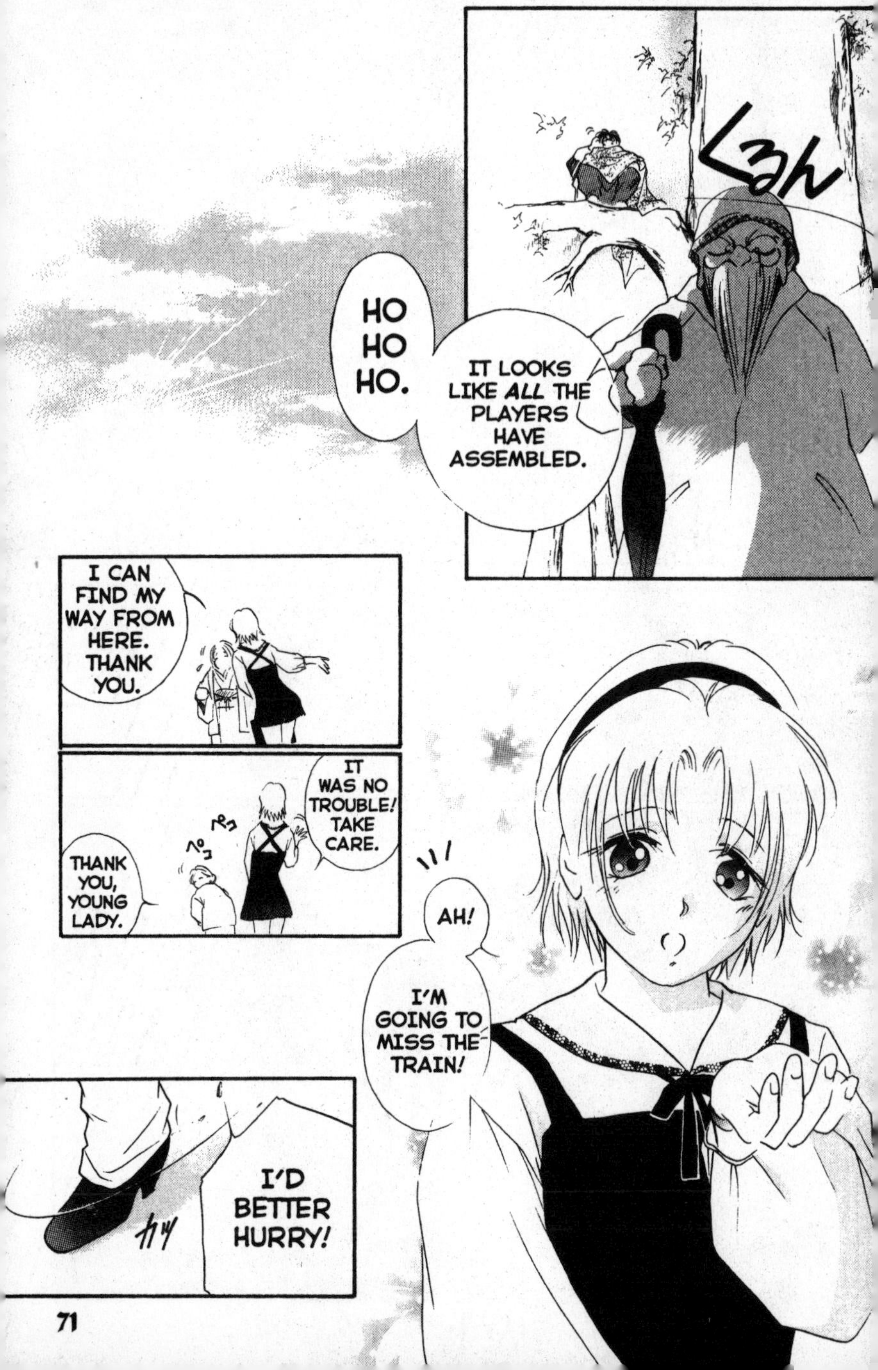
くるん
IT LOOKS LIKE ALL THE PLAYERS HAVE ASSEMBLED.
HO HO HO.
AH!
I'M GOING TO MISS THE TRAIN!
I CAN FIND MY WAY FROM HERE. THANK YOU.
IT WAS NO TROUBLE! TAKE CARE.
ペコ
ペコ
THANK YOU, YOUNG LADY.
I'D BETTER HURRY!
カツ

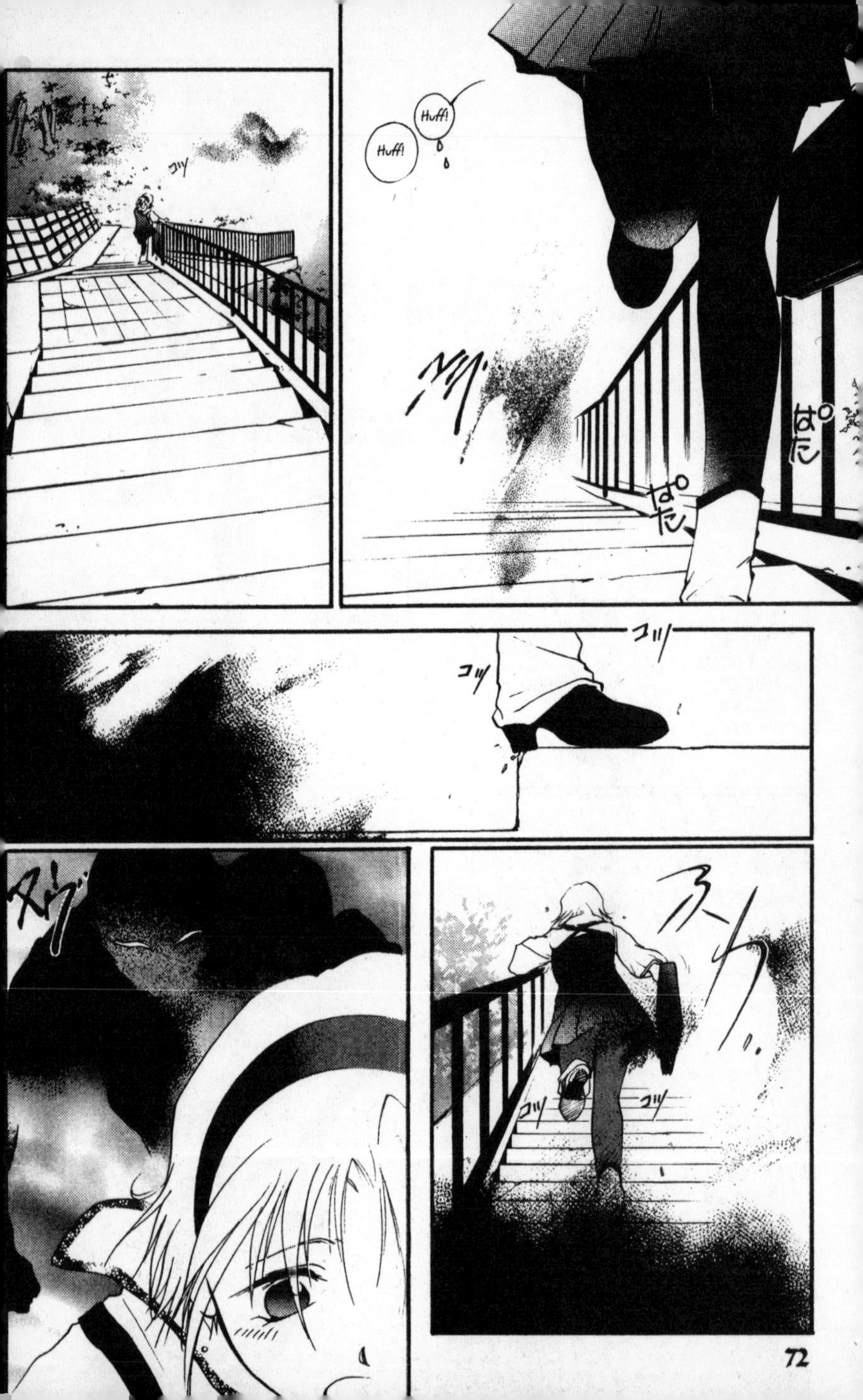
Huff!
Huff!
ぱた
ぱた
コツ
コツ
コツ
コツ
コツ

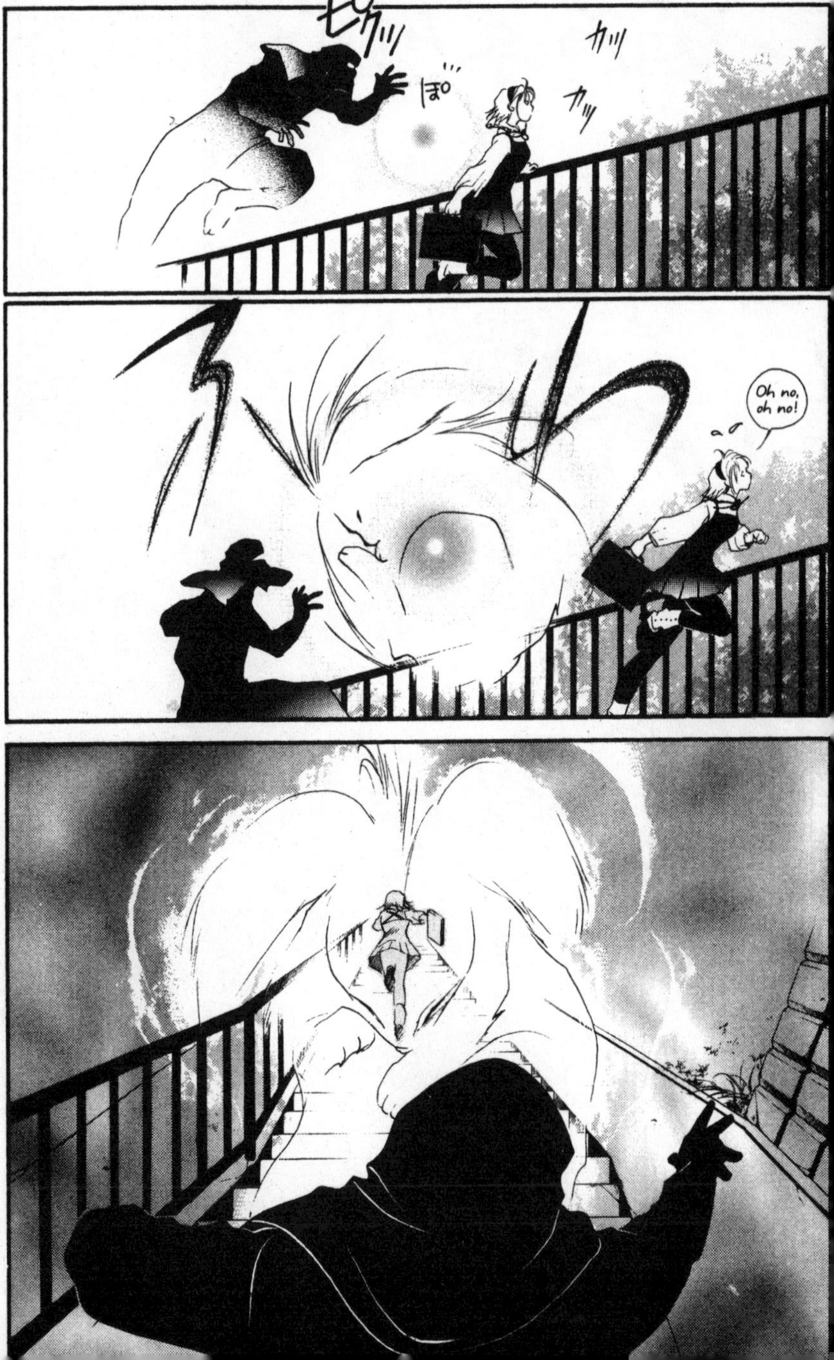
カッ
カッ
ぽ
ピクッ
Oh no, oh no!

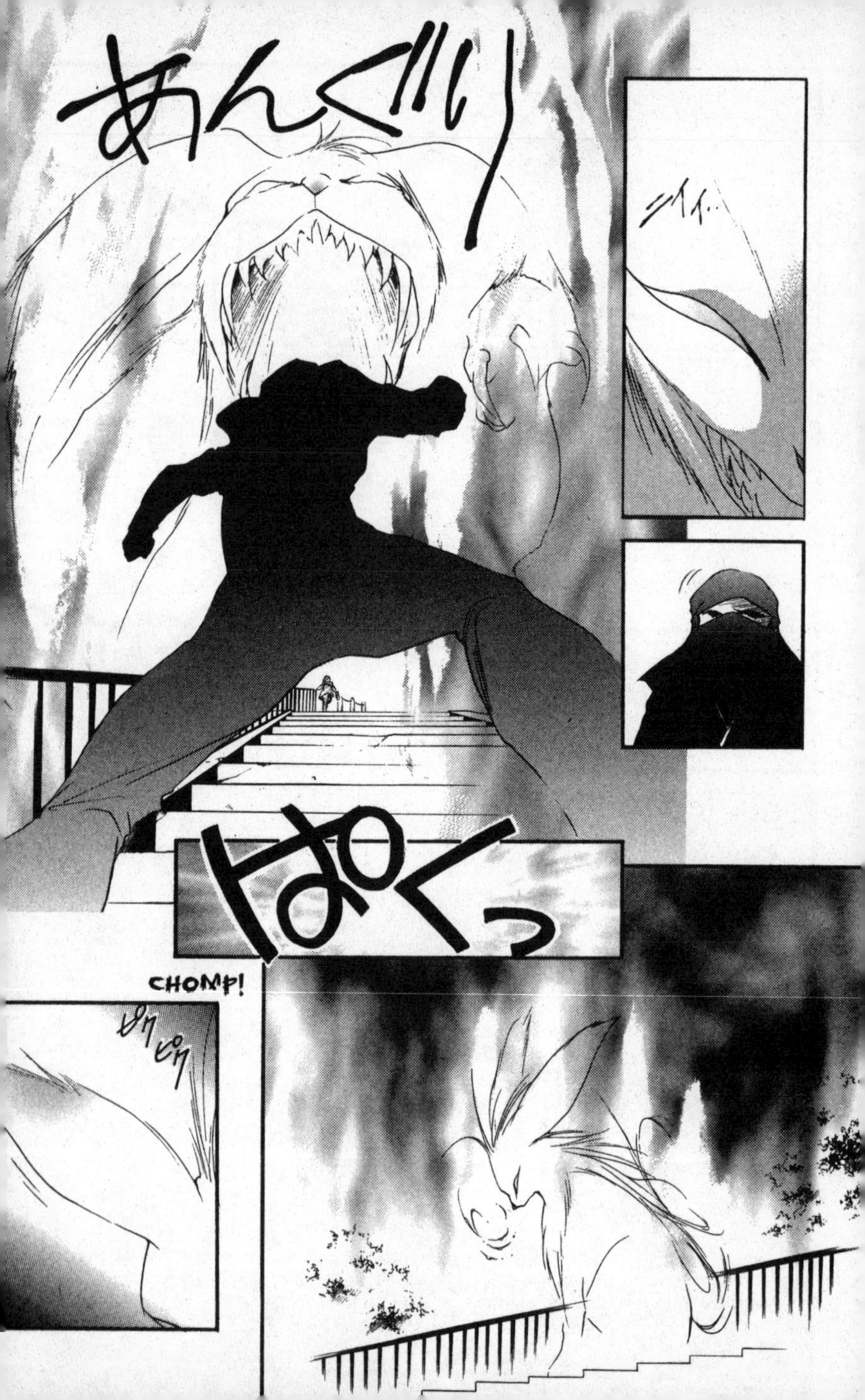
あんぐり
ジイィ..
ぱくっ
CHOMP!
ピクピク

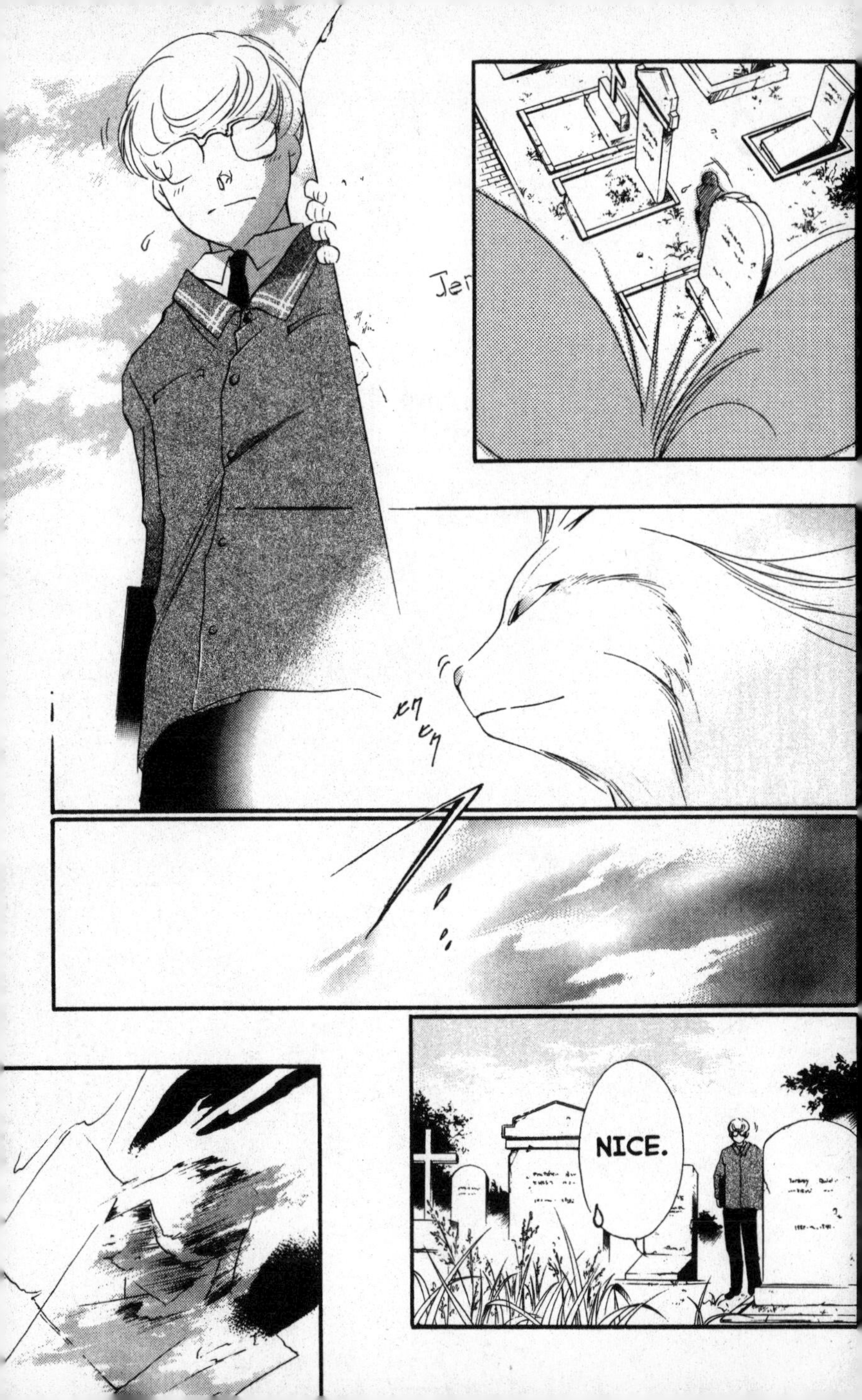
ヒク ヒク
NICE.

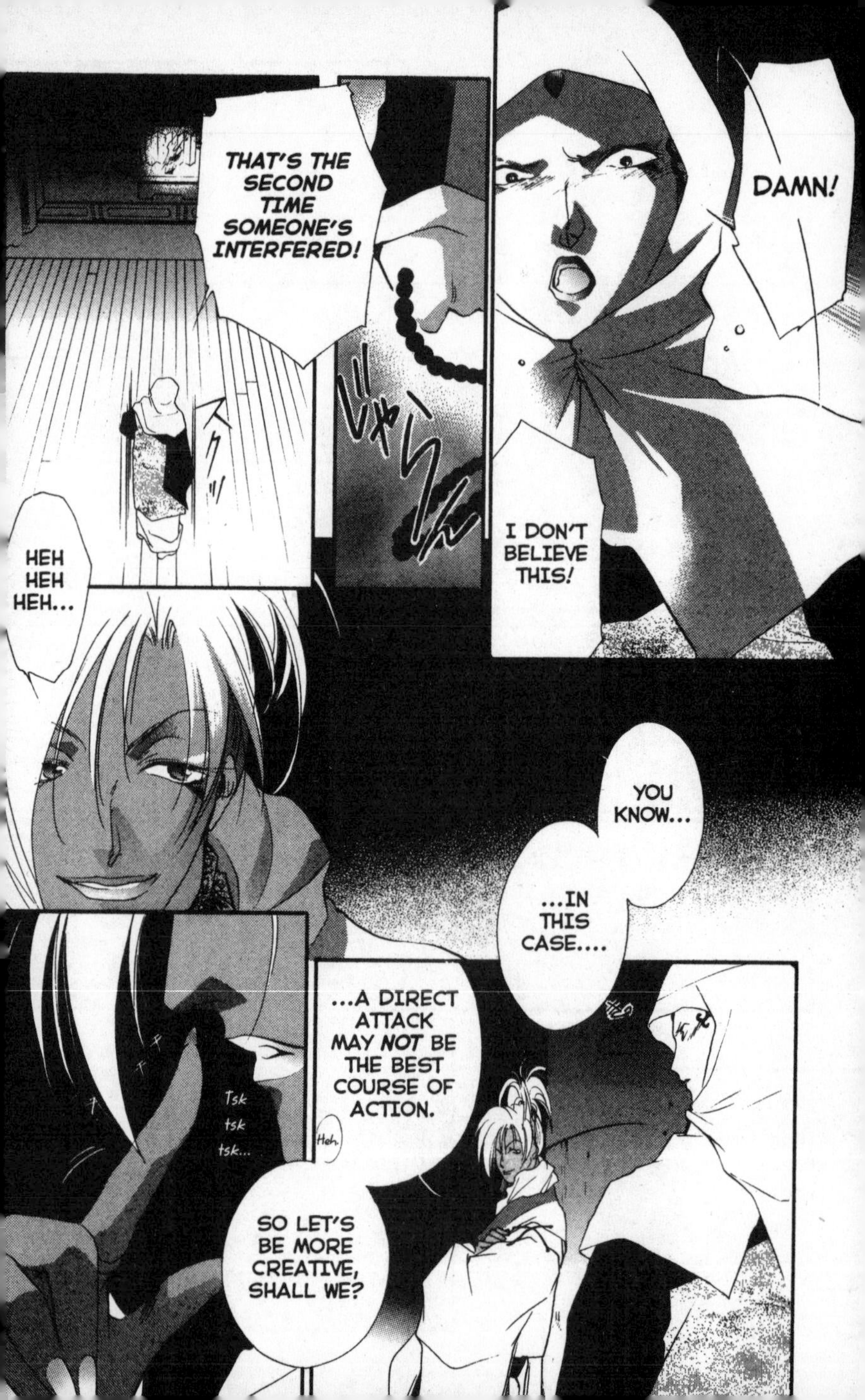
DAMN!
I DON'T BELIEVE THIS!
THAT'S THE SECOND TIME SOMEONE'S INTERFERED!
じゃらん
HEH HEH HEH...
YOU KNOW...
...IN THIS CASE....
...A DIRECT ATTACK MAY *NOT* BE THE BEST COURSE OF ACTION.
Heh.
SO LET'S BE MORE CREATIVE, SHALL WE?
Tsk tsk tsk...

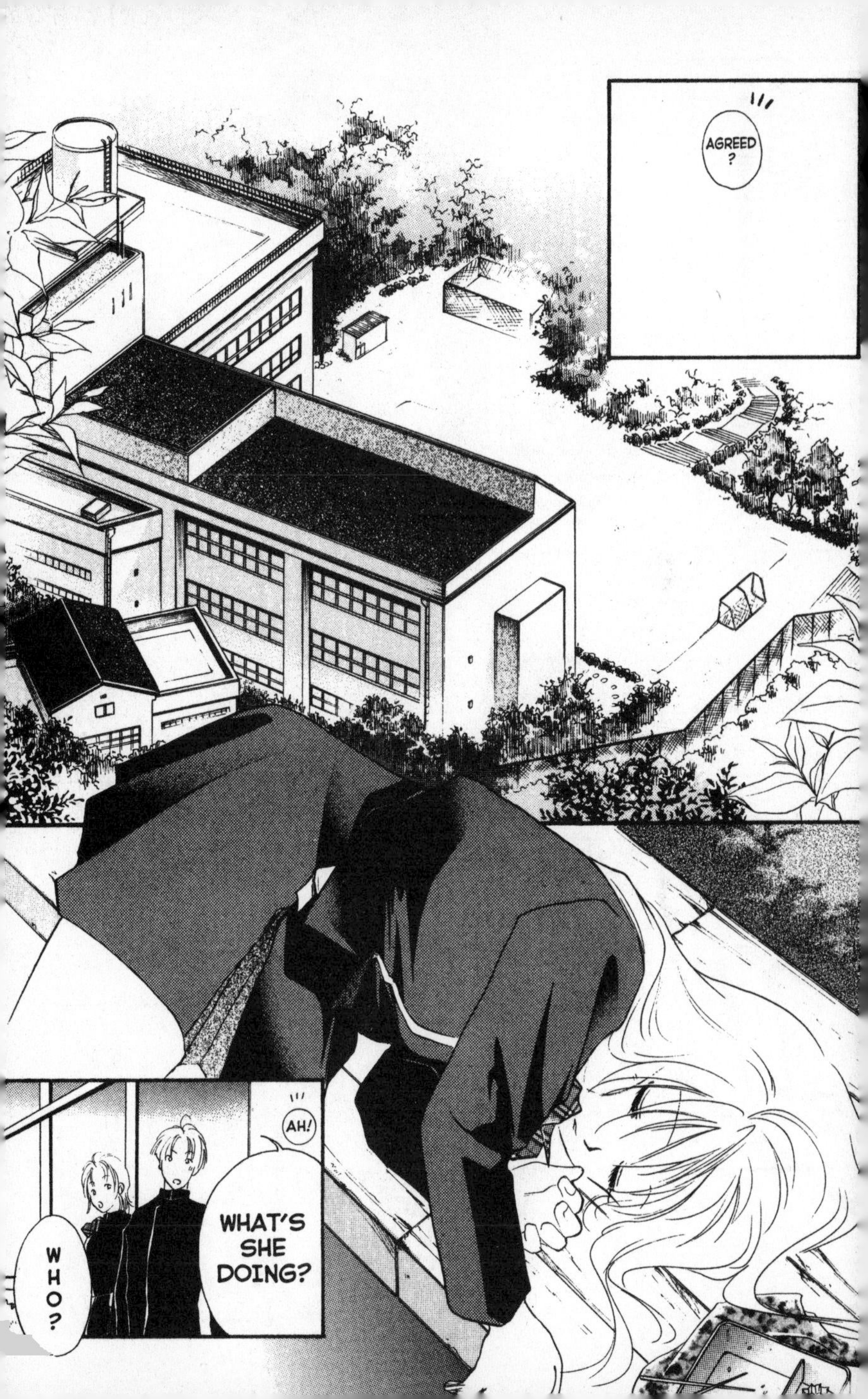
AGREED?
AH!
WHAT'S SHE DOING?
WHO?

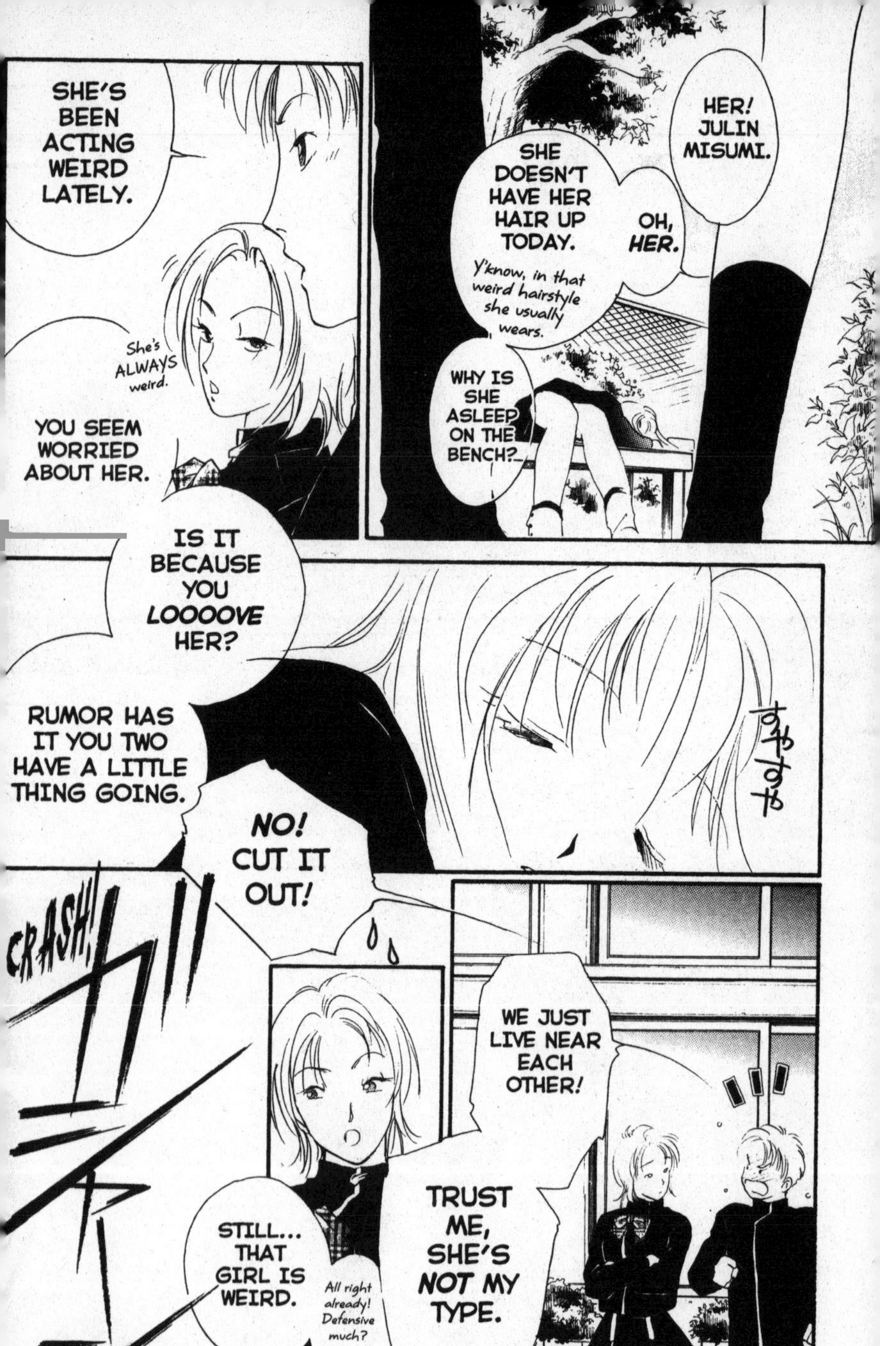
HER! JULIN MISUMI.
OH, *HER.*
SHE DOESN'T HAVE HER HAIR UP TODAY.
Y'know, in that weird hairstyle she usually wears.
WHY IS SHE ASLEEP ON THE BENCH?
SHE'S BEEN ACTING WEIRD LATELY.
She's ALWAYS weird.
YOU SEEM WORRIED ABOUT HER.
すやすや
IS IT BECAUSE YOU *LOOOOVE* HER?
RUMOR HAS IT YOU TWO HAVE A LITTLE THING GOING.
*NO!* CUT IT OUT!
WE JUST LIVE NEAR EACH OTHER!
TRUST ME, SHE'S *NOT* MY TYPE.
All right already! Defensive much?
STILL... THAT GIRL IS WEIRD.
CRASH!

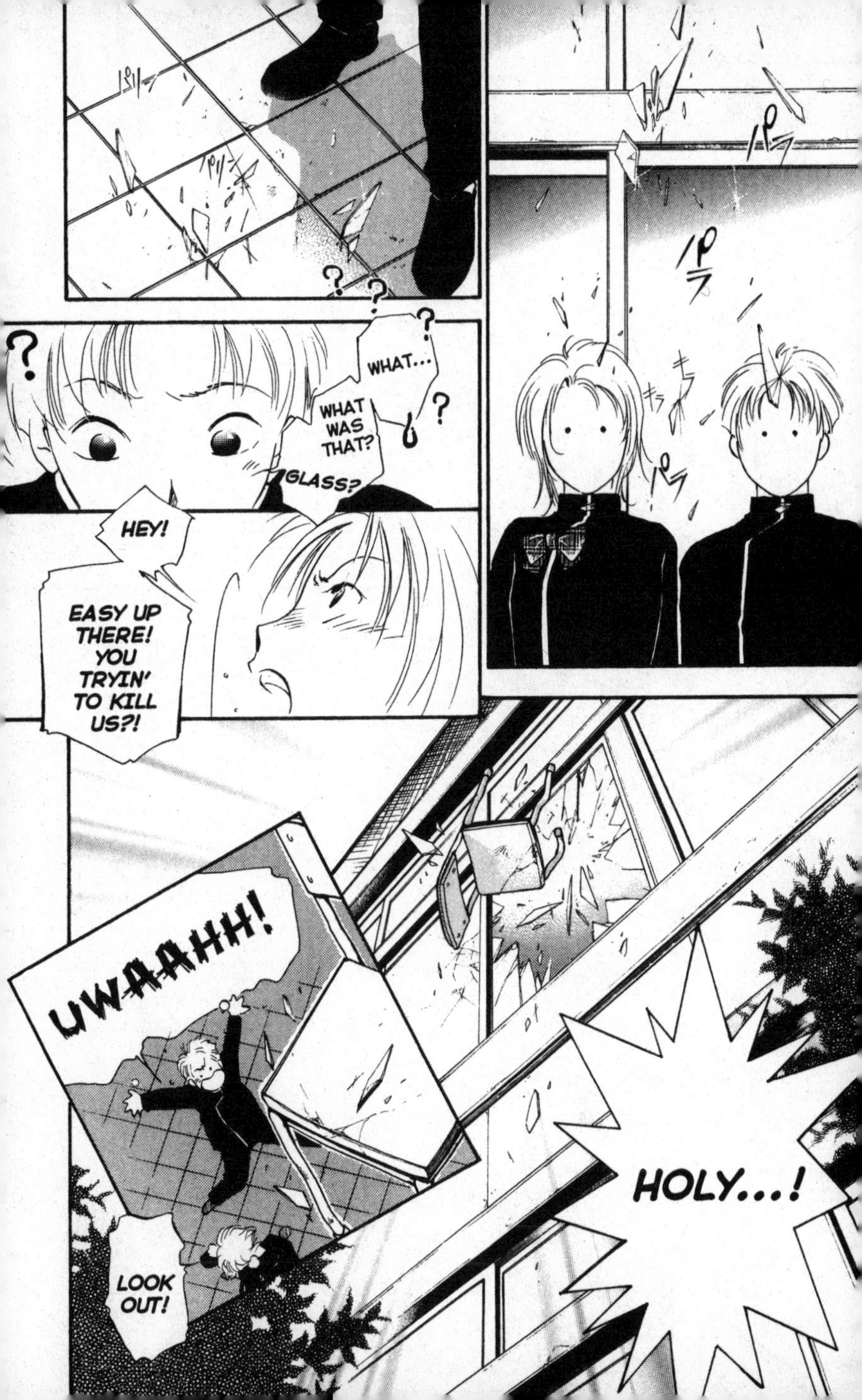
WHAT...
WHAT WAS THAT?
GLASS?
HEY!
EASY UP THERE! YOU TRYIN' TO KILL US?!
UWAAHH!
HOLY...!
LOOK OUT!

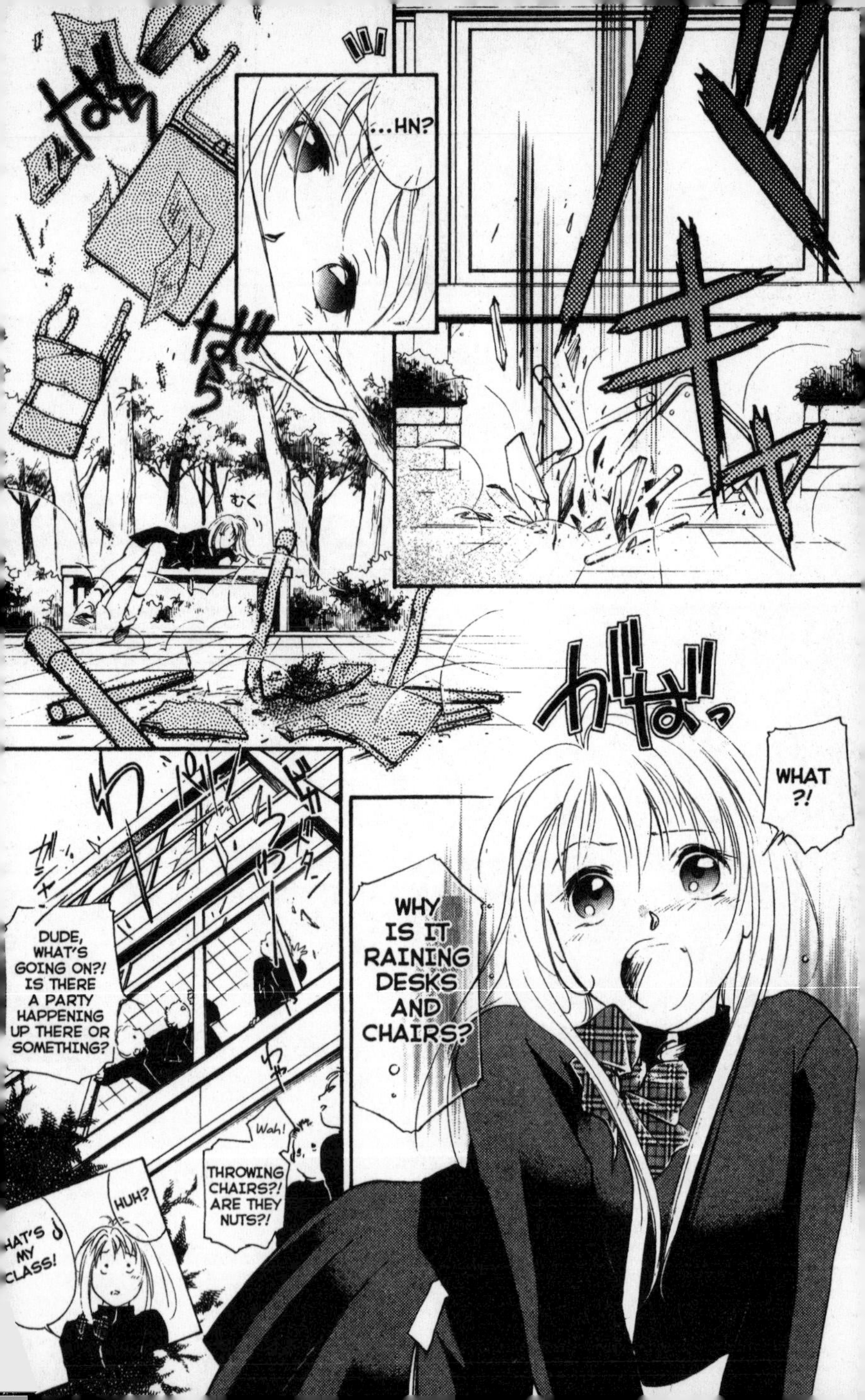
...HN?
むく
WHAT ?!
WHY IS IT RAINING DESKS AND CHAIRS?
DUDE, WHAT'S GOING ON?! IS THERE A PARTY HAPPENING UP THERE OR SOMETHING?
Wah!
THROWING CHAIRS?! ARE THEY NUTS?!
HUH?
HAT'S MY CLASS!

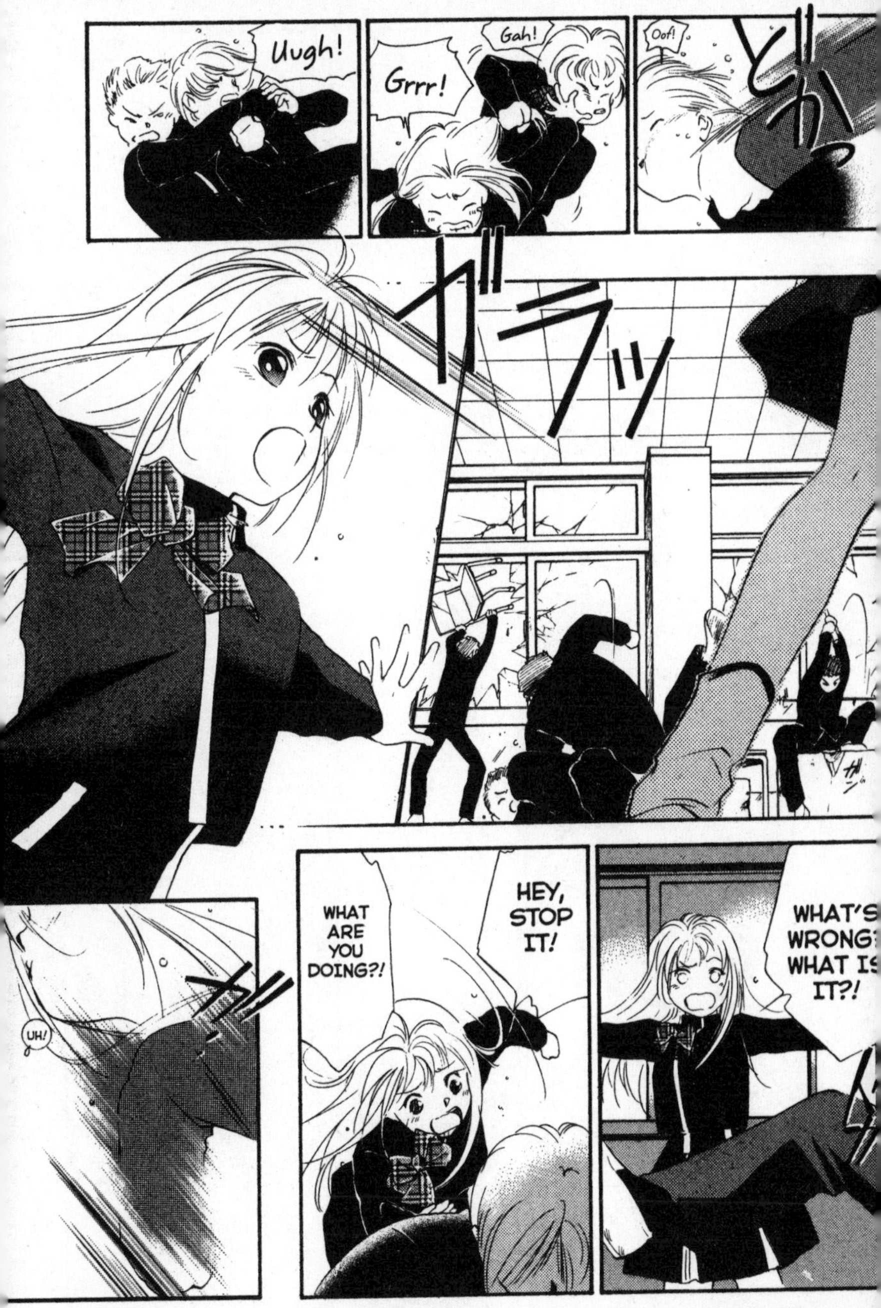
Oof!
Gah!
Grrr!
Uugh!
WHAT'S WRONG
WHAT IS IT?!
HEY, STOP IT!
WHAT ARE YOU DOING?!
UH!

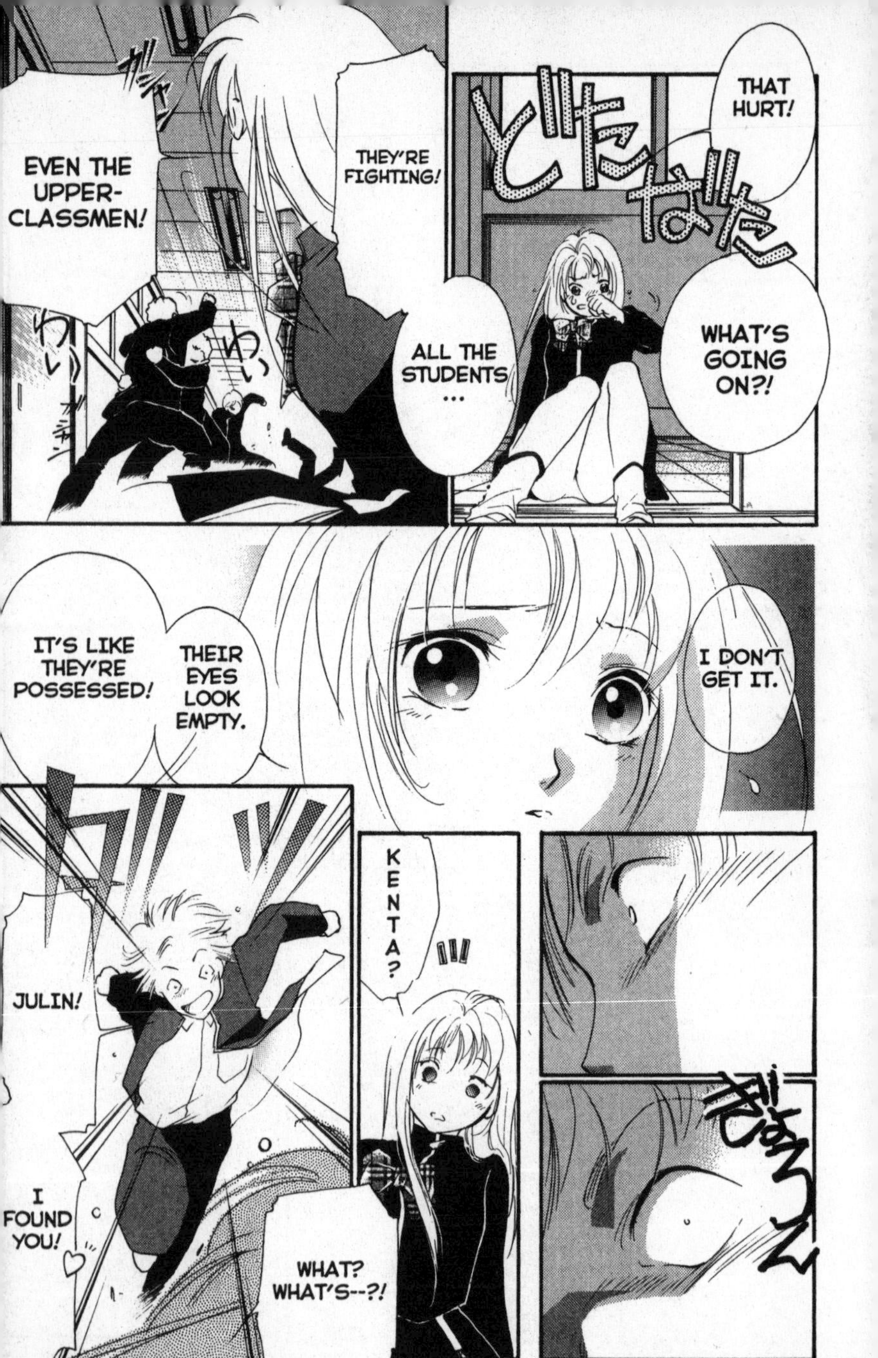
THAT HURT!
WHAT'S GOING ON?!
ALL THE STUDENTS ...
THEY'RE FIGHTING!
EVEN THE UPPER-CLASSMEN!
I DON'T GET IT.
THEIR EYES LOOK EMPTY.
IT'S LIKE THEY'RE POSSESSED!
KENTA?
WHAT? WHAT'S--?!
JULIN!
I FOUND YOU!

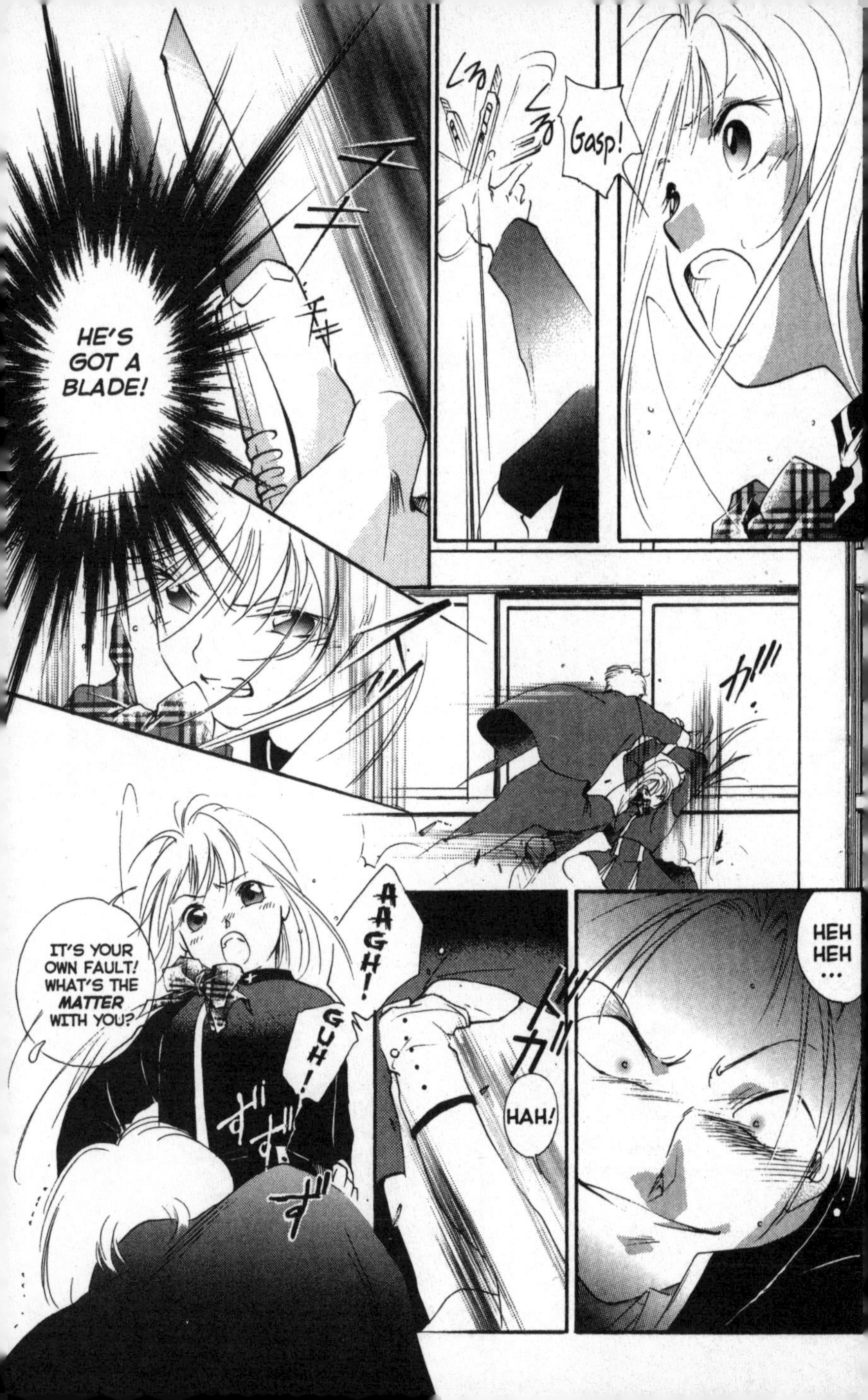
Gasp!
HE'S GOT A BLADE!
HEH HEH ...
HAH!
AAGH!
GUH!
IT'S YOUR OWN FAULT! WHAT'S THE MATTER WITH YOU?

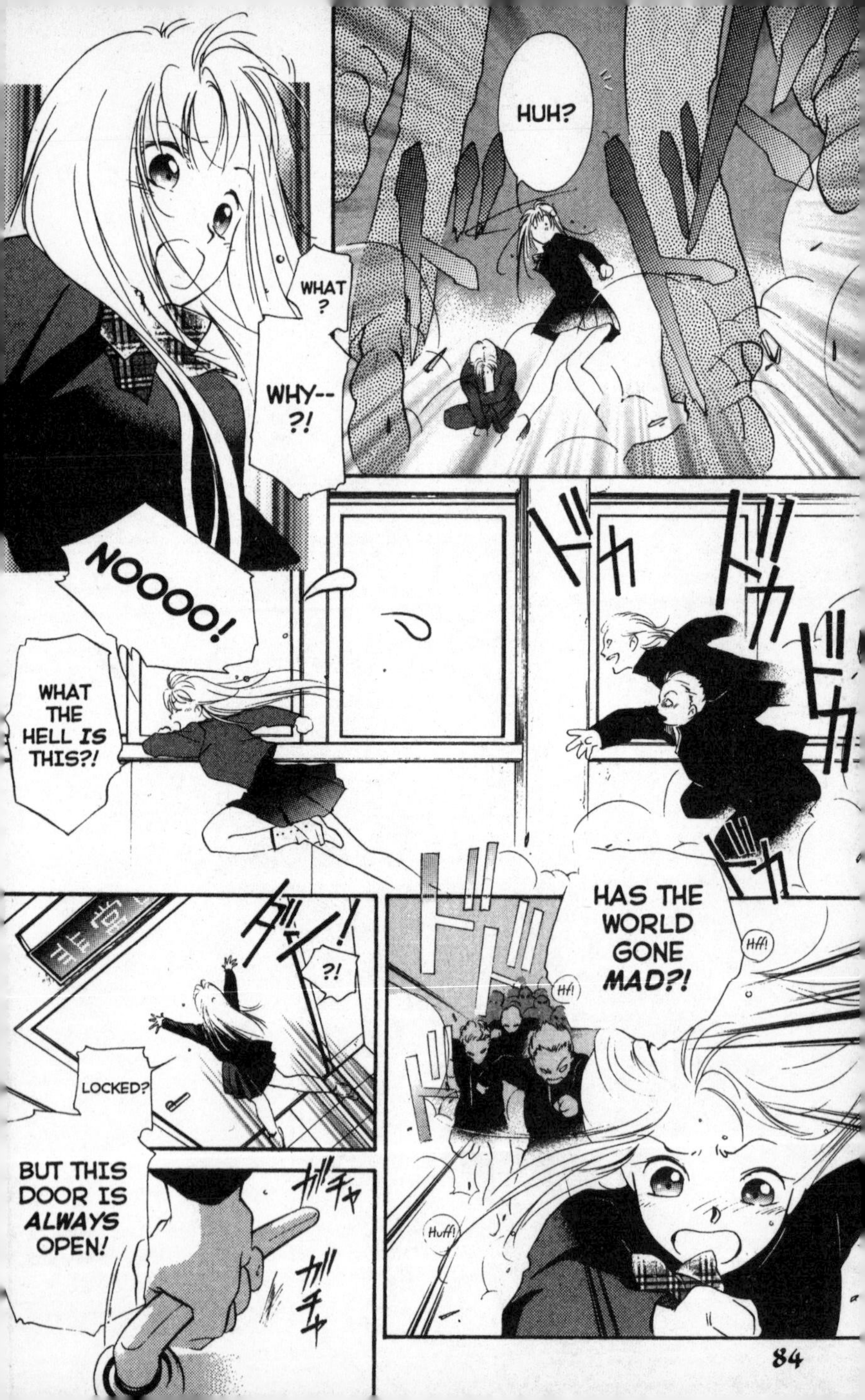
HUH?
WHAT?
WHY--?!
NOOOO!
WHAT THE HELL IS THIS?!
HAS THE WORLD GONE MAD?!
Hff!
Hff!
Huff!
?!
LOCKED?
BUT THIS DOOR IS ALWAYS OPEN!
ガチャ
ガチャ

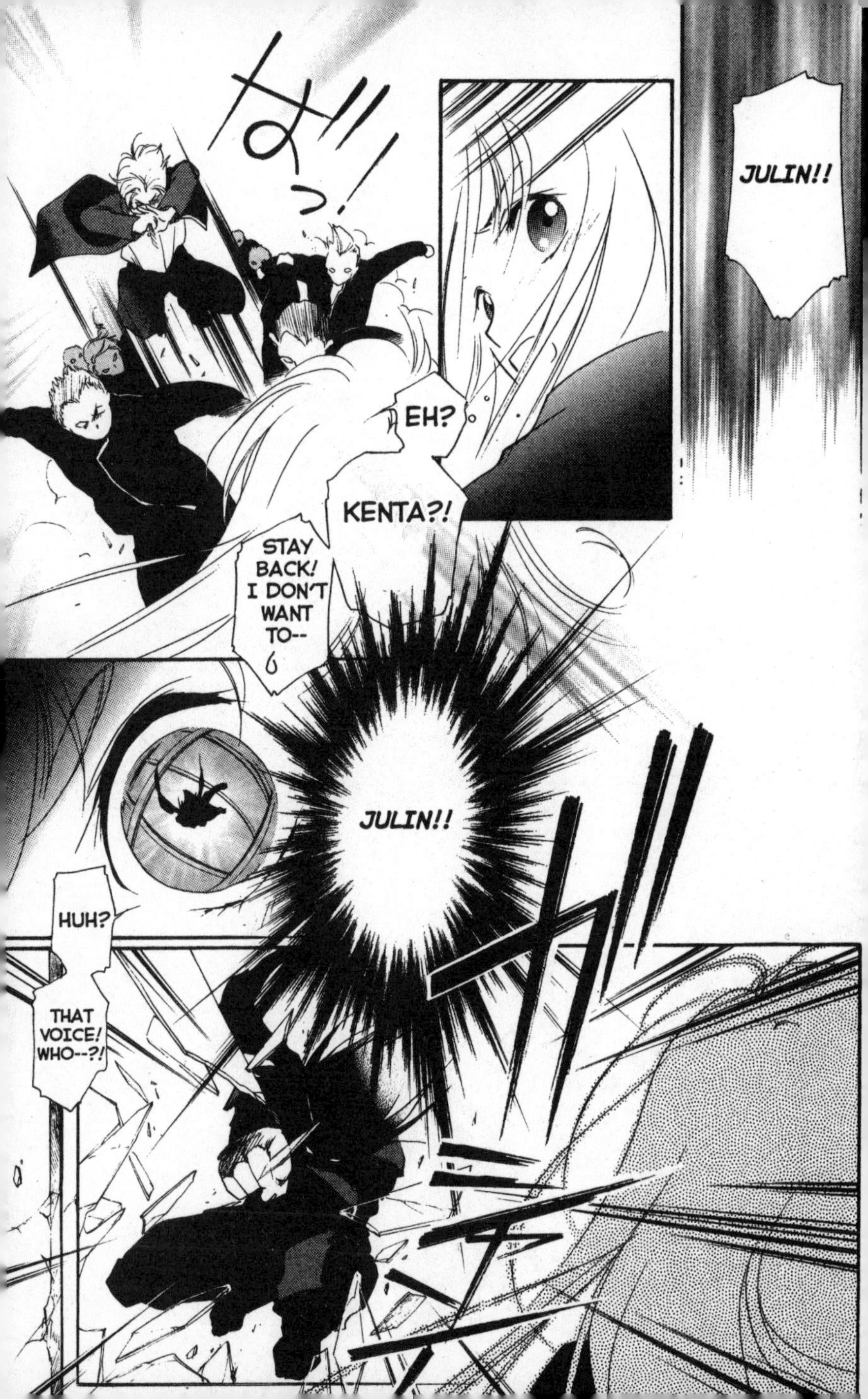
JULIN!!
EH?
KENTA?!
STAY BACK! I DON'T WANT TO--
JULIN!!
HUH?
THAT VOICE! WHO--?!

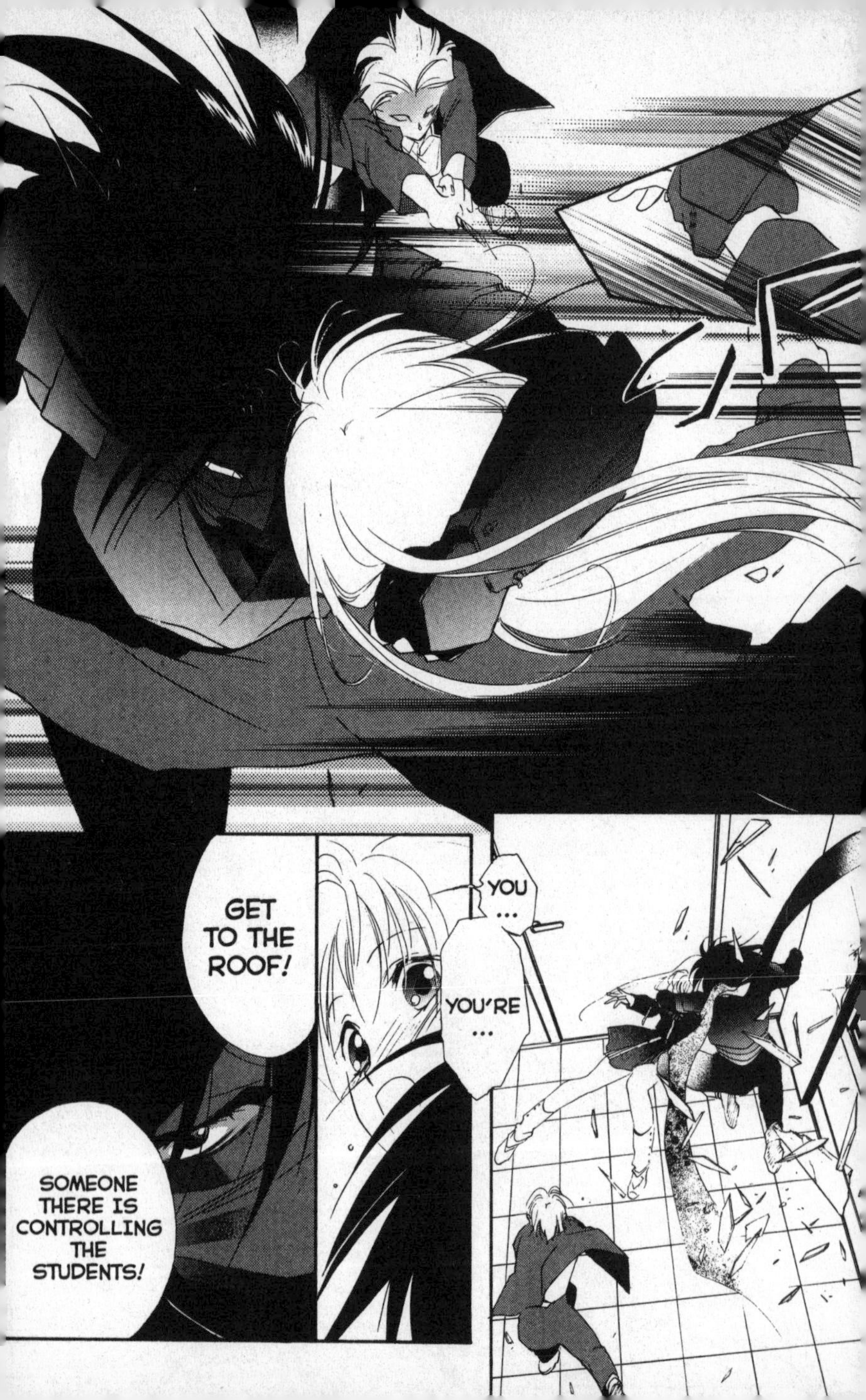
YOU ...
YOU'RE ...
GET TO THE ROOF!
SOMEONE THERE IS CONTROLLING THE STUDENTS!

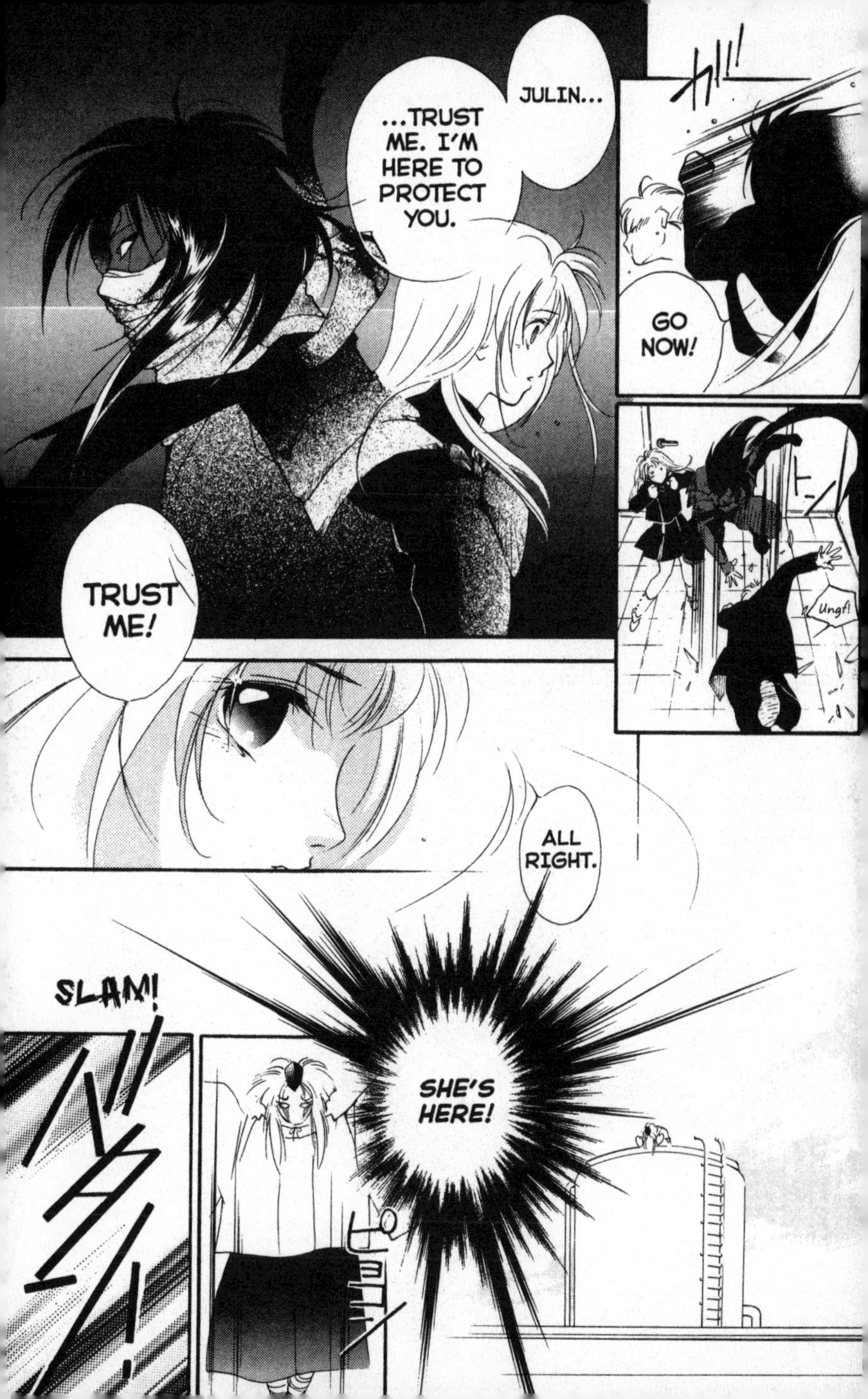
GO NOW!
Ungf!
JULIN...
...TRUST ME. I'M HERE TO PROTECT YOU.
TRUST ME!
ALL RIGHT.
SLAM!
SHE'S HERE!

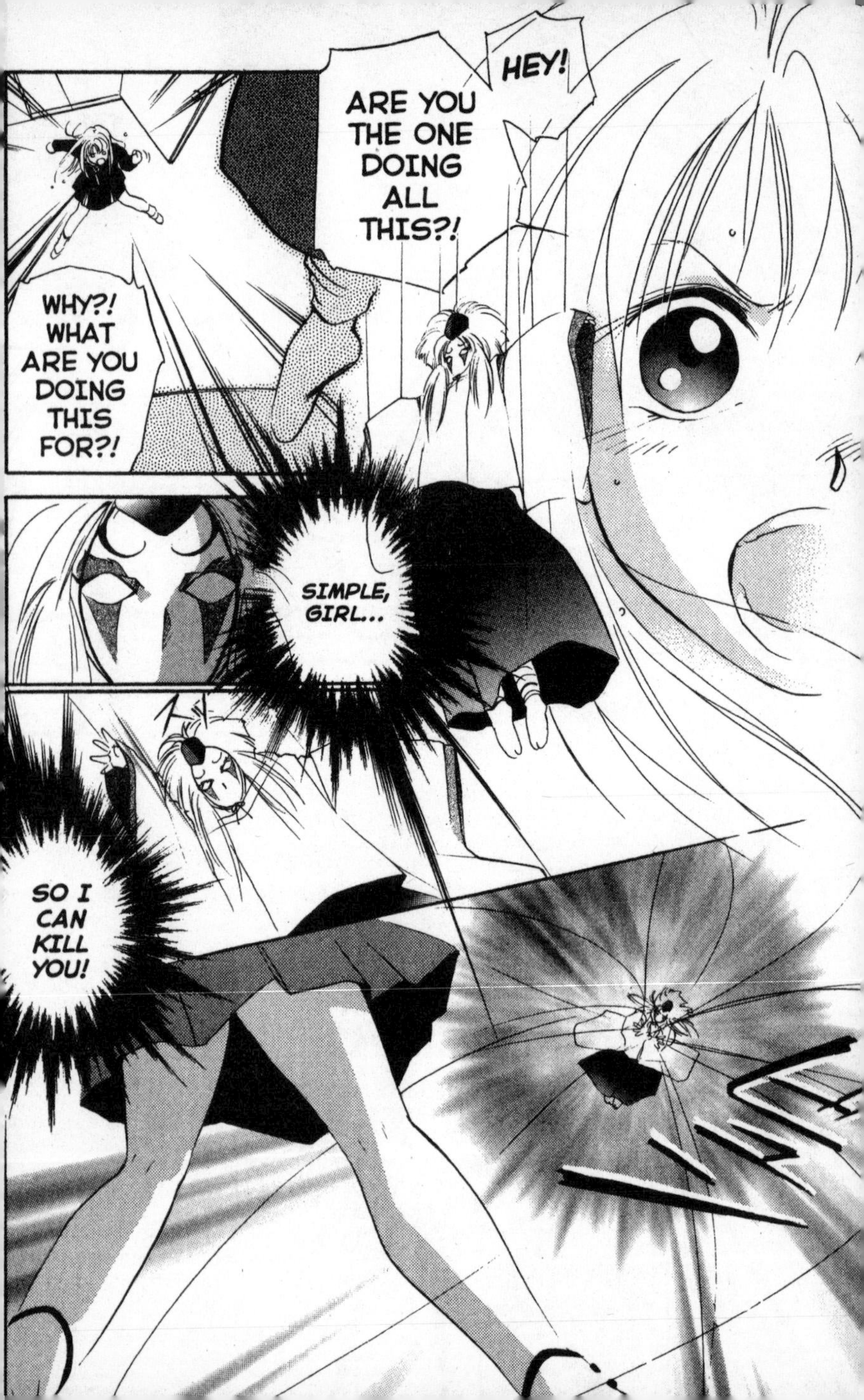
HEY!
ARE YOU THE ONE DOING ALL THIS?!
WHY?! WHAT ARE YOU DOING THIS FOR?!
SIMPLE, GIRL...
SO I CAN KILL YOU!

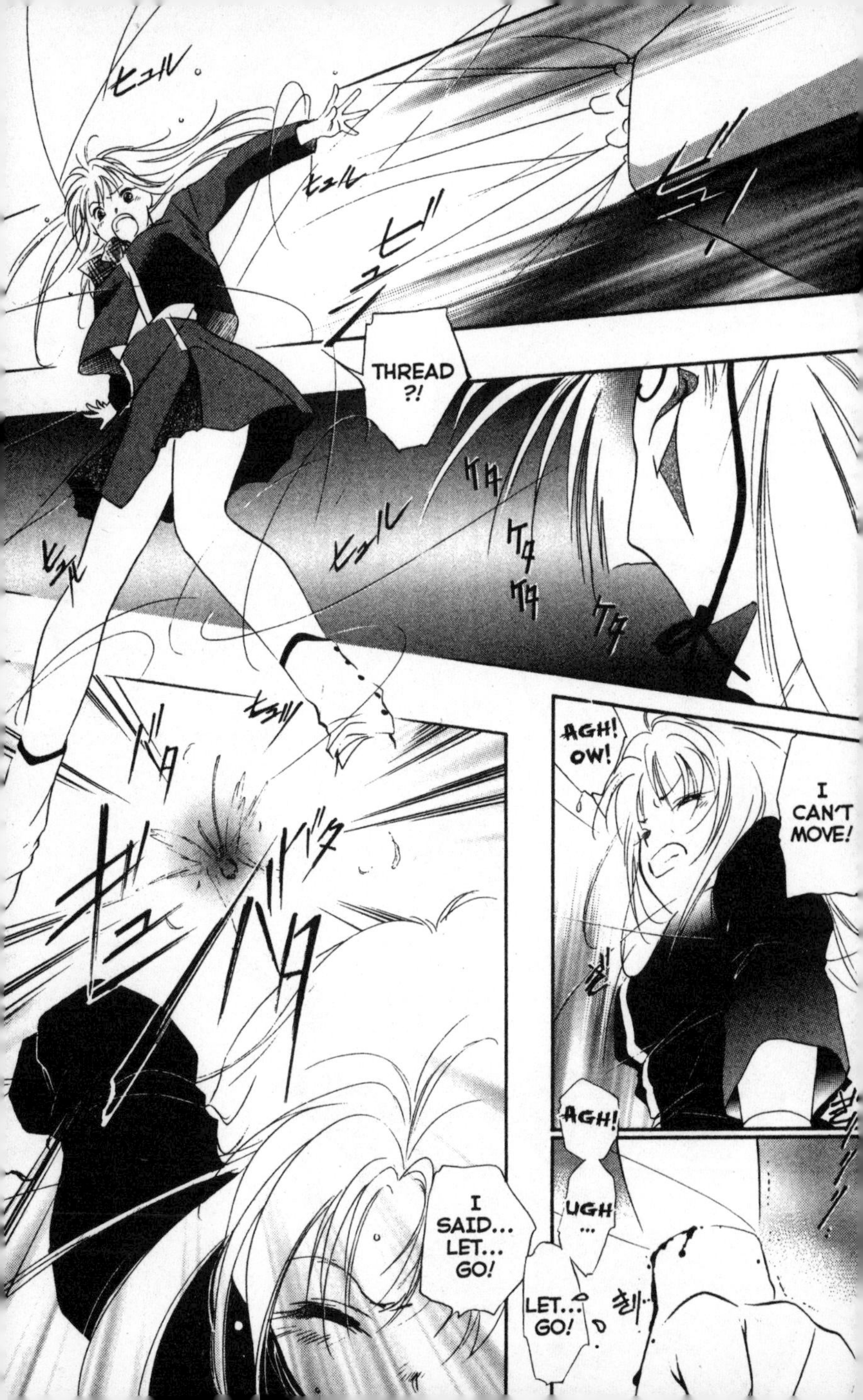
THREAD ?!
AGH! OW!
I CAN'T MOVE!
AGH!
UGH ...
LET... GO!
I SAID... LET... GO!

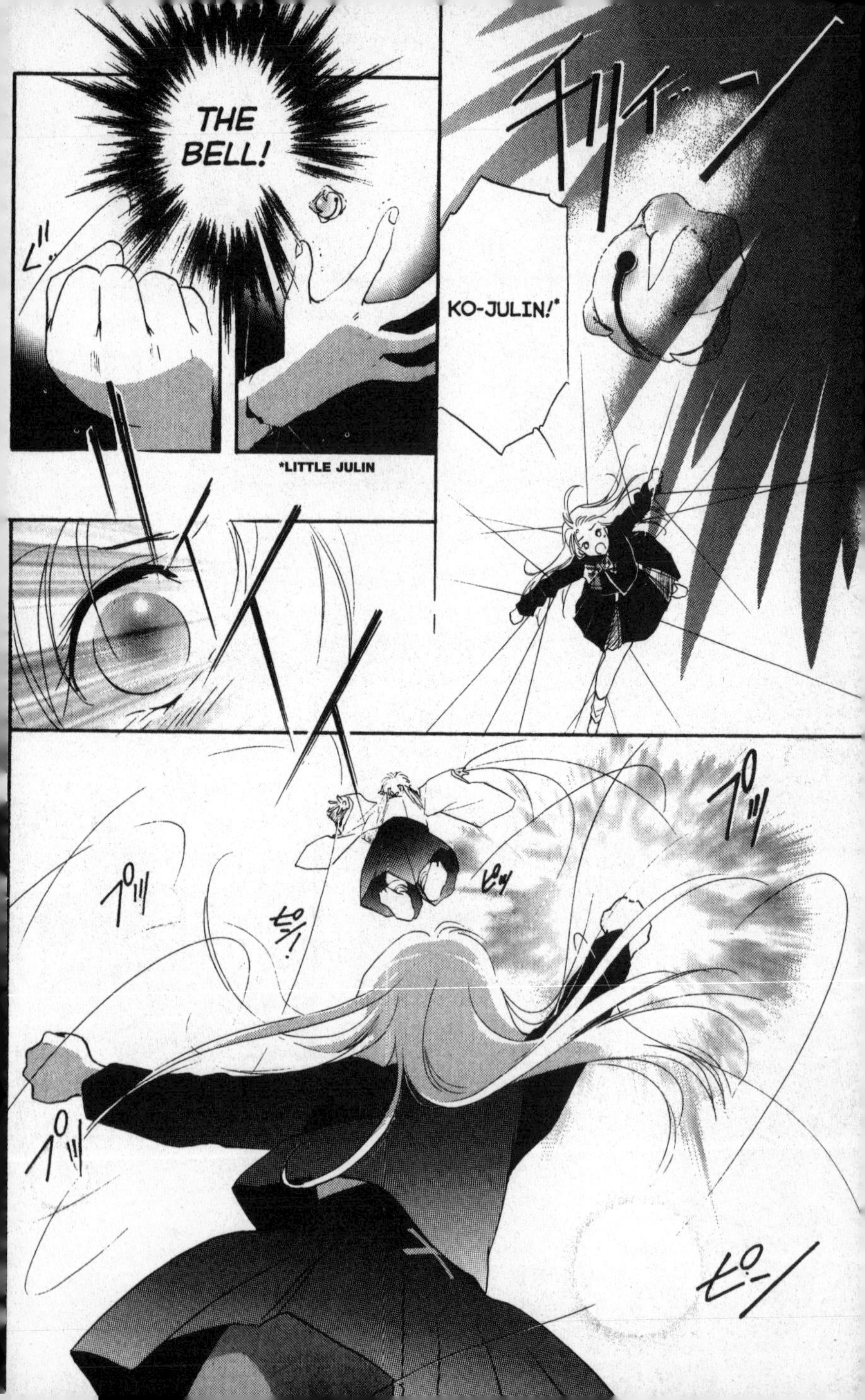
KO-JULIN!*
THE BELL!
*LITTLE JULIN

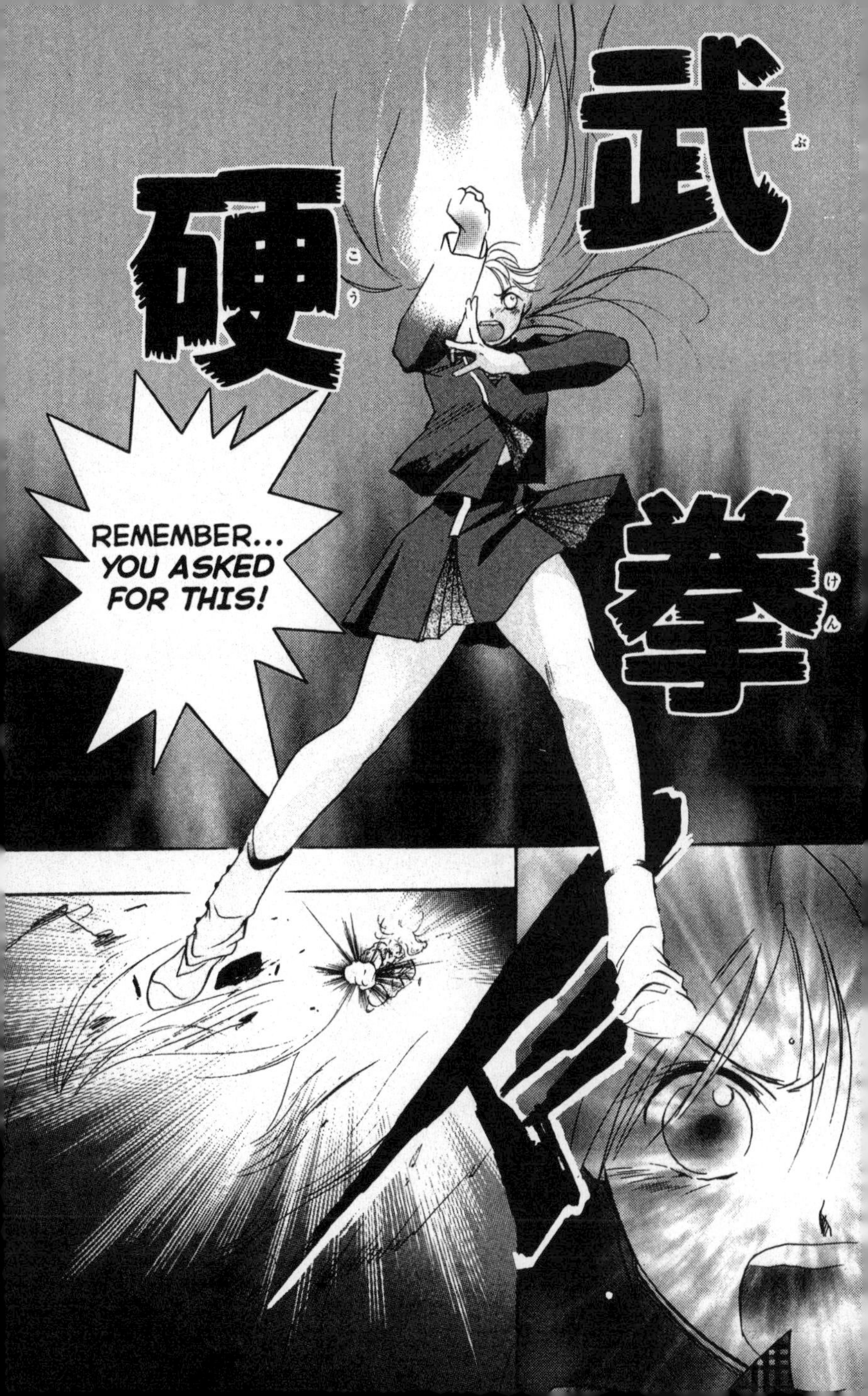
武拳
硬
REMEMBER... YOU ASKED FOR THIS!

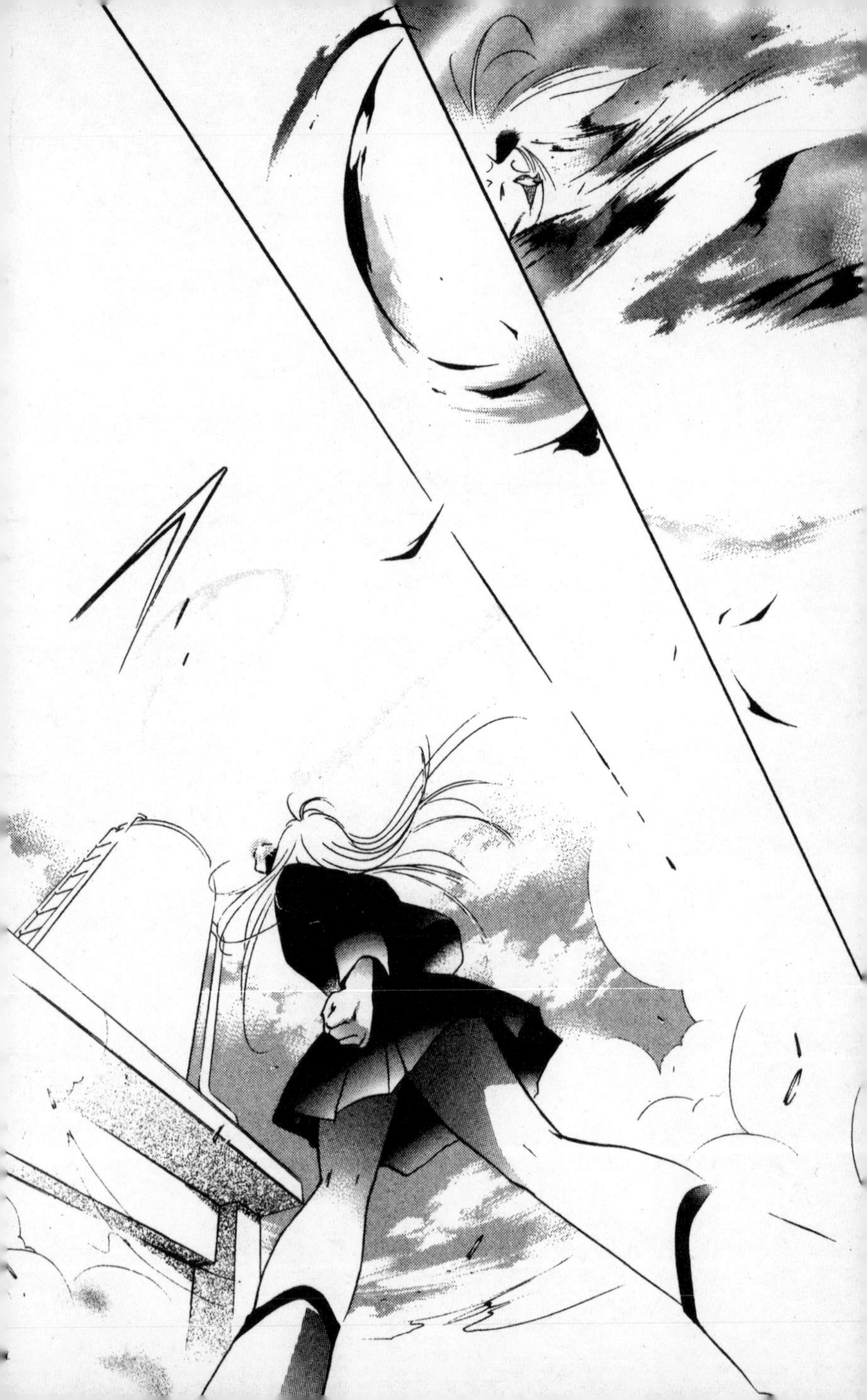

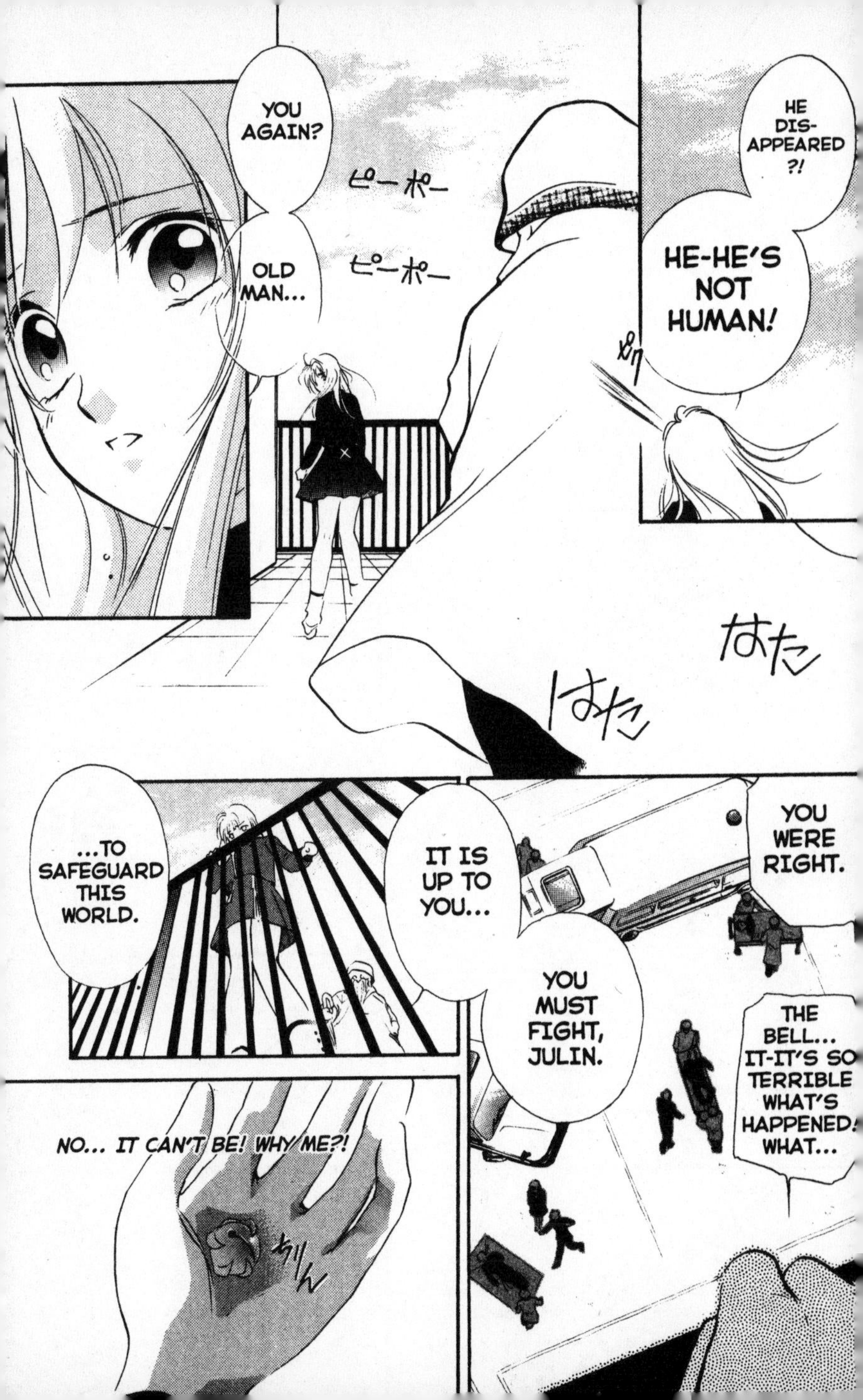
HE DIS- APPEARED ?!
HE-HE'S NOT HUMAN!
ピーポー
ピーポー
なた
はた
YOU AGAIN?
OLD MAN...
YOU WERE RIGHT.
IT IS UP TO YOU...
YOU MUST FIGHT, JULIN.
THE BELL... IT-IT'S SO TERRIBLE WHAT'S HAPPENED! WHAT...
...TO SAFEGUARD THIS WORLD.
NO... IT CAN'T BE! WHY ME?!
ちりん

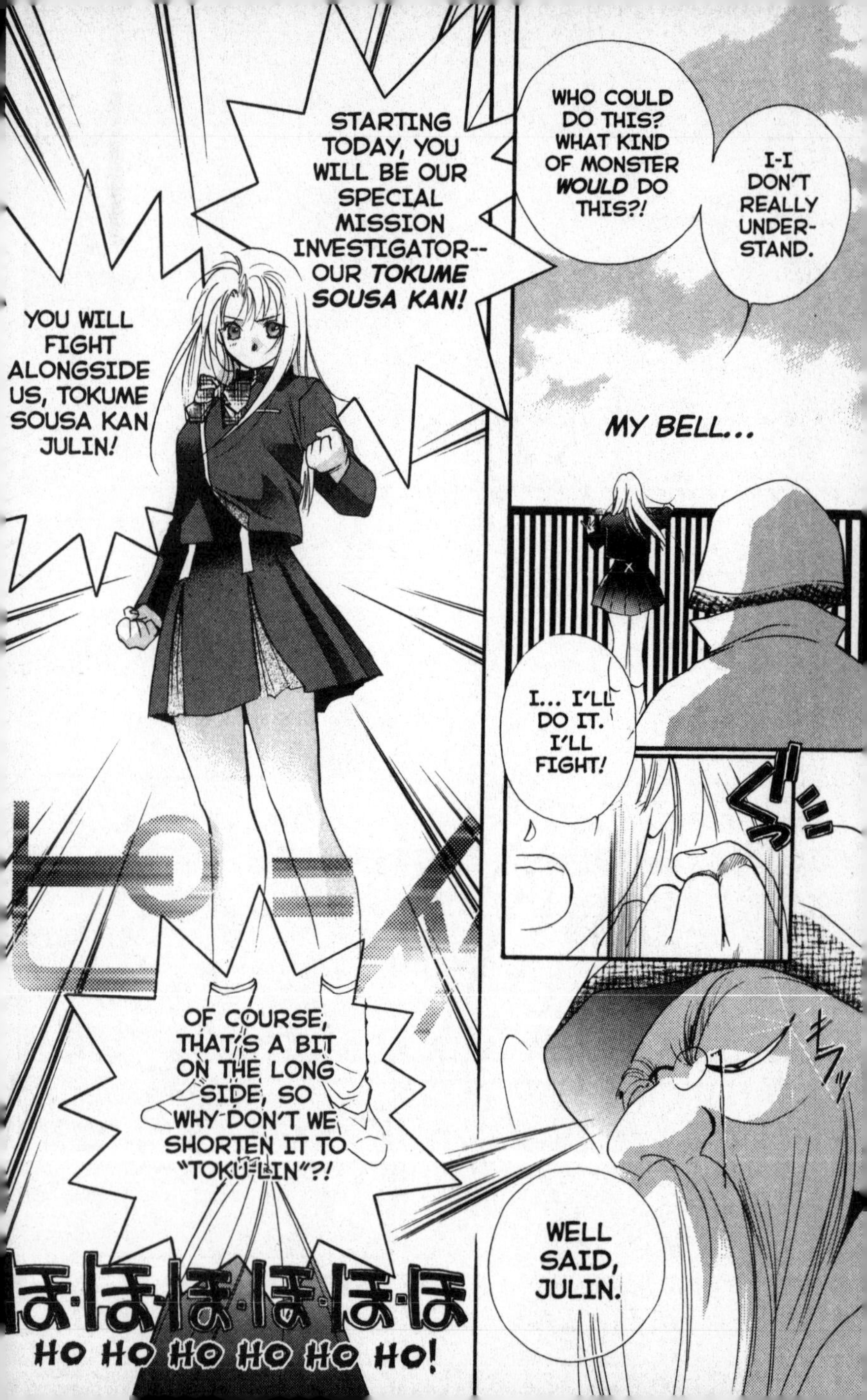

I-I DON'T REALLY UNDER-STAND.
WHO COULD DO THIS? WHAT KIND OF MONSTER *WOULD* DO THIS?!
*MY BELL...*
I... I'LL DO IT. I'LL FIGHT!
WELL SAID, JULIN.
STARTING TODAY, YOU WILL BE OUR SPECIAL MISSION INVESTIGATOR-- OUR *TOKUME SOUSA KAN!*
YOU WILL FIGHT ALONGSIDE US, TOKUME SOUSA KAN JULIN!
OF COURSE, THAT'S A BIT ON THE LONG SIDE, SO WHY DON'T WE SHORTEN IT TO "TOKU-LIN"?!
ほ・ほ・ほ・ほ・ほ・ほ
HO HO HO HO HO HO HO!

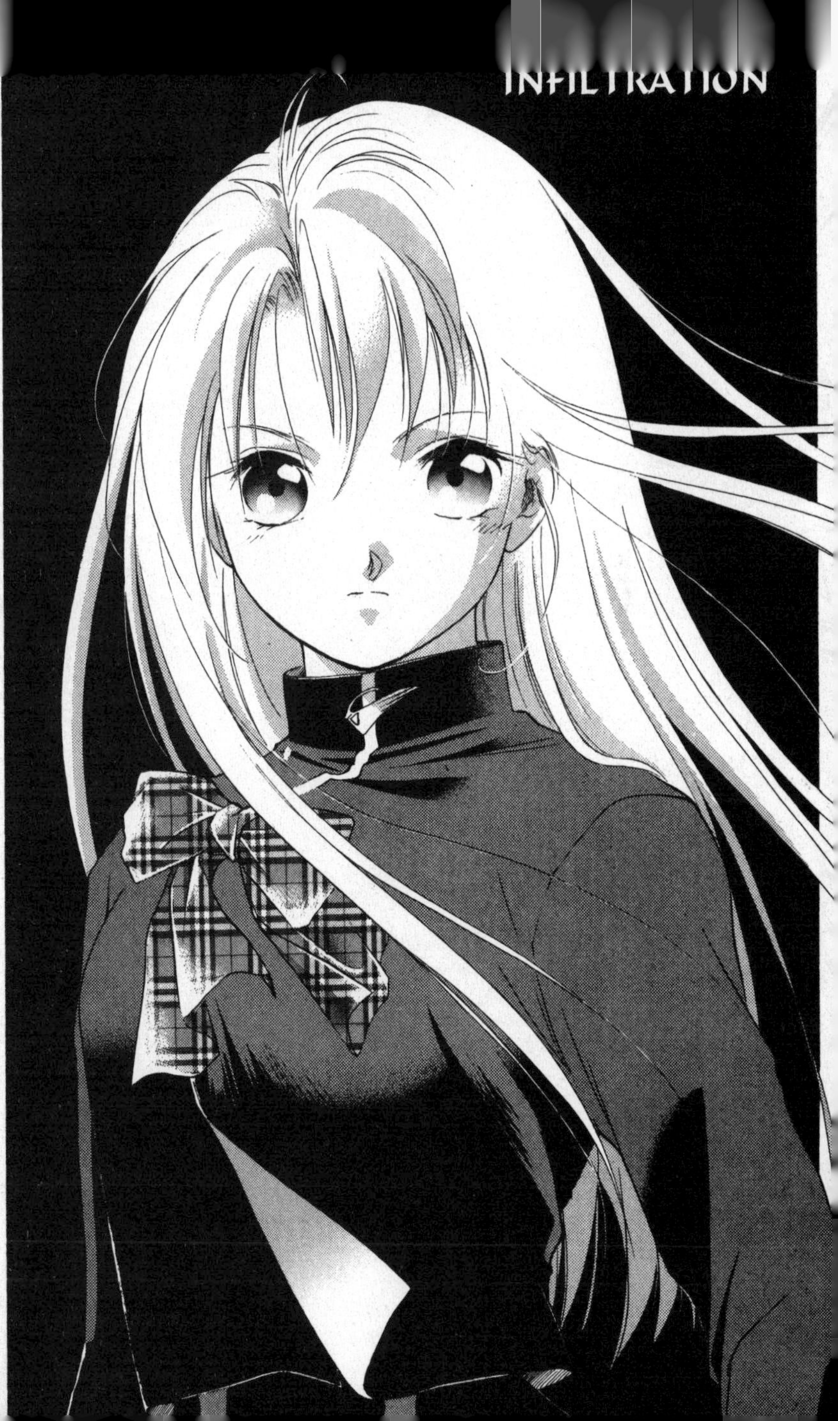
INFILTRATION

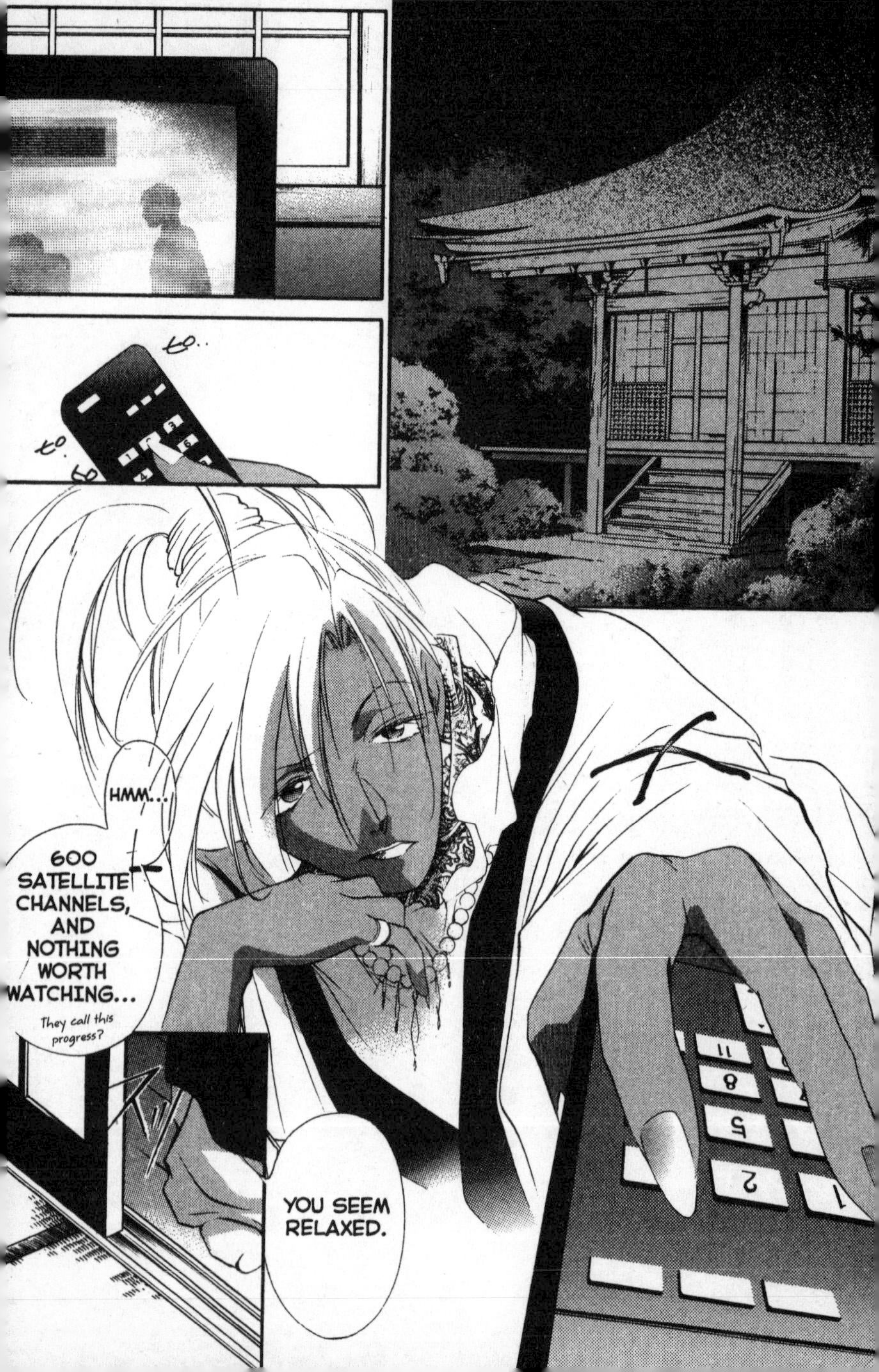
HMM...
600 SATELLITE CHANNELS, AND NOTHING WORTH WATCHING...
They call this progress?
YOU SEEM RELAXED.

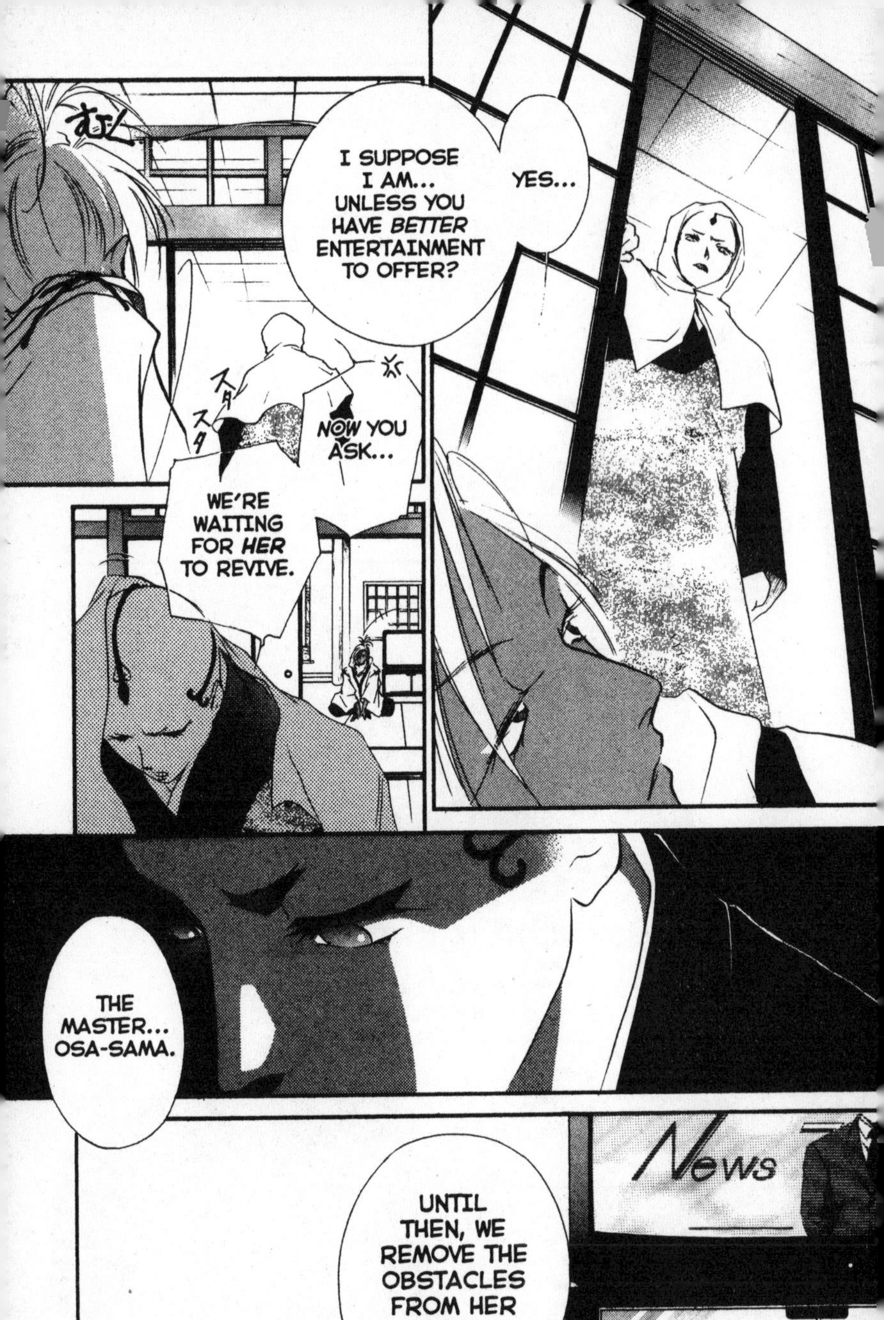
YES...
I SUPPOSE I AM... UNLESS YOU HAVE *BETTER* ENTERTAINMENT TO OFFER?
むん
スタスタ
*NOW* YOU ASK...
WE'RE WAITING FOR *HER* TO REVIVE.
THE MASTER... OSA-SAMA.
UNTIL THEN, WE REMOVE THE OBSTACLES FROM HER PATH.
News

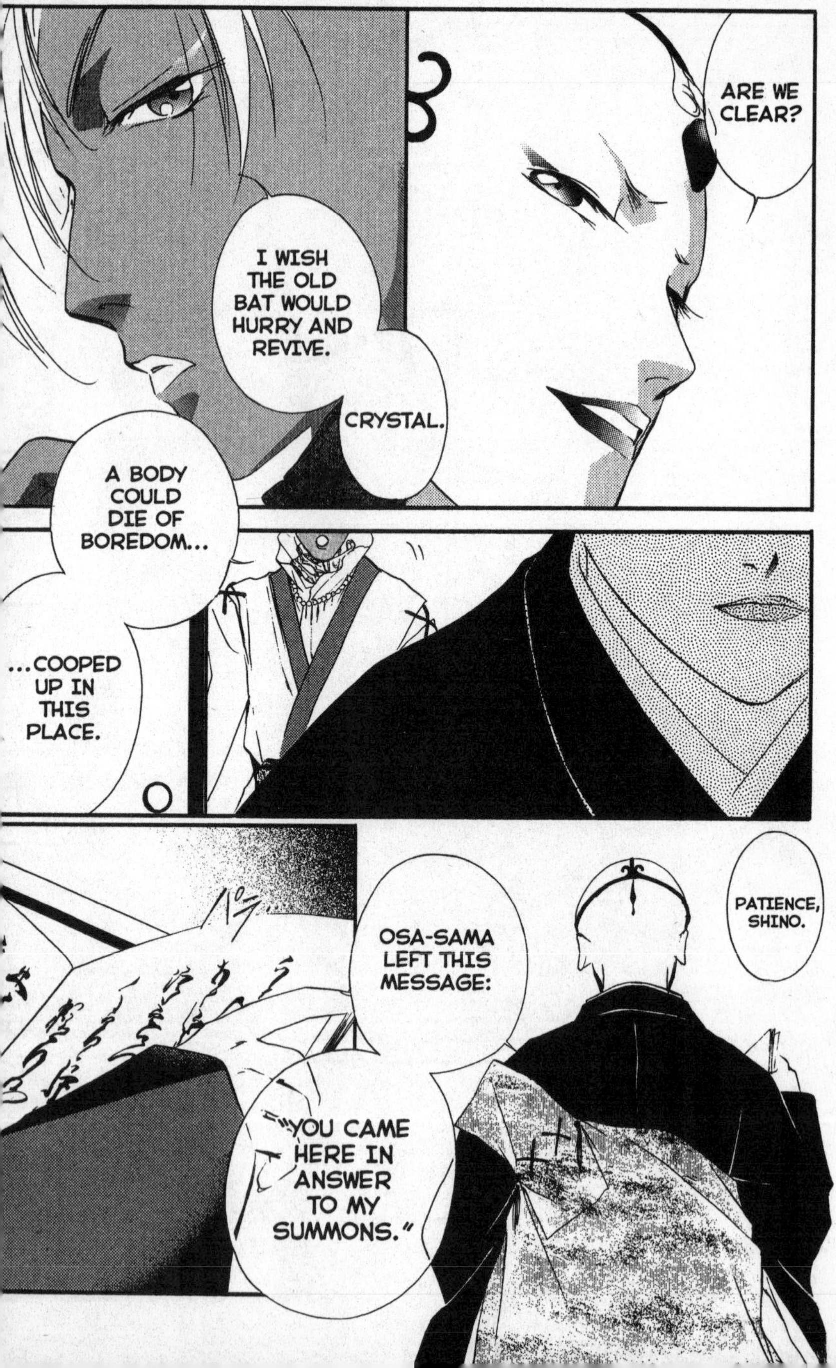
ARE WE CLEAR?
CRYSTAL.
I WISH THE OLD BAT WOULD HURRY AND REVIVE.
A BODY COULD DIE OF BOREDOM...
...COOPED UP IN THIS PLACE.
PATIENCE, SHINO.
OSA-SAMA LEFT THIS MESSAGE:
"YOU CAME HERE IN ANSWER TO MY SUMMONS."

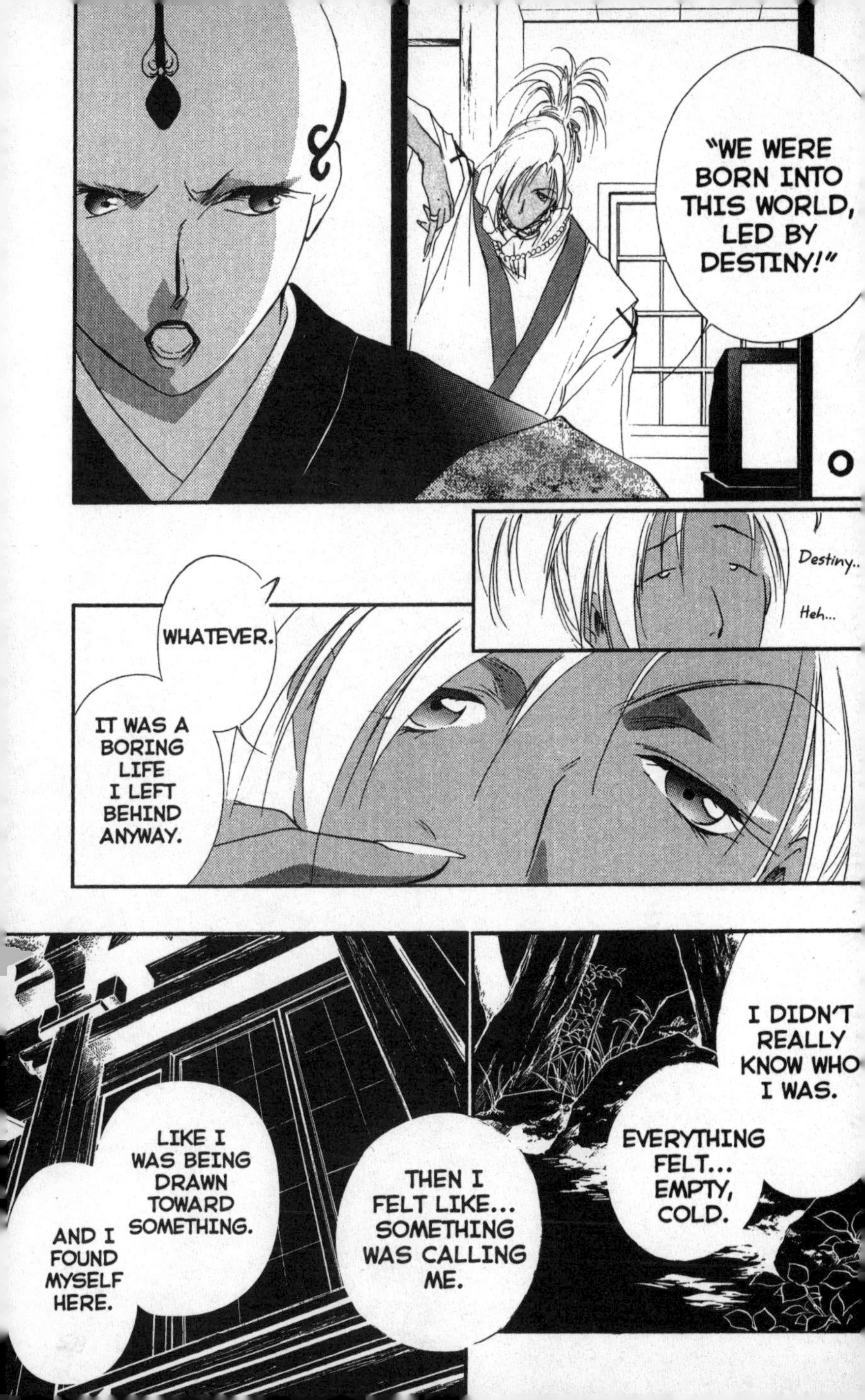
"WE WERE BORN INTO THIS WORLD, LED BY DESTINY!"
Destiny..
Heh...
WHATEVER.
IT WAS A BORING LIFE I LEFT BEHIND ANYWAY.
I DIDN'T REALLY KNOW WHO I WAS.
EVERYTHING FELT... EMPTY, COLD.
THEN I FELT LIKE... SOMETHING WAS CALLING ME.
LIKE I WAS BEING DRAWN TOWARD SOMETHING.
AND I FOUND MYSELF HERE.

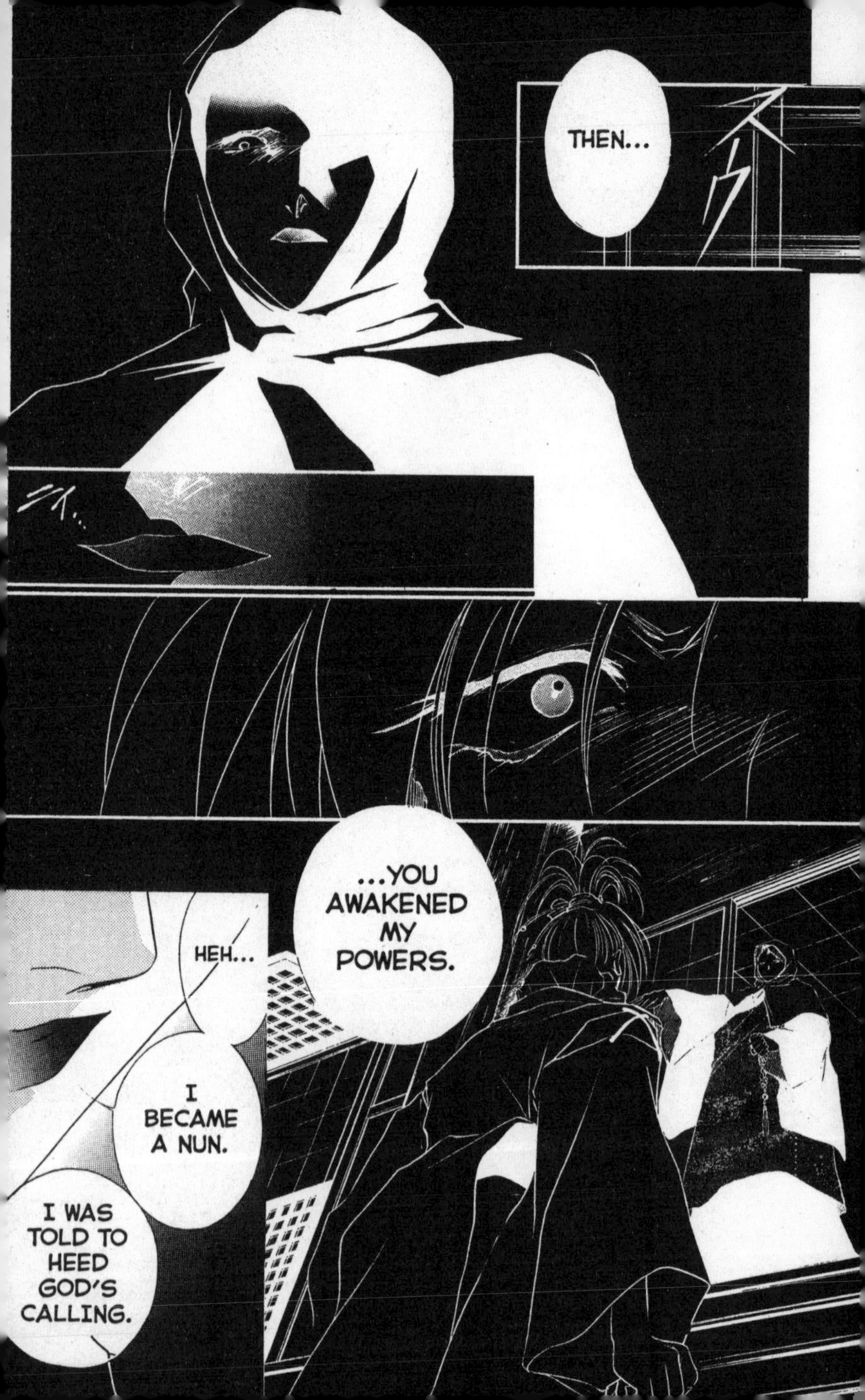
THEN...
...YOU AWAKENED MY POWERS.
HEH...
I BECAME A NUN.
I WAS TOLD TO HEED GOD'S CALLING.

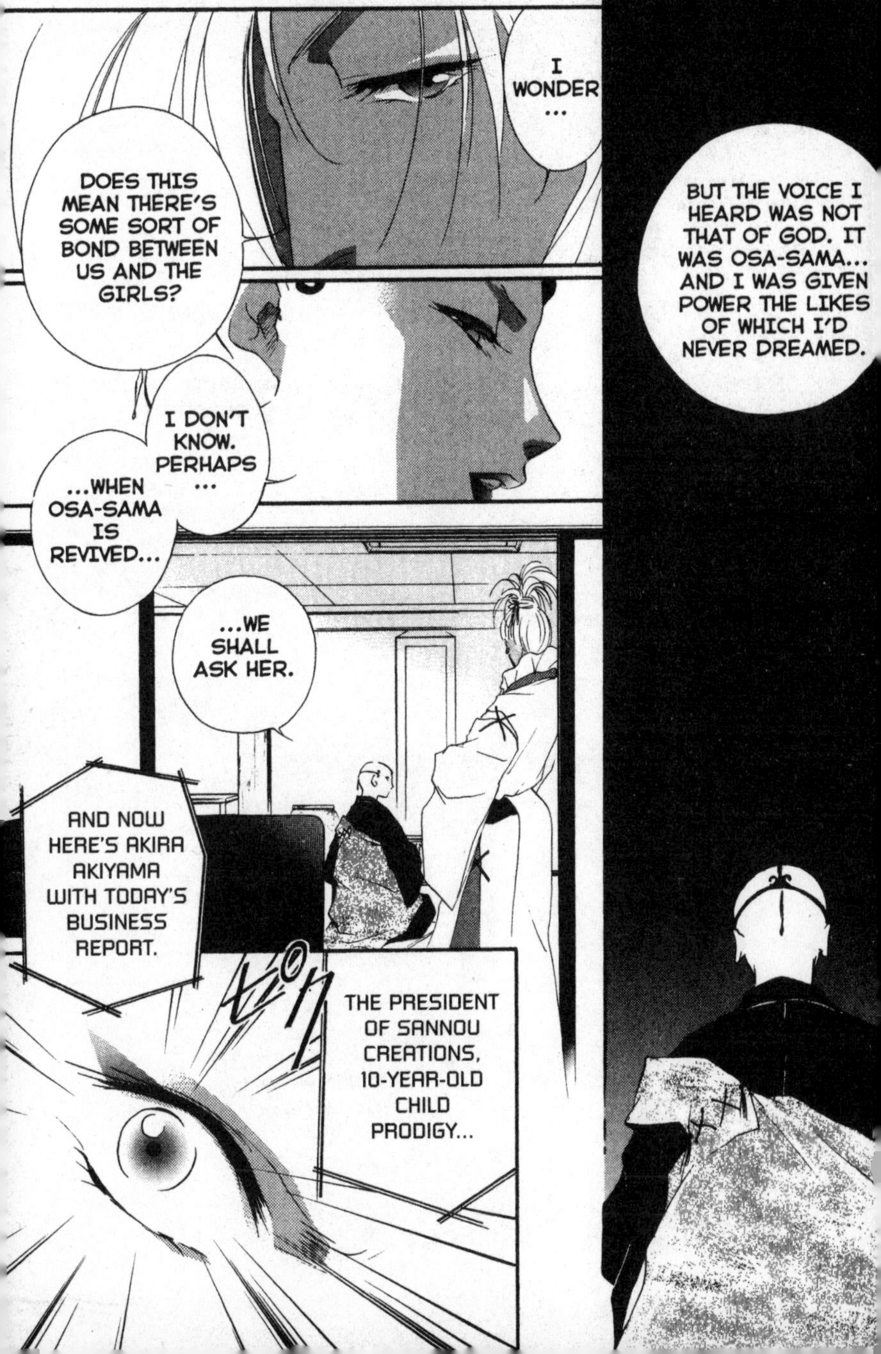
BUT THE VOICE I HEARD WAS NOT THAT OF GOD. IT WAS OSA-SAMA... AND I WAS GIVEN POWER THE LIKES OF WHICH I'D NEVER DREAMED.
I WONDER...
DOES THIS MEAN THERE'S SOME SORT OF BOND BETWEEN US AND THE GIRLS?
I DON'T KNOW. PERHAPS...
...WHEN OSA-SAMA IS REVIVED...
...WE SHALL ASK HER.
AND NOW HERE'S AKIRA AKIYAMA WITH TODAY'S BUSINESS REPORT.
THE PRESIDENT OF SANNOU CREATIONS, 10-YEAR-OLD CHILD PRODIGY...

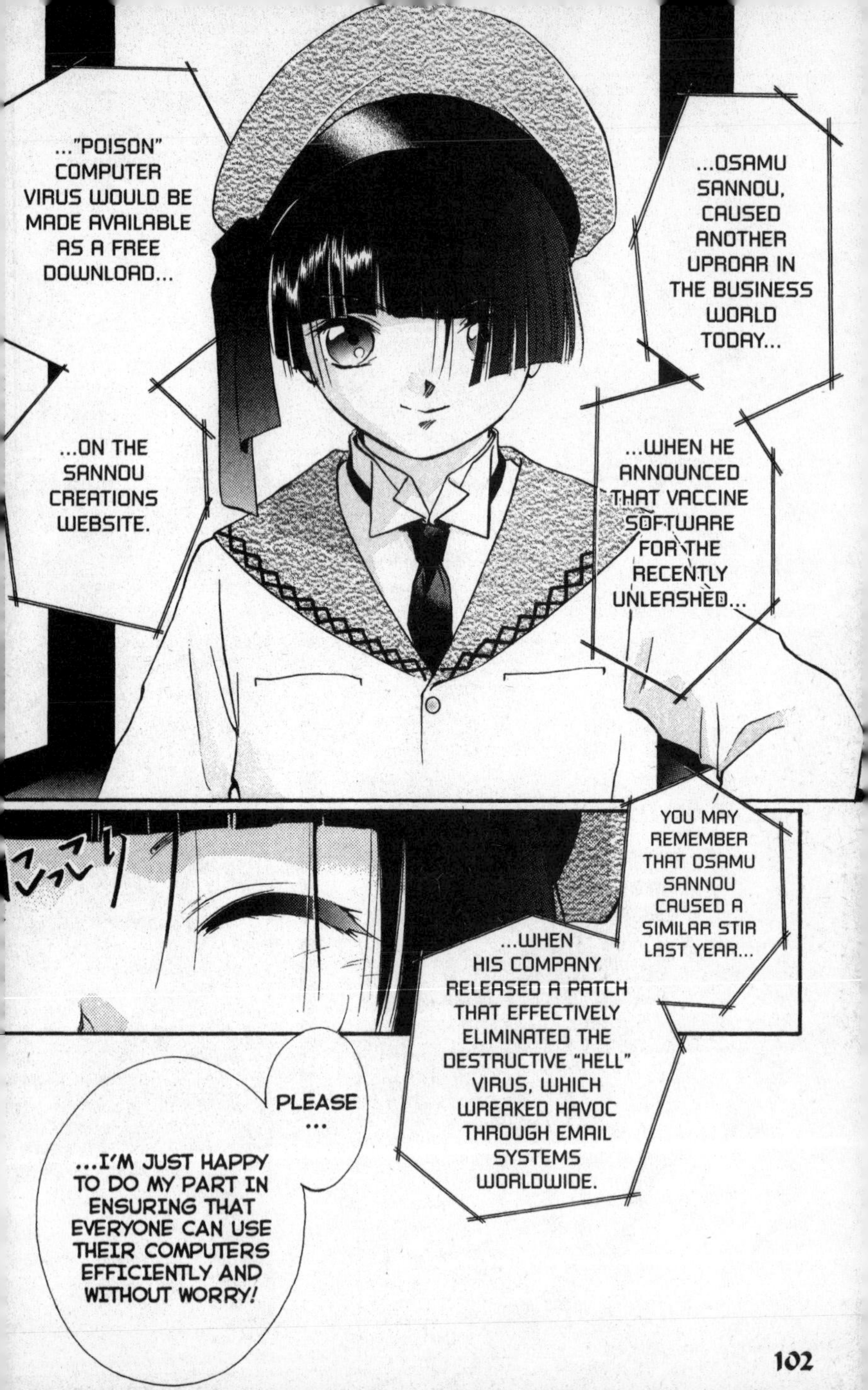
...OSAMU SANNOU, CAUSED ANOTHER UPROAR IN THE BUSINESS WORLD TODAY...
...WHEN HE ANNOUNCED THAT VACCINE SOFTWARE FOR THE RECENTLY UNLEASHED...
..."POISON" COMPUTER VIRUS WOULD BE MADE AVAILABLE AS A FREE DOWNLOAD...
...ON THE SANNOU CREATIONS WEBSITE.
YOU MAY REMEMBER THAT OSAMU SANNOU CAUSED A SIMILAR STIR LAST YEAR...
...WHEN HIS COMPANY RELEASED A PATCH THAT EFFECTIVELY ELIMINATED THE DESTRUCTIVE "HELL" VIRUS, WHICH WREAKED HAVOC THROUGH EMAIL SYSTEMS WORLDWIDE.
PLEASE ...
...I'M JUST HAPPY TO DO MY PART IN ENSURING THAT EVERYONE CAN USE THEIR COMPUTERS EFFICIENTLY AND WITHOUT WORRY!

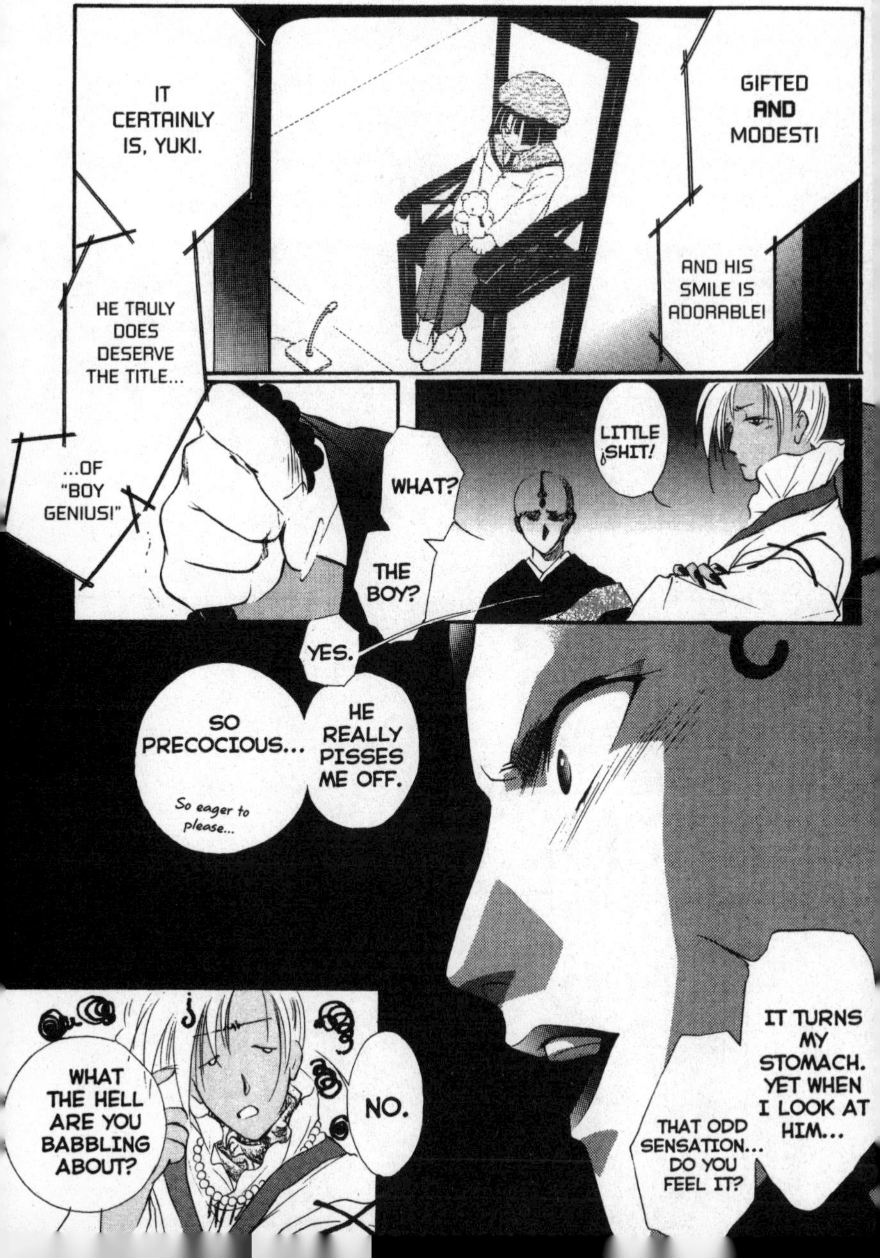
GIFTED AND MODEST!
AND HIS SMILE IS ADORABLE!
IT CERTAINLY IS, YUKI.
HE TRULY DOES DESERVE THE TITLE...
...OF "BOY GENIUS!"
LITTLE ¡SHIT!
WHAT?
THE BOY?
YES.
HE REALLY PISSES ME OFF.
SO PRECOCIOUS...
So eager to please...
IT TURNS MY STOMACH. YET WHEN I LOOK AT HIM...
THAT ODD SENSATION... DO YOU FEEL IT?
NO.
WHAT THE HELL ARE YOU BABBLING ABOUT?

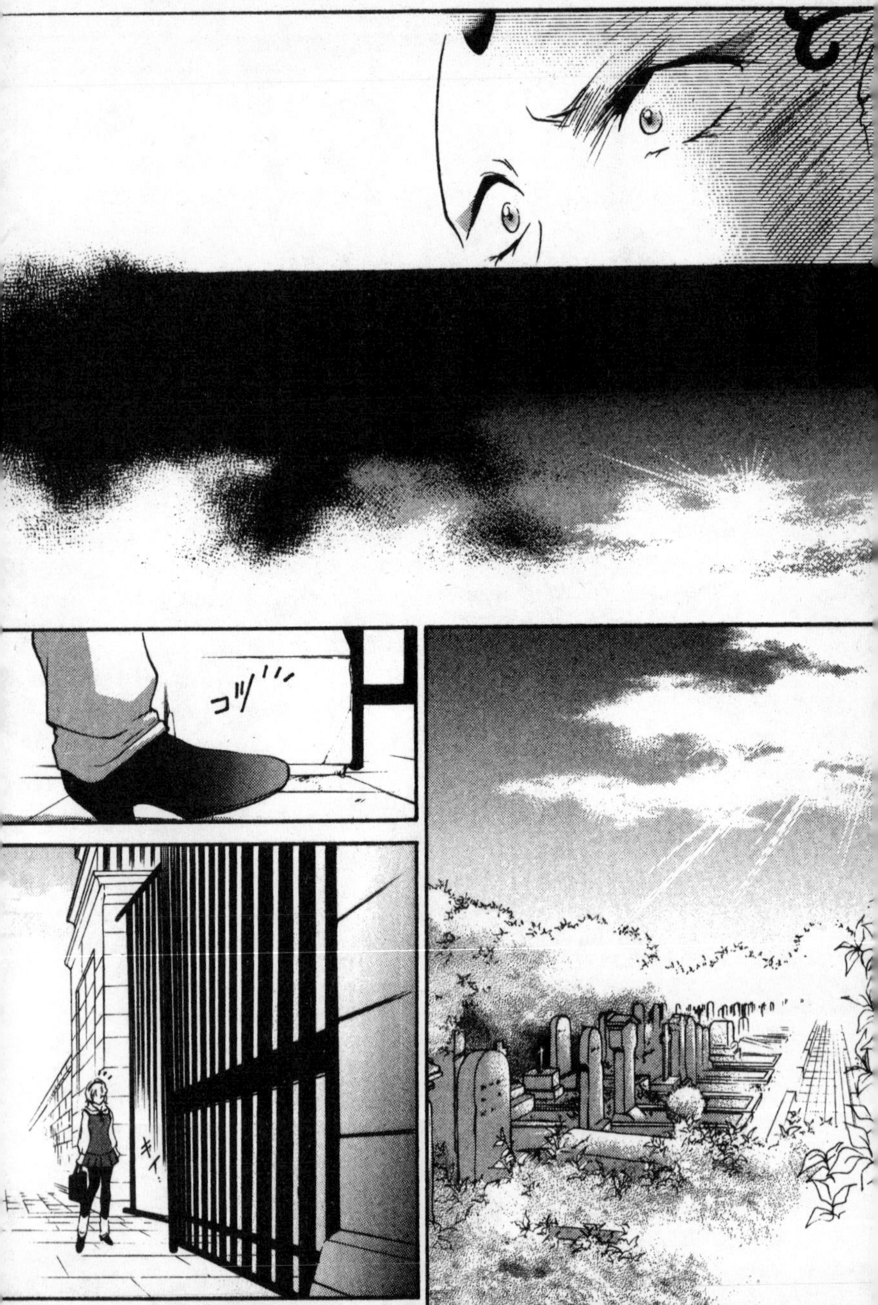
コツ
キィ…

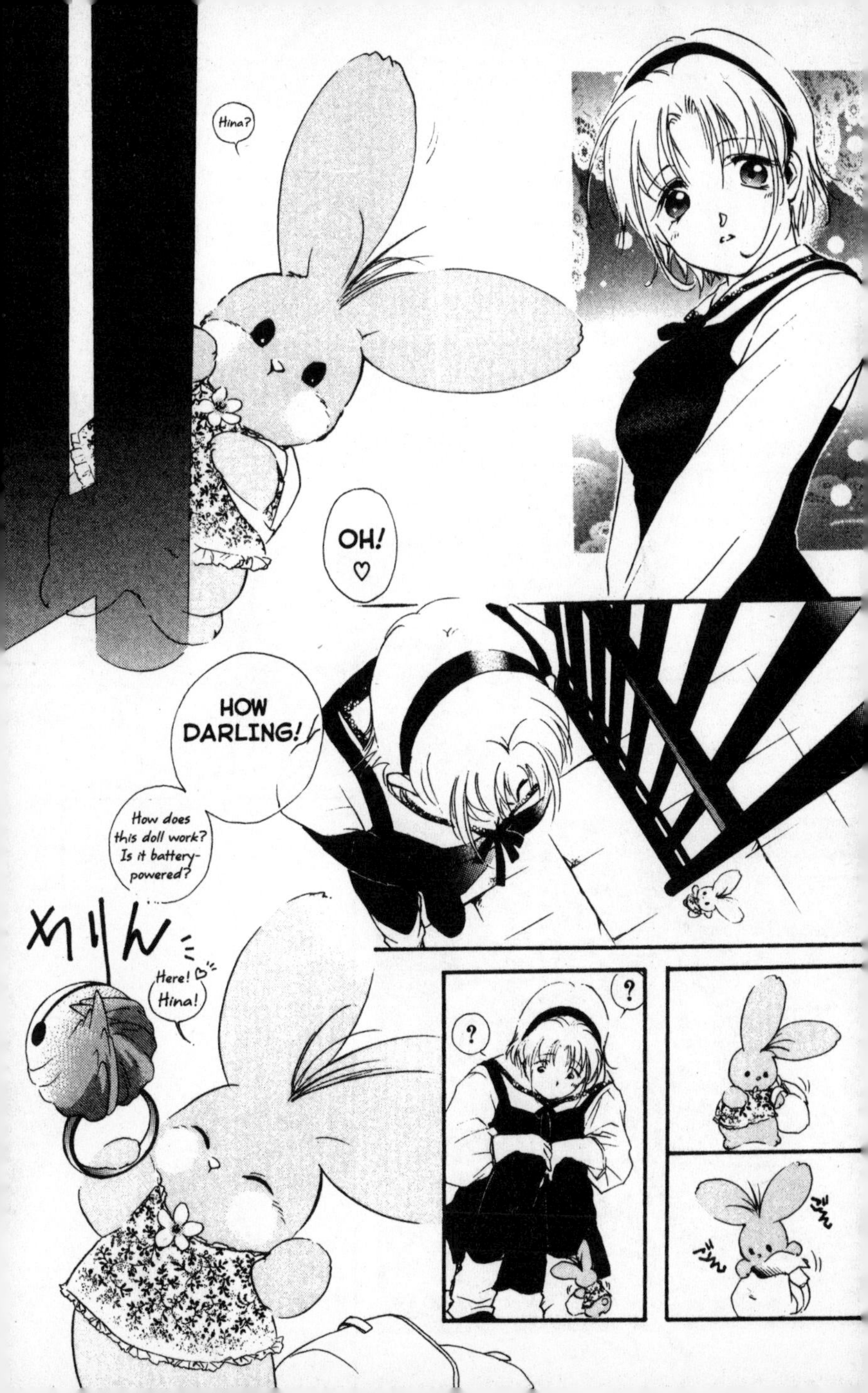
Hina?
OH! ♡
HOW DARLING!
How does this doll work? Is it battery-powered?
?
?
Here! ♡ Hina!

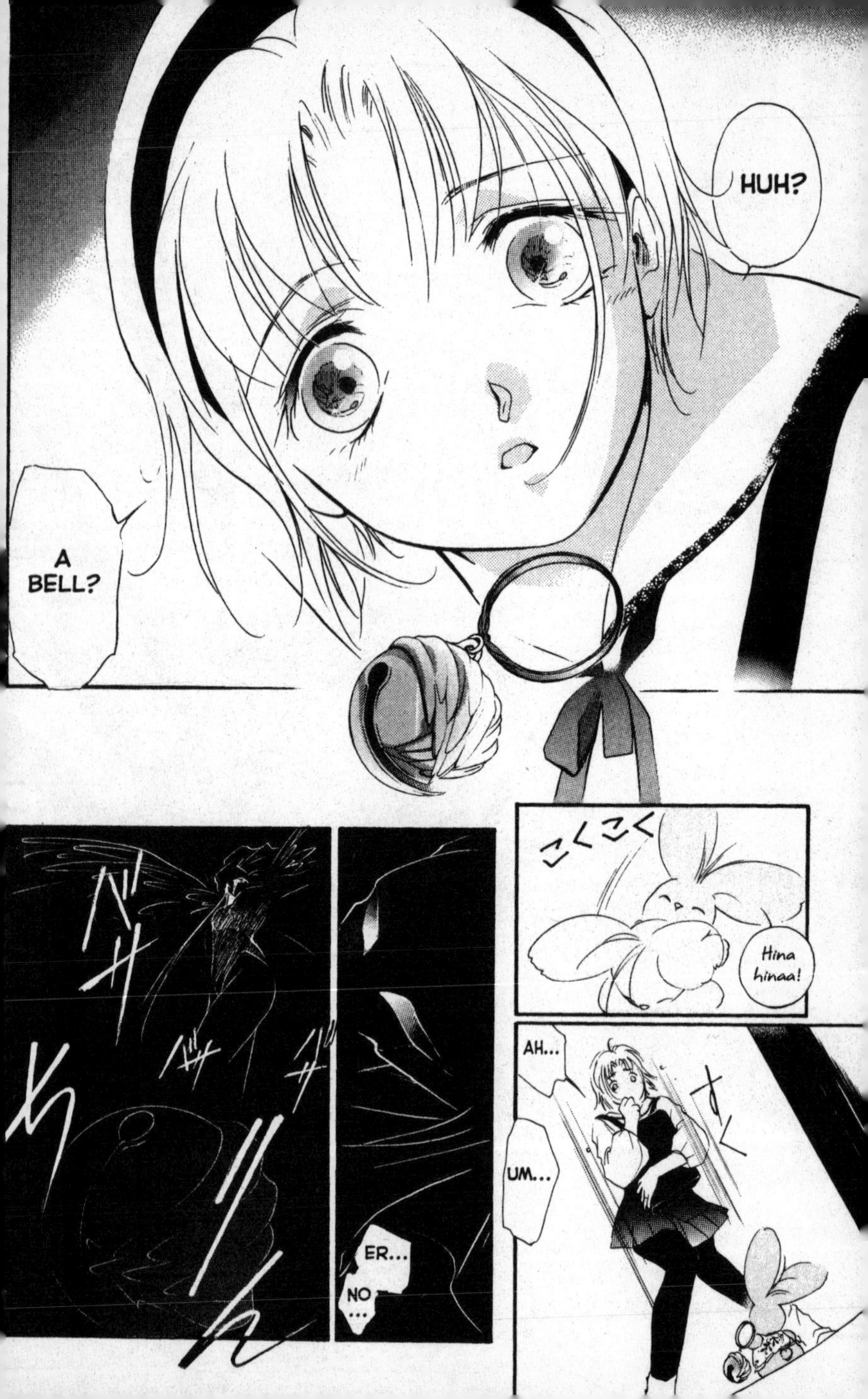
HUH?
A BELL?
こくこく
Hina hinaa!
AH...
UM...
ER...
NO ...

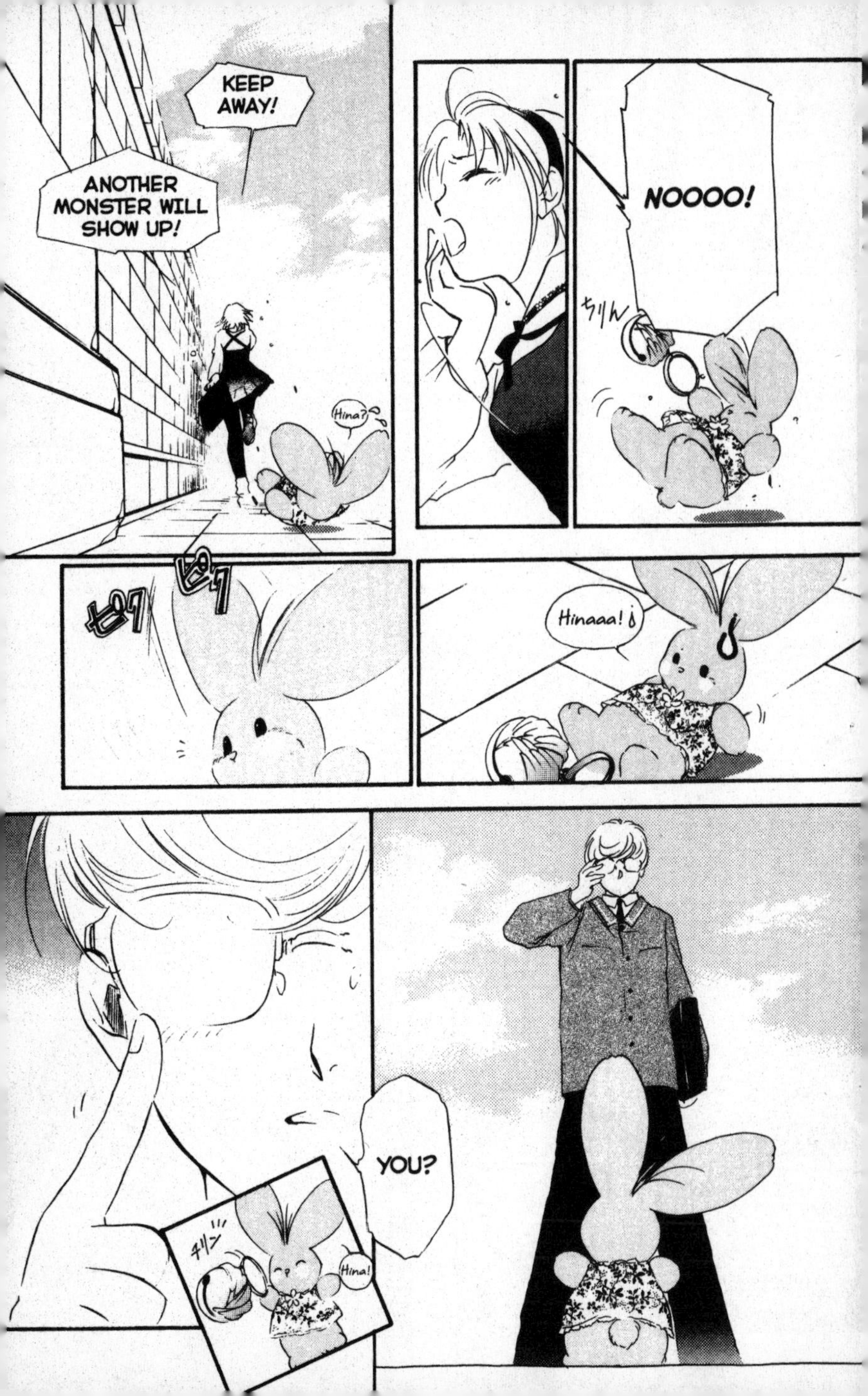
NOOOO!
ちりん
KEEP AWAY!
ANOTHER MONSTER WILL SHOW UP!
Hina?
Hinaaa!
ピク
ピク
YOU?
チリン
Hina!

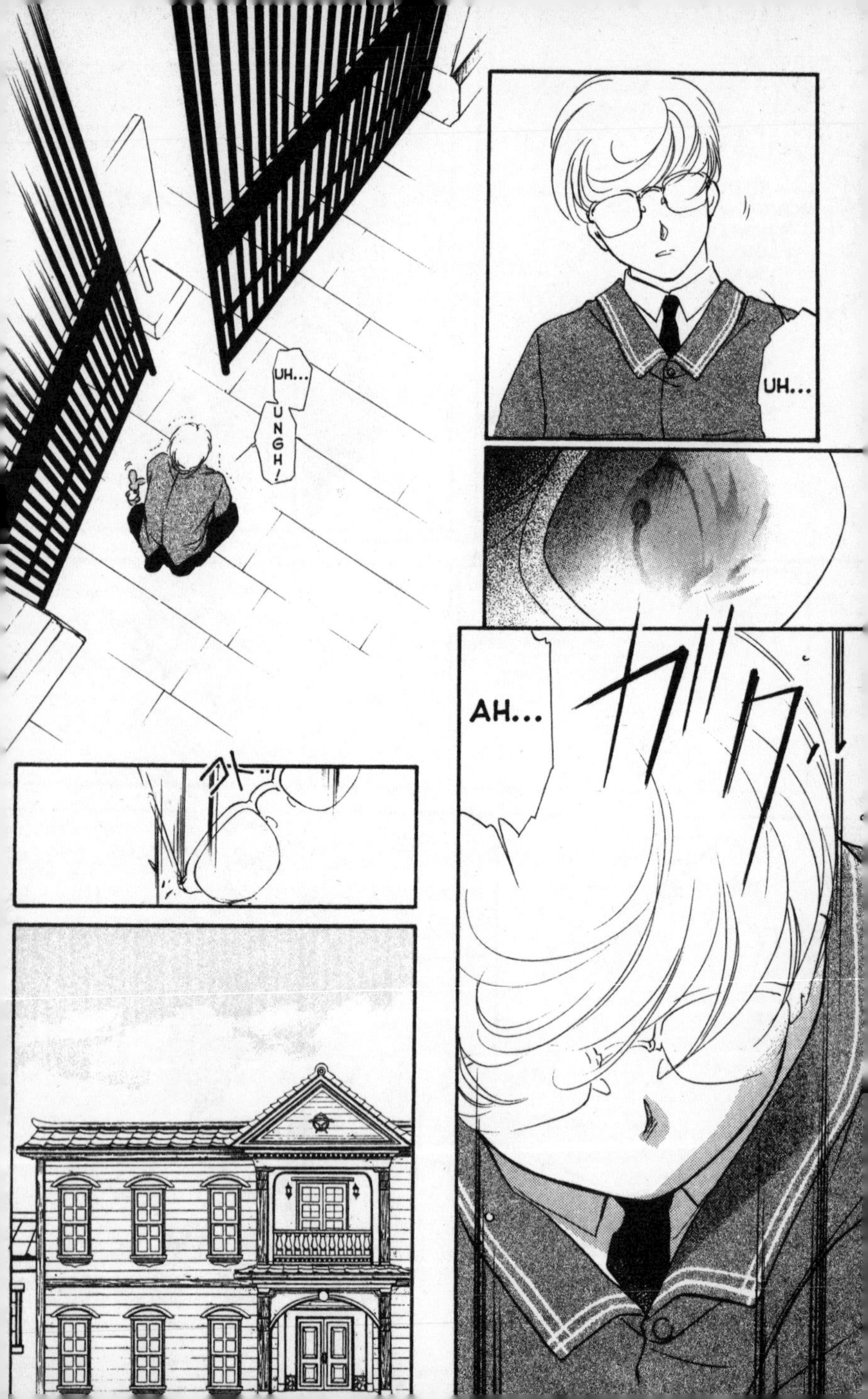
UH...
AH...
UH...
UNGH!

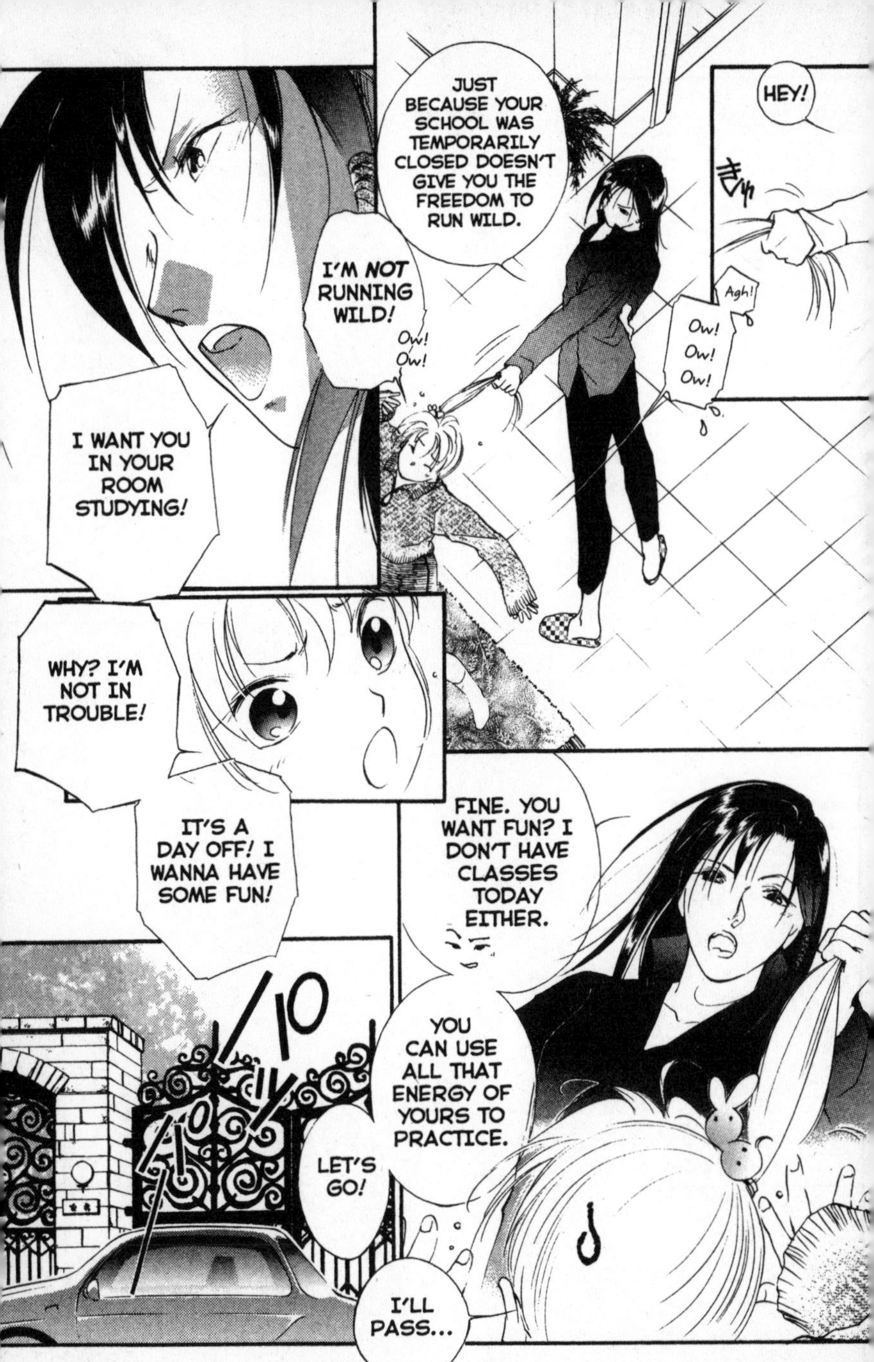
HEY!
Agh!
Ow! Ow! Ow!
JUST BECAUSE YOUR SCHOOL WAS TEMPORARILY CLOSED DOESN'T GIVE YOU THE FREEDOM TO RUN WILD.
I'M *NOT* RUNNING WILD!
Ow! Ow!
I WANT YOU IN YOUR ROOM STUDYING!
WHY? I'M NOT IN TROUBLE!
IT'S A DAY OFF! I WANNA HAVE SOME FUN!
FINE. YOU WANT FUN? I DON'T HAVE CLASSES TODAY EITHER.
YOU CAN USE ALL THAT ENERGY OF YOURS TO PRACTICE.
LET'S GO!
I'LL PASS...

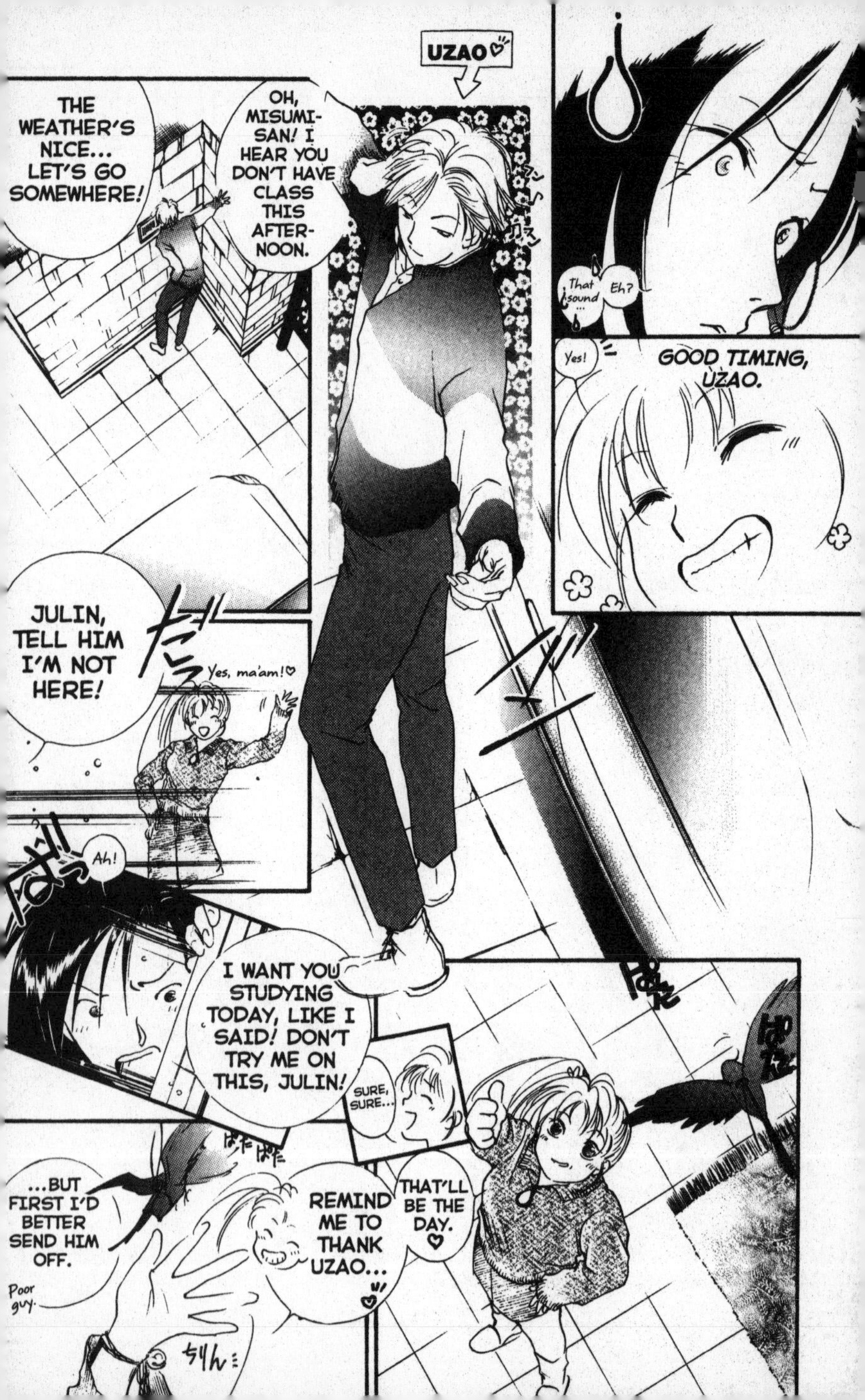
That sound...
Eh?
Yes!
GOOD TIMING, UZAO.
UZAO
OH, MISUMI-SAN! I HEAR YOU DON'T HAVE CLASS THIS AFTERNOON.
THE WEATHER'S NICE... LET'S GO SOMEWHERE!
JULIN, TELL HIM I'M NOT HERE!
Yes, ma'am!
Ah!
I WANT YOU STUDYING TODAY, LIKE I SAID! DON'T TRY ME ON THIS, JULIN!
SURE, SURE...
THAT'LL BE THE DAY.
REMIND ME TO THANK UZAO...
...BUT FIRST I'D BETTER SEND HIM OFF.
Poor guy.

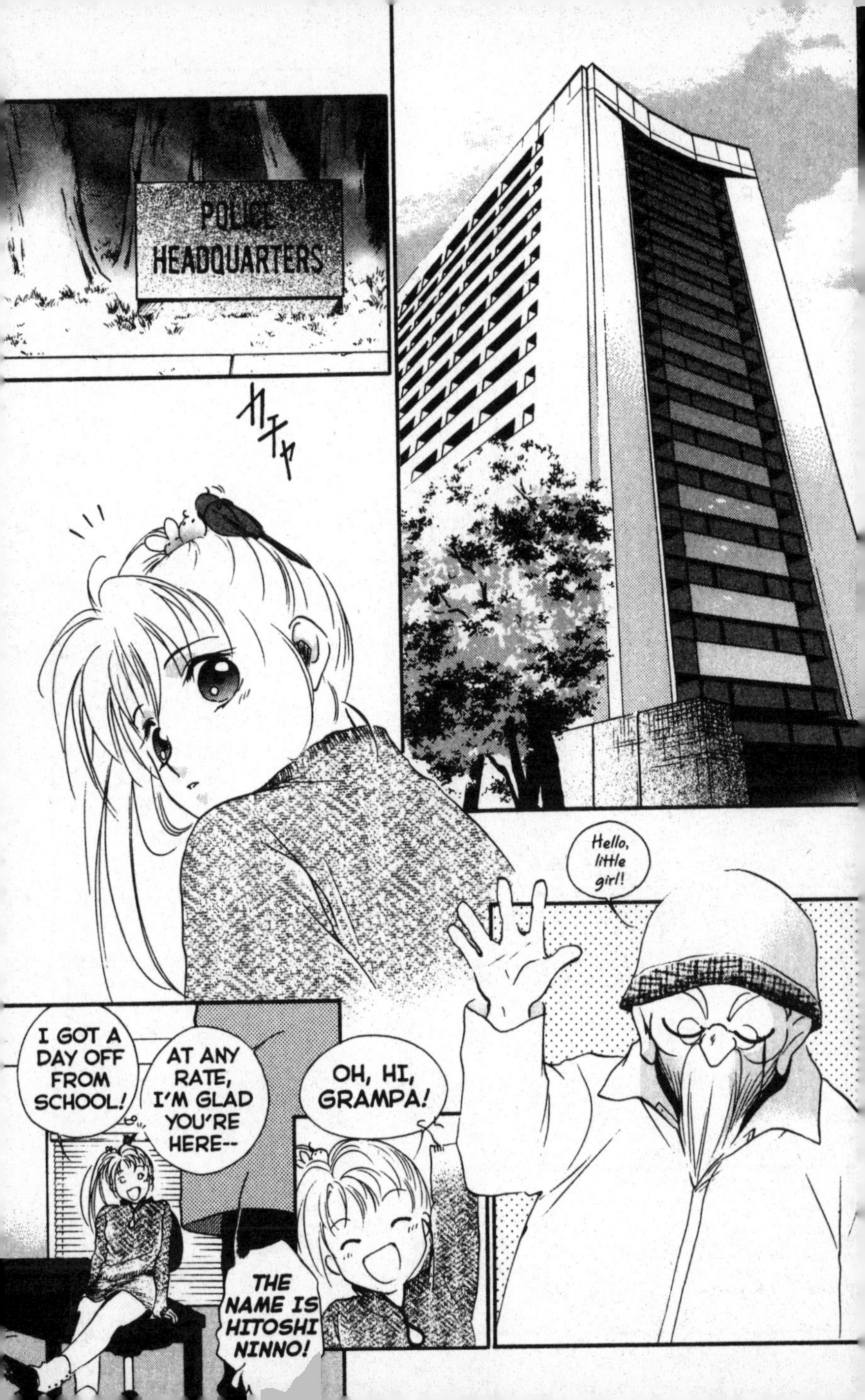
POLICE HEADQUARTERS
カチャ
Hello, little girl!
OH, HI, GRAMPA!
THE NAME IS HITOSHI NINNO!
AT ANY RATE, I'M GLAD YOU'RE HERE--
I GOT A DAY OFF FROM SCHOOL!

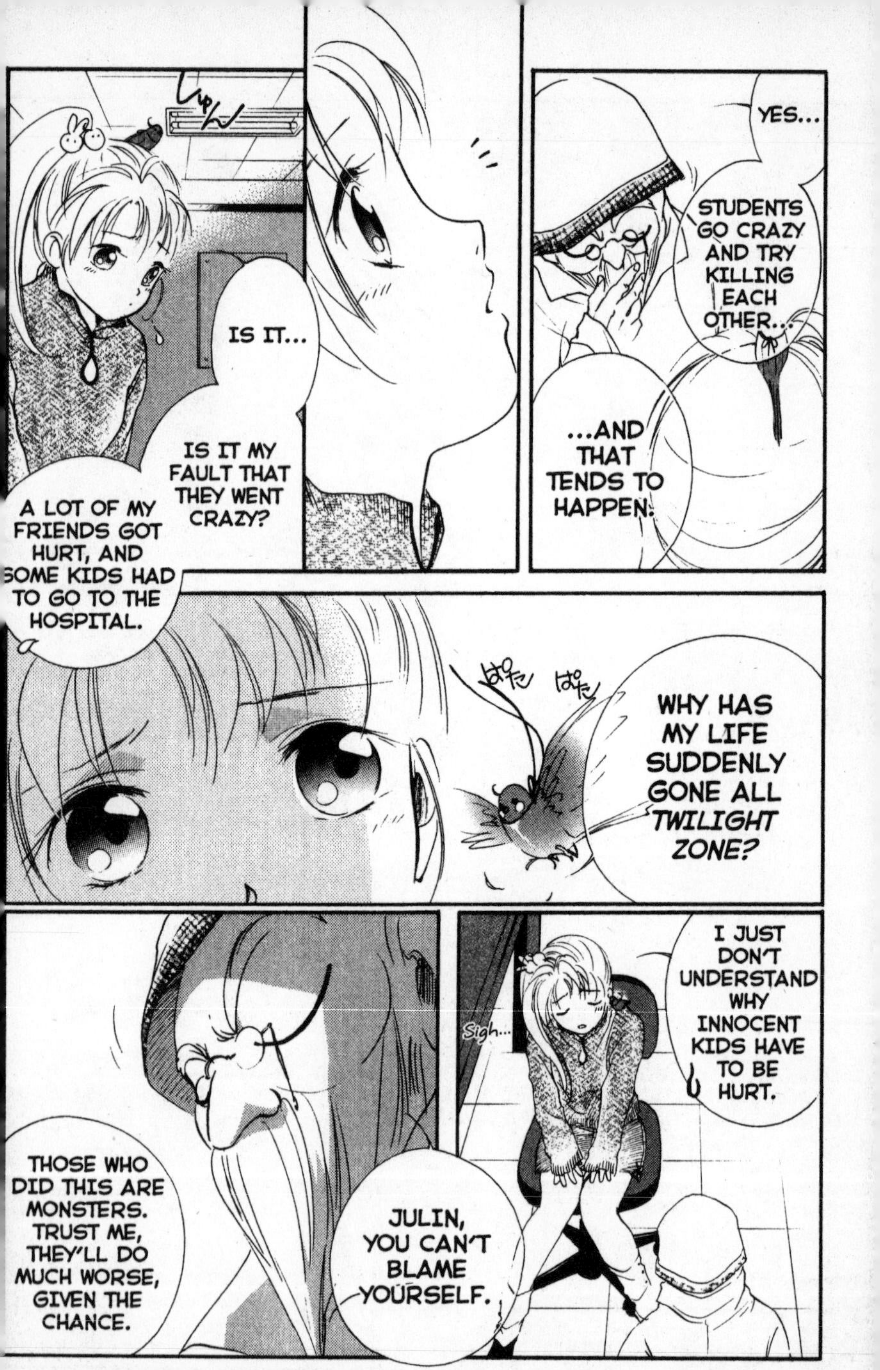
YES...
STUDENTS GO CRAZY AND TRY KILLING EACH OTHER...
...AND THAT TENDS TO HAPPEN.
しゅん
IS IT...
IS IT MY FAULT THAT THEY WENT CRAZY?
A LOT OF MY FRIENDS GOT HURT, AND SOME KIDS HAD TO GO TO THE HOSPITAL.
ぱた ぱた
WHY HAS MY LIFE SUDDENLY GONE ALL *TWILIGHT ZONE?*
I JUST DON'T UNDERSTAND WHY INNOCENT KIDS HAVE TO BE HURT.
Sigh...
JULIN, YOU CAN'T BLAME YOURSELF.
THOSE WHO DID THIS ARE MONSTERS. TRUST ME, THEY'LL DO MUCH WORSE, GIVEN THE CHANCE.

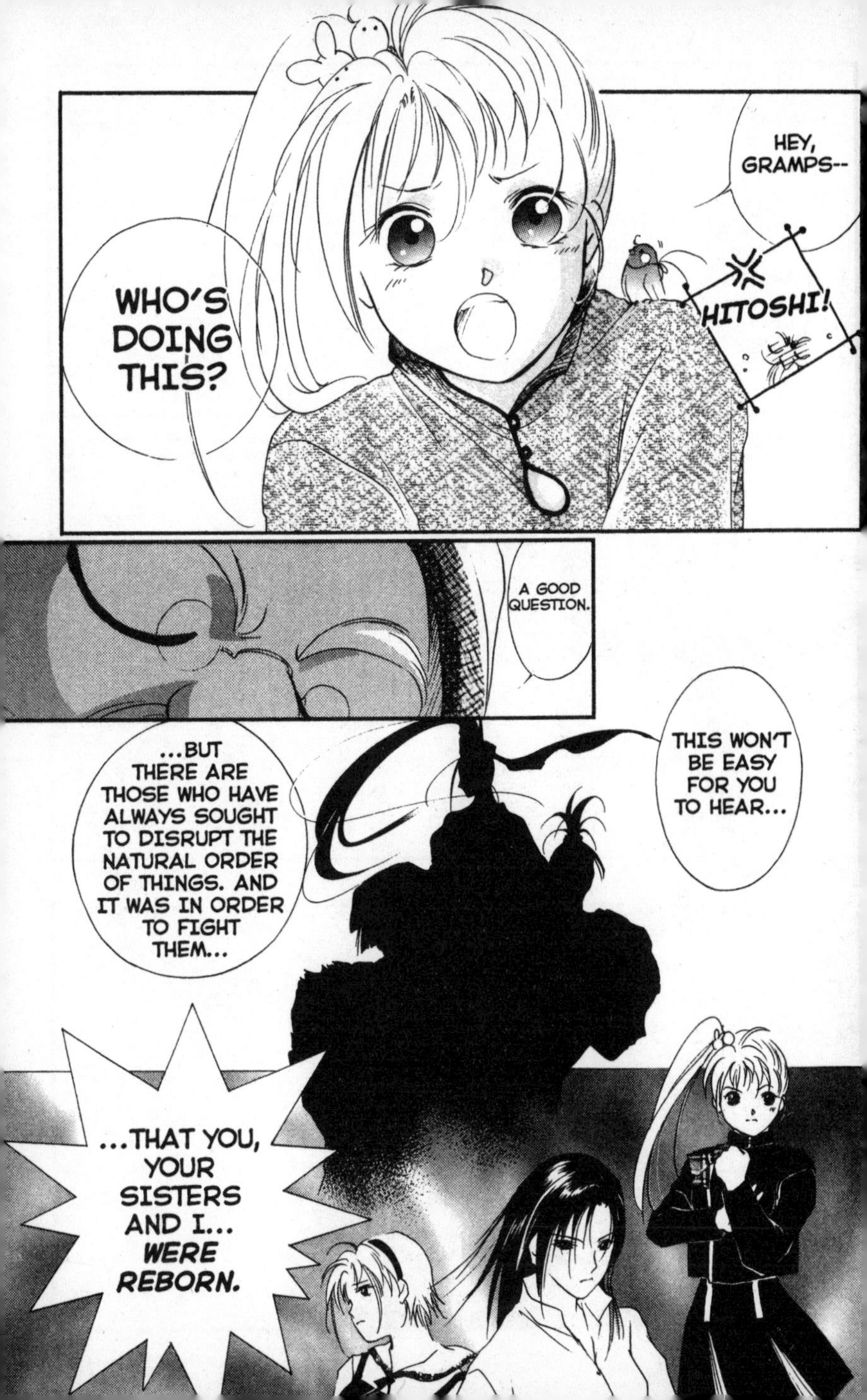
HEY, GRAMPS--
HITOSHI!
WHO'S DOING THIS?
A GOOD QUESTION.
THIS WON'T BE EASY FOR YOU TO HEAR...
...BUT THERE ARE THOSE WHO HAVE ALWAYS SOUGHT TO DISRUPT THE NATURAL ORDER OF THINGS. AND IT WAS IN ORDER TO FIGHT THEM...
...THAT YOU, YOUR SISTERS AND I... *WERE REBORN.*

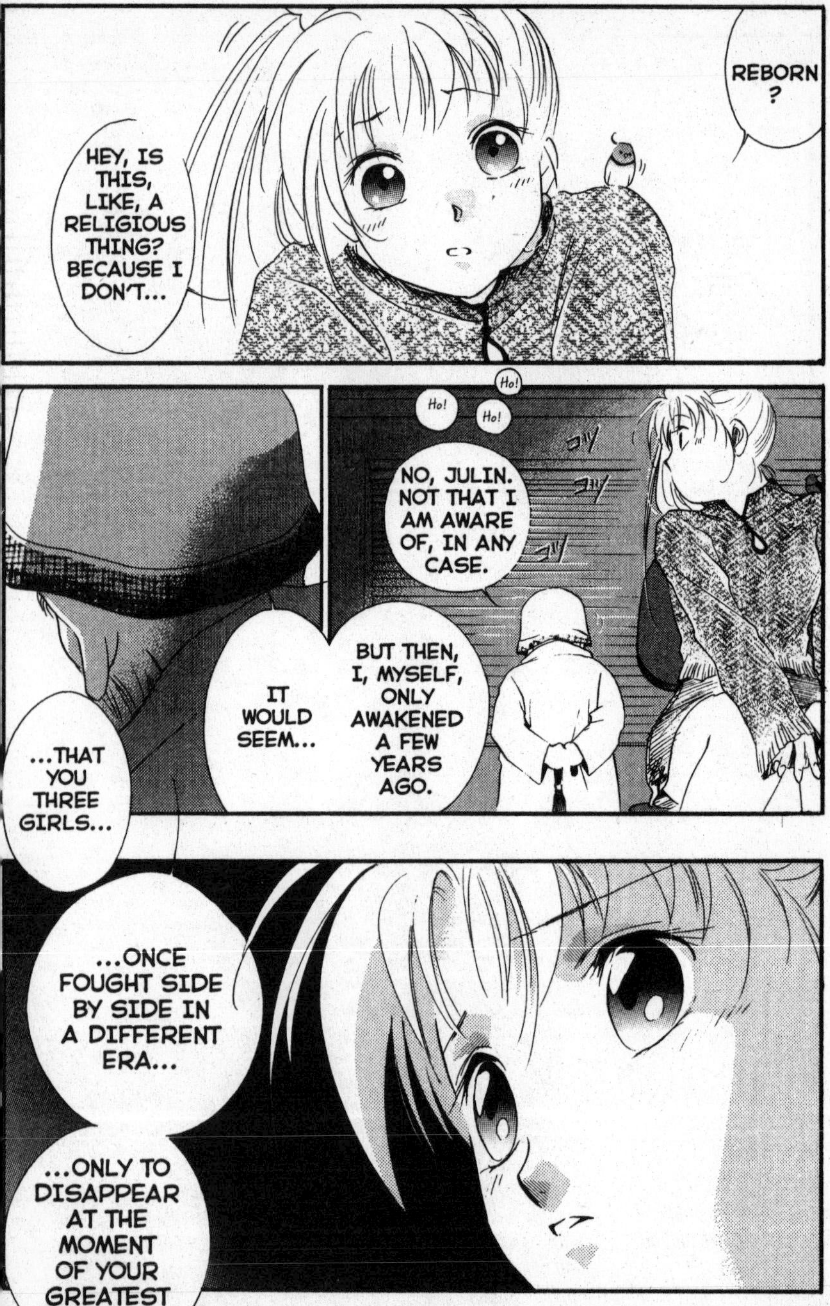
REBORN ?
HEY, IS THIS, LIKE, A RELIGIOUS THING? BECAUSE I DON'T...
Ho!
Ho!
Ho!
NO, JULIN. NOT THAT I AM AWARE OF, IN ANY CASE.
BUT THEN, I, MYSELF, ONLY AWAKENED A FEW YEARS AGO.
IT WOULD SEEM...
...THAT YOU THREE GIRLS...
...ONCE FOUGHT SIDE BY SIDE IN A DIFFERENT ERA...
...ONLY TO DISAPPEAR AT THE MOMENT OF YOUR GREATEST TRIUMPH.

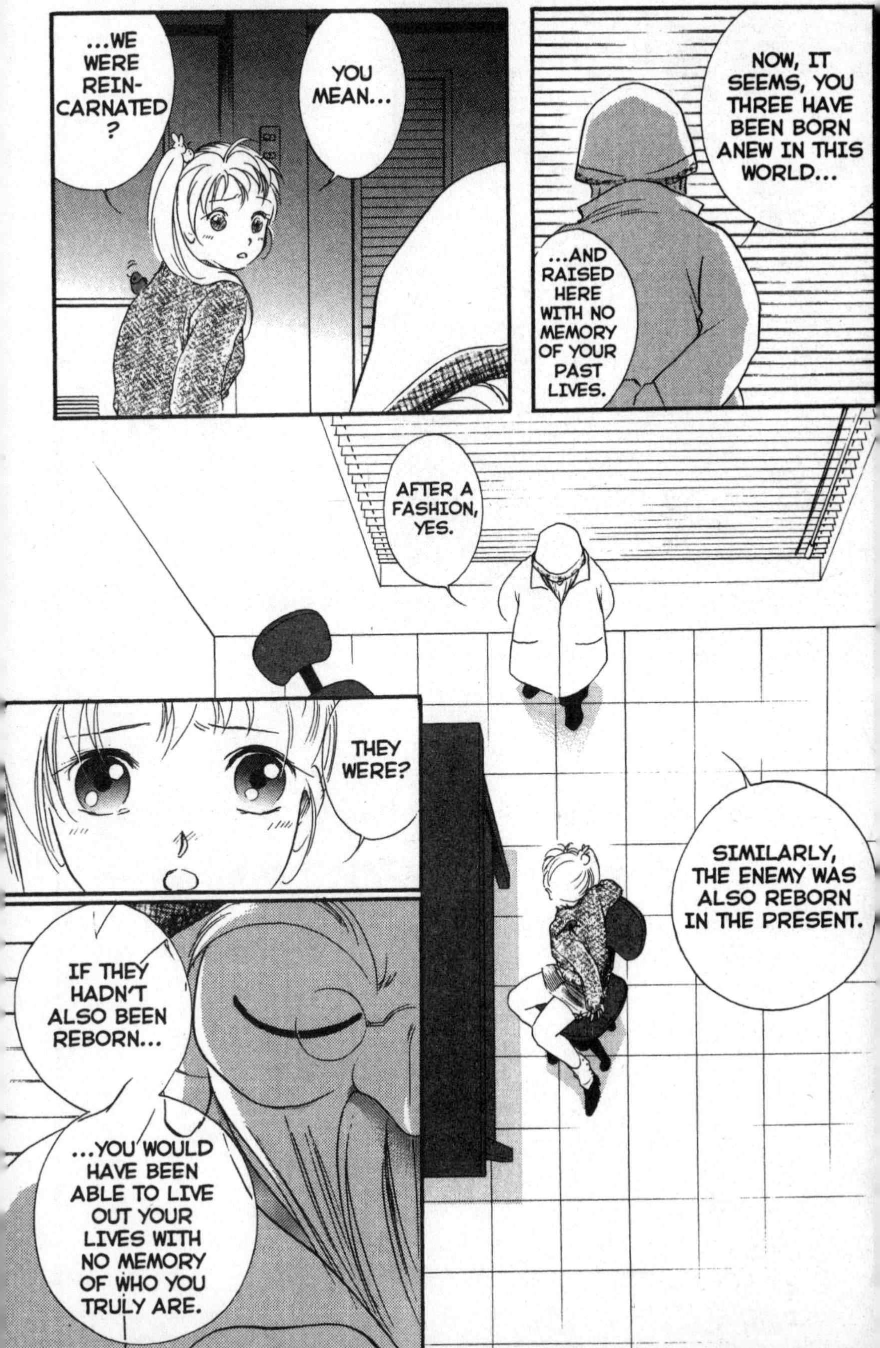
NOW, IT SEEMS, YOU THREE HAVE BEEN BORN ANEW IN THIS WORLD...
...AND RAISED HERE WITH NO MEMORY OF YOUR PAST LIVES.
YOU MEAN...
...WE WERE REIN-CARNATED?
AFTER A FASHION, YES.
SIMILARLY, THE ENEMY WAS ALSO REBORN IN THE PRESENT.
THEY WERE?
IF THEY HADN'T ALSO BEEN REBORN...
...YOU WOULD HAVE BEEN ABLE TO LIVE OUT YOUR LIVES WITH NO MEMORY OF WHO YOU TRULY ARE.

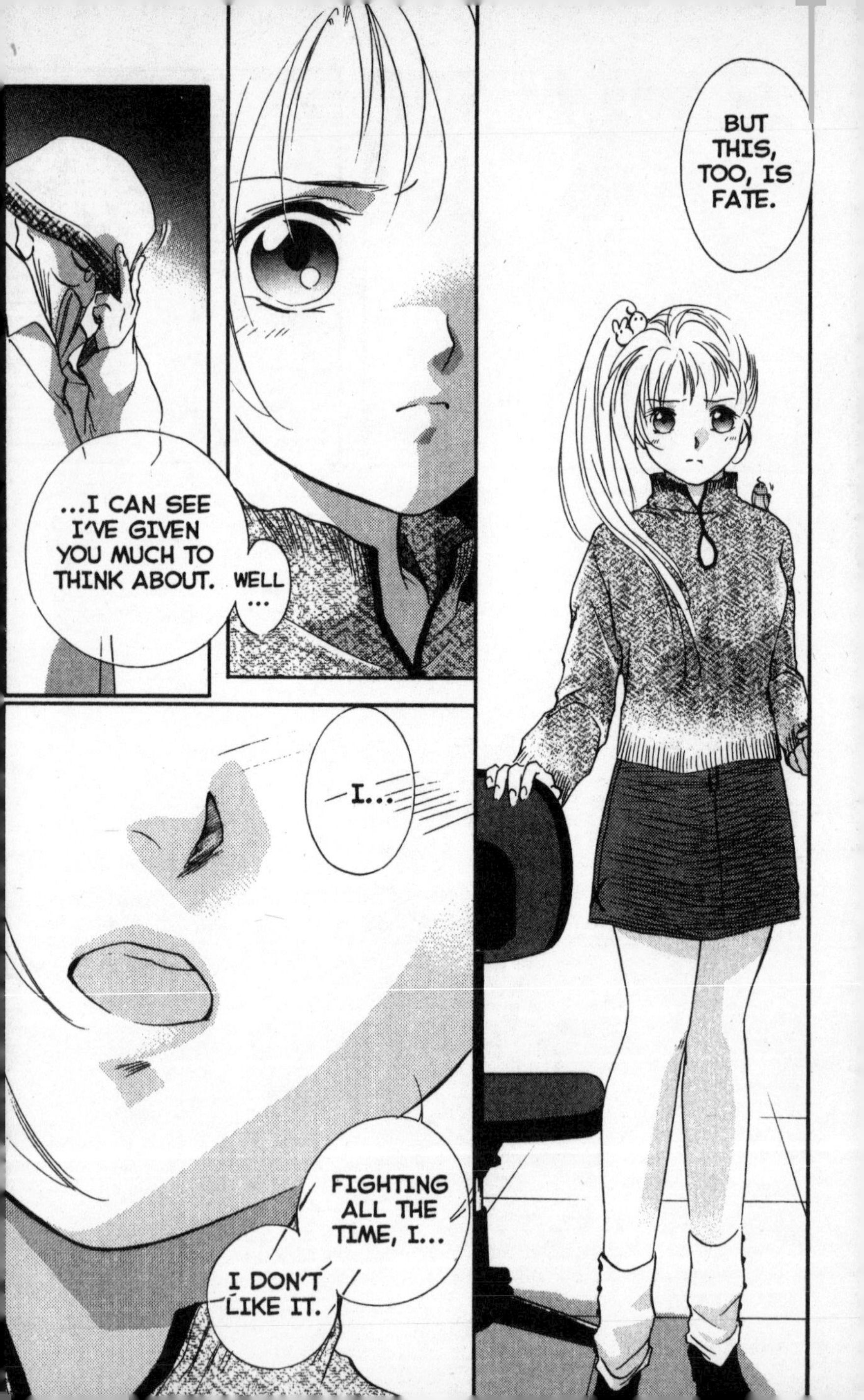
BUT THIS, TOO, IS FATE.
...I CAN SEE I'VE GIVEN YOU MUCH TO THINK ABOUT.
WELL ...
I...
FIGHTING ALL THE TIME, I...
I DON'T LIKE IT.

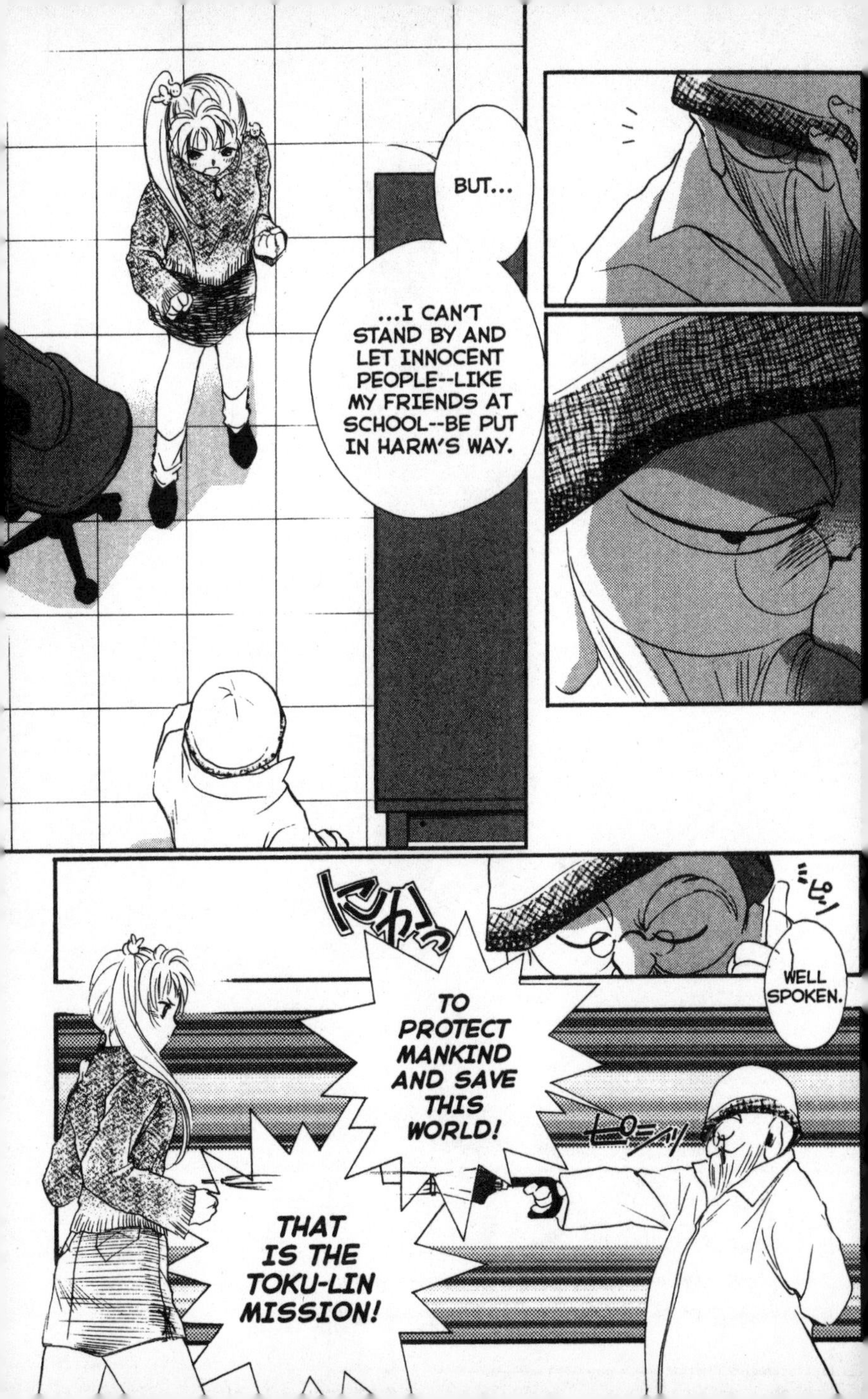
BUT...
...I CAN'T STAND BY AND LET INNOCENT PEOPLE--LIKE MY FRIENDS AT SCHOOL--BE PUT IN HARM'S WAY.
WELL SPOKEN.
TO PROTECT MANKIND AND SAVE THIS WORLD!
THAT IS THE TOKU-LIN MISSION!

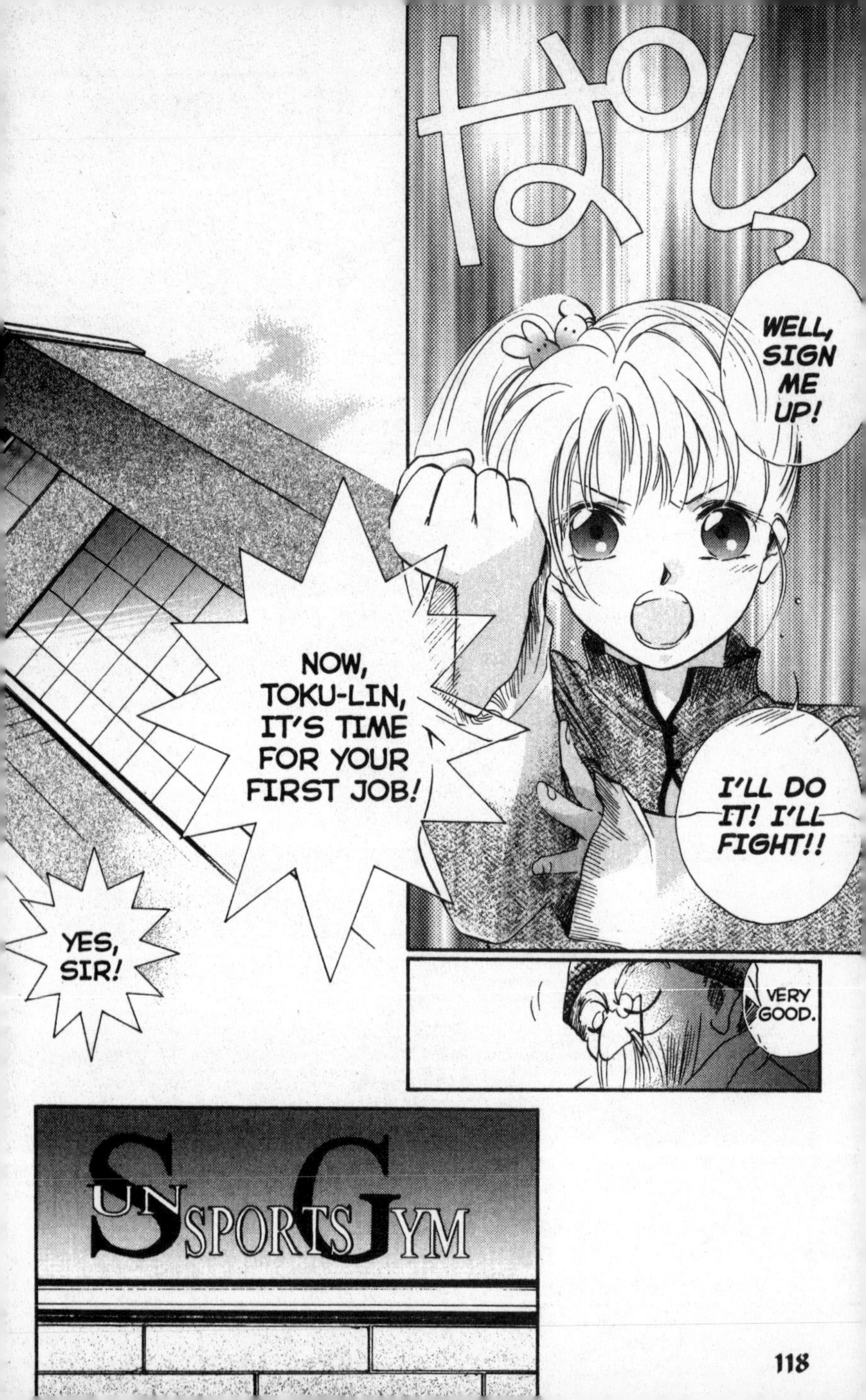
はい
WELL, SIGN ME UP!
I'LL DO IT! I'LL FIGHT!!
VERY GOOD.
NOW, TOKU-LIN, IT'S TIME FOR YOUR FIRST JOB!
YES, SIR!
SUN SPORTS GYM

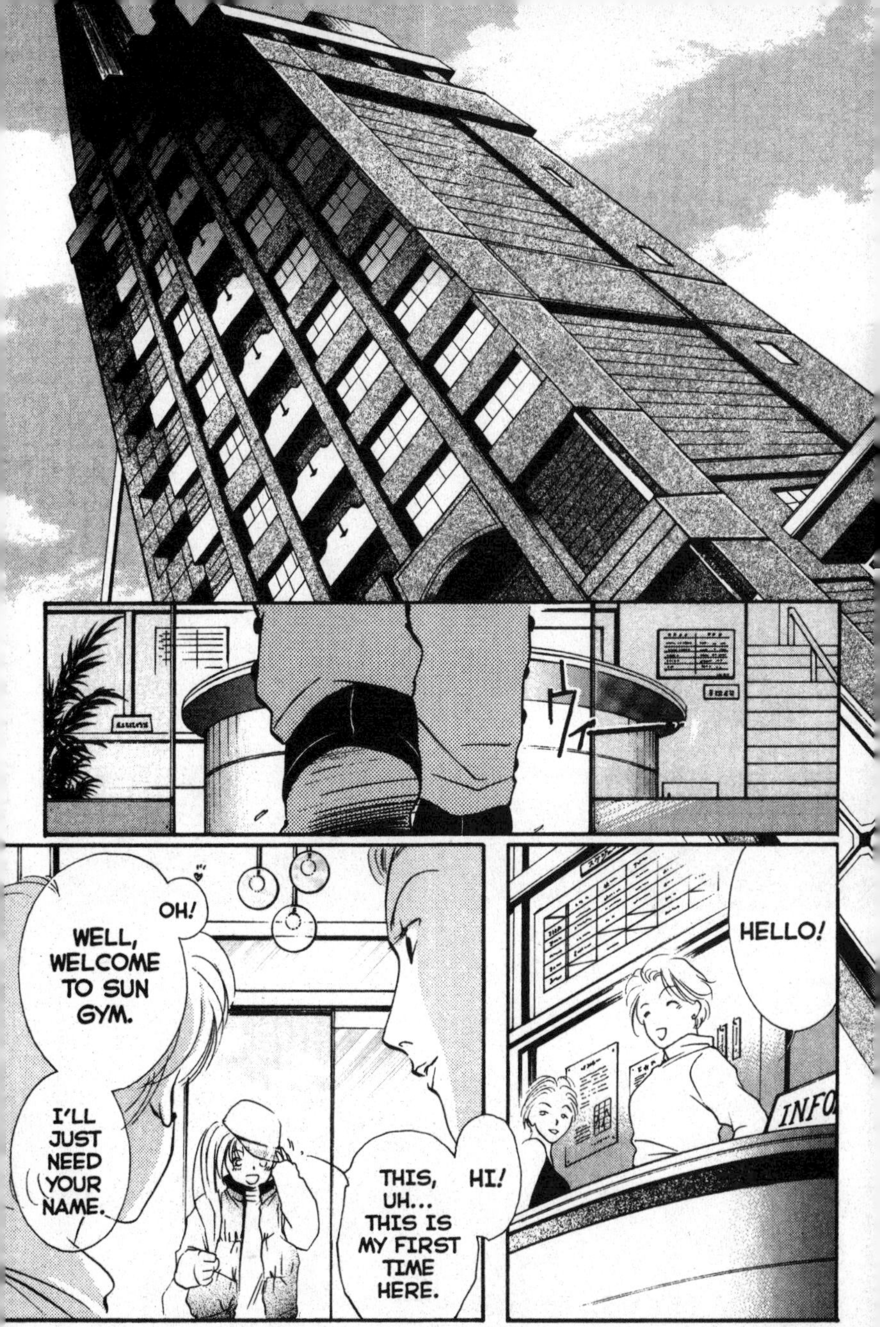
ウィ
HELLO!
INFO
HI! THIS, UH... THIS IS MY FIRST TIME HERE.
OH!
WELL, WELCOME TO SUN GYM.
I'LL JUST NEED YOUR NAME.

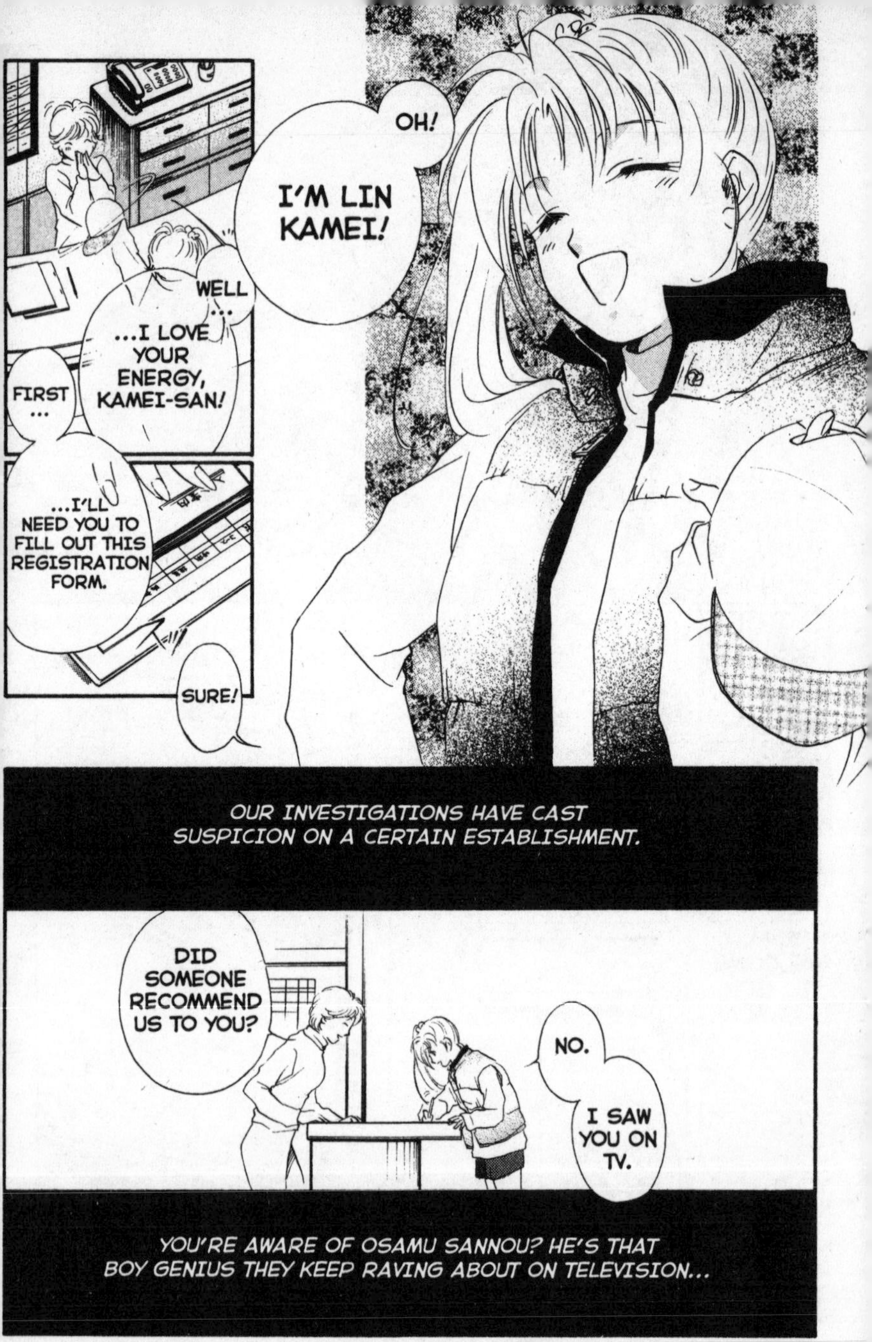
OH!
I'M LIN KAMEI!
WELL...
...I LOVE YOUR ENERGY, KAMEI-SAN!
FIRST...
...I'LL NEED YOU TO FILL OUT THIS REGISTRATION FORM.
SURE!
OUR INVESTIGATIONS HAVE CAST SUSPICION ON A CERTAIN ESTABLISHMENT.
DID SOMEONE RECOMMEND US TO YOU?
NO.
I SAW YOU ON TV.
YOU'RE AWARE OF OSAMU SANNOU? HE'S THAT BOY GENIUS THEY KEEP RAVING ABOUT ON TELEVISION...

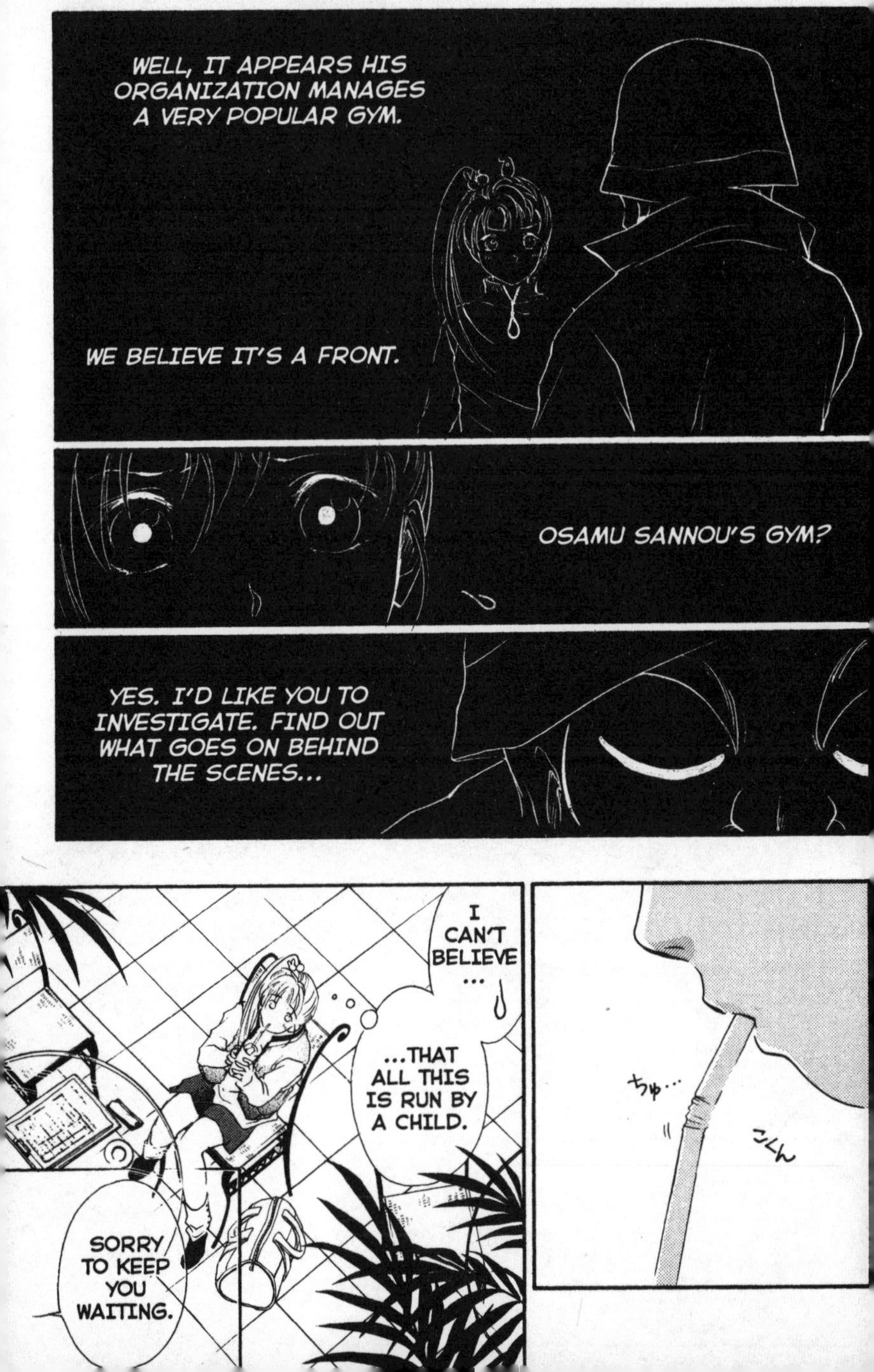
WELL, IT APPEARS HIS ORGANIZATION MANAGES A VERY POPULAR GYM.
WE BELIEVE IT'S A FRONT.
OSAMU SANNOU'S GYM?
YES. I'D LIKE YOU TO INVESTIGATE. FIND OUT WHAT GOES ON BEHIND THE SCENES...
ちゅ…
こくん
I CAN'T BELIEVE...
...THAT ALL THIS IS RUN BY A CHILD.
SORRY TO KEEP YOU WAITING.

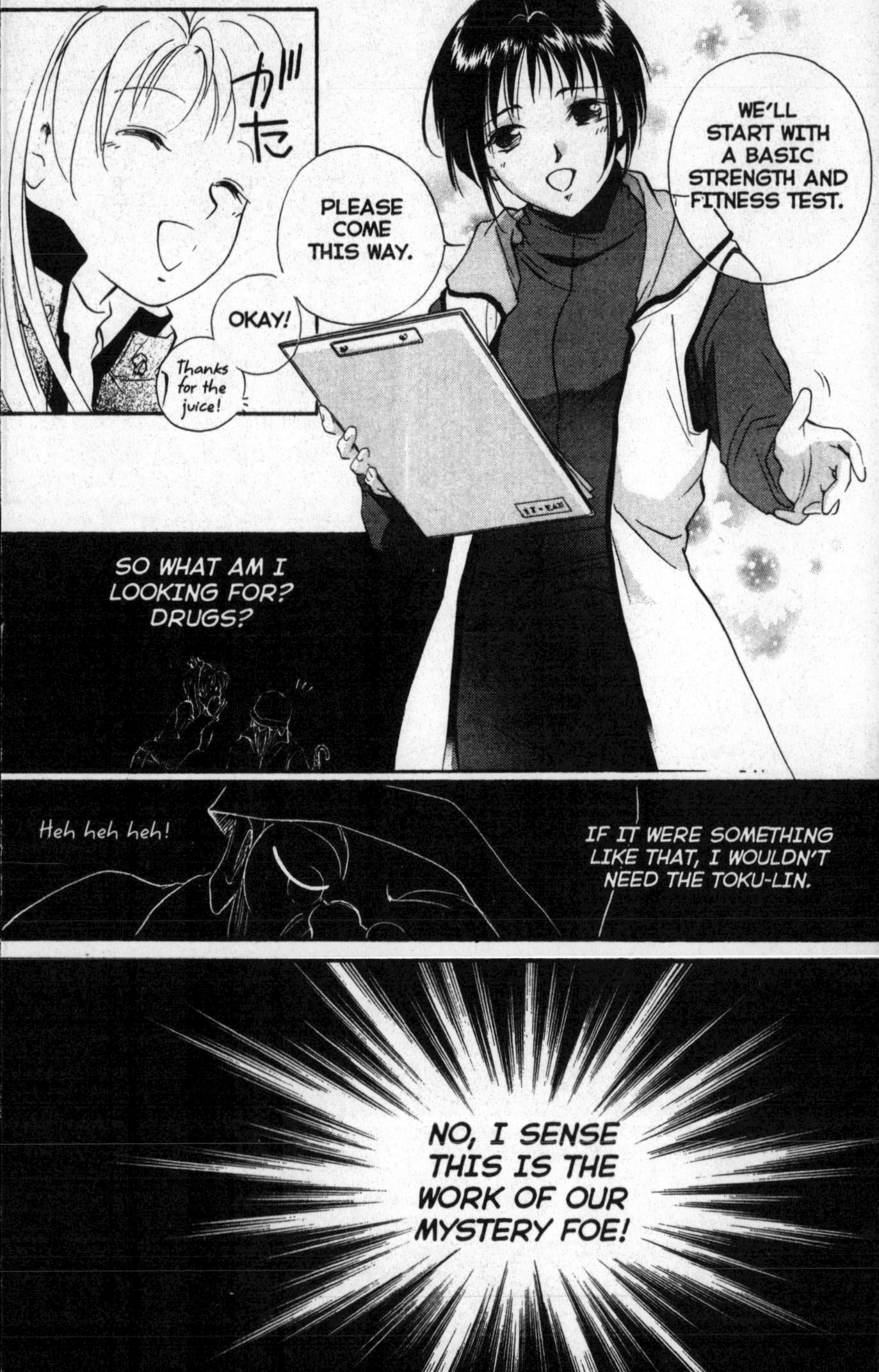
WE'LL START WITH A BASIC STRENGTH AND FITNESS TEST.
PLEASE COME THIS WAY.
ガた
OKAY!
Thanks for the juice!
SO WHAT AM I LOOKING FOR? DRUGS?
IF IT WERE SOMETHING LIKE THAT, I WOULDN'T NEED THE TOKU-LIN.
Heh heh heh!
NO, I SENSE THIS IS THE WORK OF OUR MYSTERY FOE!

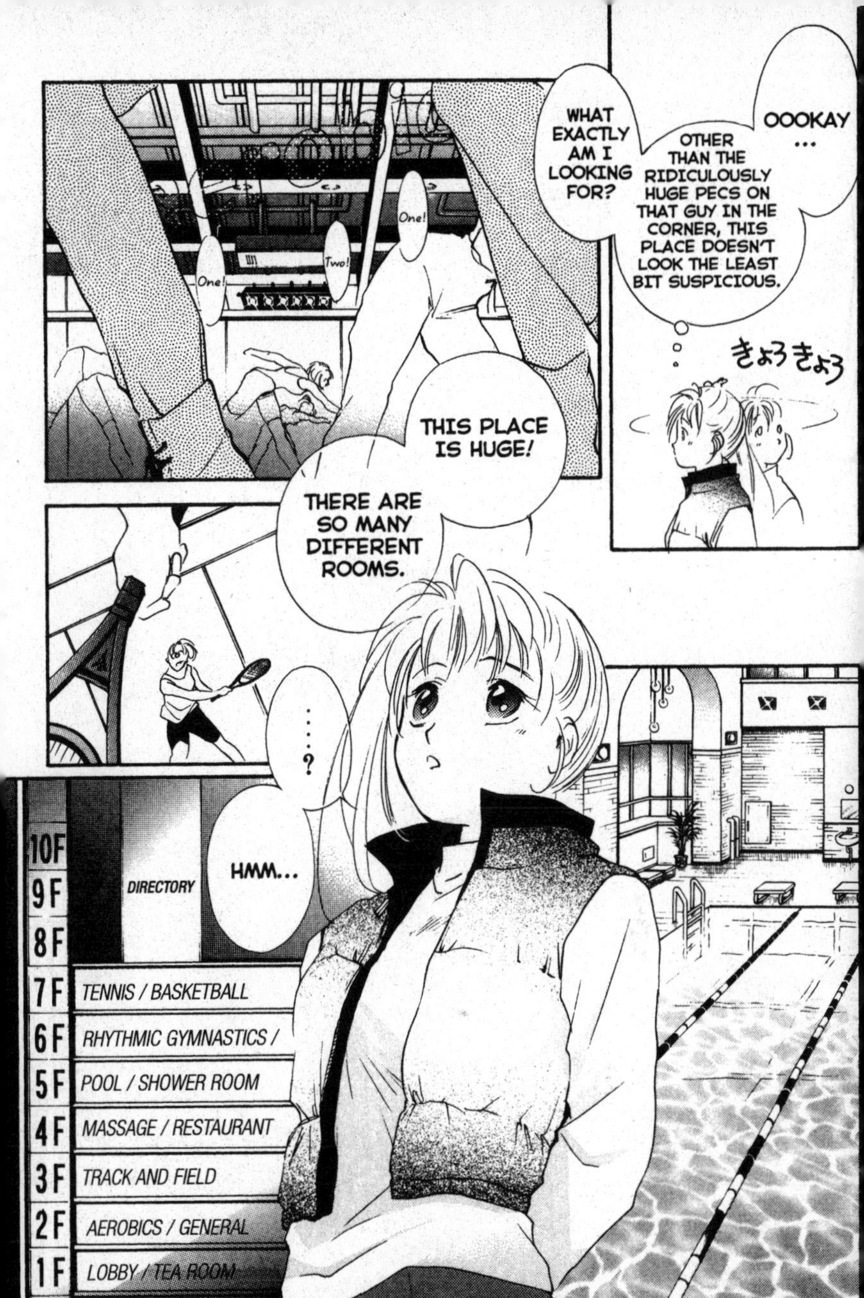
OOOKAY ...
OTHER THAN THE RIDICULOUSLY HUGE PECS ON THAT GUY IN THE CORNER, THIS PLACE DOESN'T LOOK THE LEAST BIT SUSPICIOUS.
WHAT EXACTLY AM I LOOKING FOR?
きょろきょろ
One!
Two!
One!
THIS PLACE IS HUGE!
THERE ARE SO MANY DIFFERENT ROOMS.
....?
HMM...
DIRECTORY
10F
9F
8F
7F TENNIS / BASKETBALL
6F RHYTHMIC GYMNASTICS /
5F POOL / SHOWER ROOM
4F MASSAGE / RESTAURANT
3F TRACK AND FIELD
2F AEROBICS / GENERAL
1F LOBBY / TEA ROOM
B1F PARKING LOT

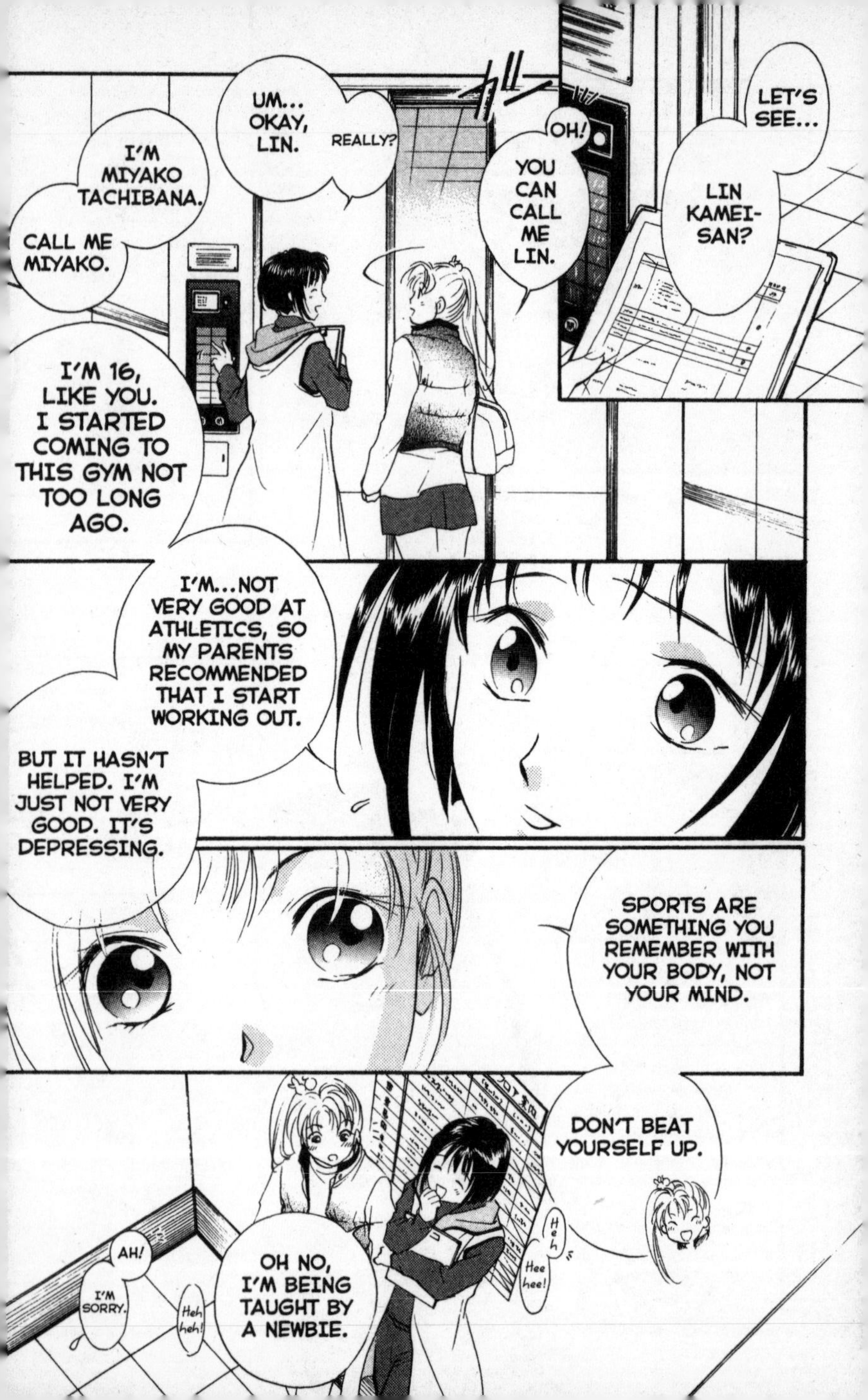
LET'S SEE...
LIN KAMEI-SAN?
OH!
YOU CAN CALL ME LIN.
UM... OKAY, LIN.
REALLY?
I'M MIYAKO TACHIBANA.
CALL ME MIYAKO.
I'M 16, LIKE YOU. I STARTED COMING TO THIS GYM NOT TOO LONG AGO.
I'M...NOT VERY GOOD AT ATHLETICS, SO MY PARENTS RECOMMENDED THAT I START WORKING OUT.
BUT IT HASN'T HELPED. I'M JUST NOT VERY GOOD. IT'S DEPRESSING.
SPORTS ARE SOMETHING YOU REMEMBER WITH YOUR BODY, NOT YOUR MIND.
DON'T BEAT YOURSELF UP.
Heh heh
Hee hee!
OH NO, I'M BEING TAUGHT BY A NEWBIE.
Heh heh!
AH!
I'M SORRY.

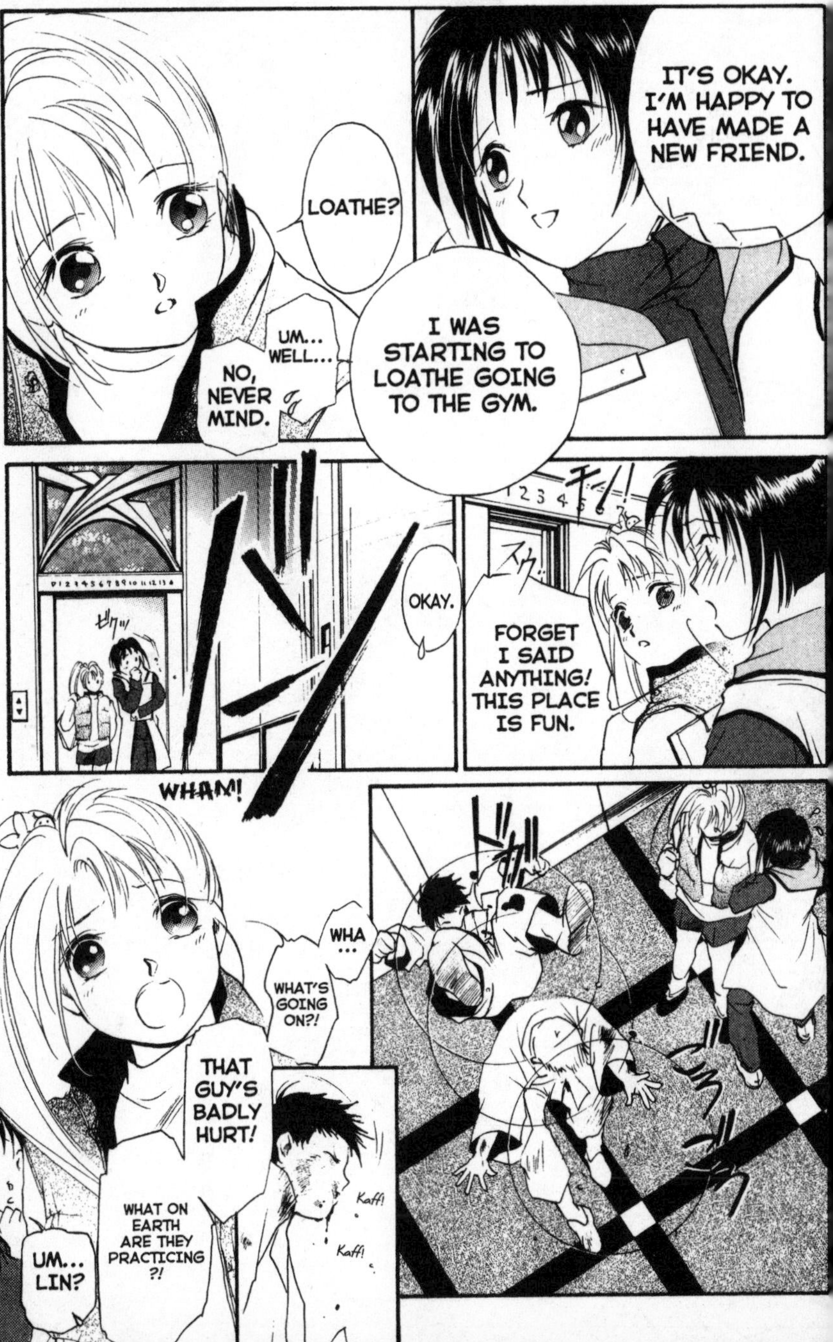
IT'S OKAY. I'M HAPPY TO HAVE MADE A NEW FRIEND.
I WAS STARTING TO LOATHE GOING TO THE GYM.
LOATHE?
UM... WELL...
NO, NEVER MIND.
FORGET I SAID ANYTHING! THIS PLACE IS FUN.
OKAY.
WHAM!
WHA...
WHAT'S GOING ON?!
THAT GUY'S BADLY HURT!
Kaff!
Kaff!
WHAT ON EARTH ARE THEY PRACTICING?!
UM... LIN?

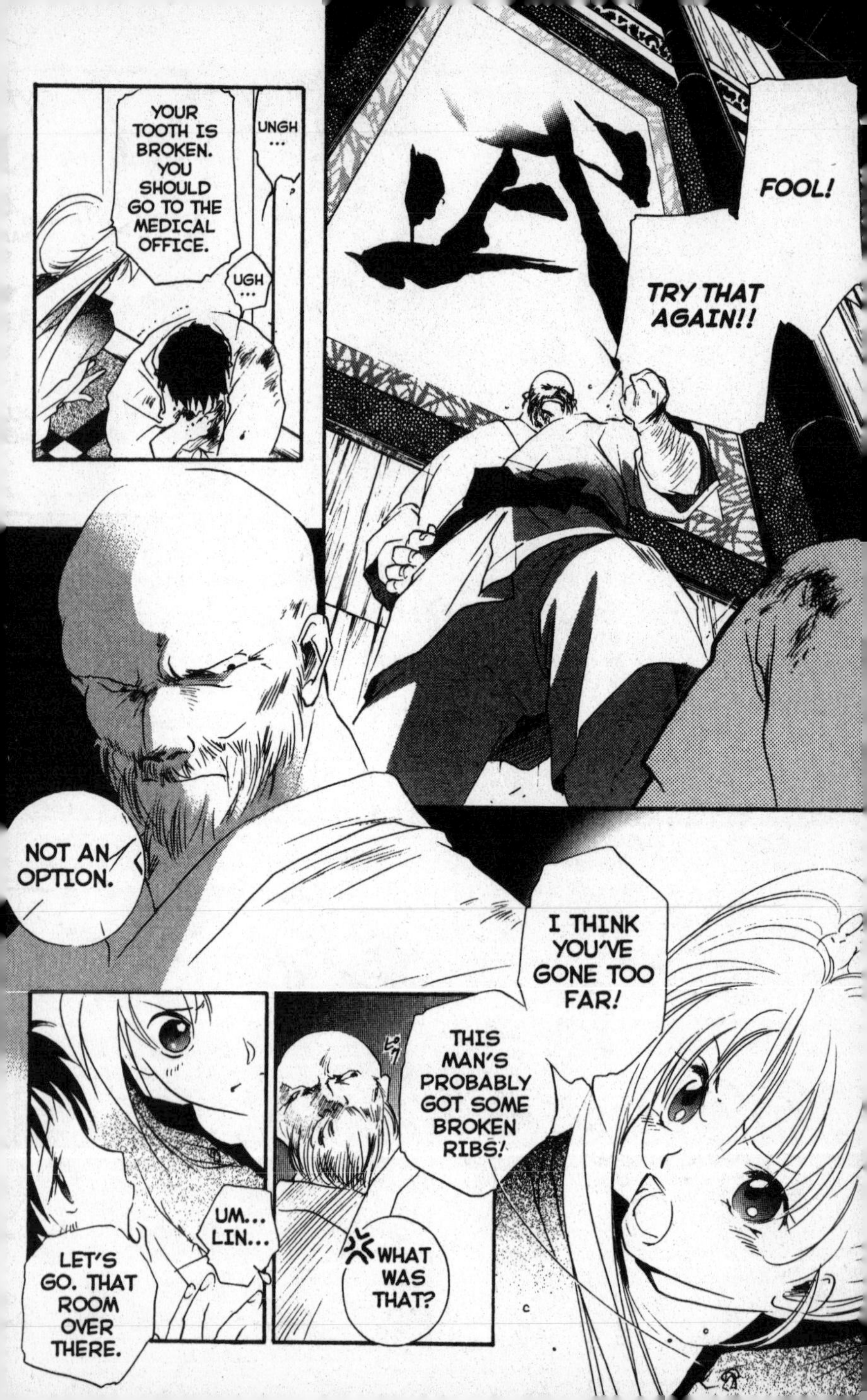
FOOL!
TRY THAT AGAIN!!
UNGH...
YOUR TOOTH IS BROKEN. YOU SHOULD GO TO THE MEDICAL OFFICE.
UGH...
NOT AN OPTION.
I THINK YOU'VE GONE TOO FAR!
THIS MAN'S PROBABLY GOT SOME BROKEN RIBS!
WHAT WAS THAT?
UM... LIN...
LET'S GO. THAT ROOM OVER THERE.

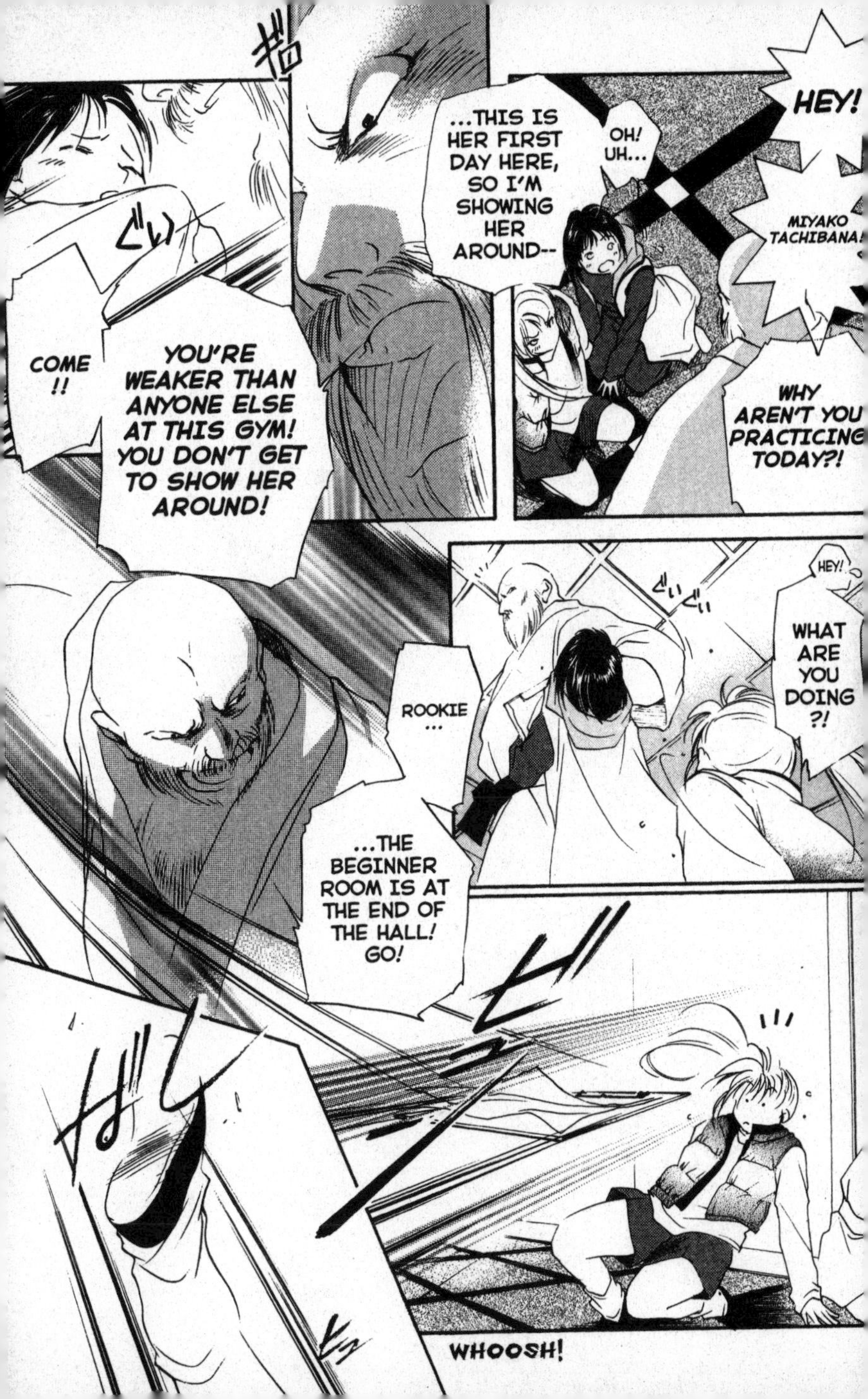
HEY!
MIYAKO TACHIBANA!
WHY AREN'T YOU PRACTICING TODAY?!
OH! UH...
...THIS IS HER FIRST DAY HERE, SO I'M SHOWING HER AROUND--
YOU'RE WEAKER THAN ANYONE ELSE AT THIS GYM! YOU DON'T GET TO SHOW HER AROUND!
COME !!
HEY!
WHAT ARE YOU DOING ?!
ROOKIE ...
...THE BEGINNER ROOM IS AT THE END OF THE HALL! GO!
WHOOSH!

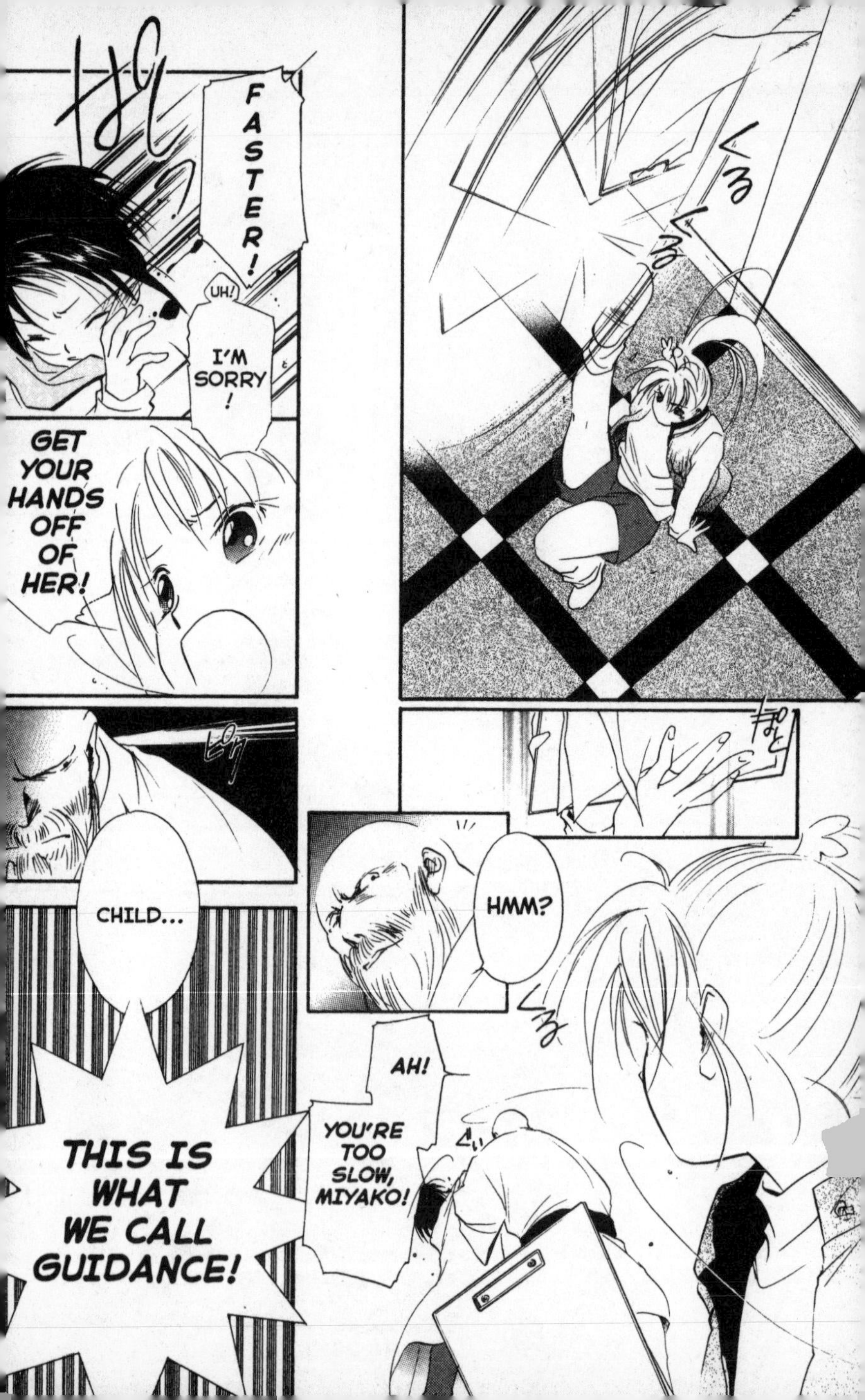
くる くる
FASTER!
UH!
I'M SORRY!
GET YOUR HANDS OFF OF HER!
HMM?
CHILD...
くる
AH!
YOU'RE TOO SLOW, MIYAKO!
THIS IS WHAT WE CALL GUIDANCE!

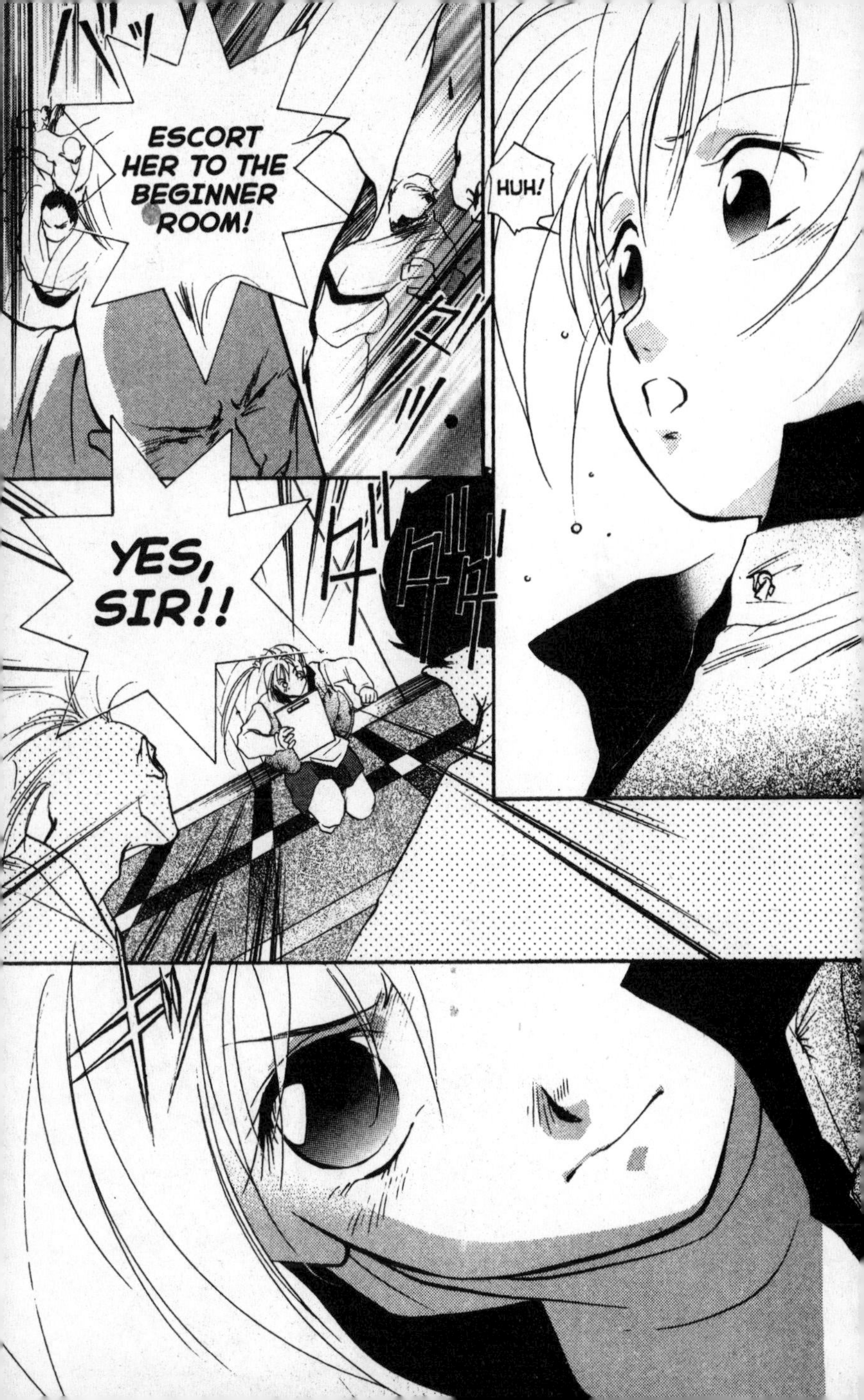
HUH!
ESCORT HER TO THE BEGINNER ROOM!
YES, SIR!!

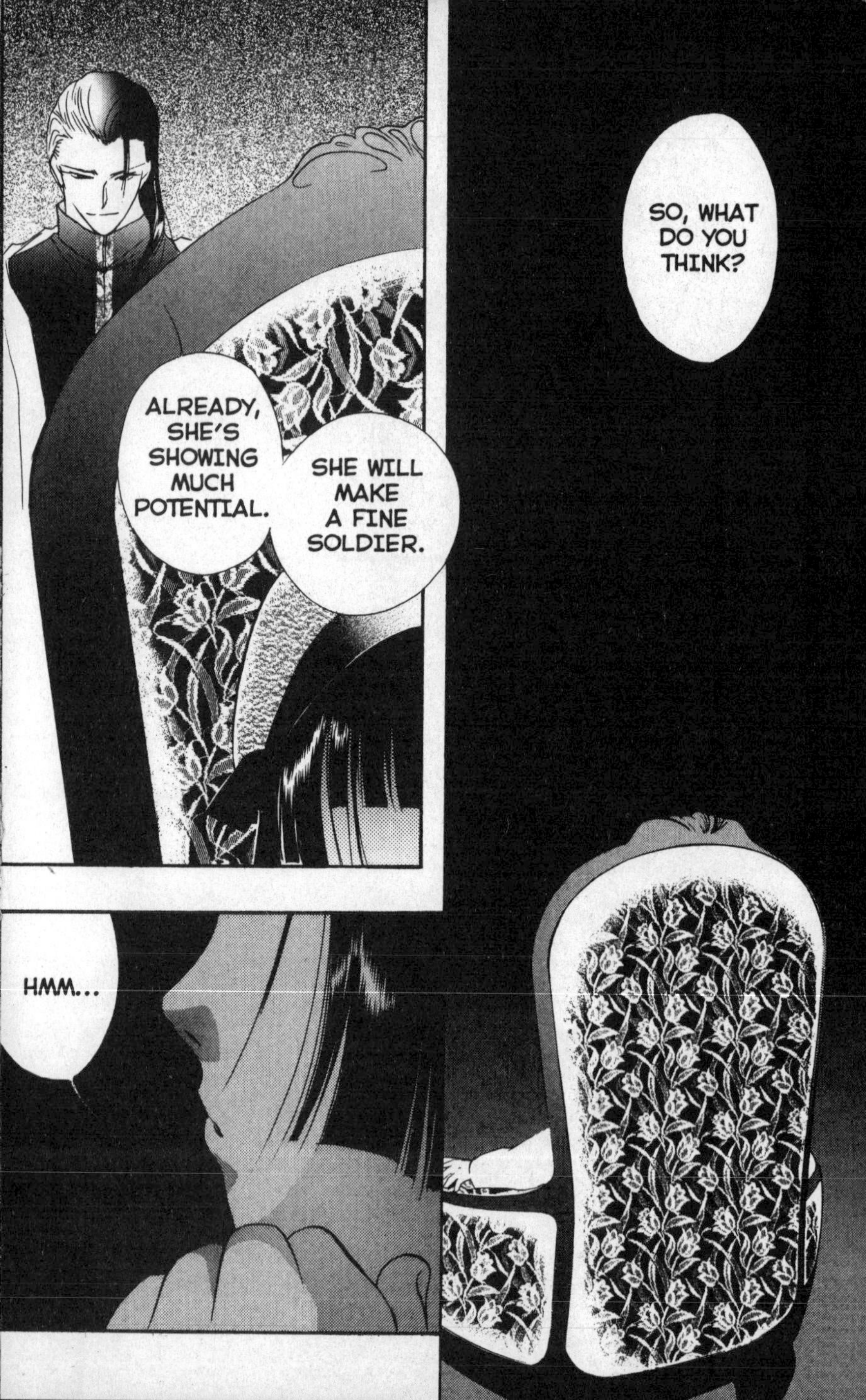
SO, WHAT DO YOU THINK?
ALREADY, SHE'S SHOWING MUCH POTENTIAL.
SHE WILL MAKE A FINE SOLDIER.
HMM...

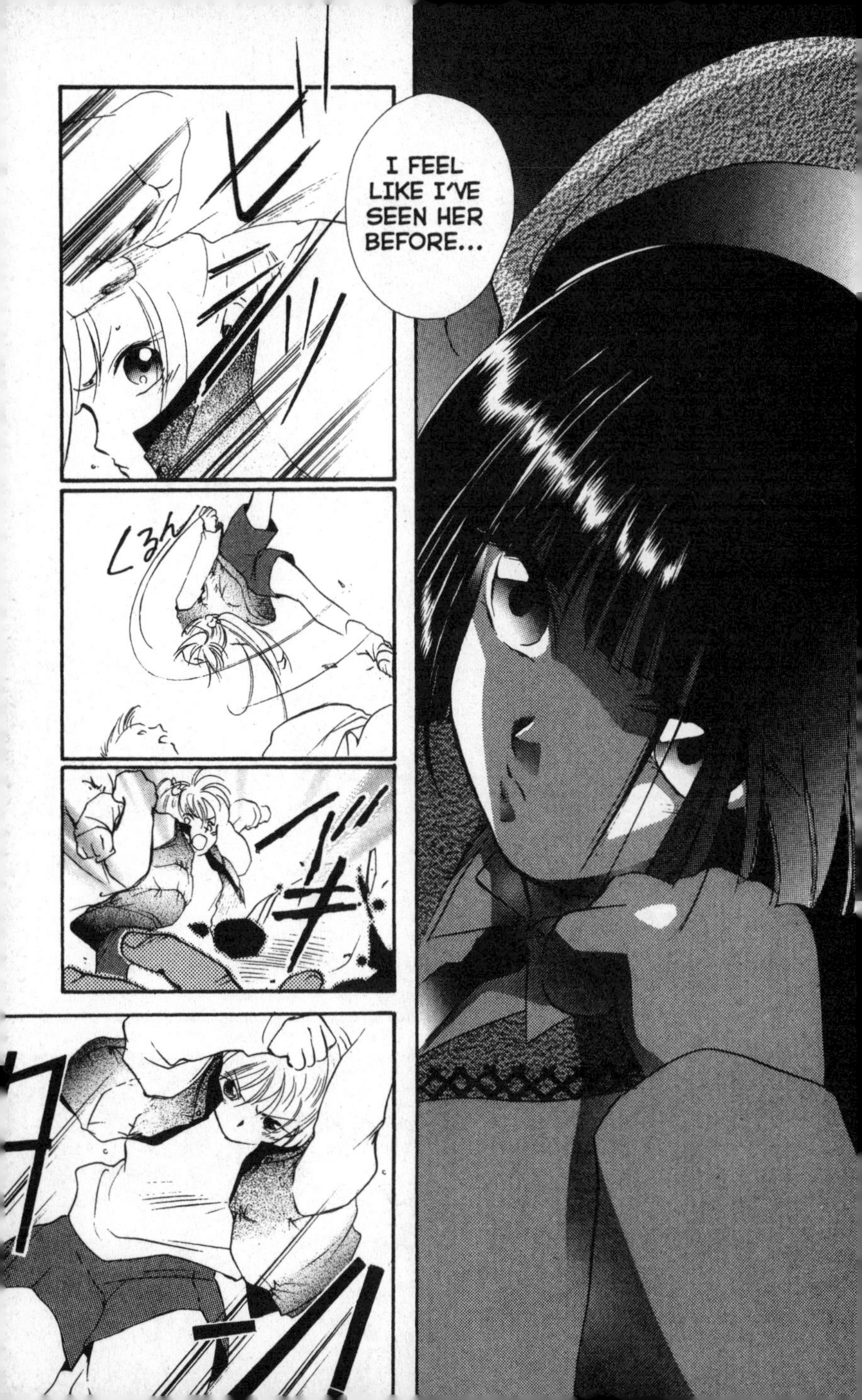
I FEEL LIKE I'VE SEEN HER BEFORE...
くるん

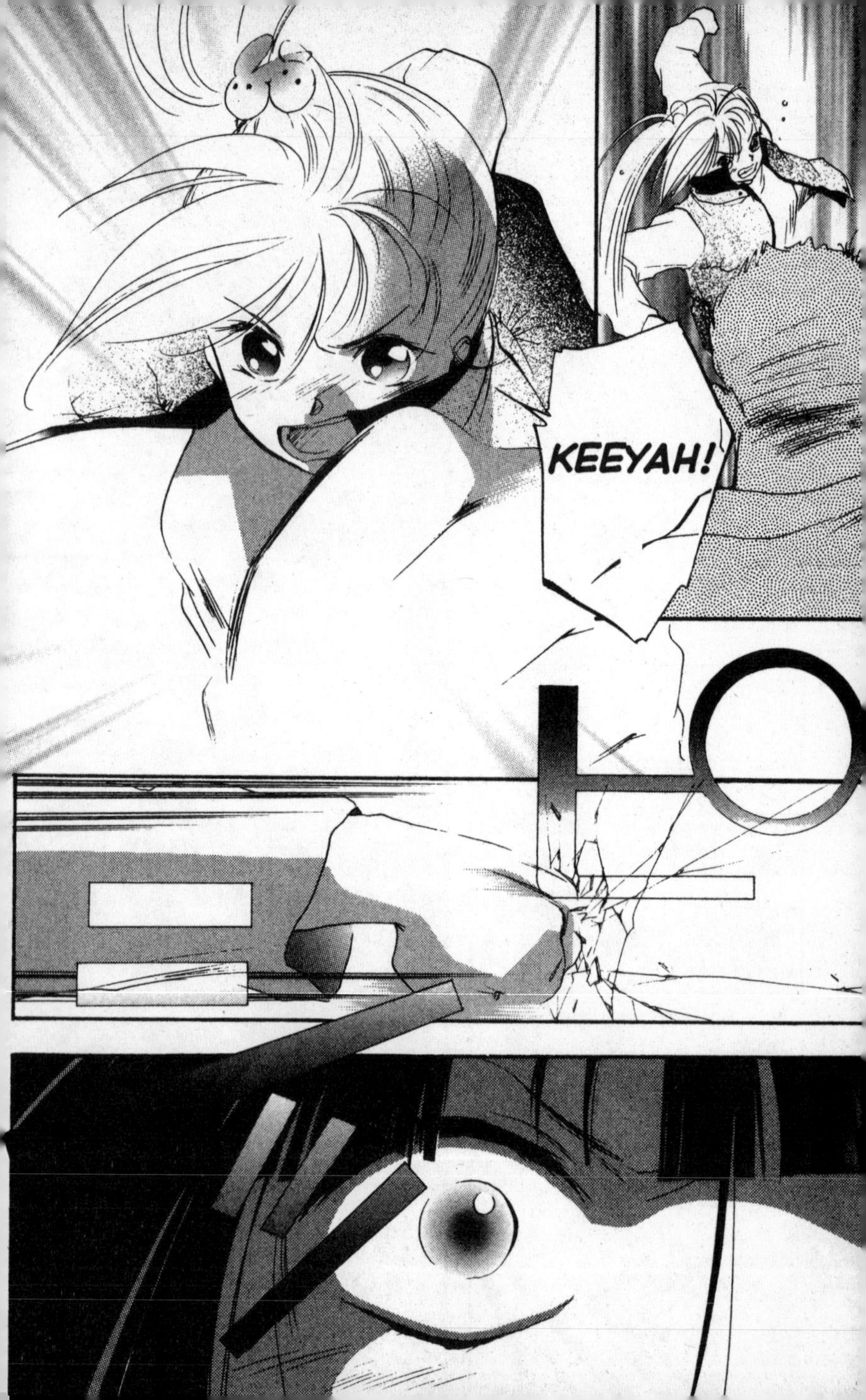
KEEYAH!

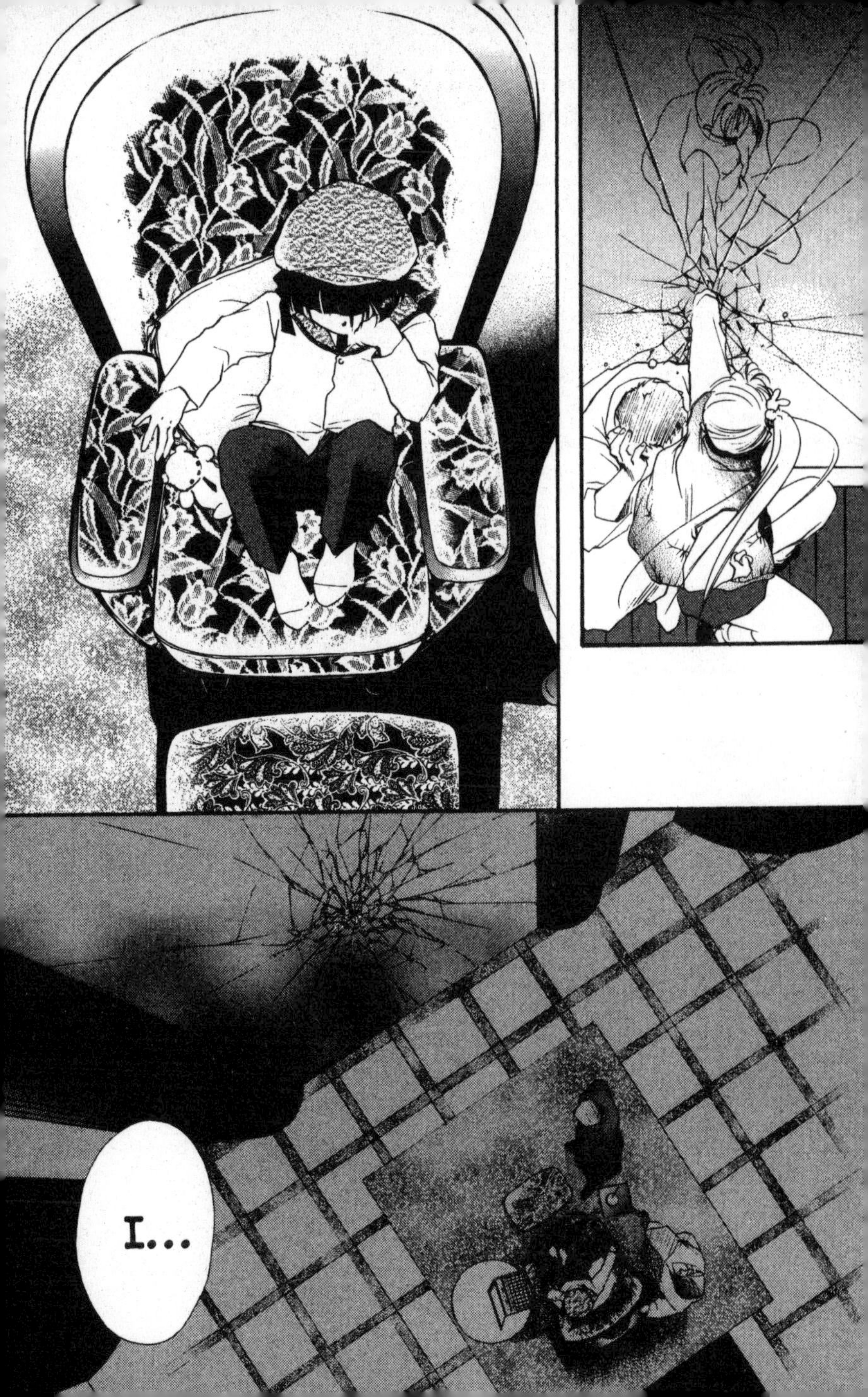
I...

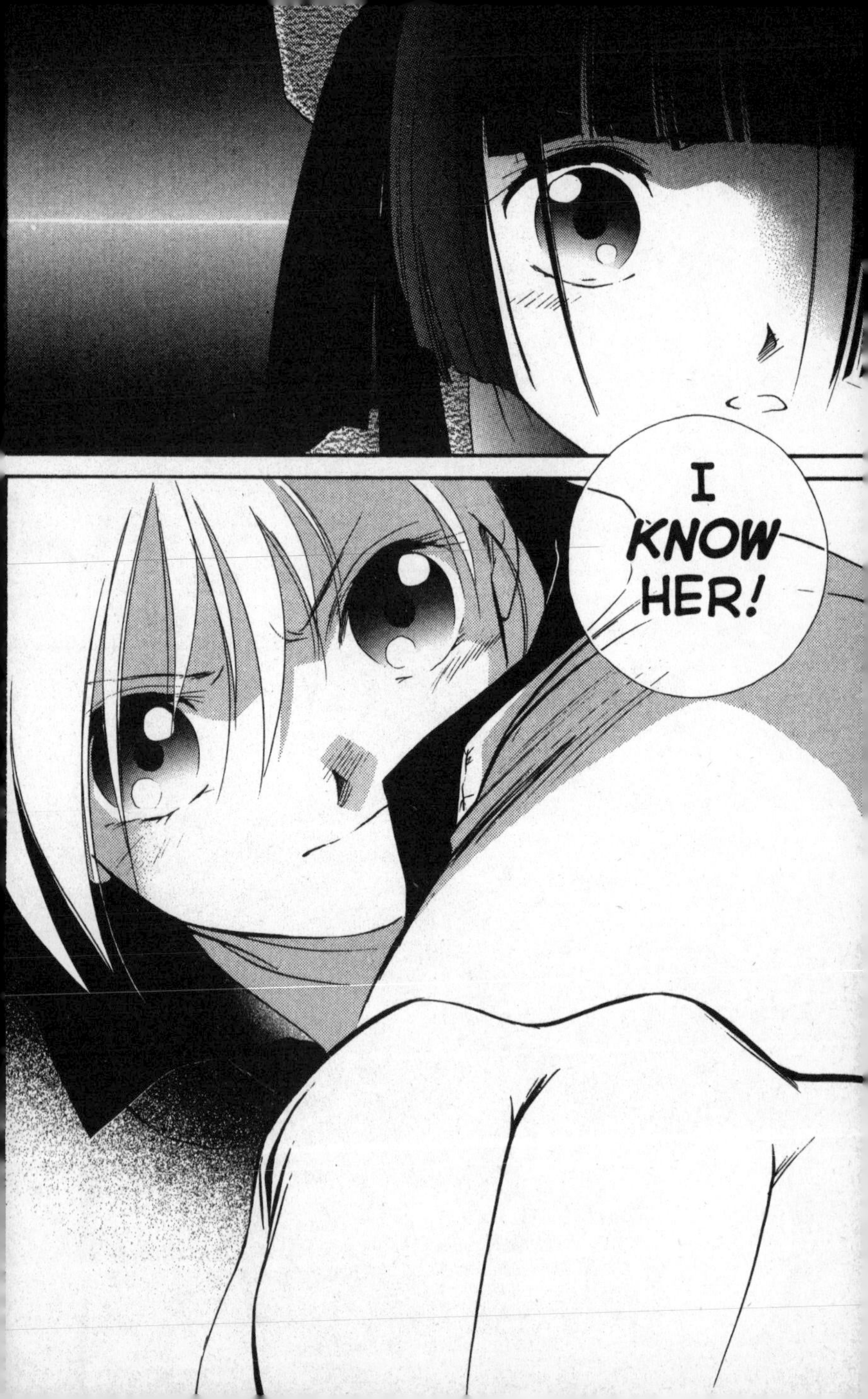
I KNOW HER!

*WHAT IS THIS?*

*I FEEL...UNEASY.*

*WHO ON EARTH IS SHE?!*

# THE DEMON
# AWAKES

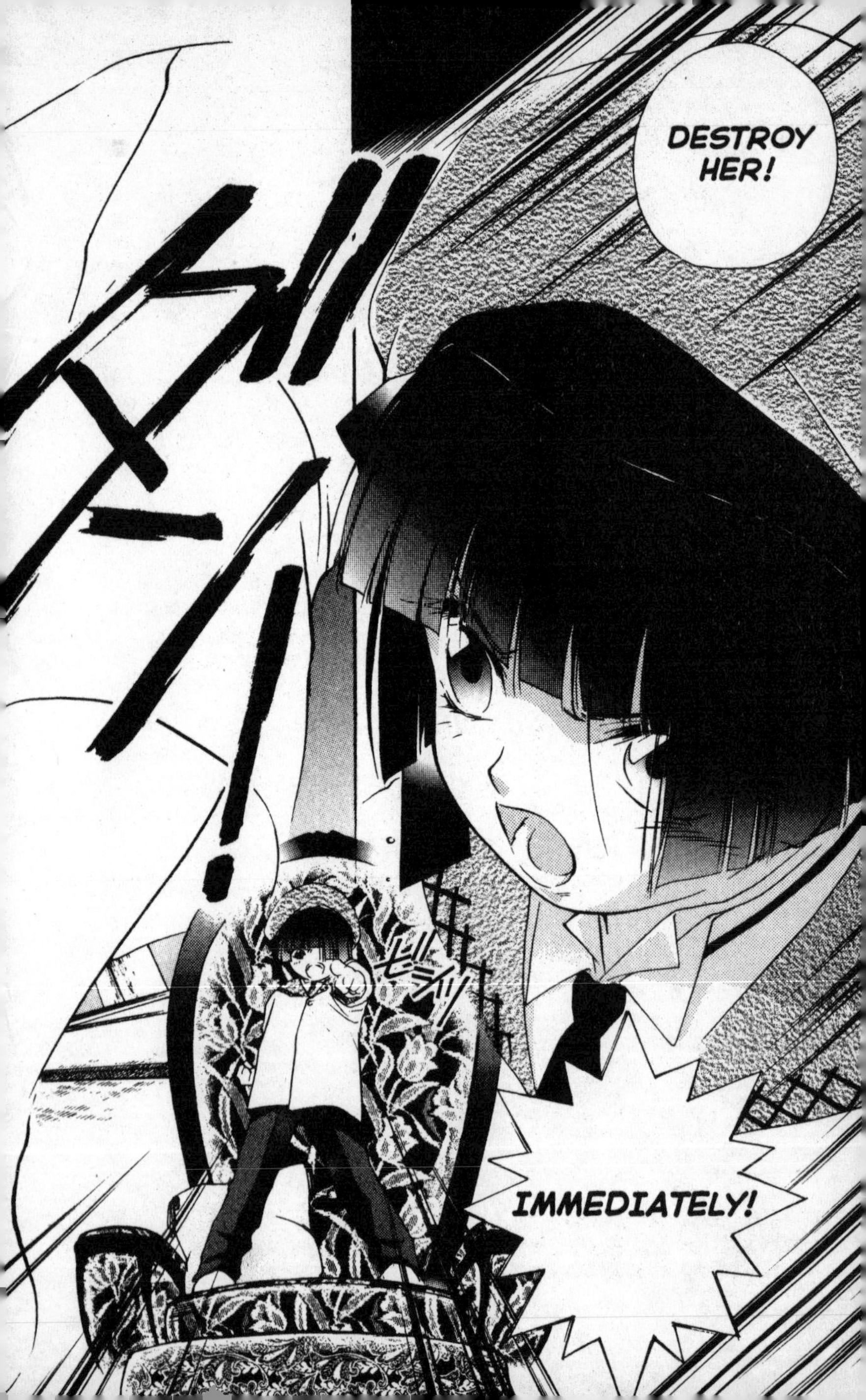
DESTROY HER!
IMMEDIATELY!

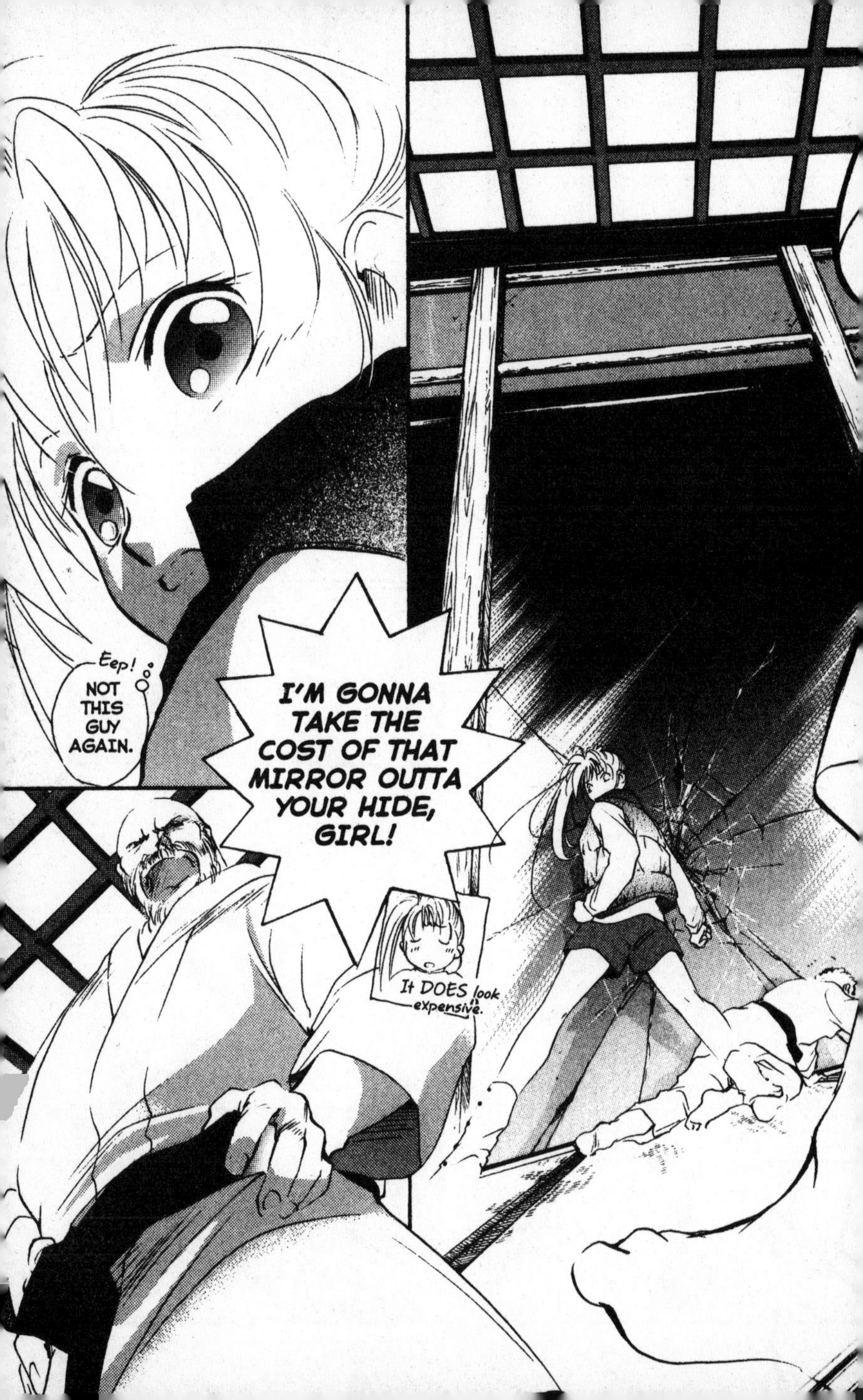
Eep!
NOT THIS GUY AGAIN.
I'M GONNA TAKE THE COST OF THAT MIRROR OUTTA YOUR HIDE, GIRL!
It DOES look expensive.

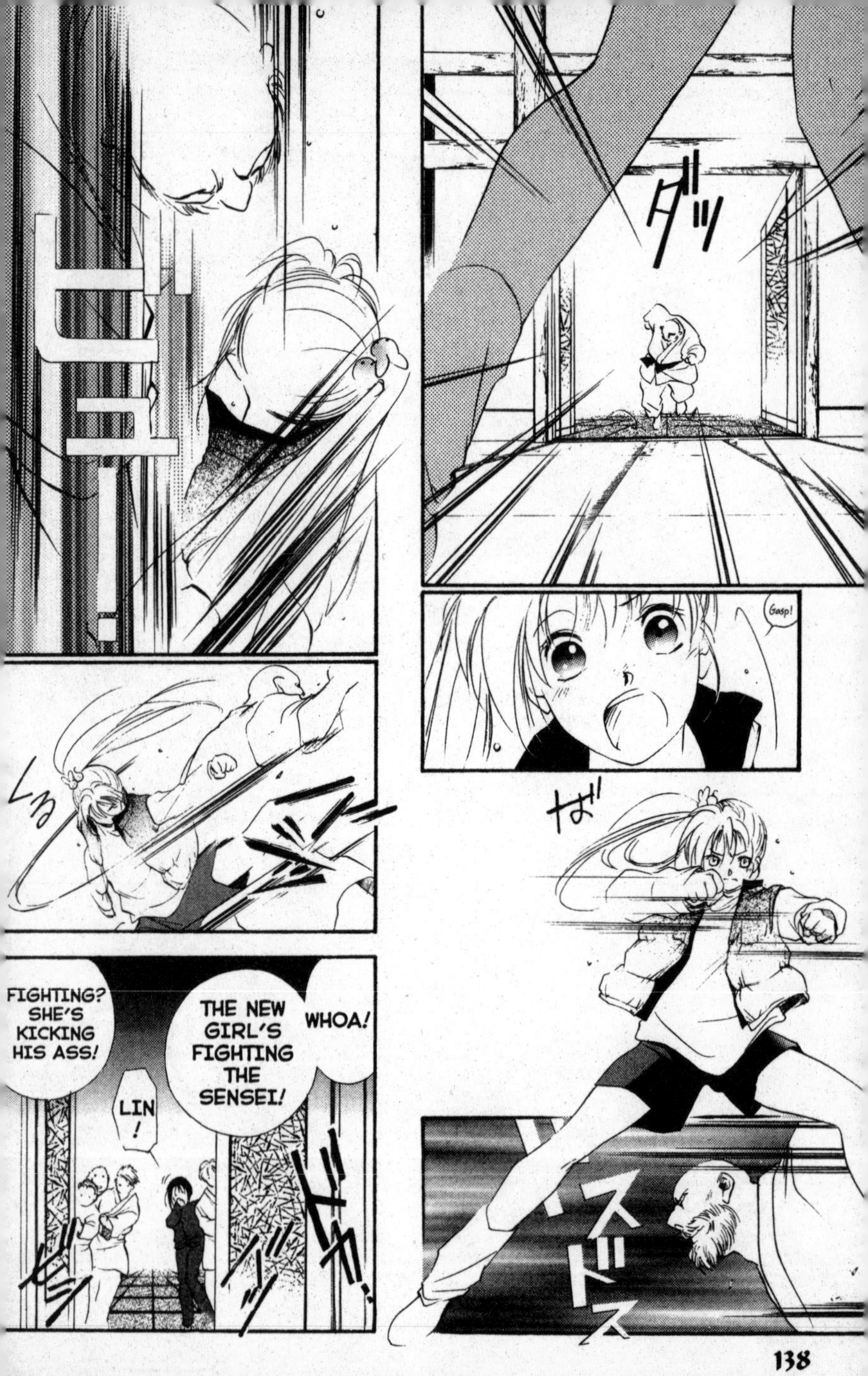
ダッ
Gasp!
WHOA!
THE NEW GIRL'S FIGHTING THE SENSEI!
FIGHTING? SHE'S KICKING HIS ASS!
LIN!

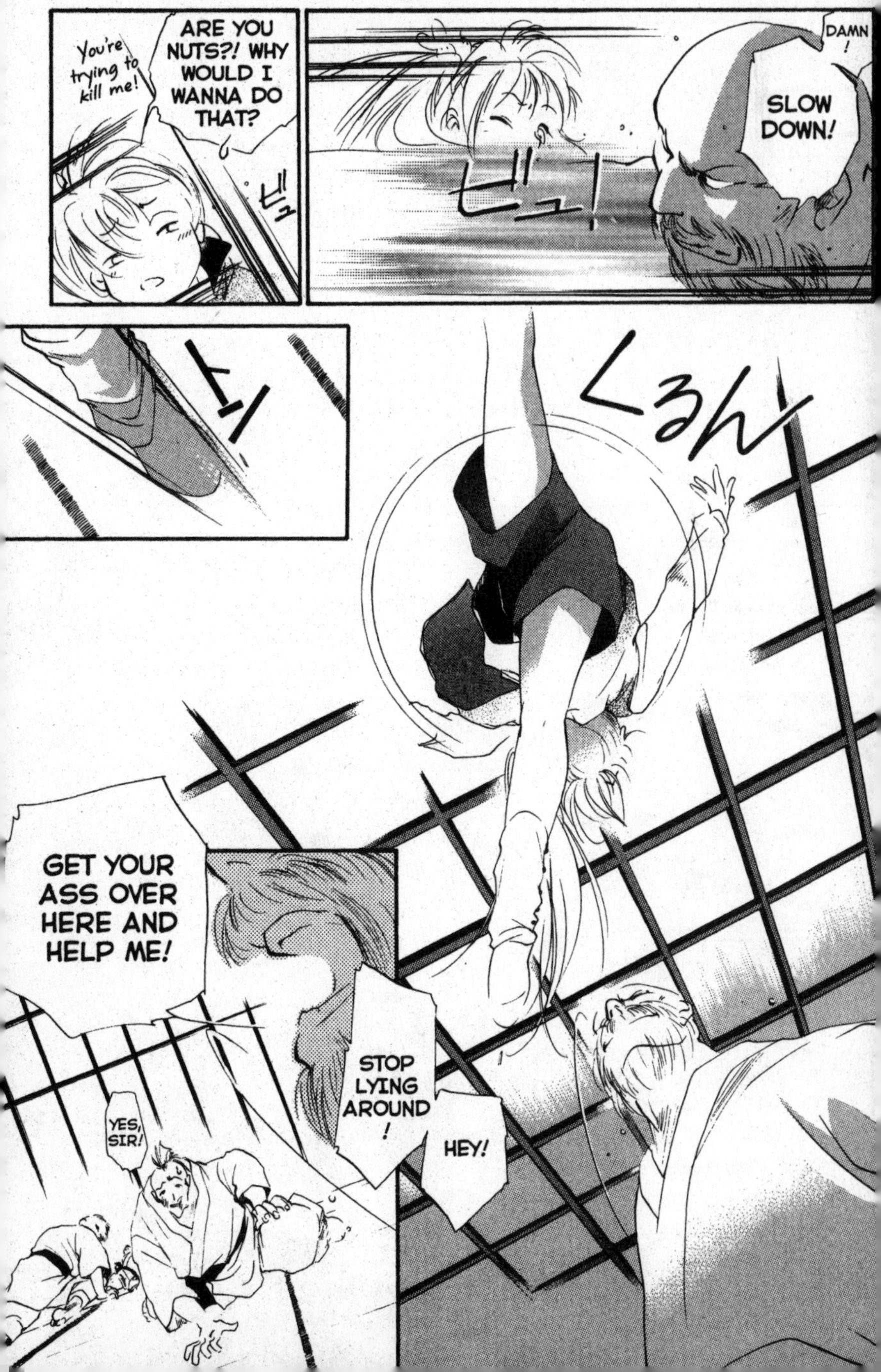
DAMN!
SLOW DOWN!
ビュ!
You're trying to kill me!
ARE YOU NUTS?! WHY WOULD I WANNA DO THAT?
くるん
HEY!
STOP LYING AROUND!
GET YOUR ASS OVER HERE AND HELP ME!
YES, SIR!

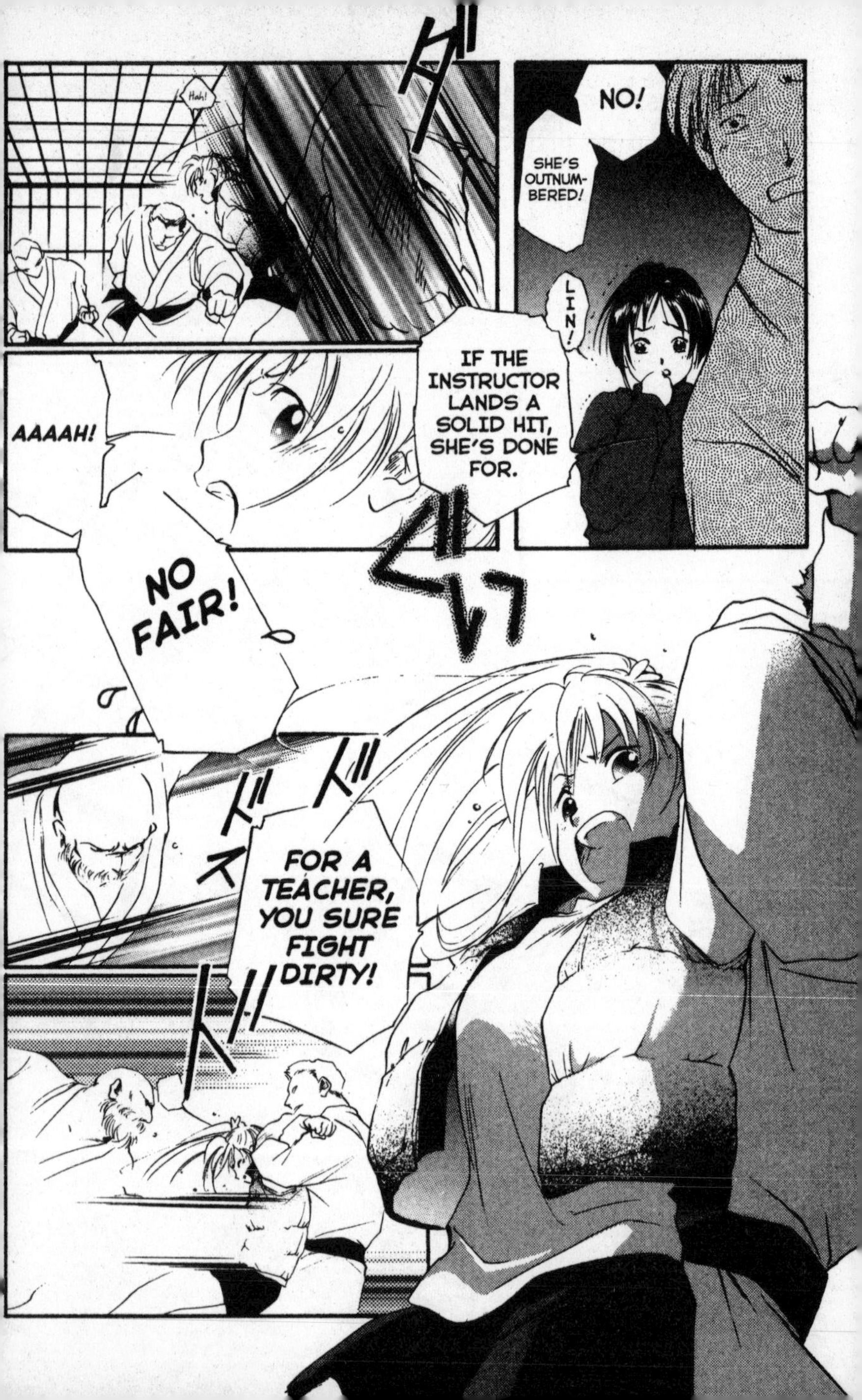
NO!
SHE'S OUTNUMBERED!
LIN!
Hah!
IF THE INSTRUCTOR LANDS A SOLID HIT, SHE'S DONE FOR.
AAAAH!
NO FAIR!
FOR A TEACHER, YOU SURE FIGHT DIRTY!

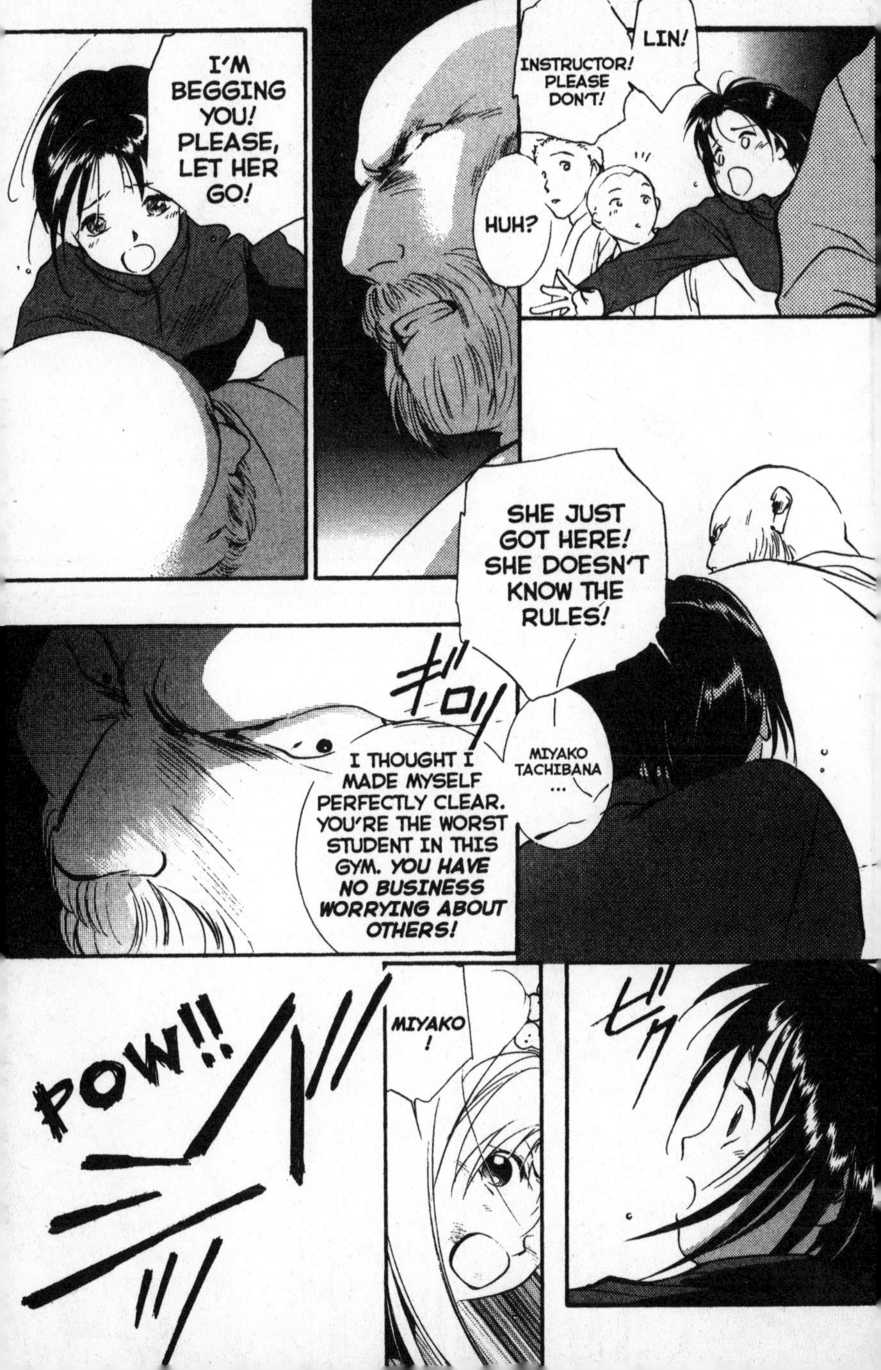
LIN!
INSTRUCTOR! PLEASE DON'T!
HUH?
I'M BEGGING YOU! PLEASE, LET HER GO!
SHE JUST GOT HERE! SHE DOESN'T KNOW THE RULES!
MIYAKO TACHIBANA ...
I THOUGHT I MADE MYSELF PERFECTLY CLEAR. YOU'RE THE WORST STUDENT IN THIS GYM. *YOU HAVE NO BUSINESS WORRYING ABOUT OTHERS!*
MIYAKO!
POW!!

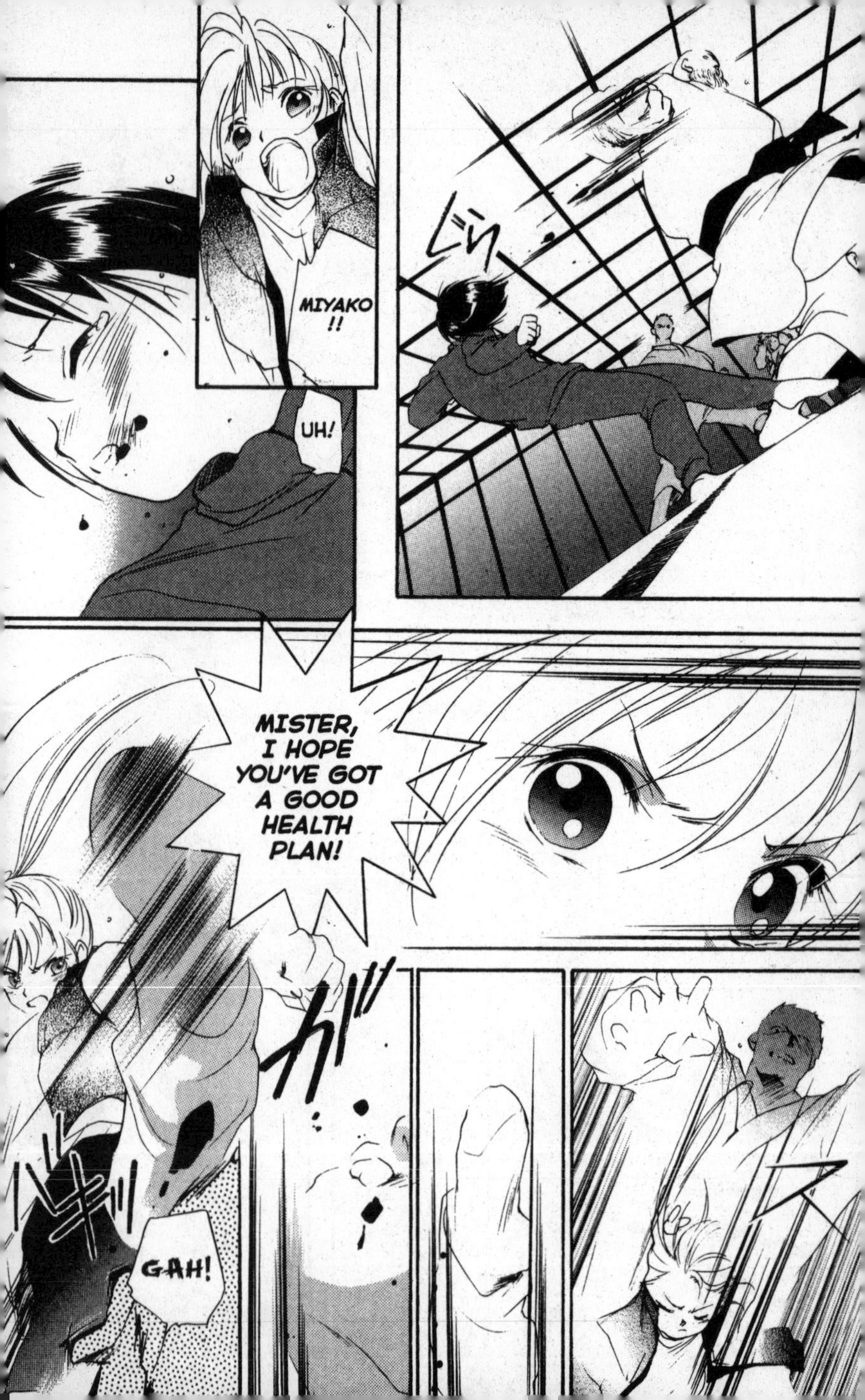
MIYAKO !!
UH!
MISTER, I HOPE YOU'VE GOT A GOOD HEALTH PLAN!
GAH!

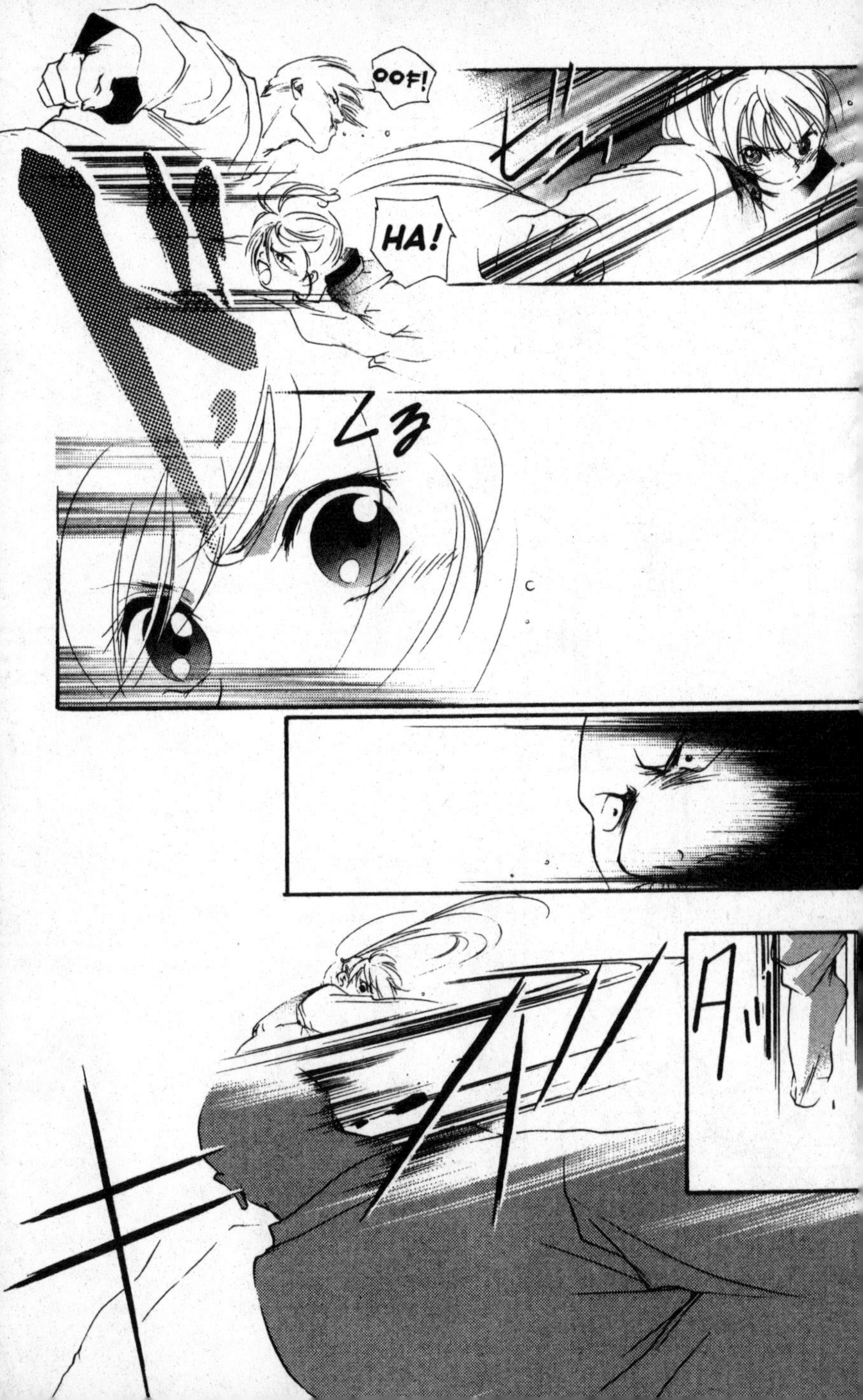
HA!
OOF!

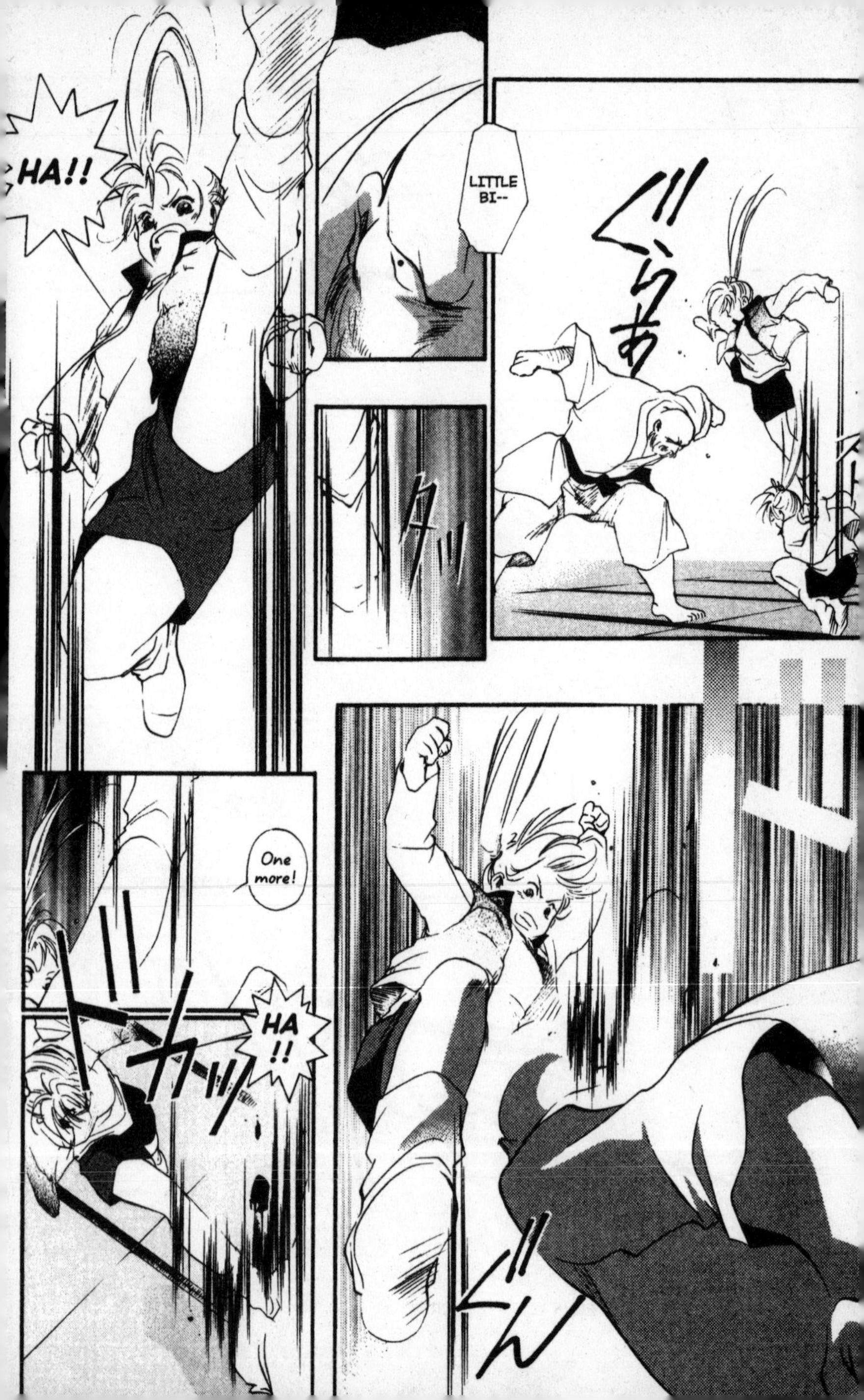
LITTLE BI--
HA!!
One more!
HA !!

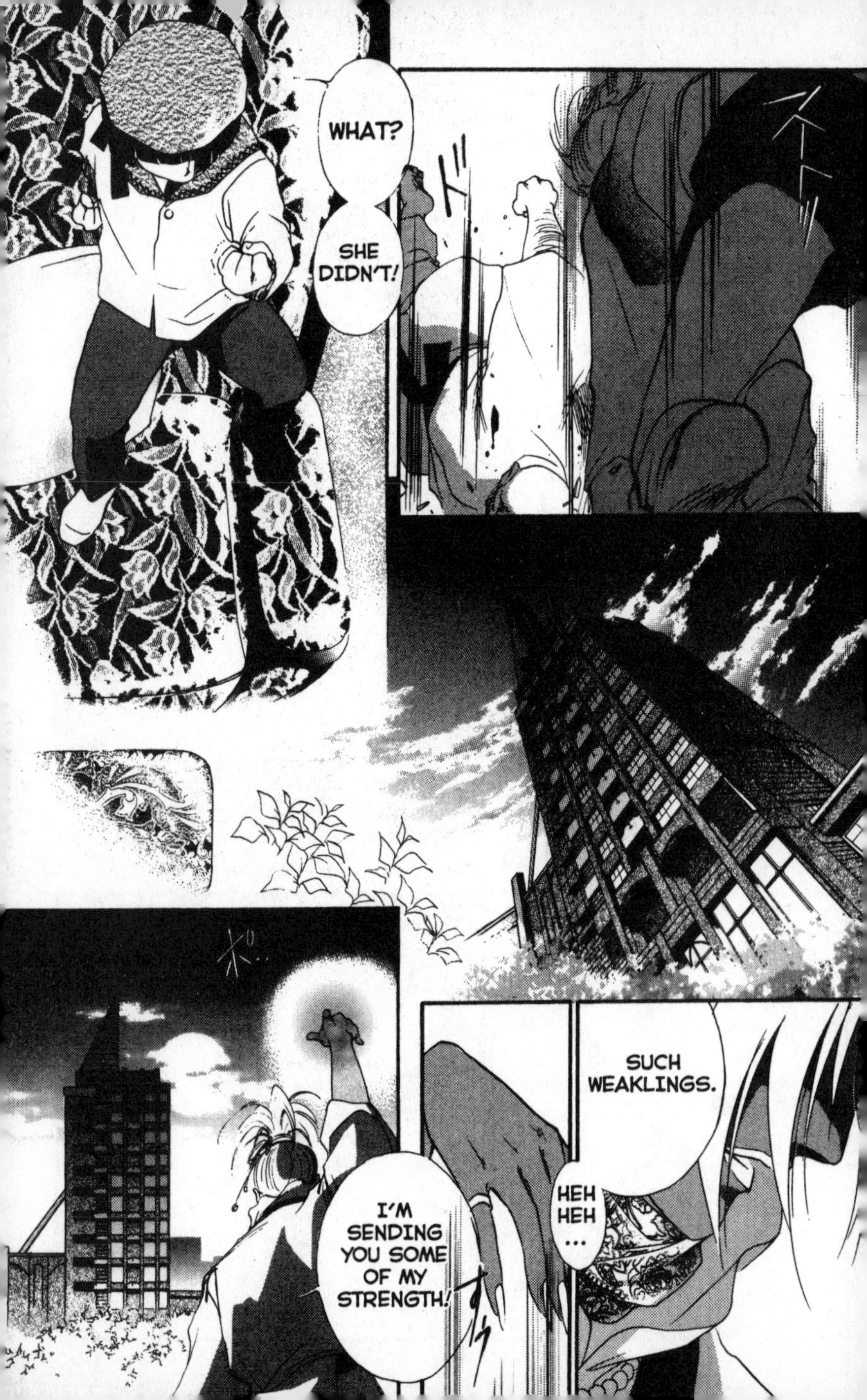
WHAT?
SHE DIDN'T!
SUCH WEAKLINGS.
HEH HEH ...
I'M SENDING YOU SOME OF MY STRENGTH!

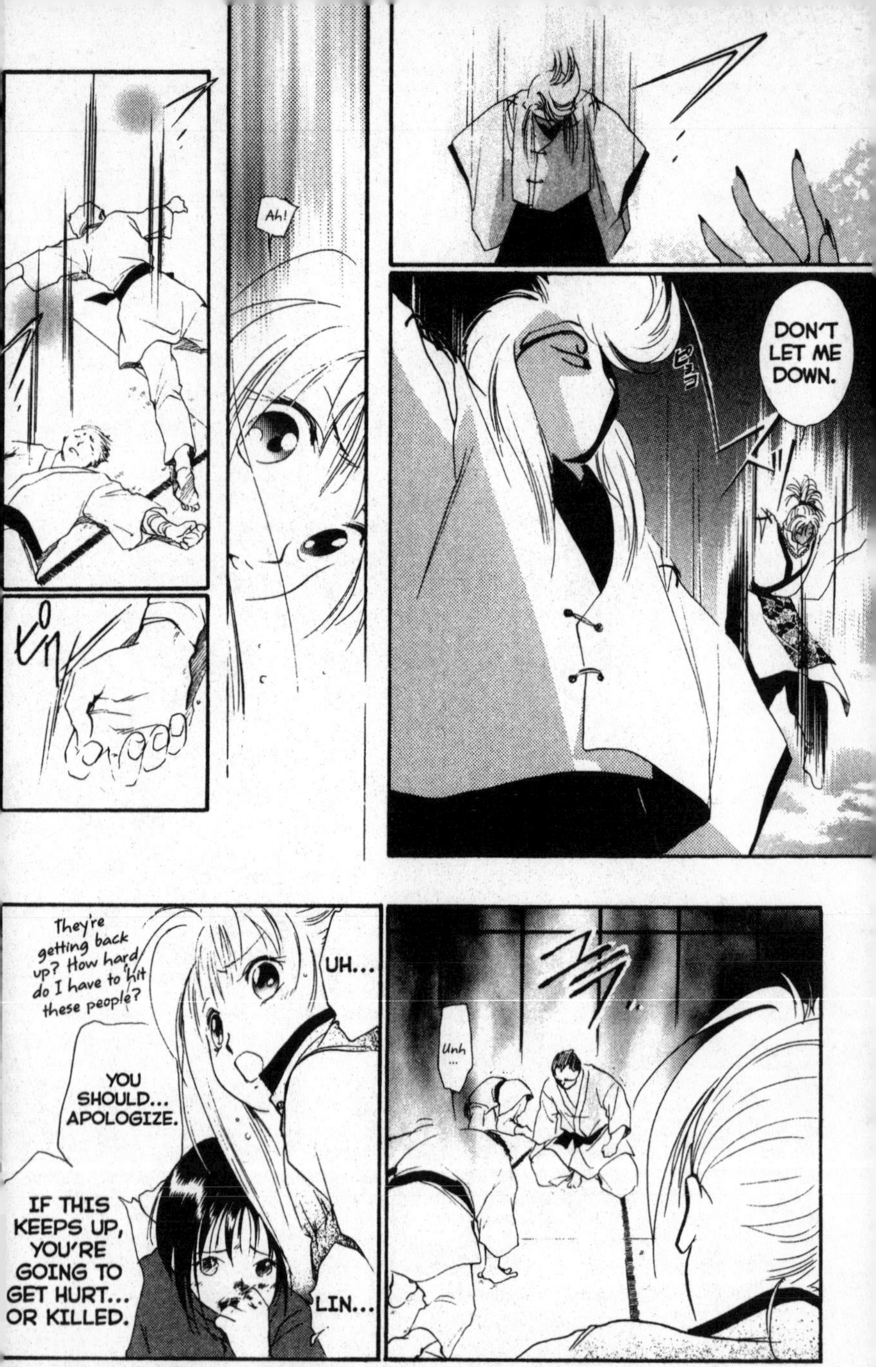

DON'T LET ME DOWN.
Ah!
Unh...
UH...
They're getting back up? How hard do I have to hit these people?
YOU SHOULD... APOLOGIZE.
IF THIS KEEPS UP, YOU'RE GOING TO GET HURT... OR KILLED.
LIN...

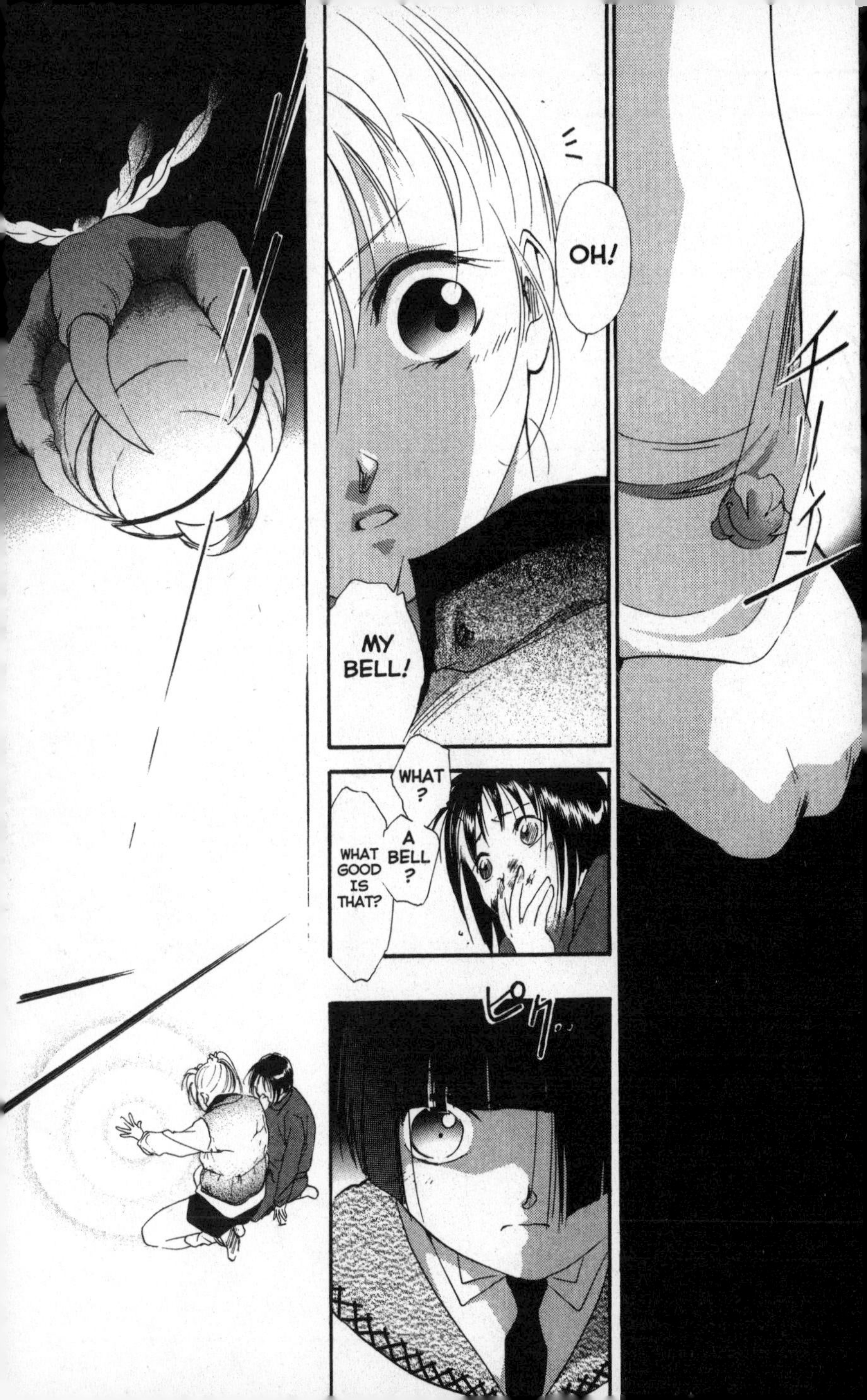
OH!
MY BELL!
WHAT?
A BELL?
WHAT GOOD IS THAT?

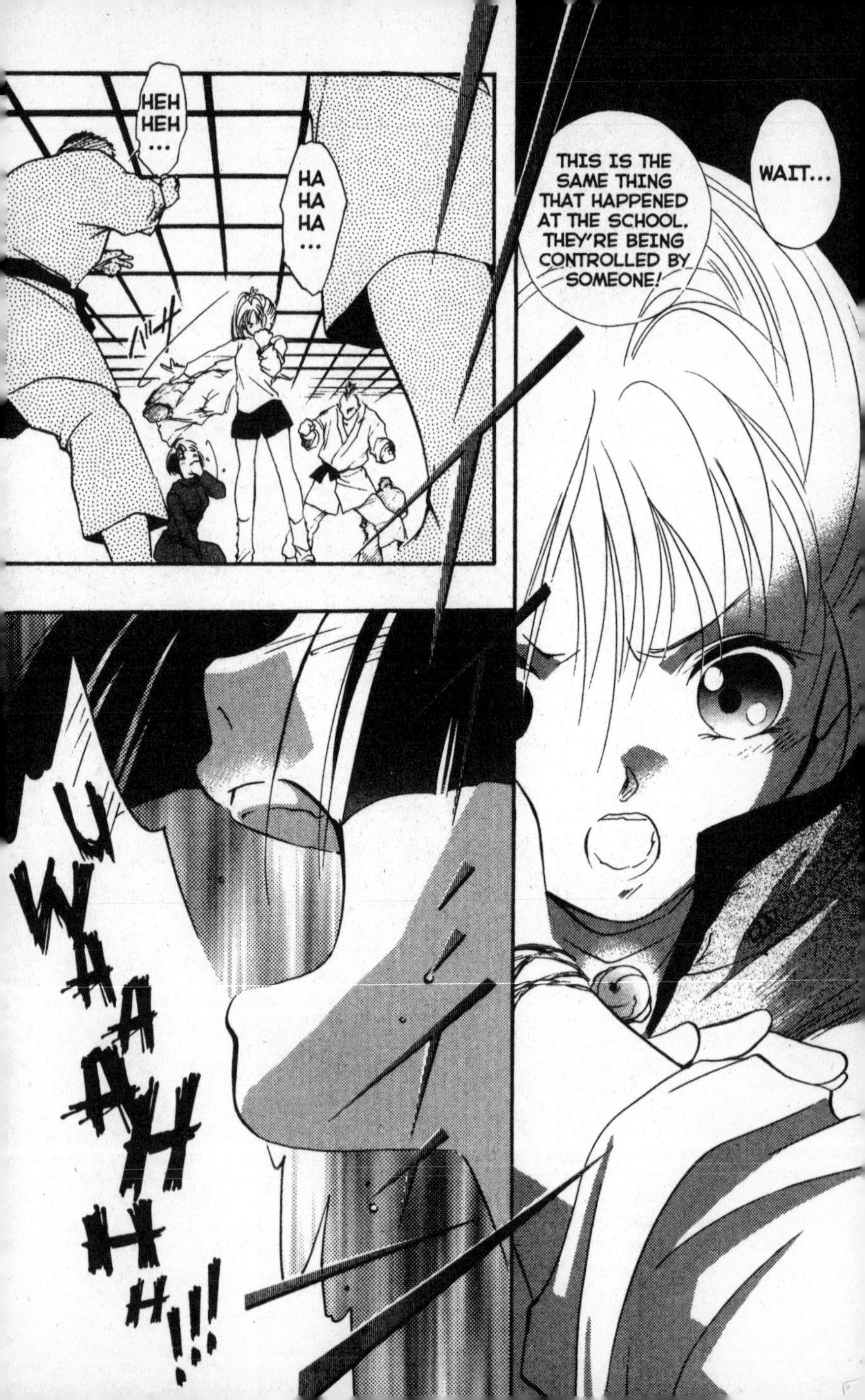
WAIT...
THIS IS THE SAME THING THAT HAPPENED AT THE SCHOOL. THEY'RE BEING CONTROLLED BY SOMEONE!
HA HA HA...
HEH HEH...
UWAAAHHHH!!!

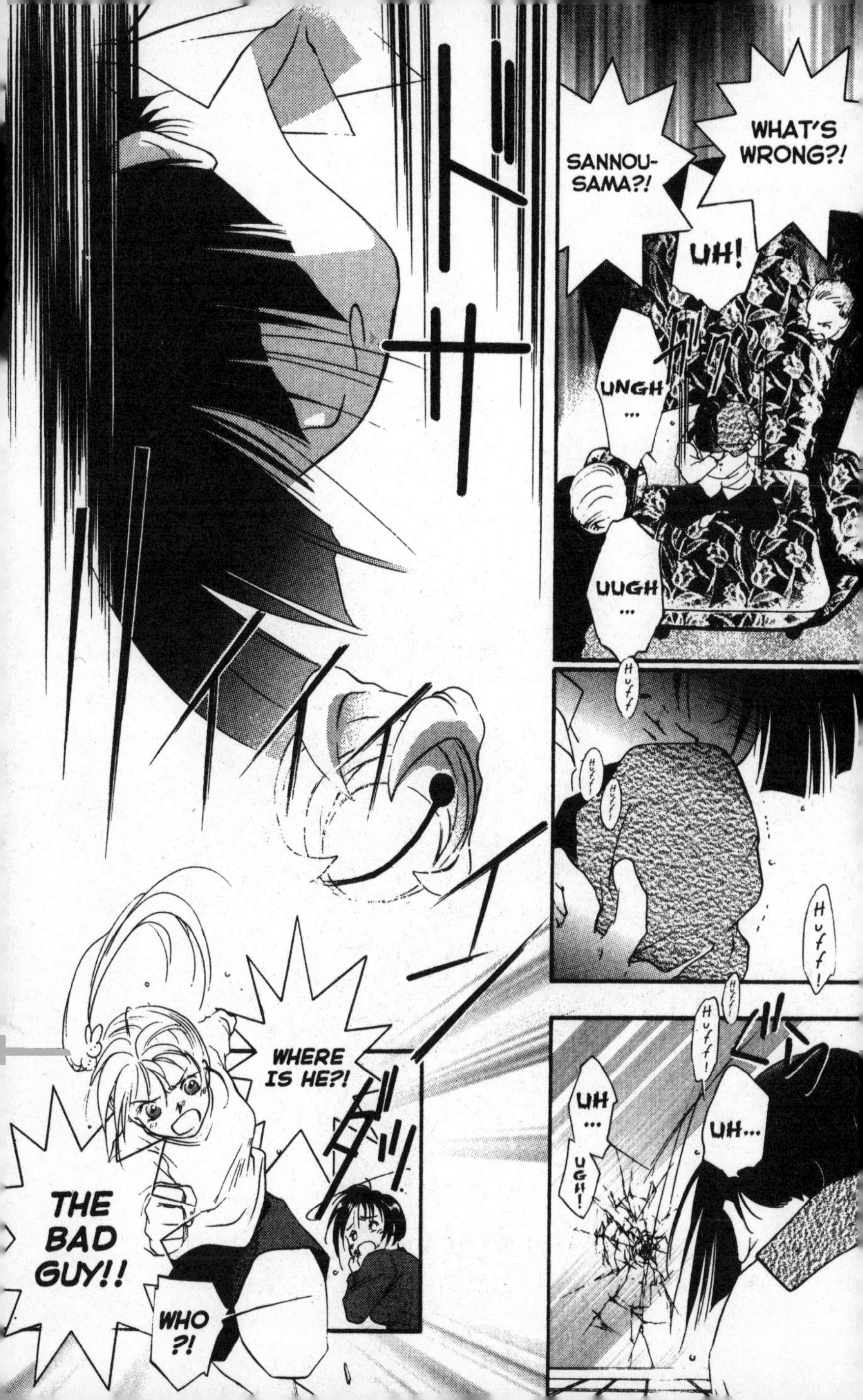
WHAT'S WRONG?!
SANNOU-SAMA?!
UH!
UNGH...
UUGH...
Huff
Huff!
Huff!
Huff!
Huff!
Huff!
UH...
UH...
UGH!
WHERE IS HE?!
THE BAD GUY!!
WHO?!

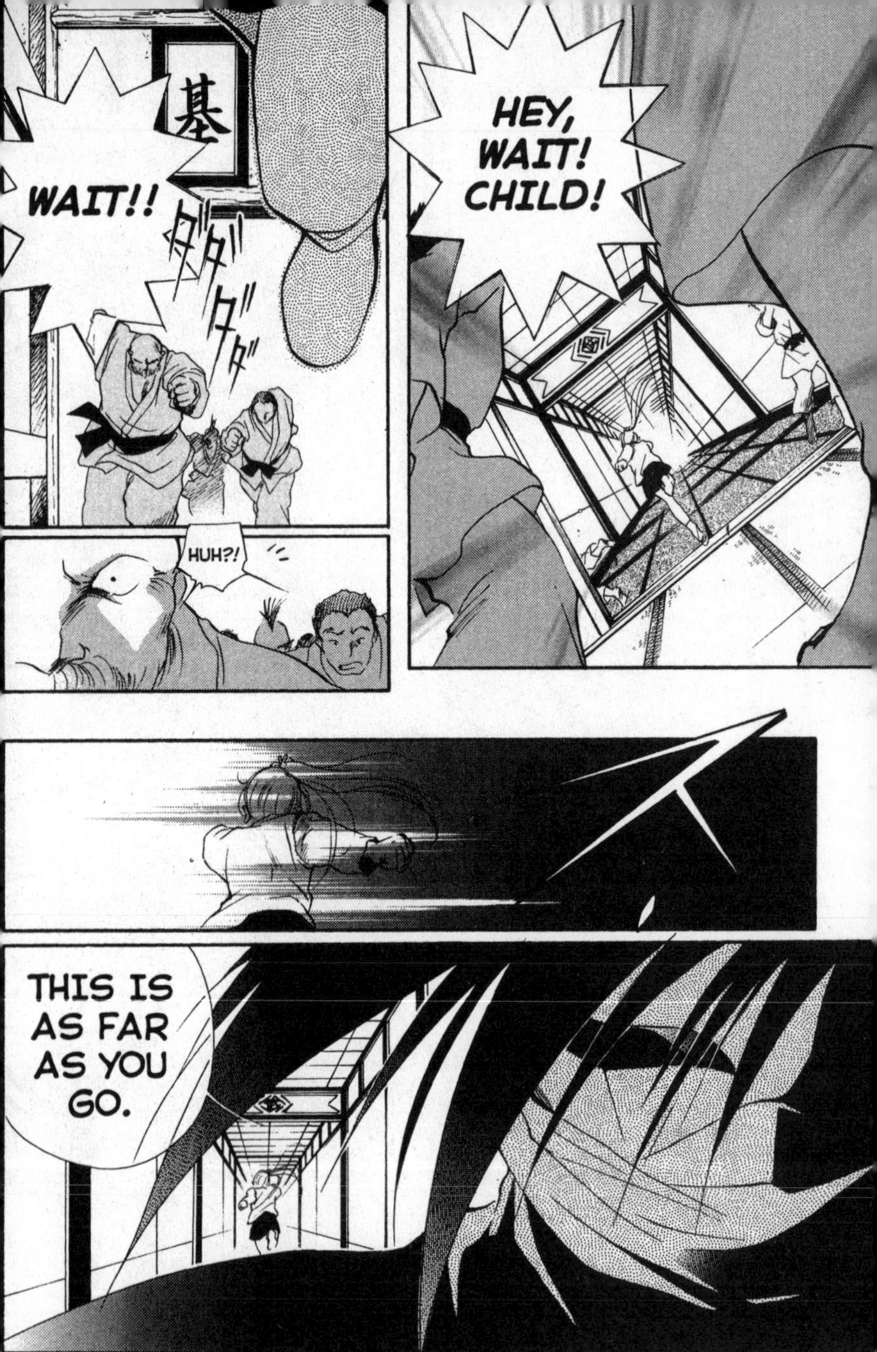
HEY, WAIT! CHILD!
基
WAIT!!
ダダダダ
HUH?!
THIS IS AS FAR AS YOU GO.

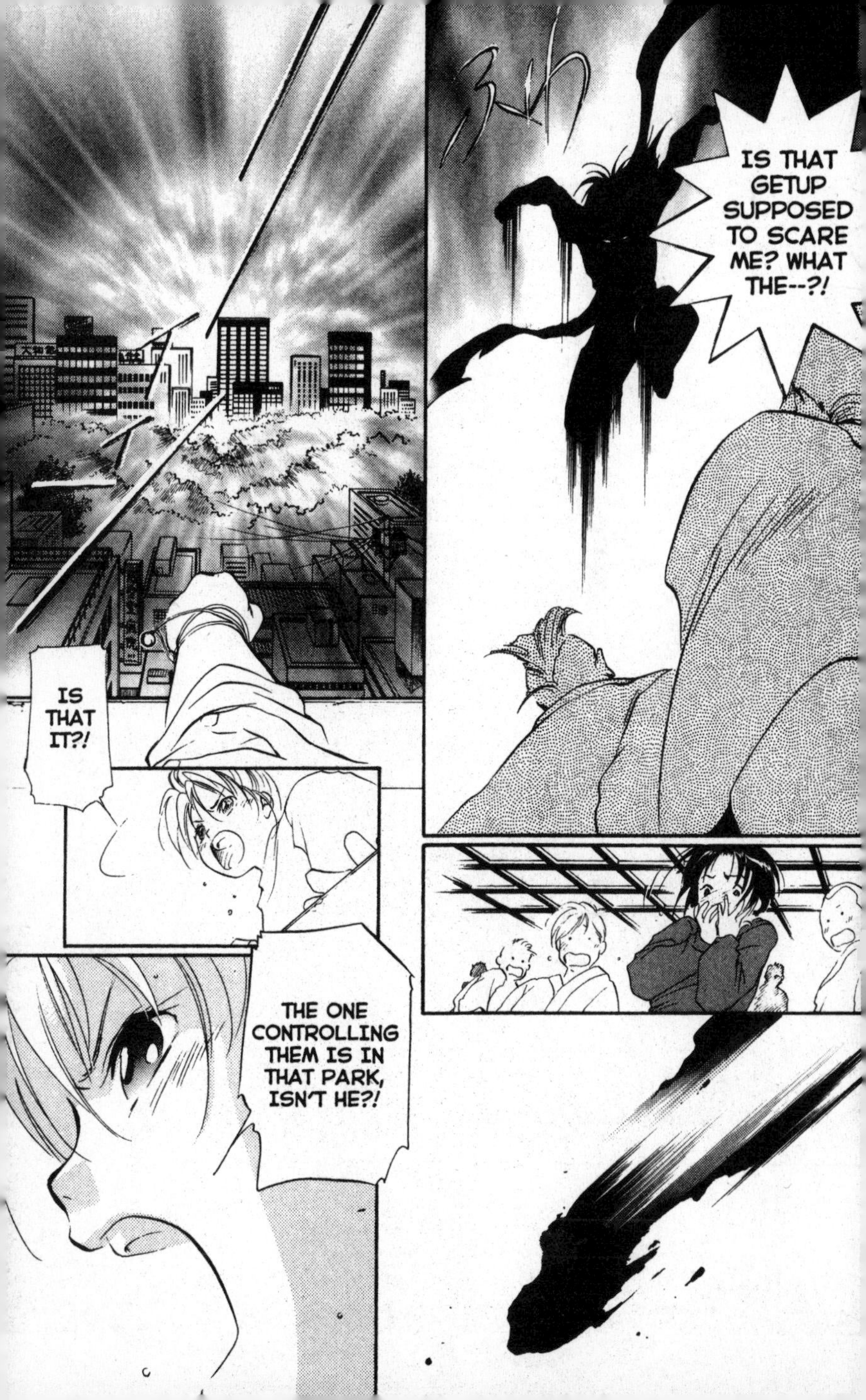
IS THAT GETUP SUPPOSED TO SCARE ME? WHAT THE--?!
IS THAT IT?!
THE ONE CONTROLLING THEM IS IN THAT PARK, ISN'T HE?!

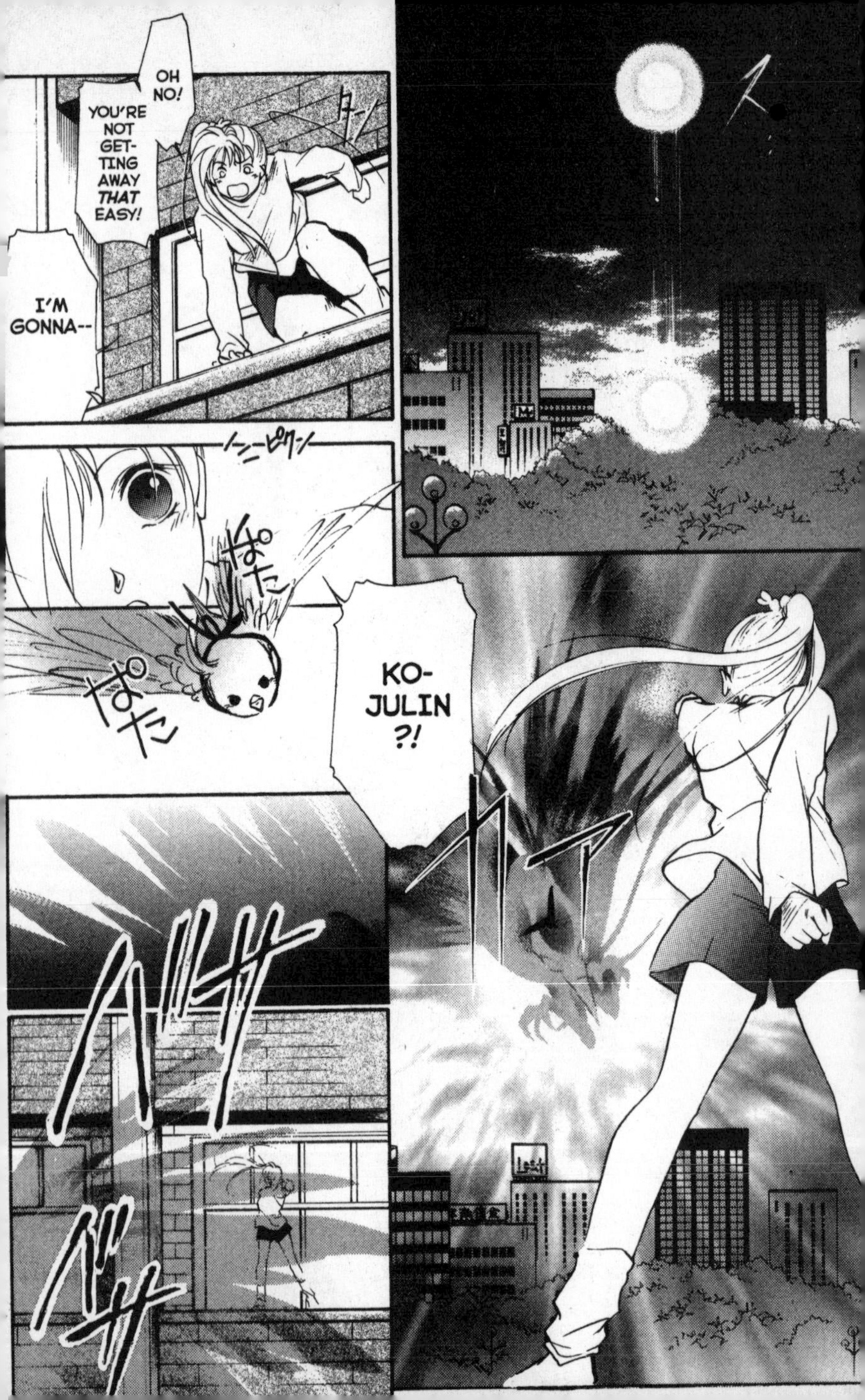
OH NO! YOU'RE NOT GETTING AWAY THAT EASY!
I'M GONNA--
KO-JULIN ?!

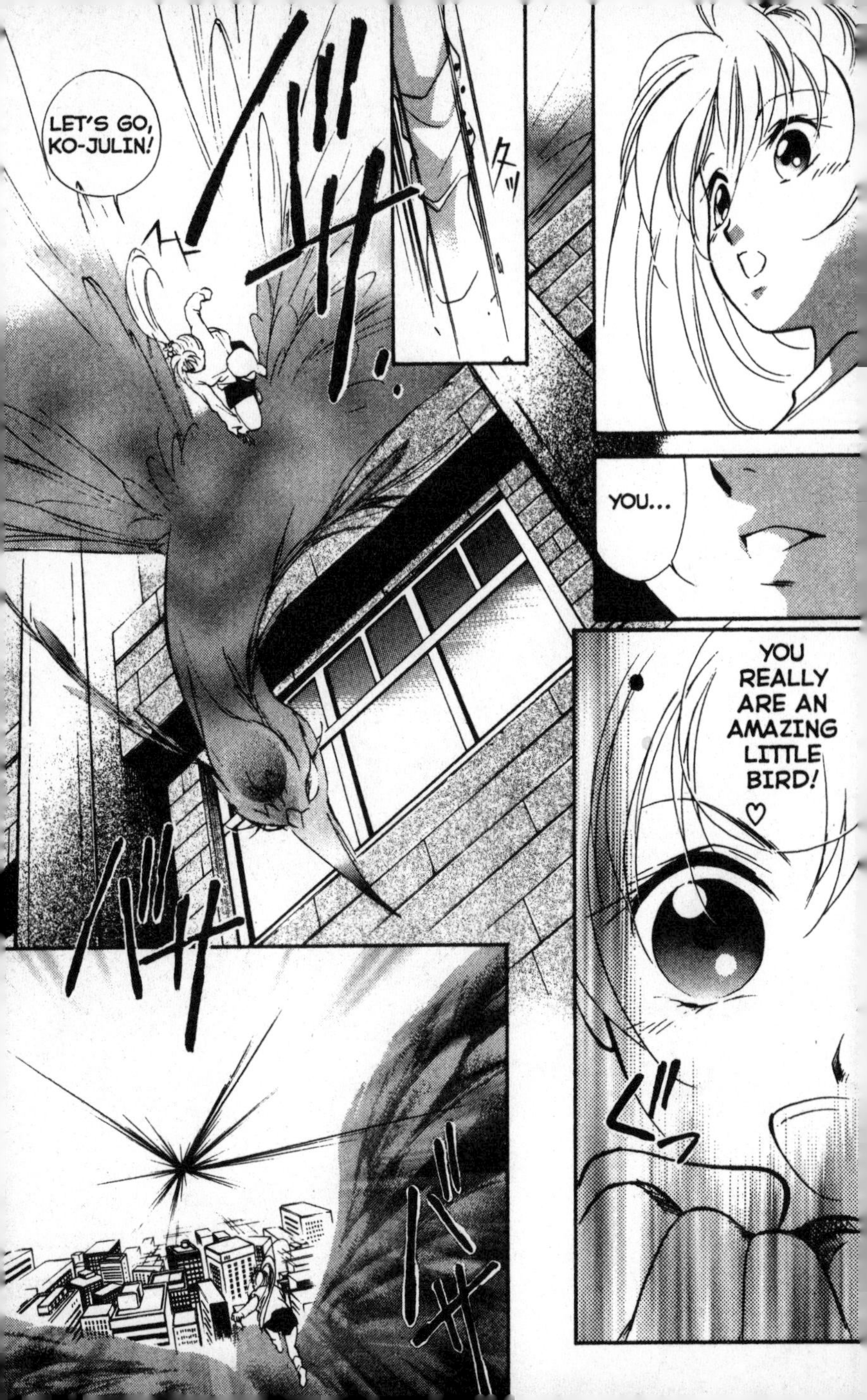
YOU...
YOU REALLY ARE AN AMAZING LITTLE BIRD! ♡
LET'S GO, KO-JULIN!

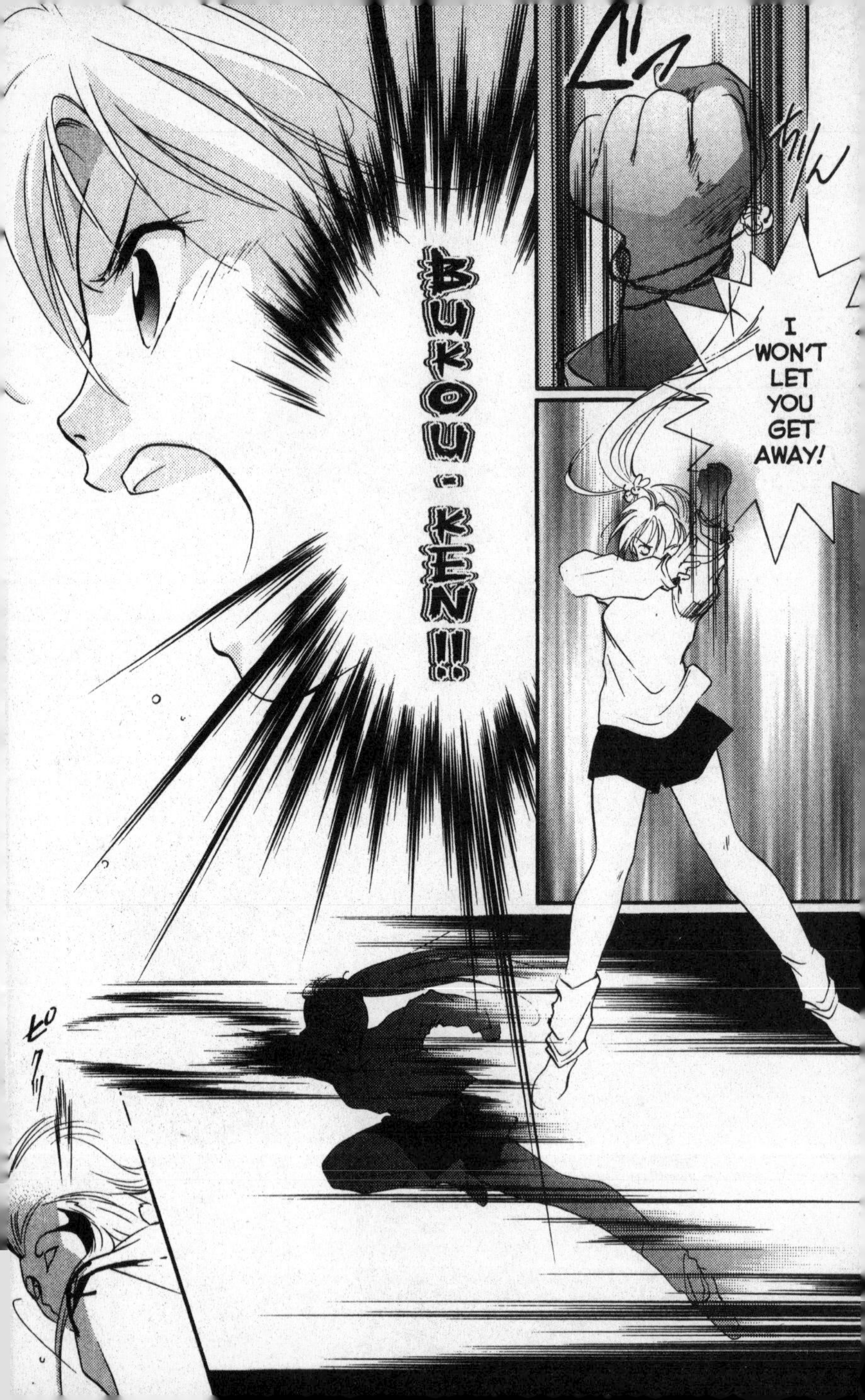
I WON'T LET YOU GET AWAY!
BUKOU-KEN!!

美澄
Misu

I'M
HOME!

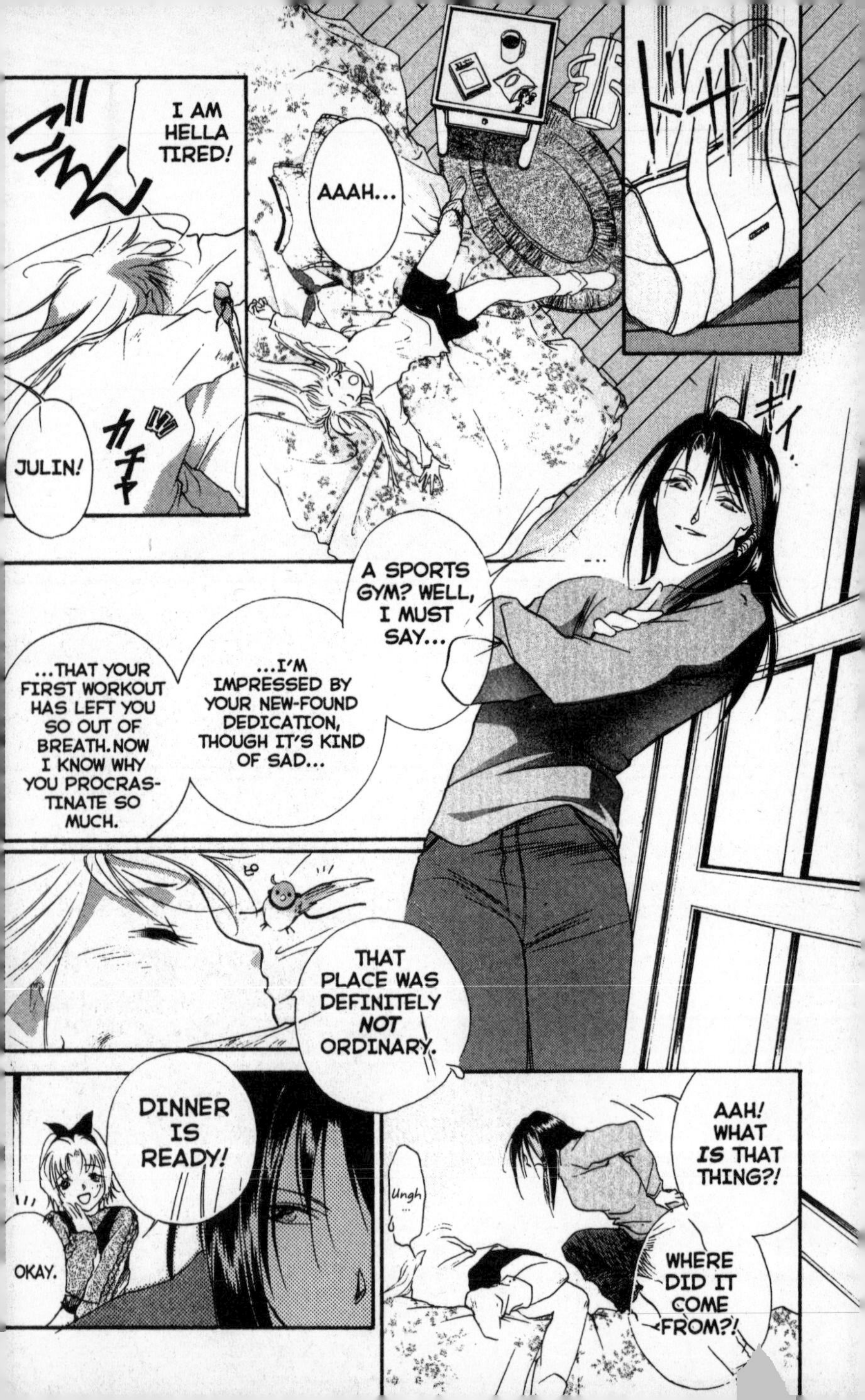
ドサッ
AAAH...
I AM HELLA TIRED!
ごろん
JULIN!
ガチャ
ギイ…
A SPORTS GYM? WELL, I MUST SAY...
...I'M IMPRESSED BY YOUR NEW-FOUND DEDICATION, THOUGH IT'S KIND OF SAD...
...THAT YOUR FIRST WORKOUT HAS LEFT YOU SO OUT OF BREATH. NOW I KNOW WHY YOU PROCRASTINATE SO MUCH.
THAT PLACE WAS DEFINITELY *NOT* ORDINARY.
AAH! WHAT *IS* THAT THING?!
WHERE DID IT COME FROM?!
Ungh...
DINNER IS READY!
OKAY.

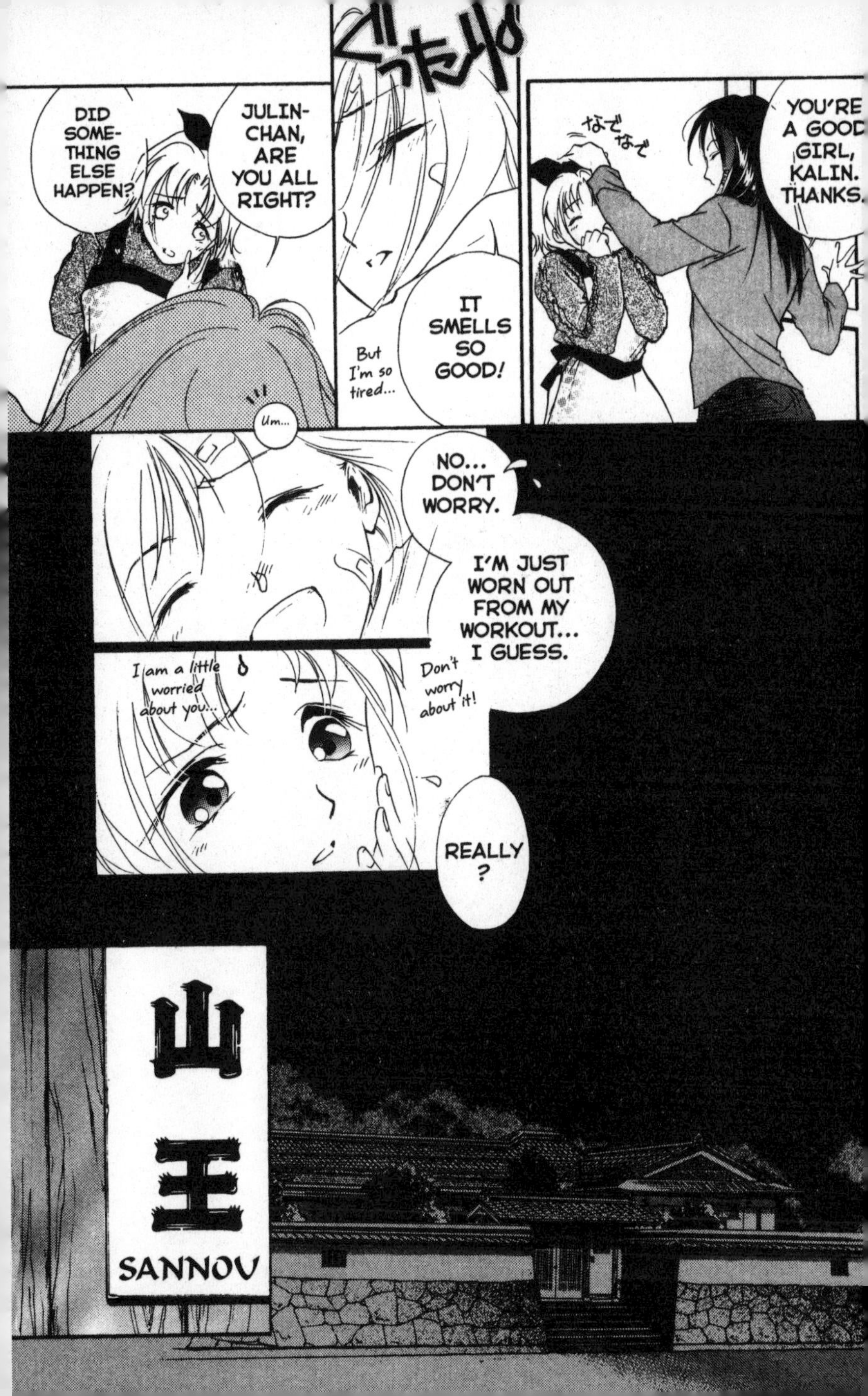

なでなで
YOU'RE A GOOD GIRL, KALIN. THANKS.
ぐったり
IT SMELLS SO GOOD!
But I'm so tired...
JULIN-CHAN, ARE YOU ALL RIGHT?
DID SOMETHING ELSE HAPPEN?
Um...
NO... DON'T WORRY.
I'M JUST WORN OUT FROM MY WORKOUT... I GUESS.
Don't worry about it!
I am a little worried about you...
REALLY?
山王
SANNOU

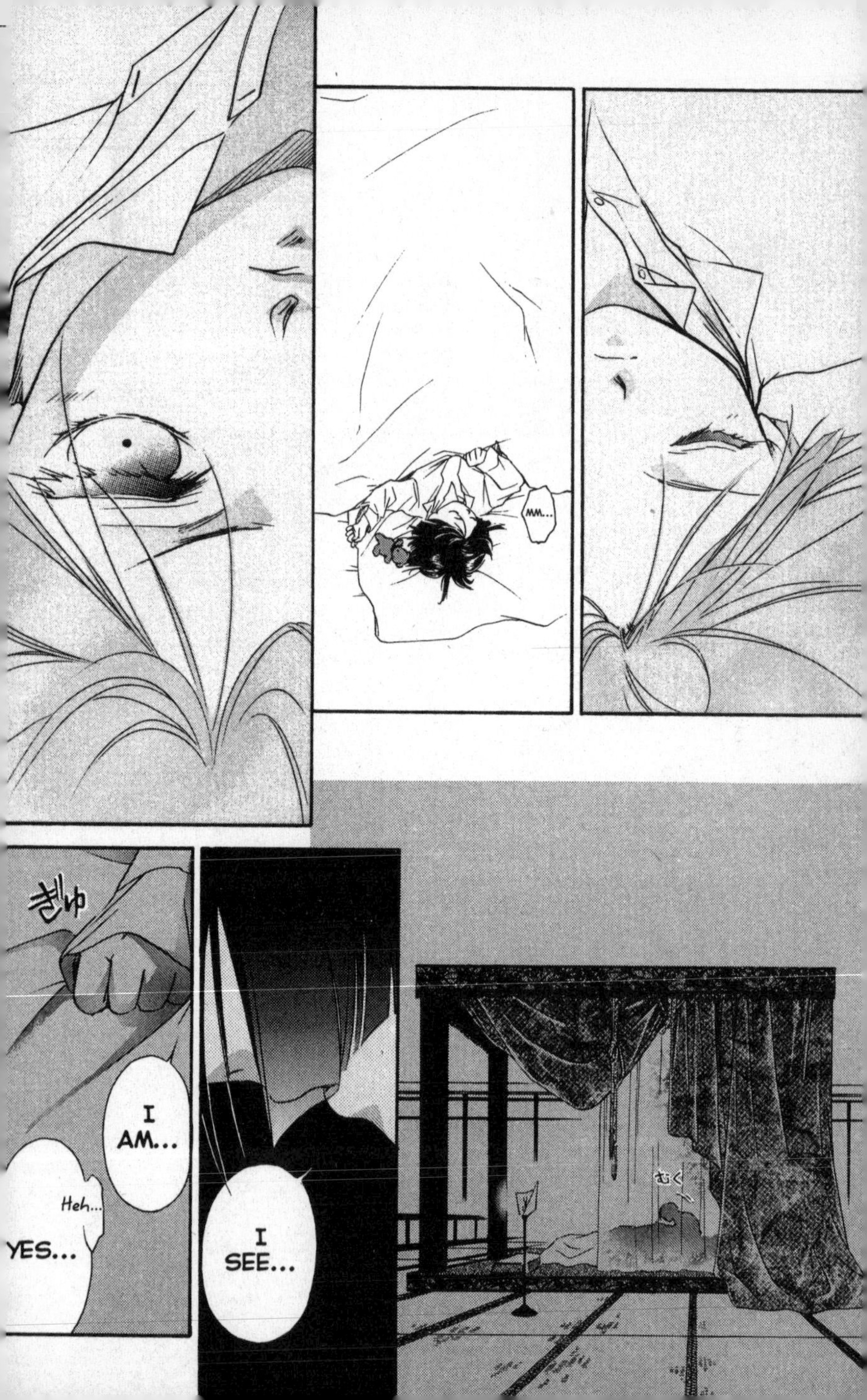
MM...
むく
I SEE...
ぎゅ
I AM...
Heh...
YES...

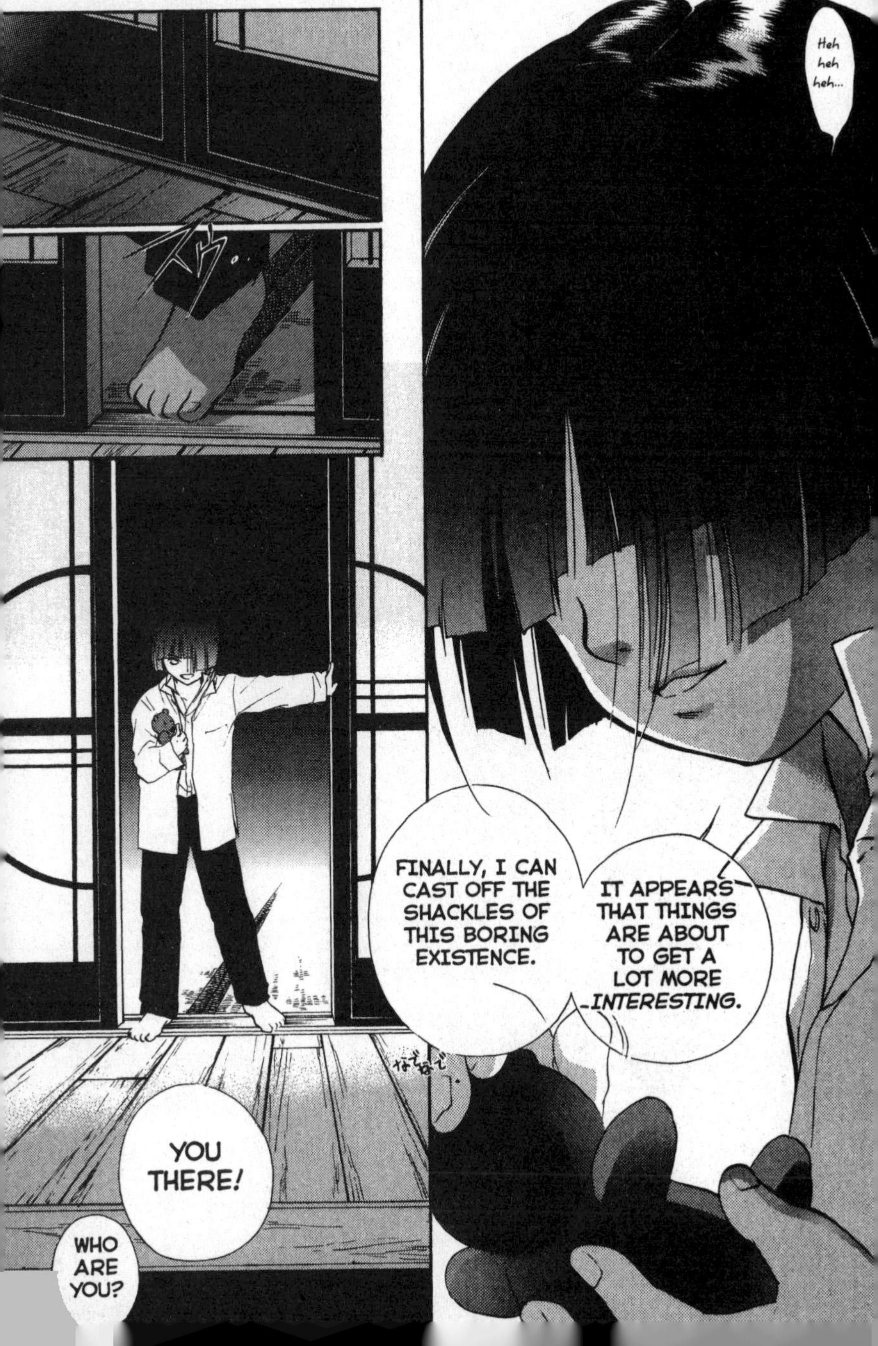
Heh heh heh...
IT APPEARS THAT THINGS ARE ABOUT TO GET A LOT MORE INTERESTING.
FINALLY, I CAN CAST OFF THE SHACKLES OF THIS BORING EXISTENCE.
なでなで
YOU THERE!
WHO ARE YOU?

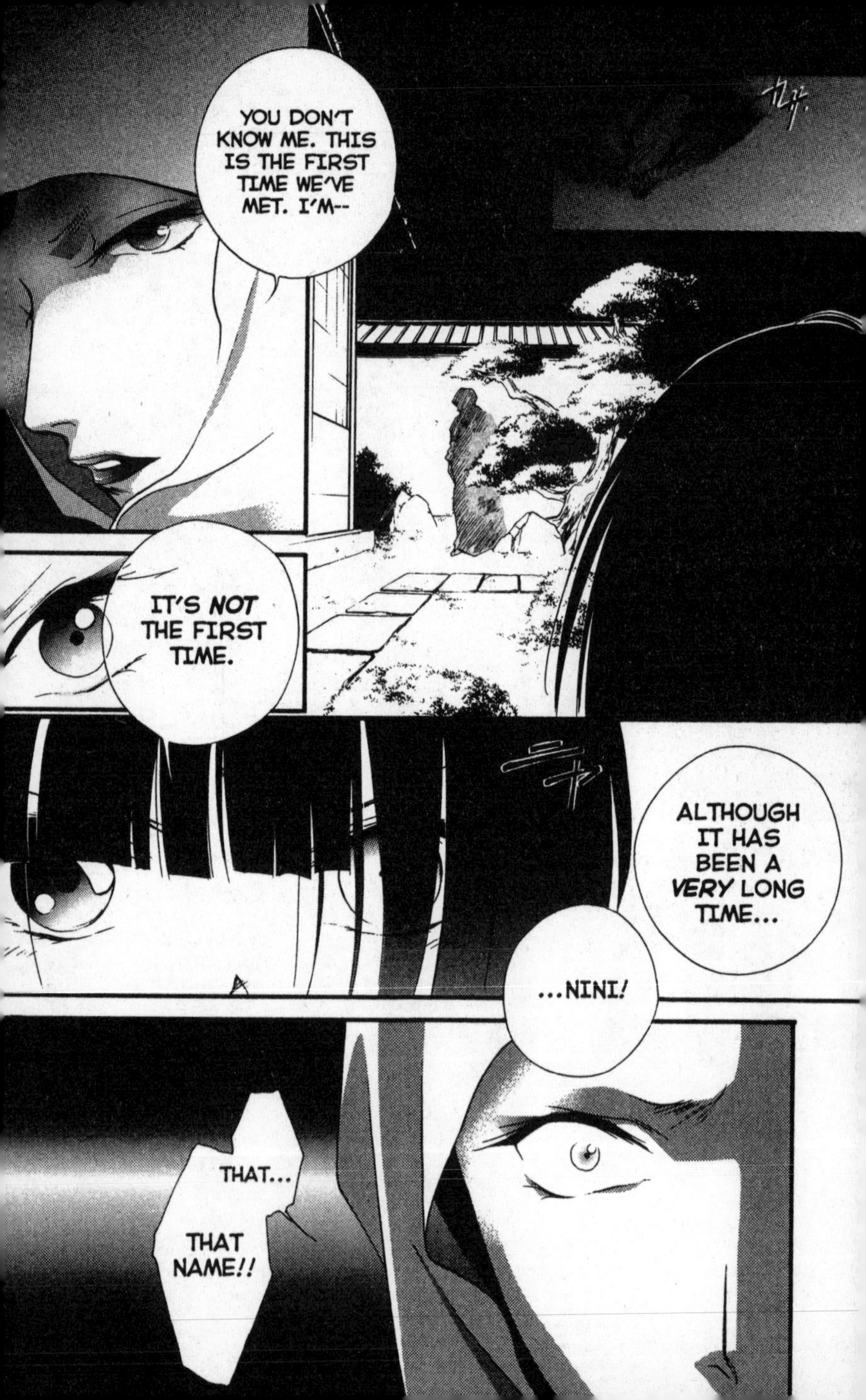
YOU DON'T KNOW ME. THIS IS THE FIRST TIME WE'VE MET. I'M--
IT'S *NOT* THE FIRST TIME.
ALTHOUGH IT HAS BEEN A *VERY* LONG TIME...
...NINI!
THAT...
THAT NAME!!

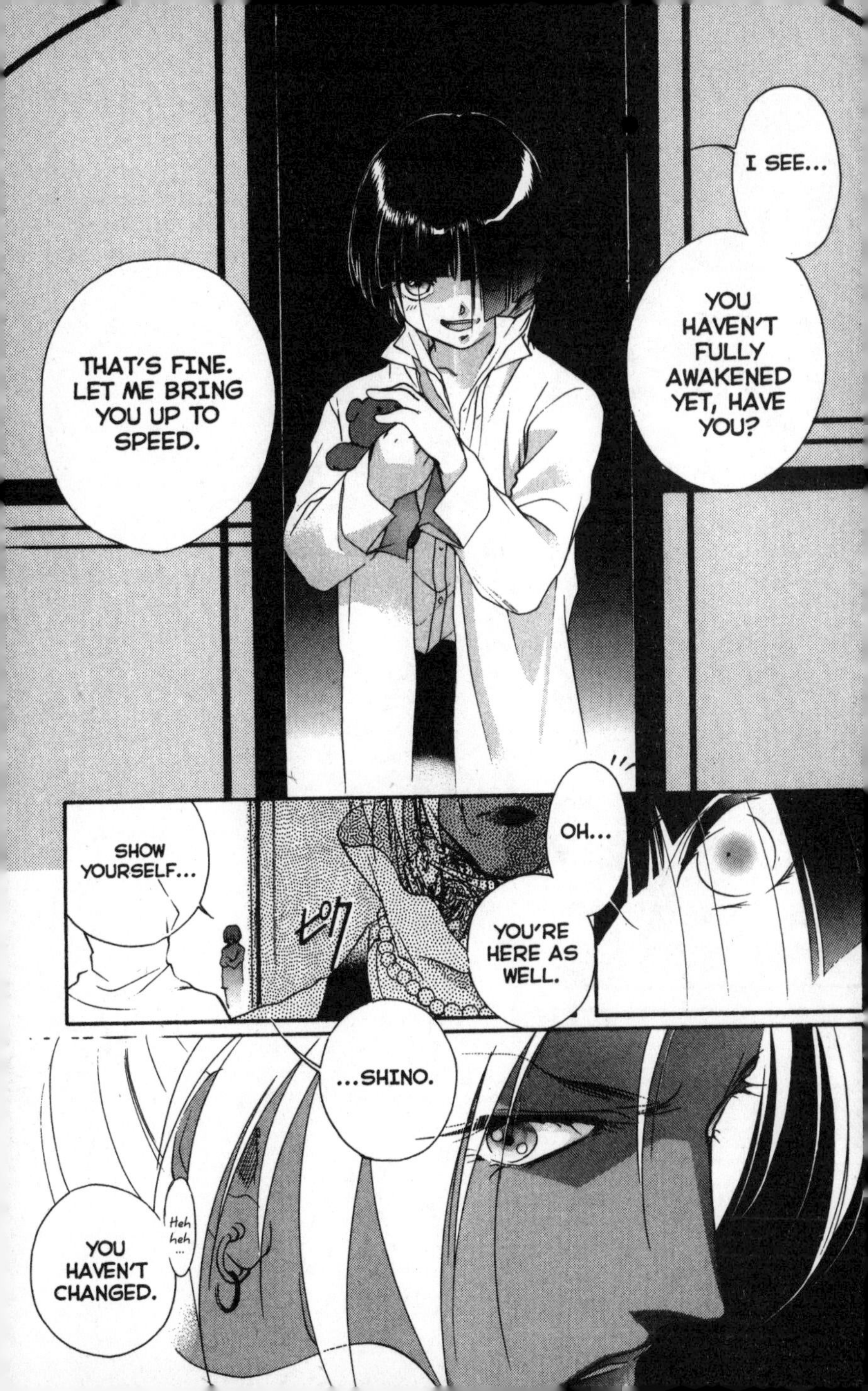
I SEE...
YOU HAVEN'T FULLY AWAKENED YET, HAVE YOU?
THAT'S FINE. LET ME BRING YOU UP TO SPEED.
OH...
YOU'RE HERE AS WELL.
SHOW YOURSELF...
...SHINO.
Heh heh...
YOU HAVEN'T CHANGED.

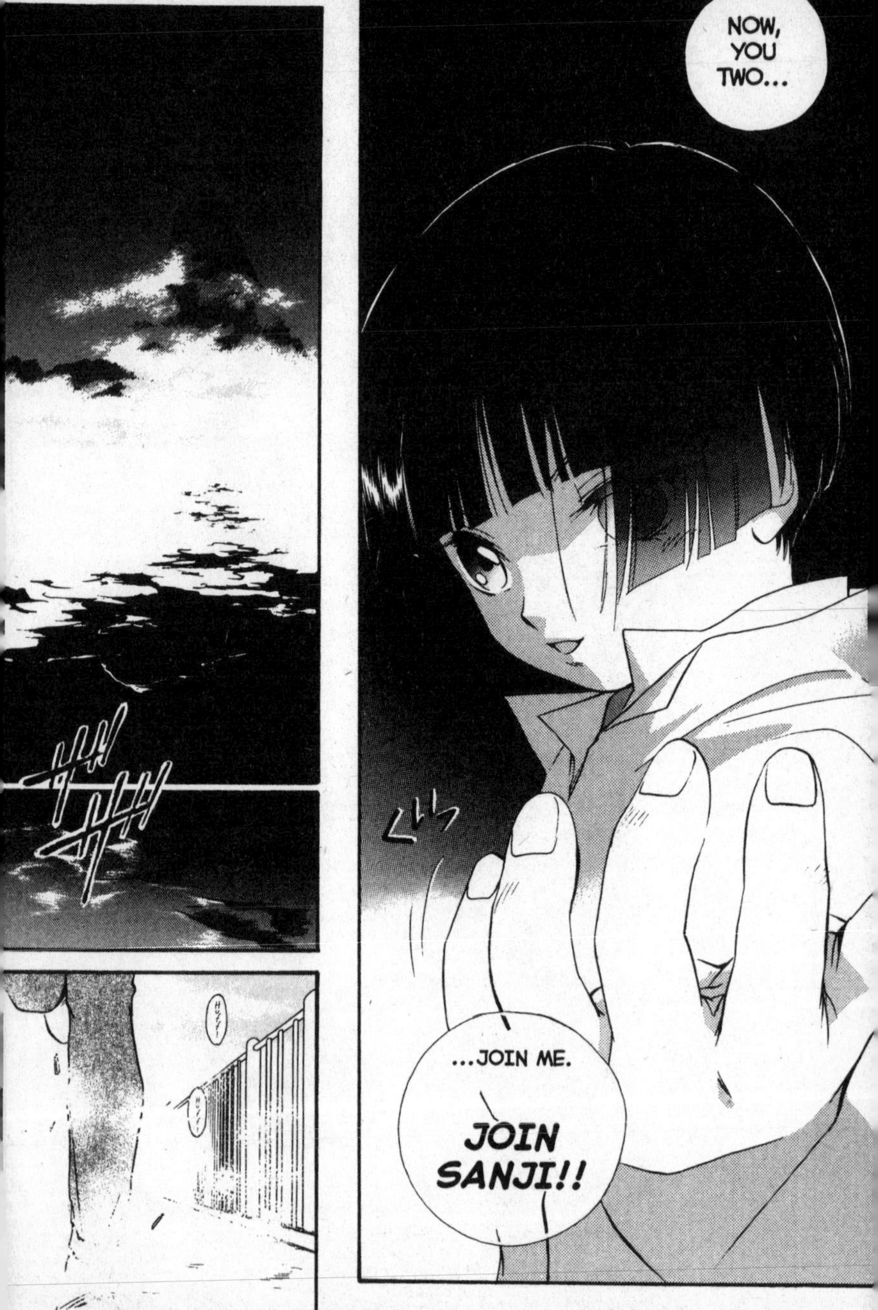
NOW, YOU TWO...
...JOIN ME.
JOIN SANJI!!

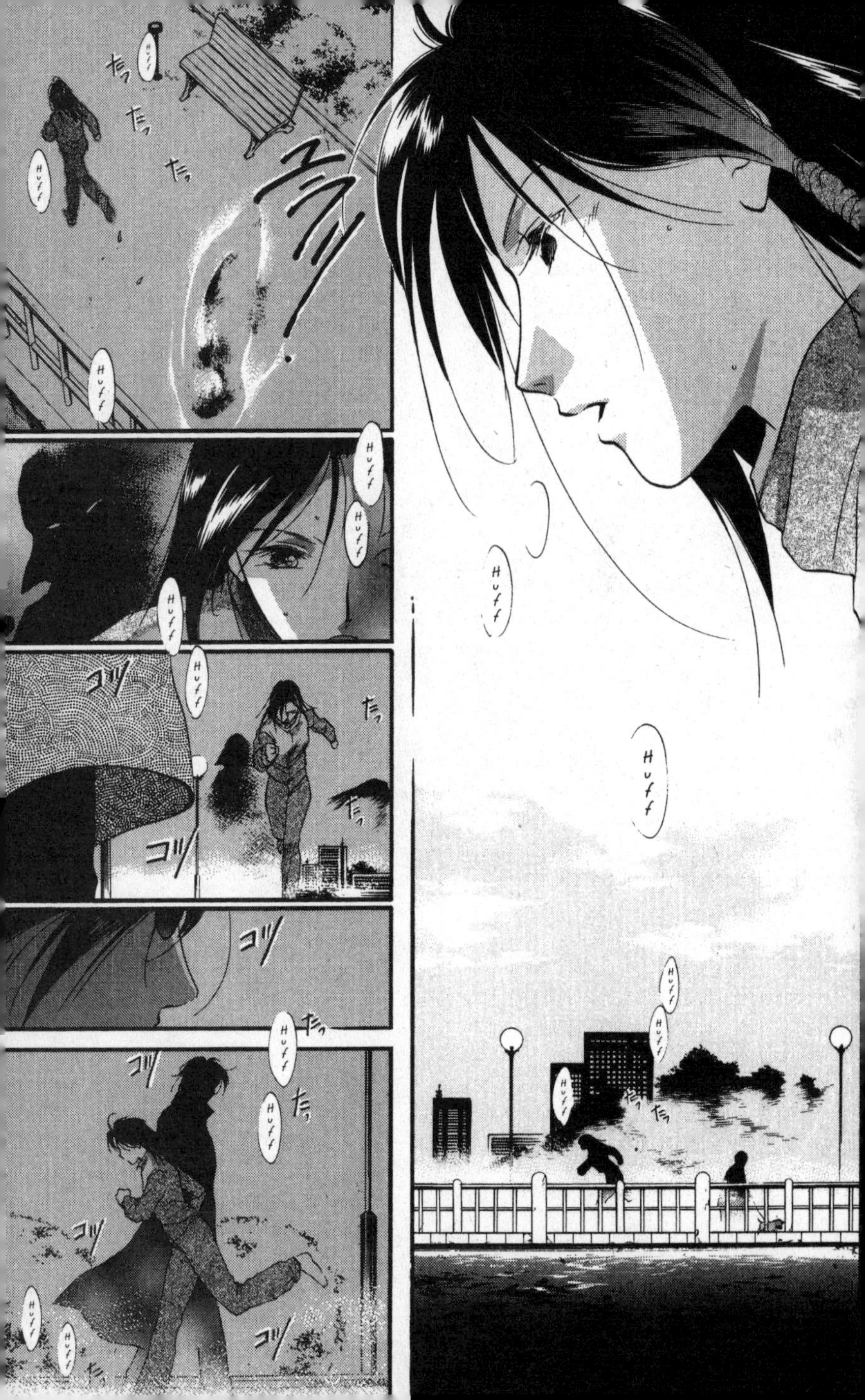
Huff
Huff
Huff
Huff
Huff
たっ
たっ
Huff
たっ
たっ
たっ
Huff
Huff
Huff
Huff
Huff
Huff
コツ
たっ
たっ
コツ
コツ
たっ
Huff
たっ
Huff
コツ
コツ
Huff
Huff
コツ
たっ

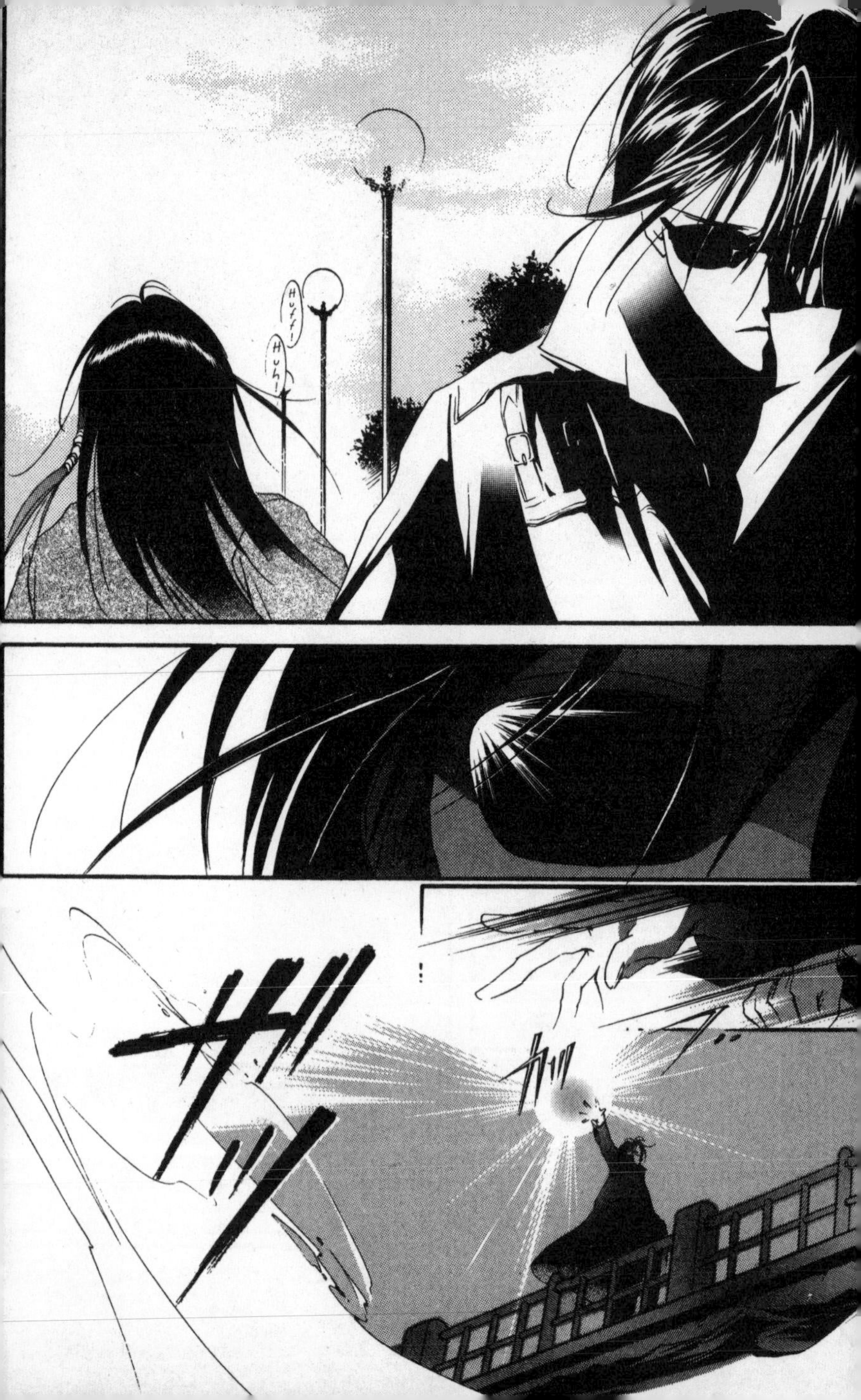
Huff!
Huh!
!
カッ
ザッ

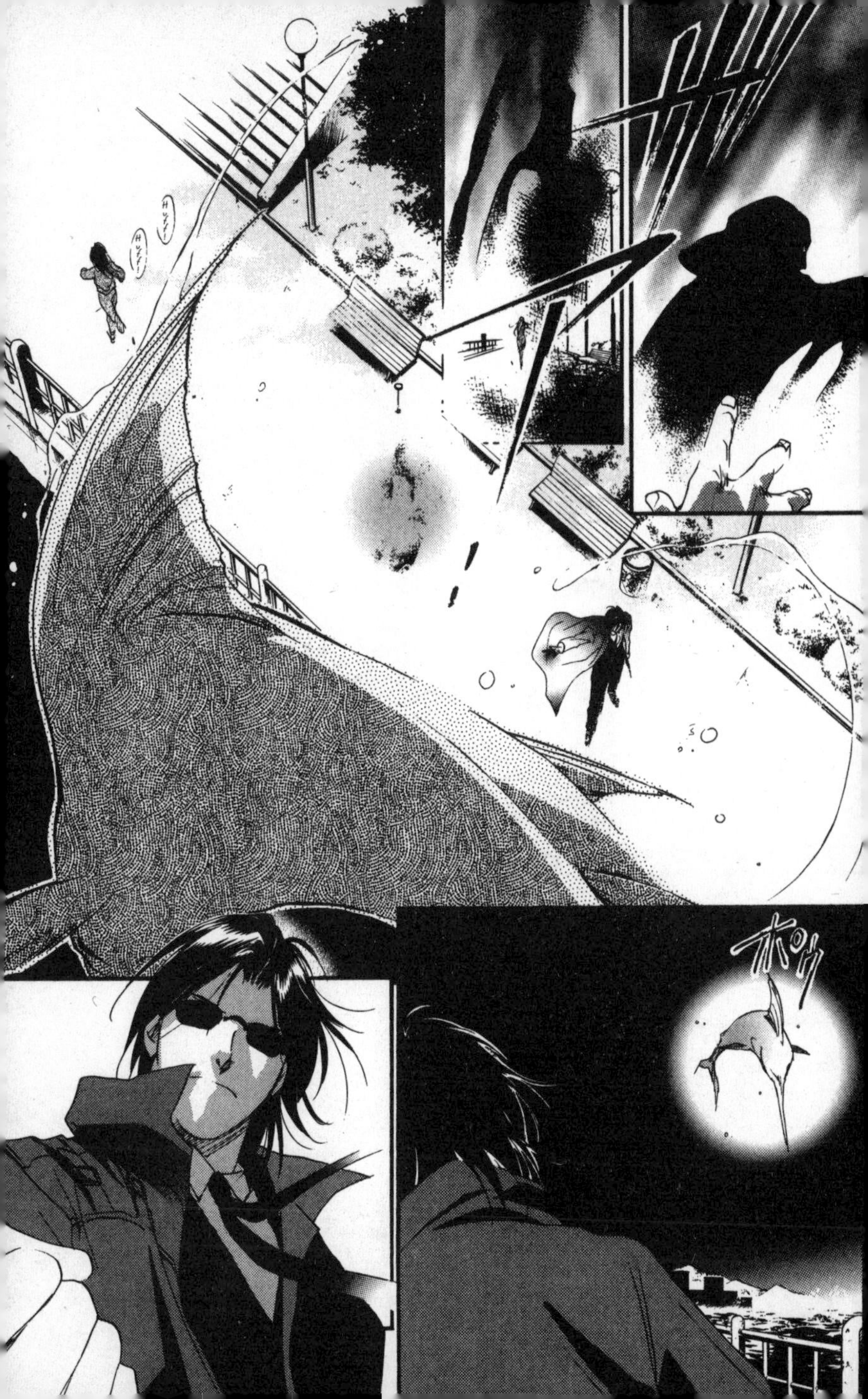
HUFF!
HUFF!

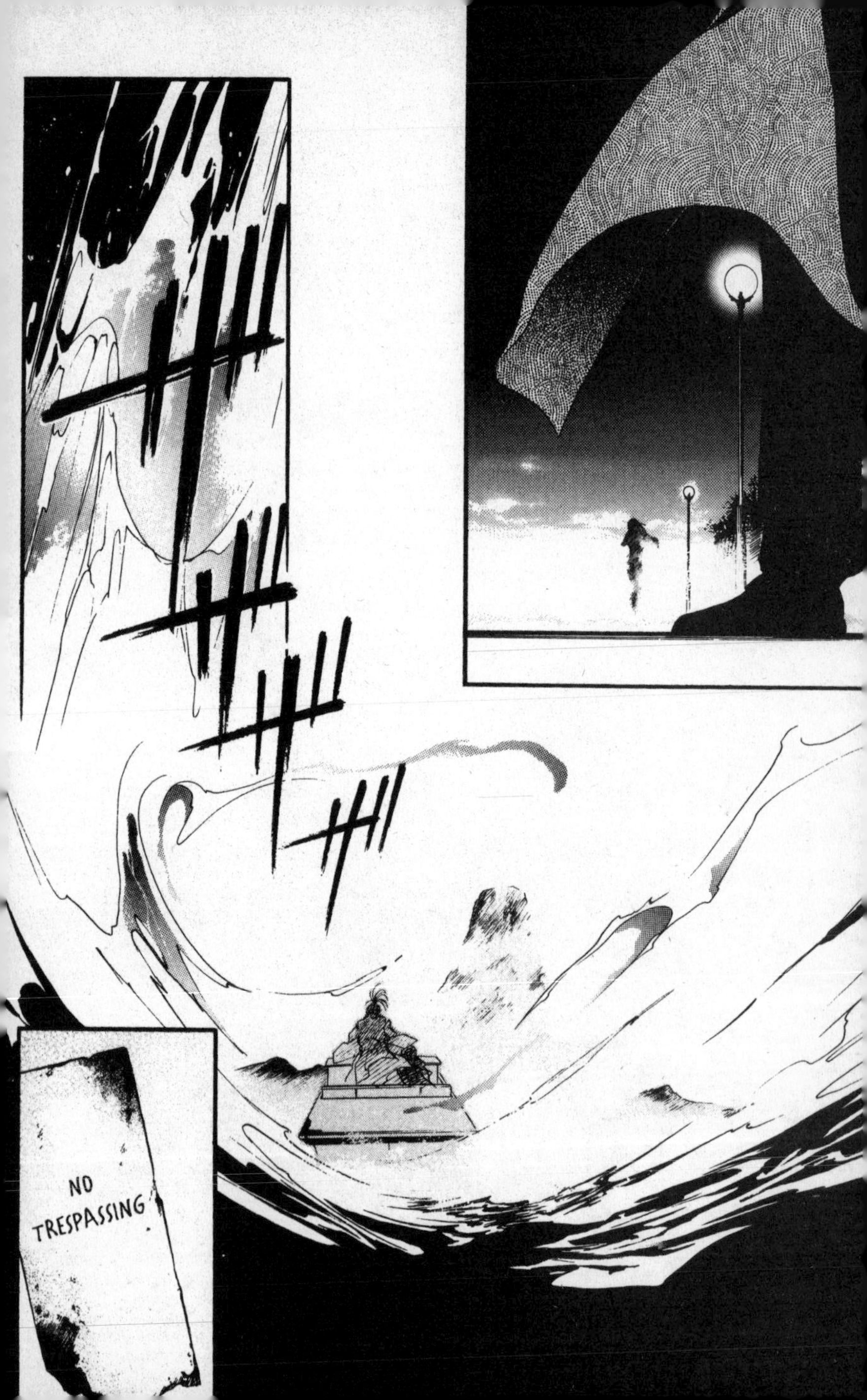
NO TRESPASSING

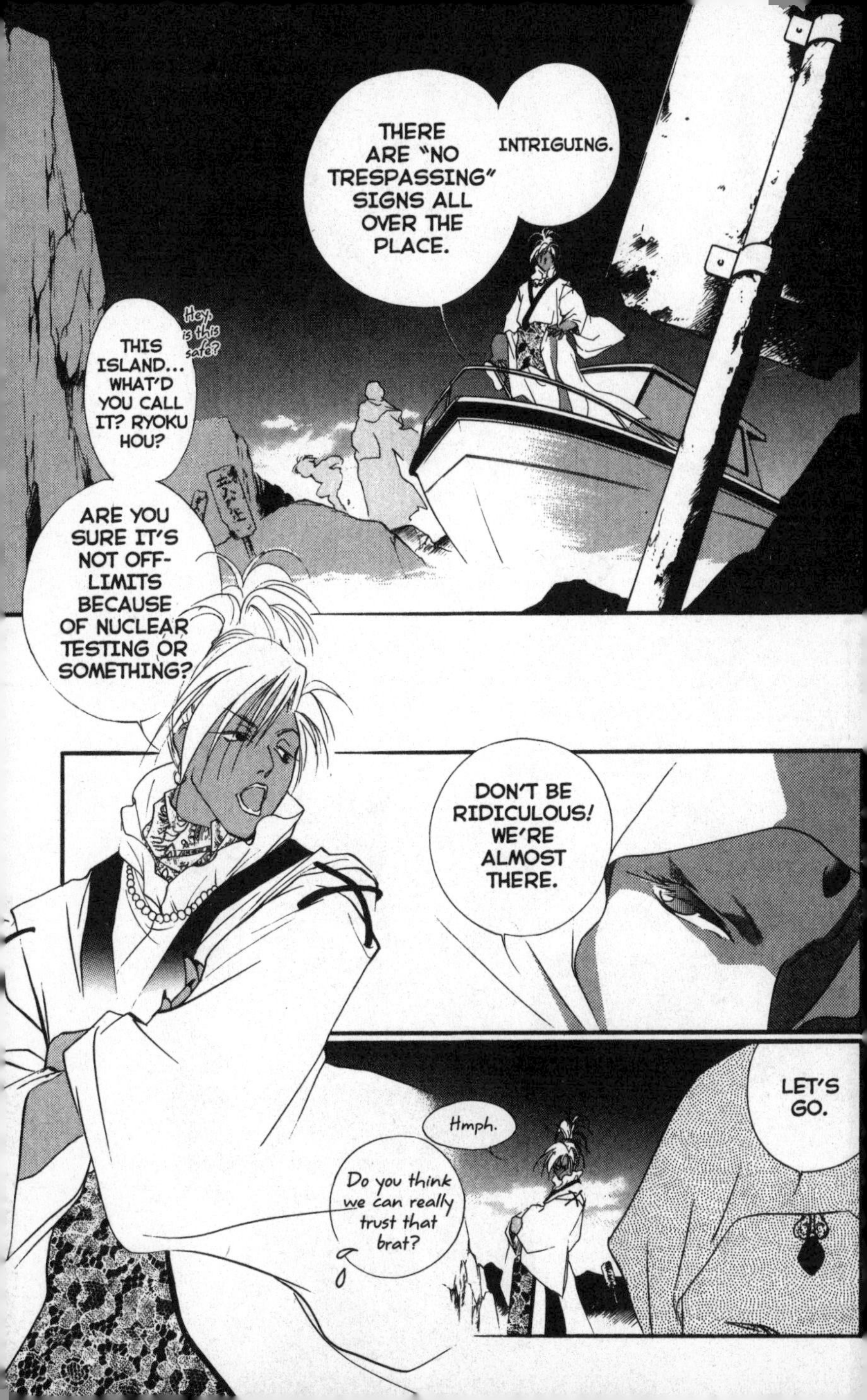
INTRIGUING.
THERE ARE "NO TRESPASSING" SIGNS ALL OVER THE PLACE.
Hey, is this safe?
THIS ISLAND... WHAT'D YOU CALL IT? RYOKU HOU?
ARE YOU SURE IT'S NOT OFF-LIMITS BECAUSE OF NUCLEAR TESTING OR SOMETHING?
DON'T BE RIDICULOUS! WE'RE ALMOST THERE.
LET'S GO.
Hmph.
Do you think we can really trust that brat?

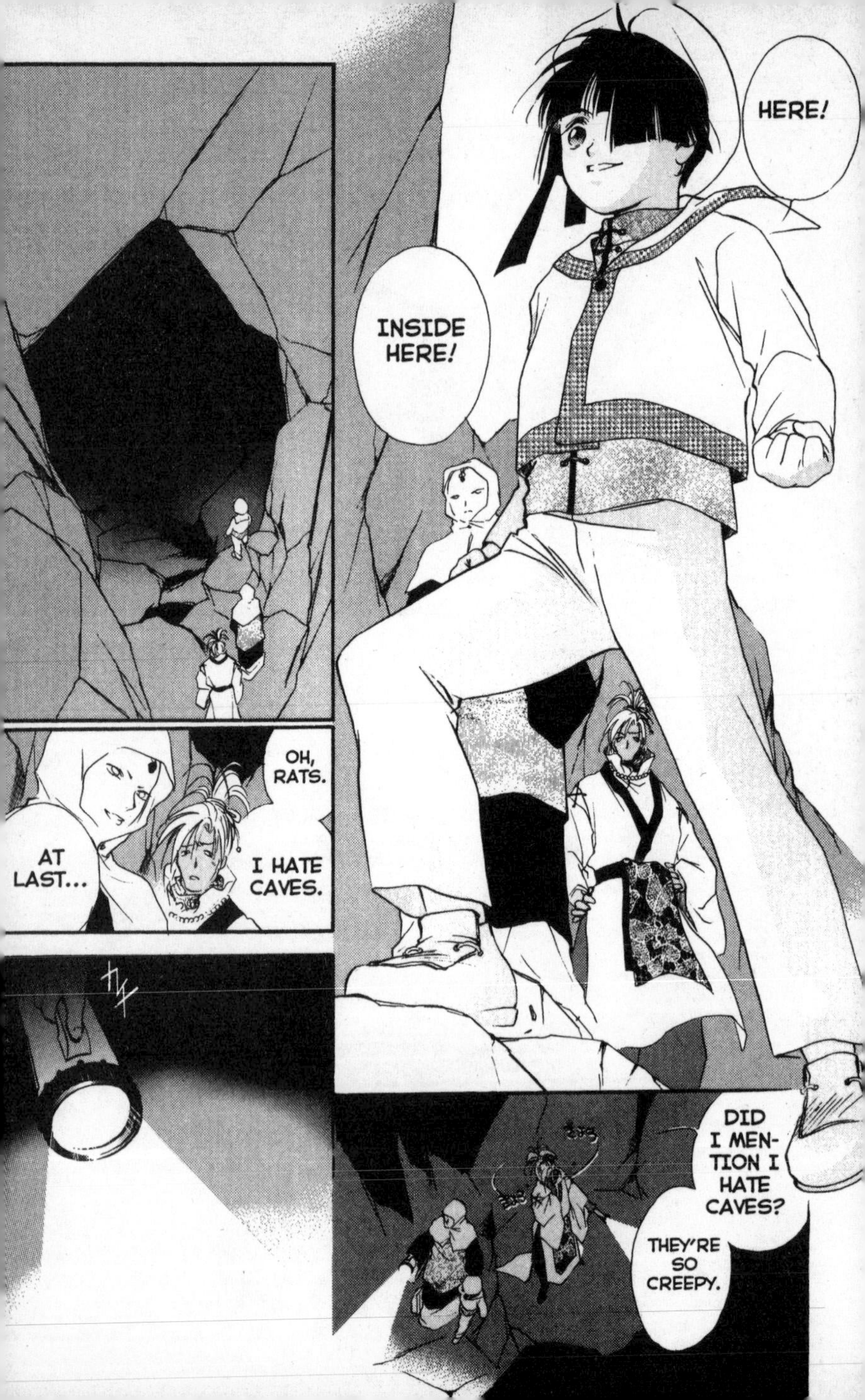
HERE!
INSIDE HERE!
OH, RATS.
I HATE CAVES.
AT LAST...
DID I MENTION I HATE CAVES?
THEY'RE SO CREEPY.

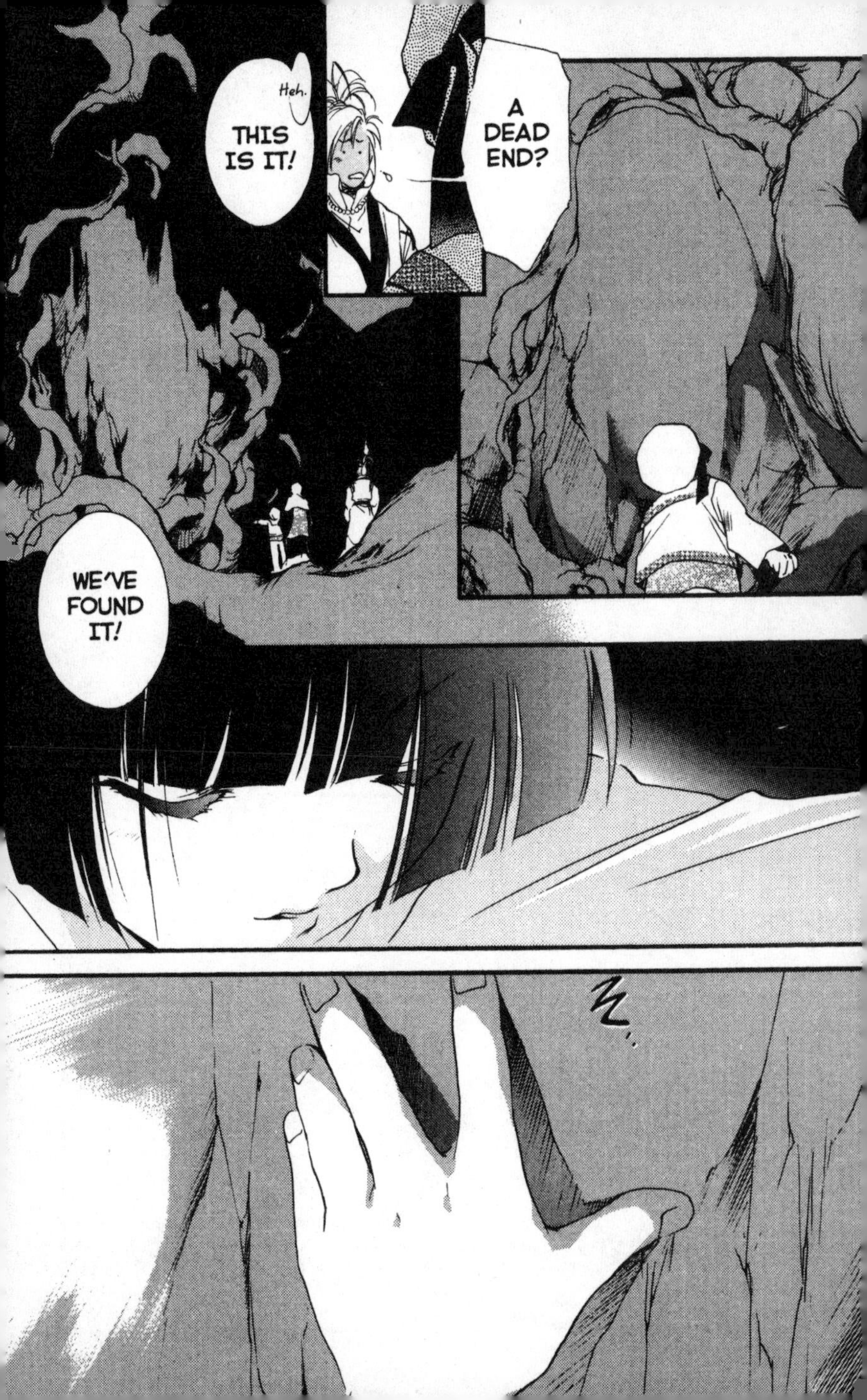
A DEAD END?
Heh.
THIS IS IT!
WE'VE FOUND IT!

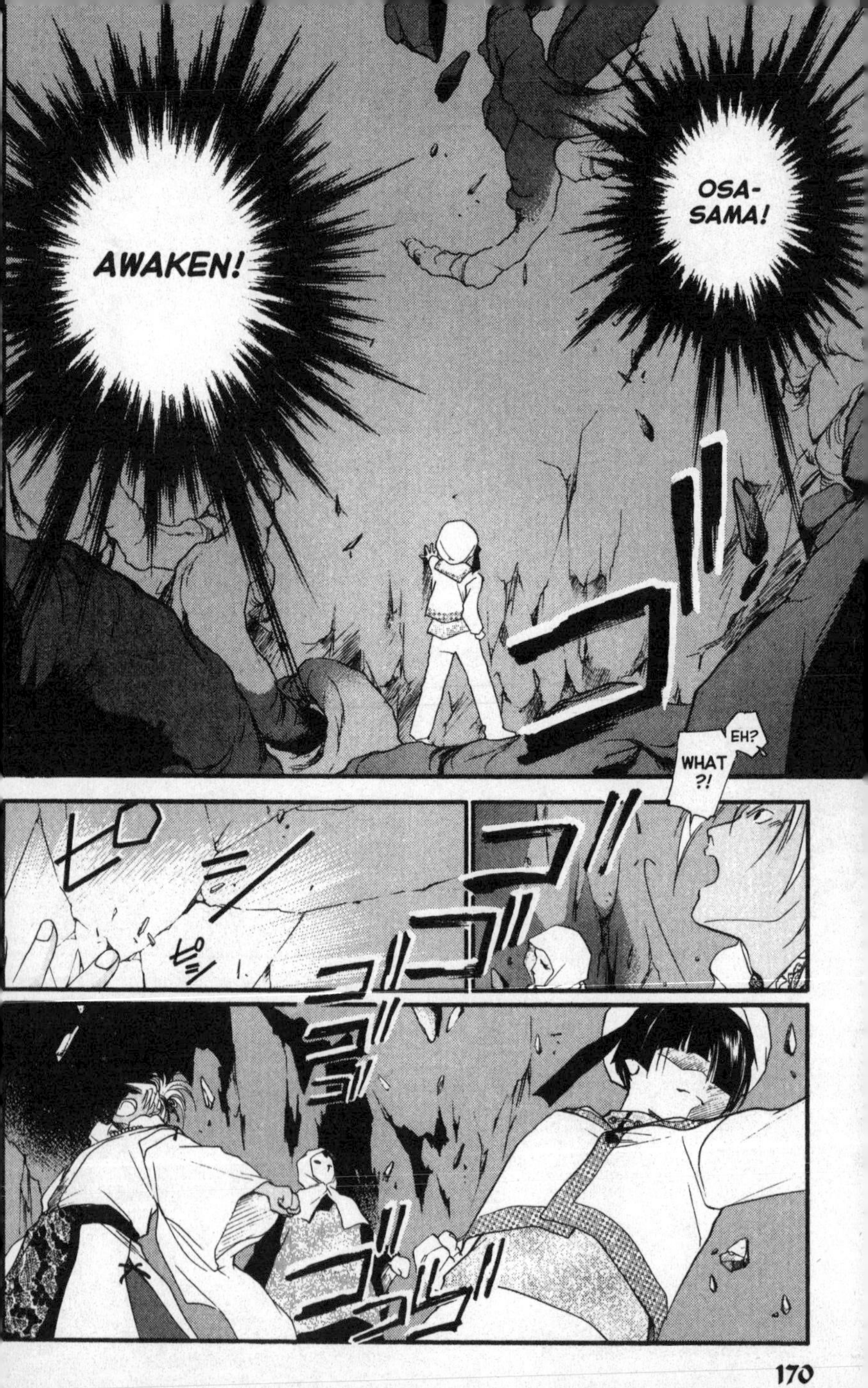
OSA-SAMA!
AWAKEN!
EH?
WHAT?!

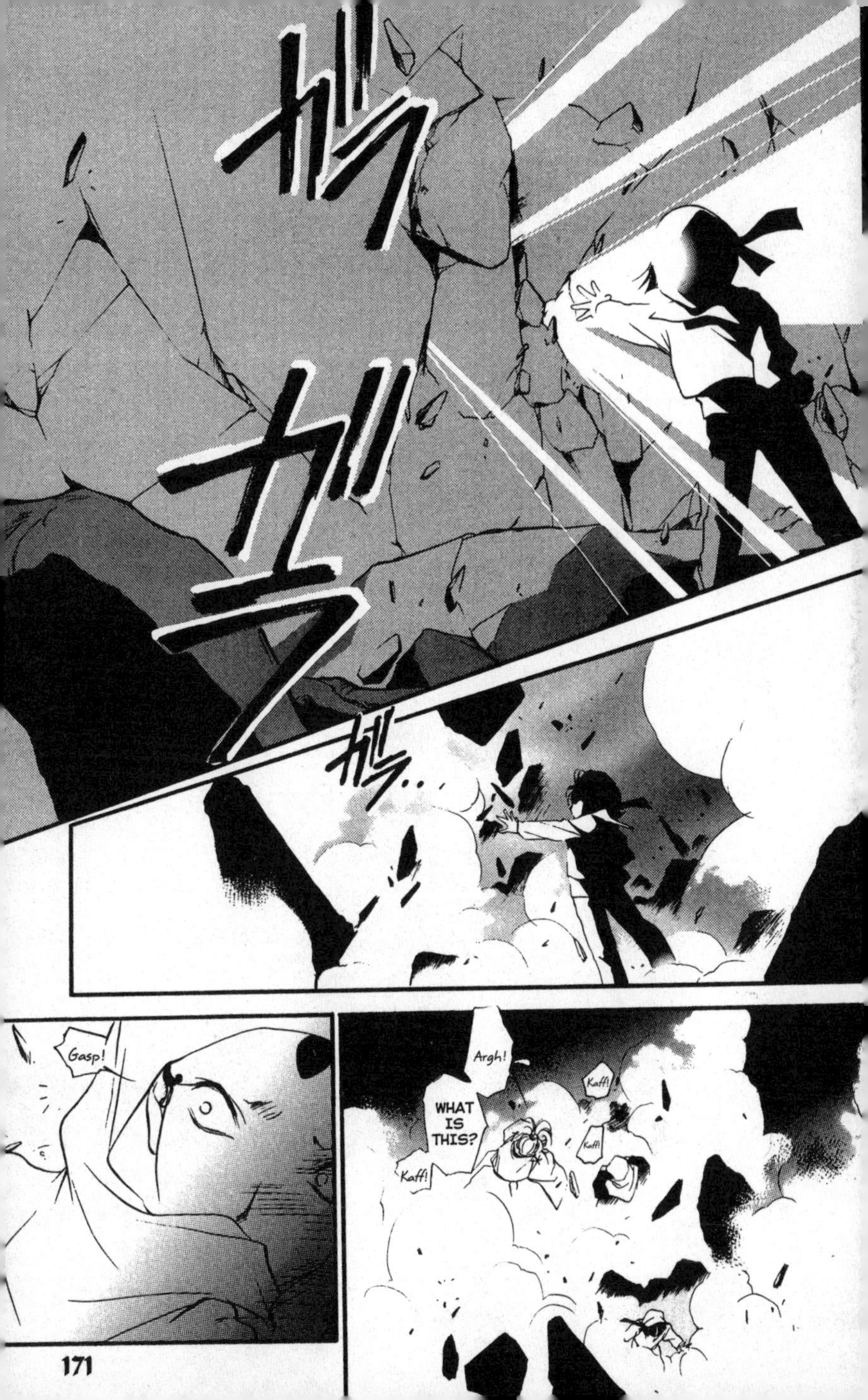
Argh!
Kaff!
WHAT IS THIS?
Kaff!
Kaff!
Gasp!

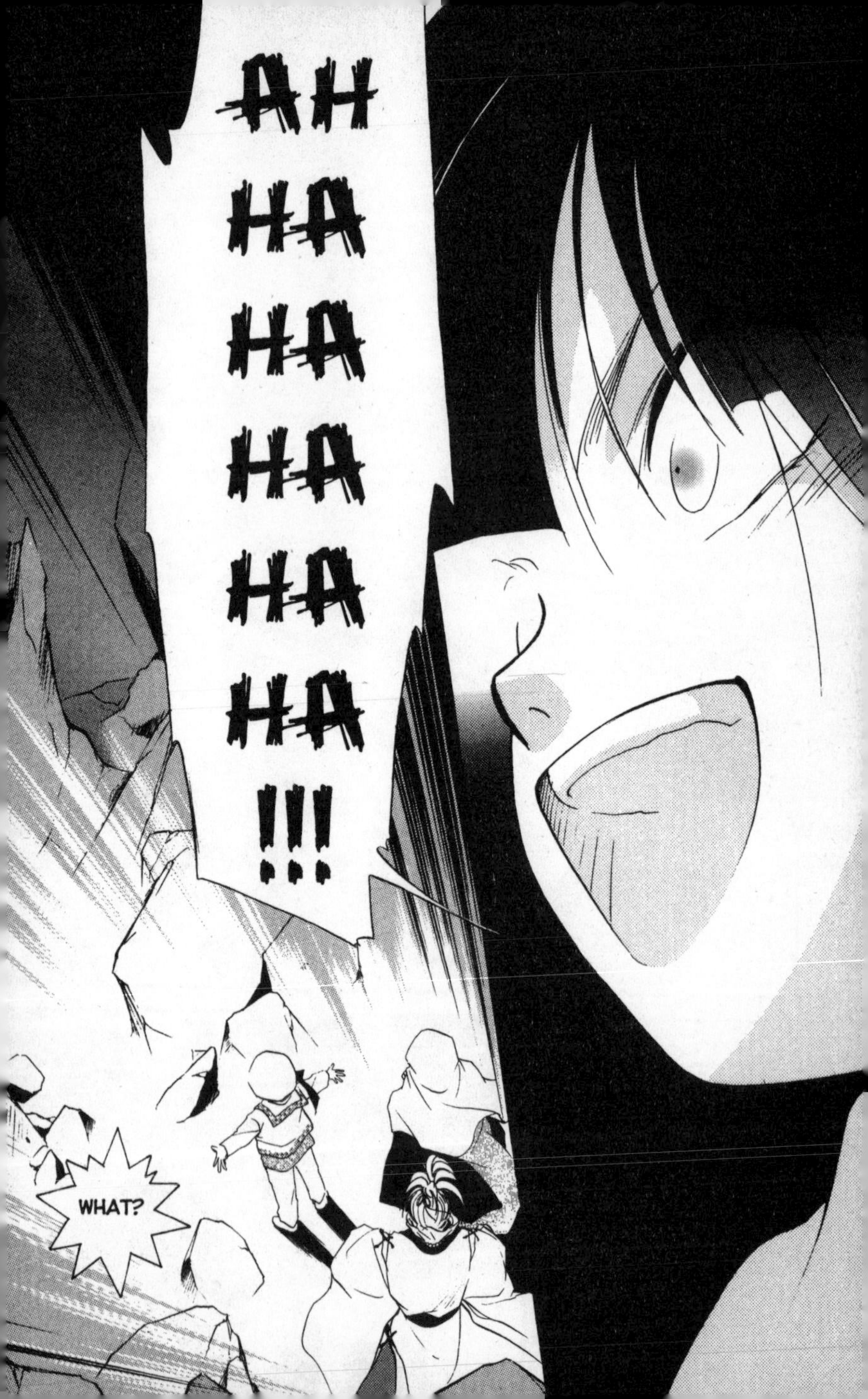
AH HA HA HA HA HA !!!
WHAT?

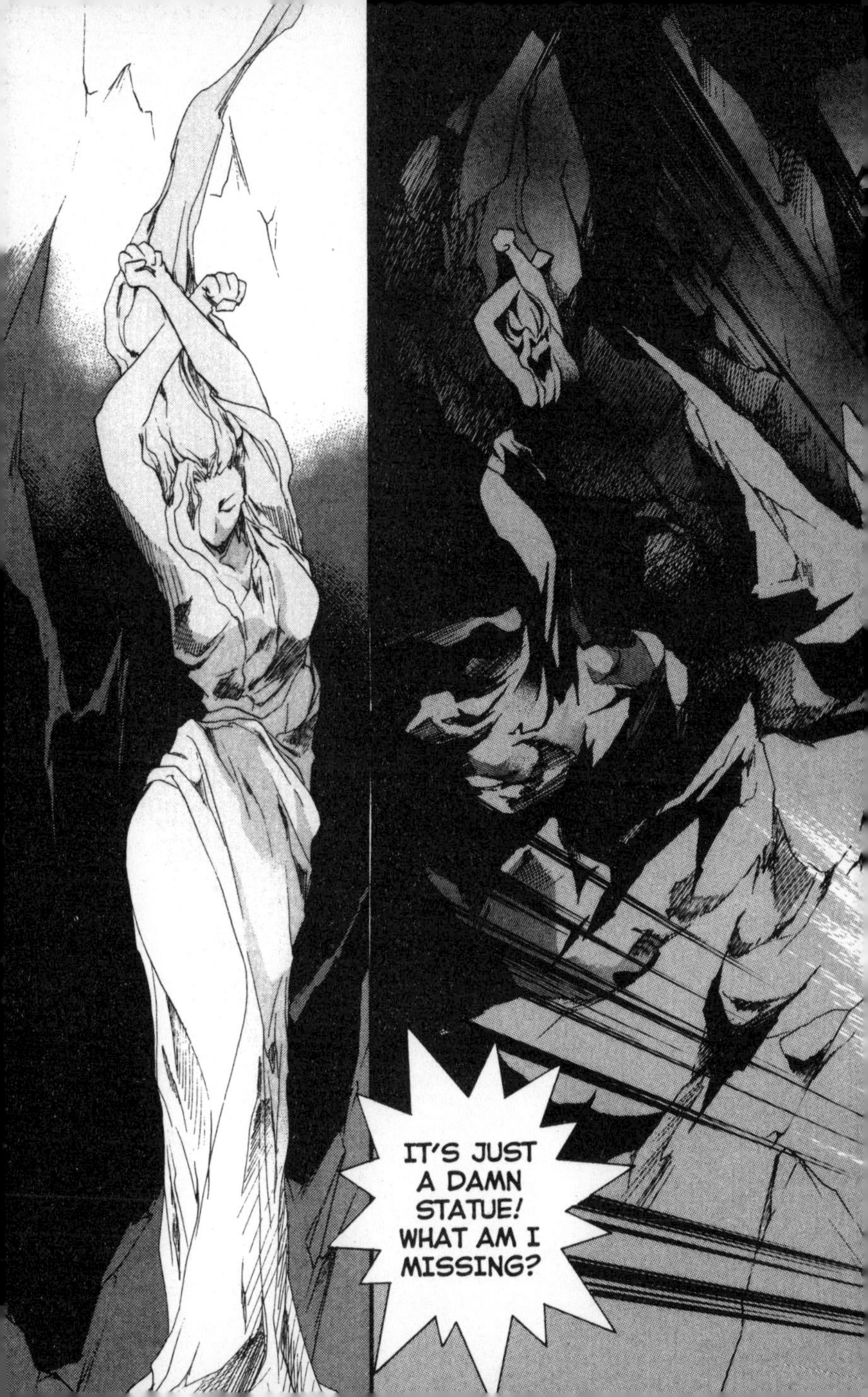
IT'S JUST A DAMN STATUE! WHAT AM I MISSING?

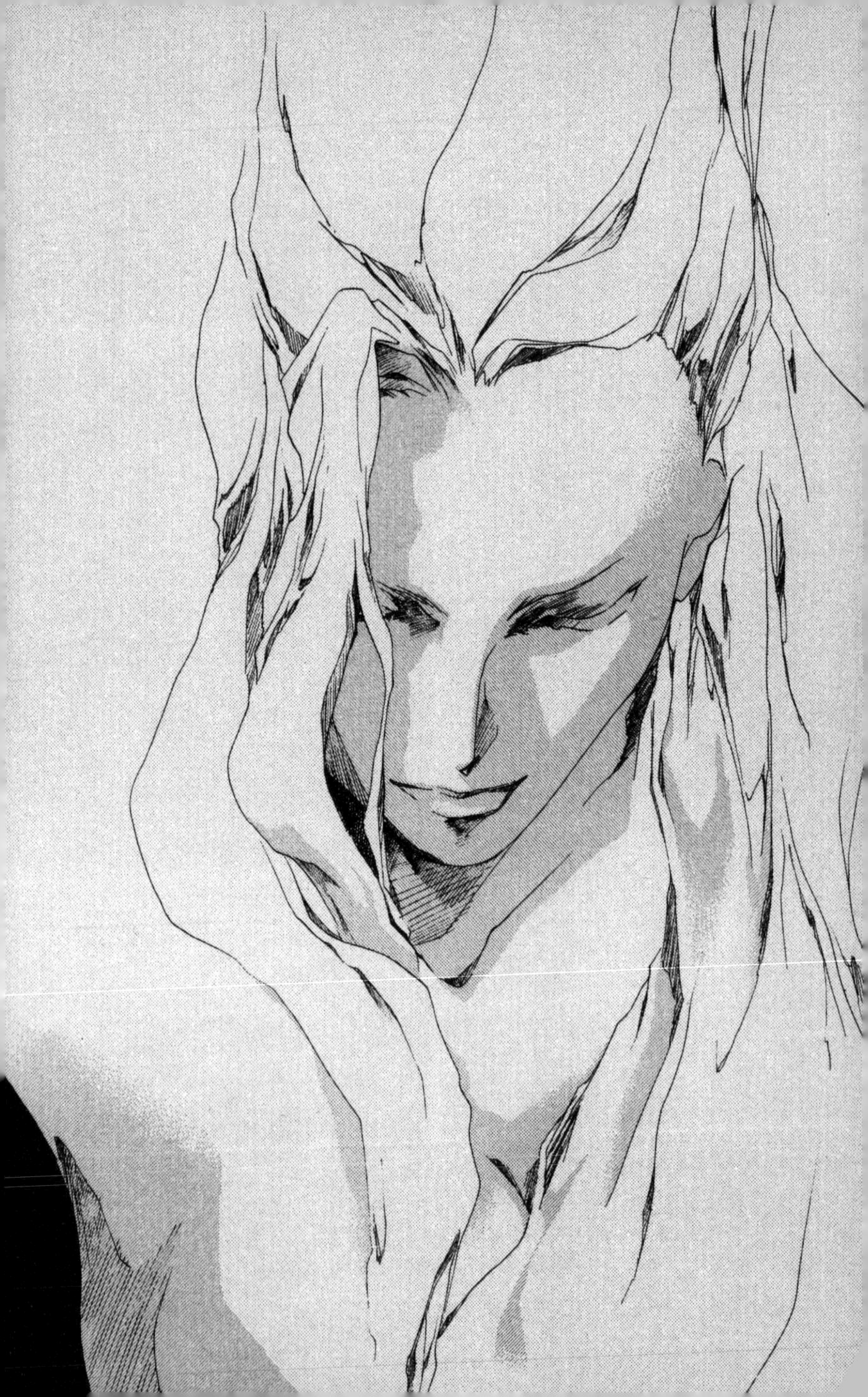

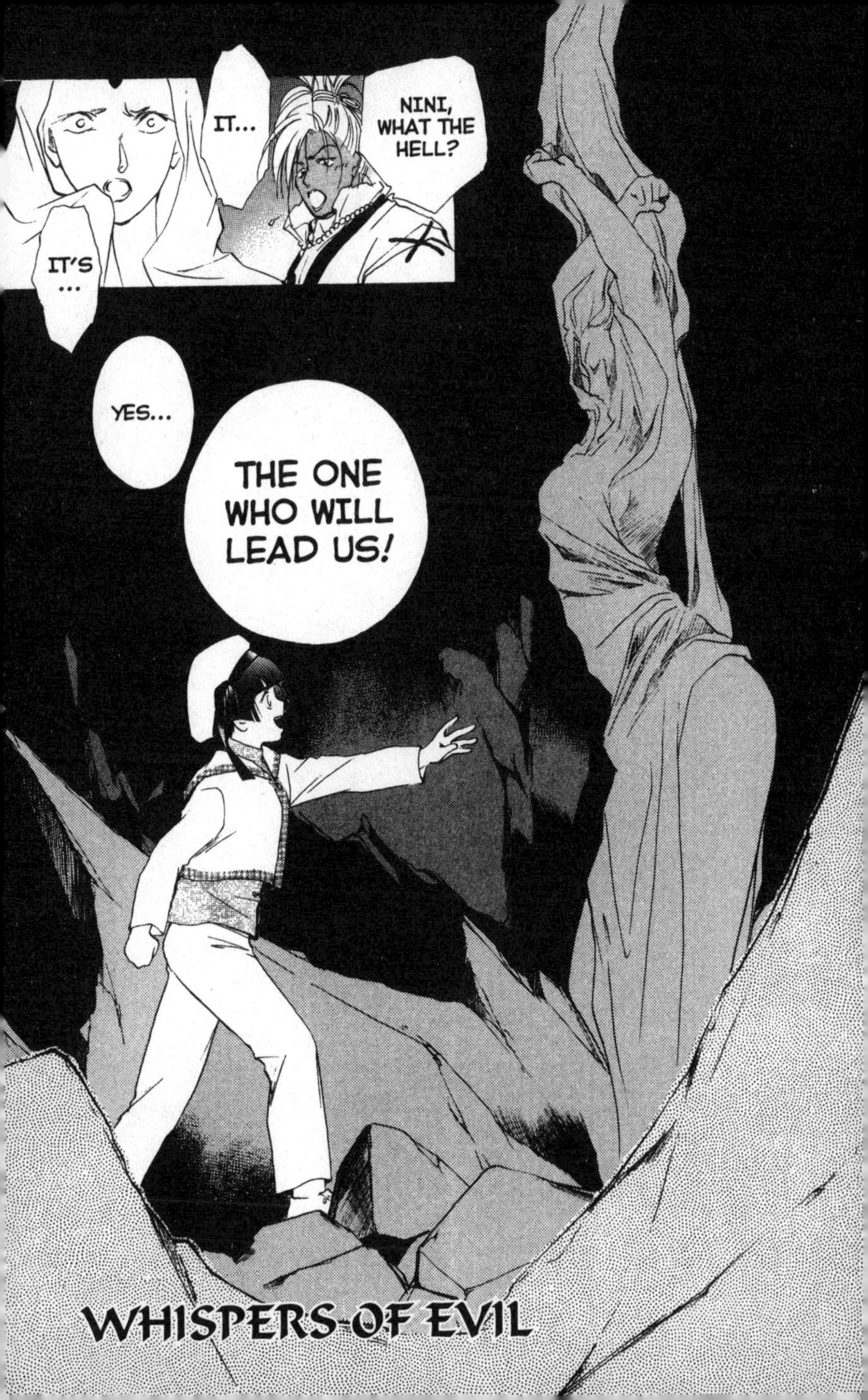
NINI, WHAT THE HELL?
IT...
IT'S ...
YES...
THE ONE WHO WILL LEAD US!
WHISPERS OF EVIL

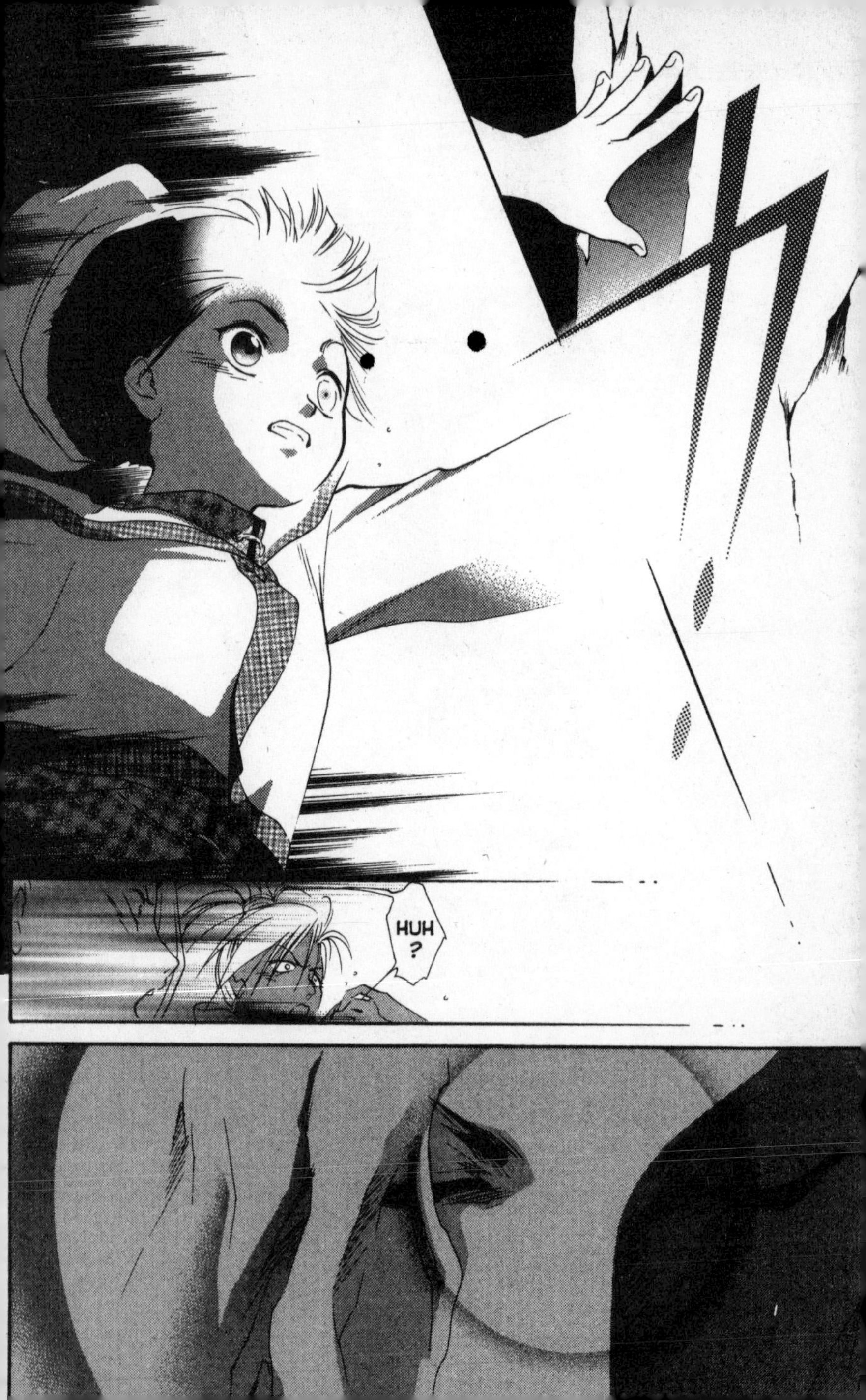
HUH ?

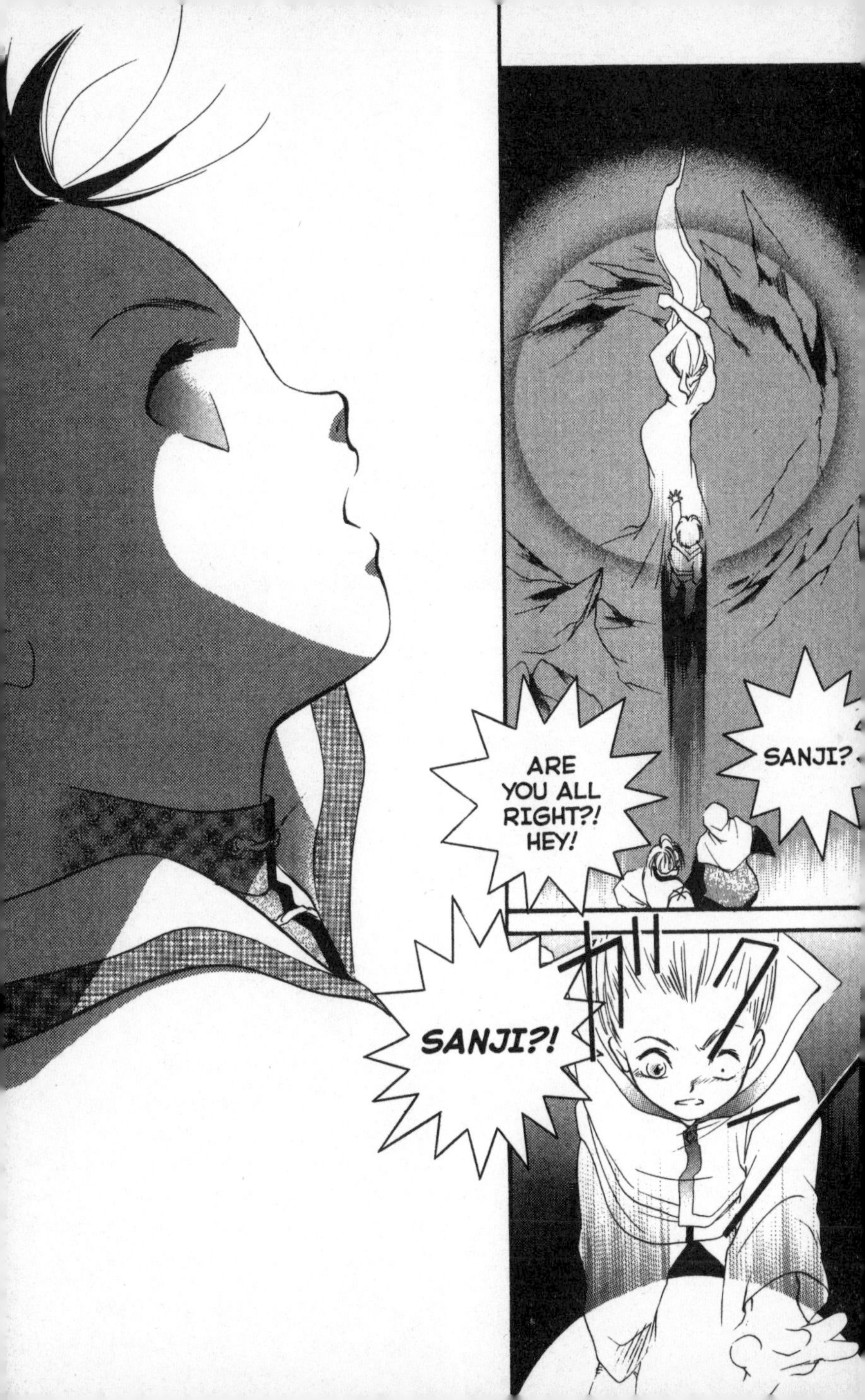
SANJI?
ARE YOU ALL RIGHT?! HEY!
SANJI?!

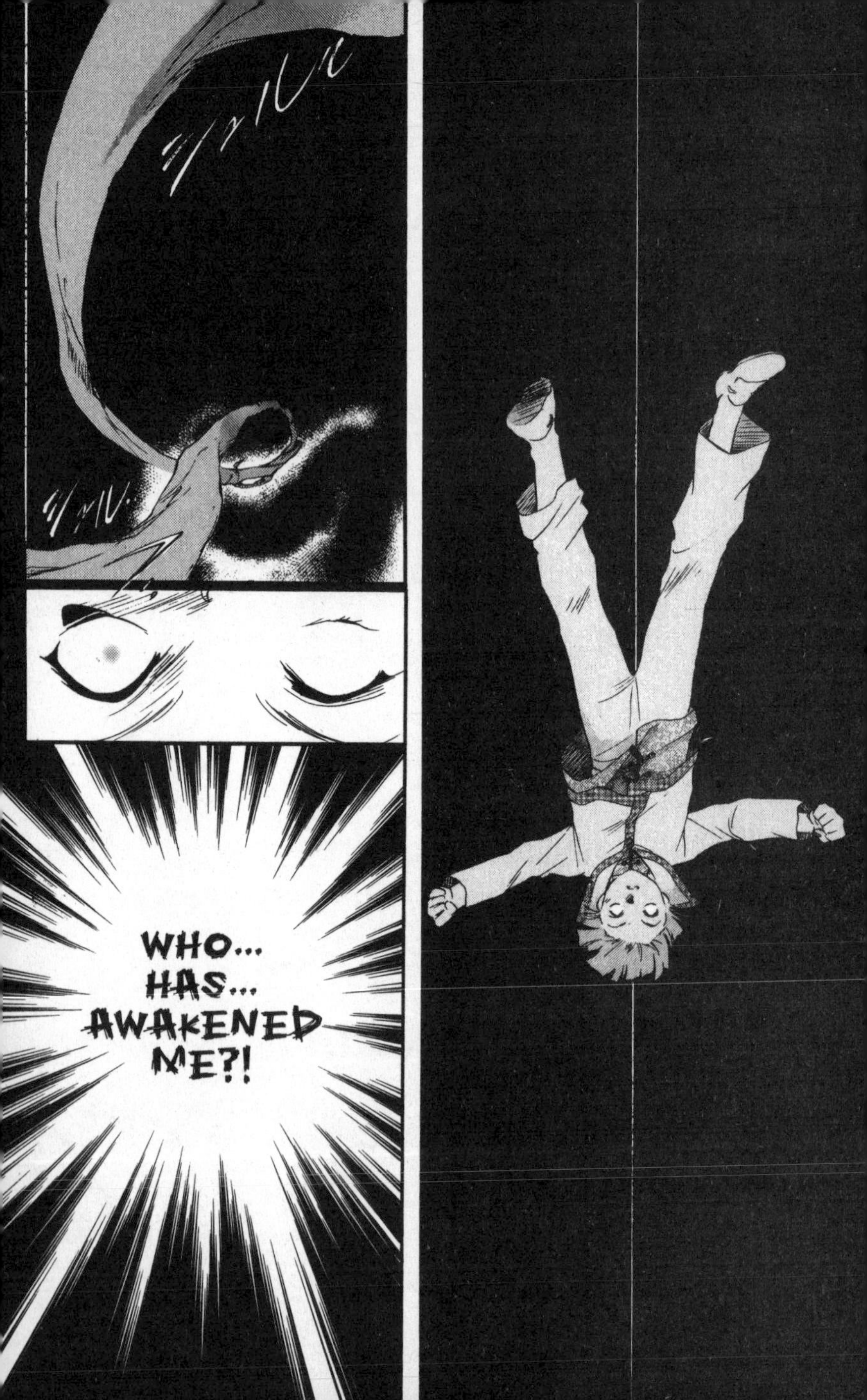
WHO... HAS... AWAKENED ME?!

MY DEAR SANJI...

YOU UNDER-STAND, DON'T YOU?

THAT VOICE...

I REMEMBER...

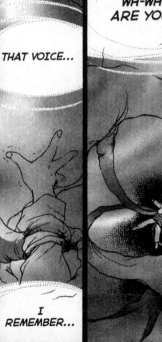

WH-WHO ARE YOU?!

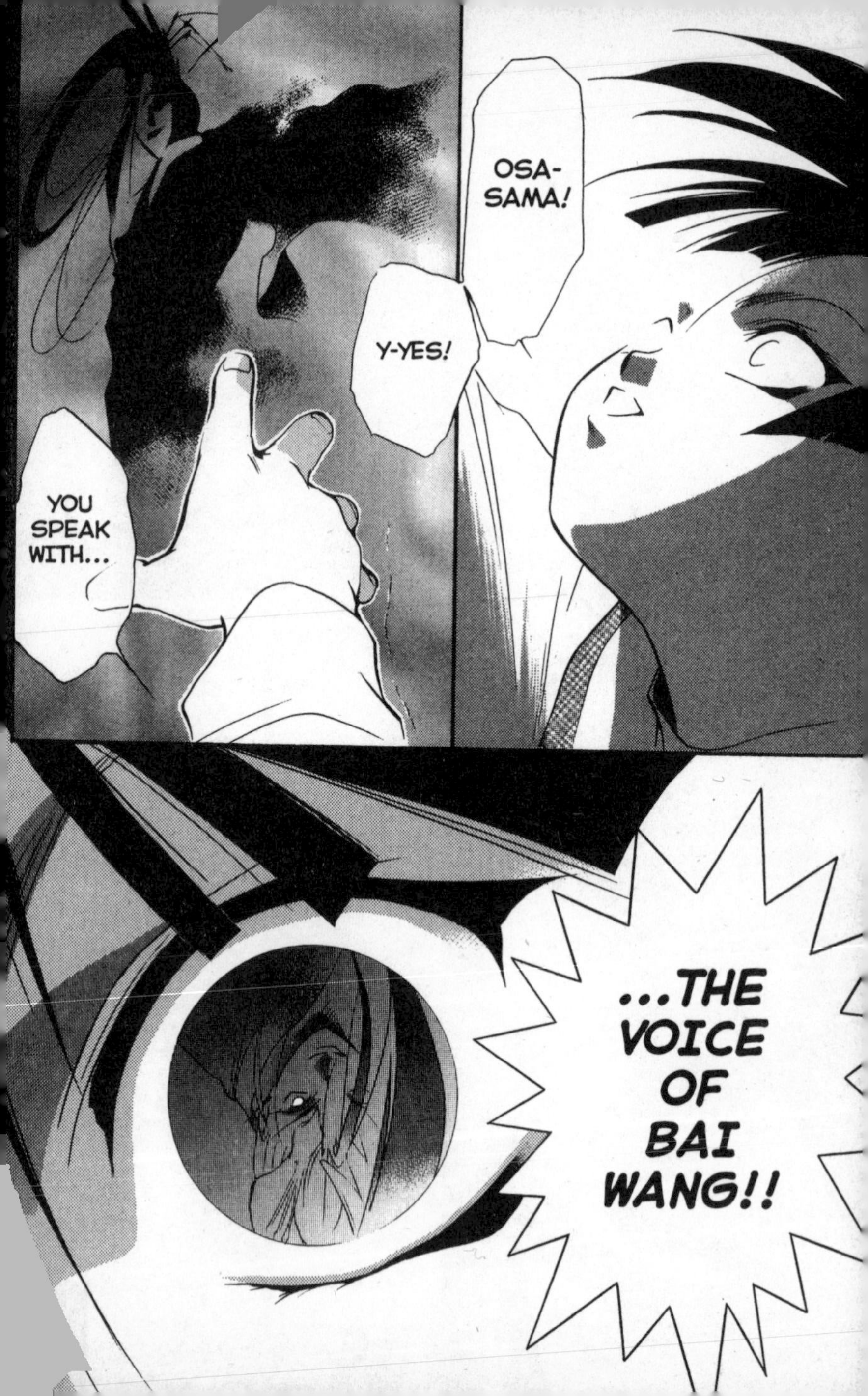
OSA-SAMA!
Y-YES!
YOU SPEAK WITH...
...THE VOICE OF BAI WANG!!

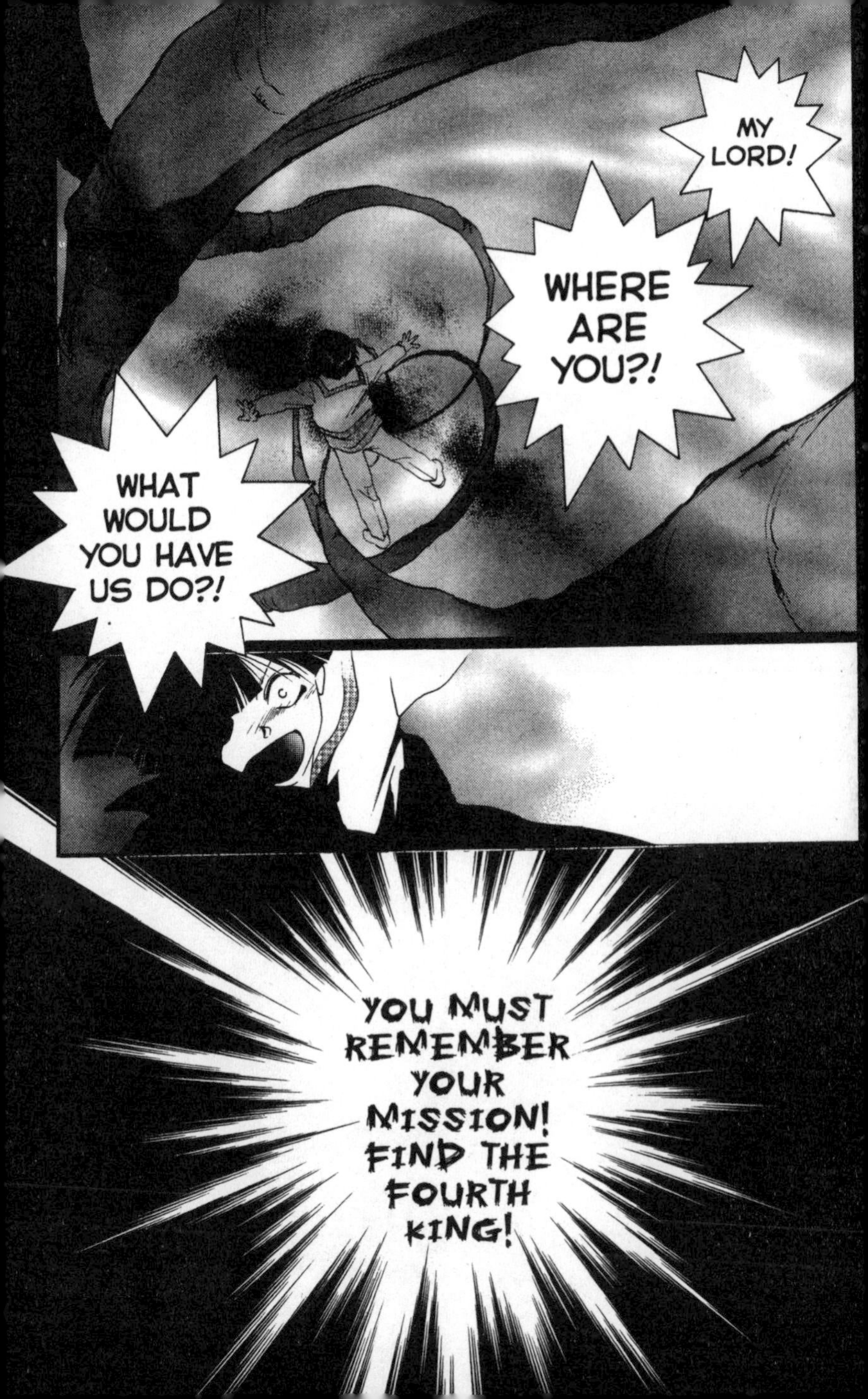
MY LORD!
WHERE ARE YOU?!
WHAT WOULD YOU HAVE US DO?!
YOU MUST REMEMBER YOUR MISSION! FIND THE FOURTH KING!

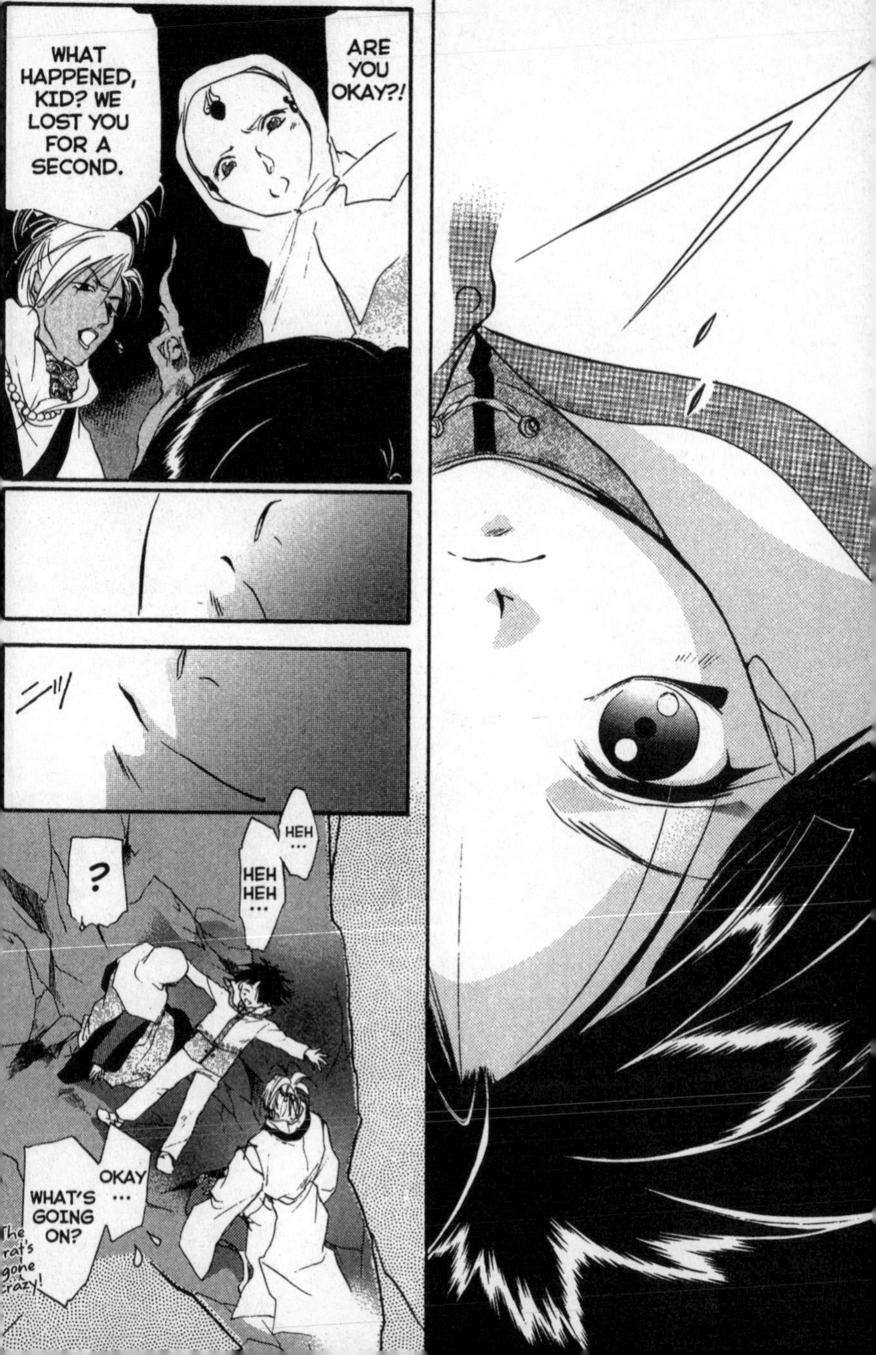
ARE YOU OKAY?!
WHAT HAPPENED, KID? WE LOST YOU FOR A SECOND.
ニッ
HEH ... HEH HEH ...
?
OKAY ... WHAT'S GOING ON?
The rat's gone crazy!

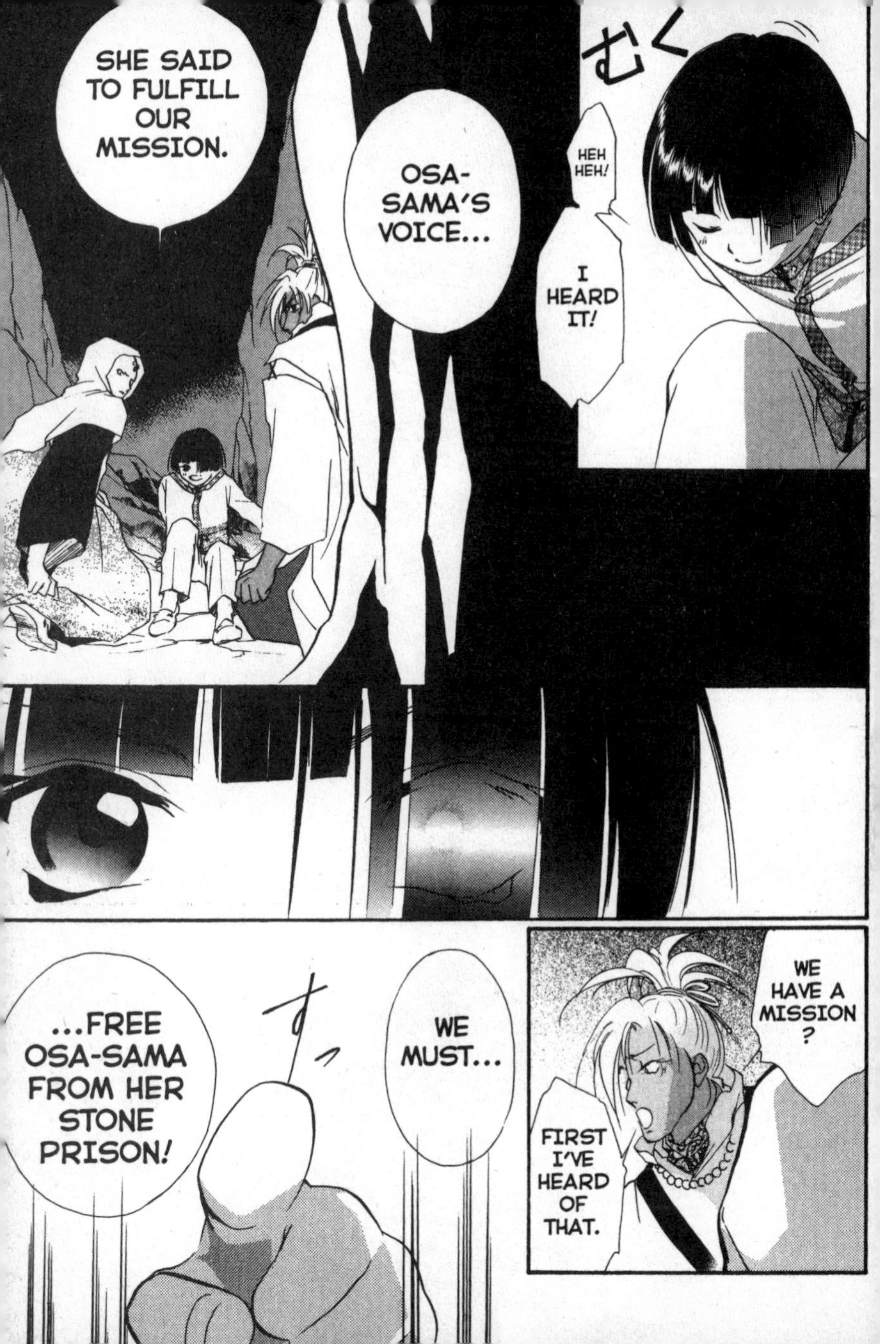
むく
HEH HEH!
I HEARD IT!
OSA-SAMA'S VOICE...
SHE SAID TO FULFILL OUR MISSION.
WE HAVE A MISSION?
FIRST I'VE HEARD OF THAT.
す
WE MUST...
...FREE OSA-SAMA FROM HER STONE PRISON!

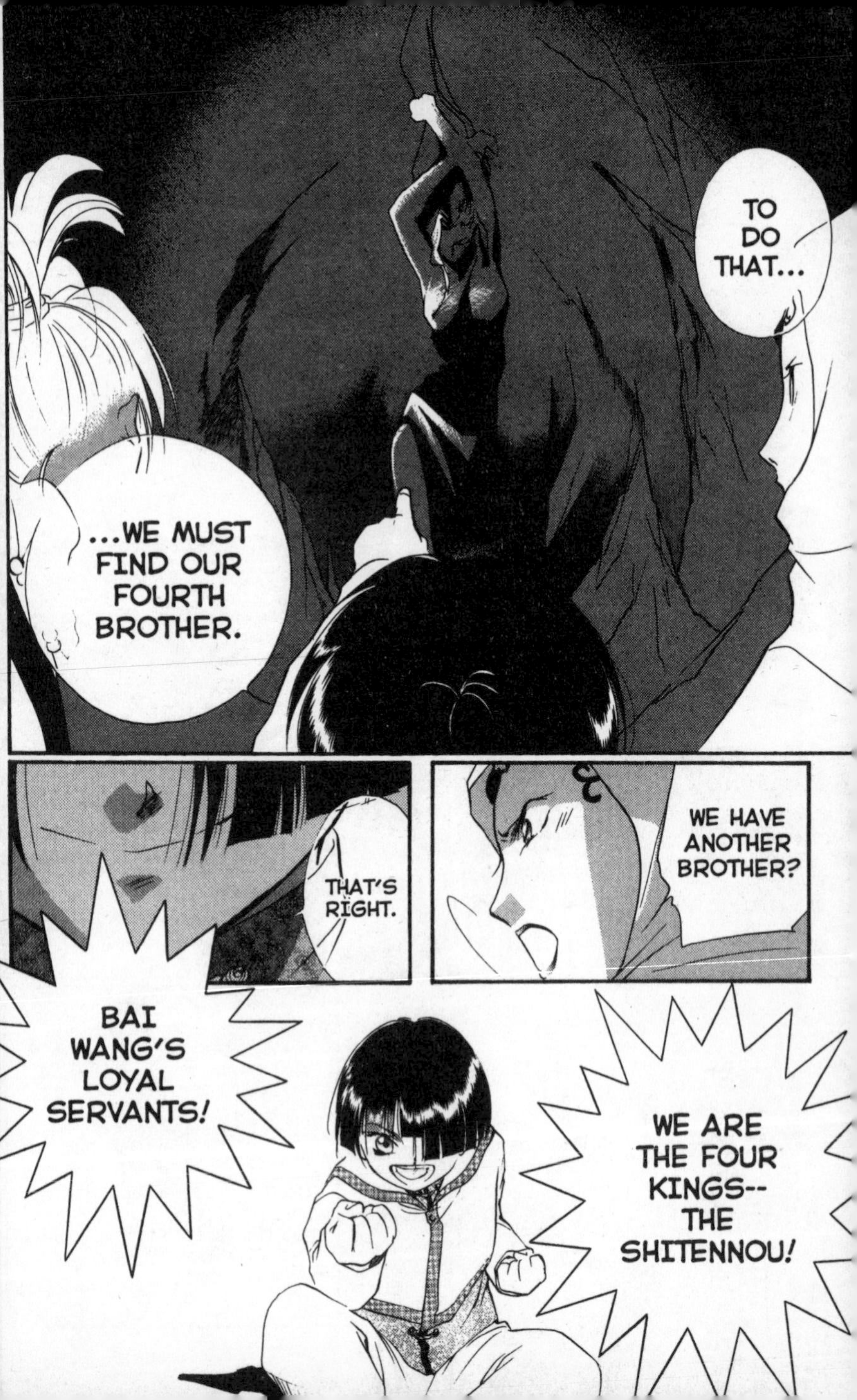
TO DO THAT...
...WE MUST FIND OUR FOURTH BROTHER.
WE HAVE ANOTHER BROTHER?
THAT'S RIGHT.
WE ARE THE FOUR KINGS-- THE SHITENNOU!
BAI WANG'S LOYAL SERVANTS!

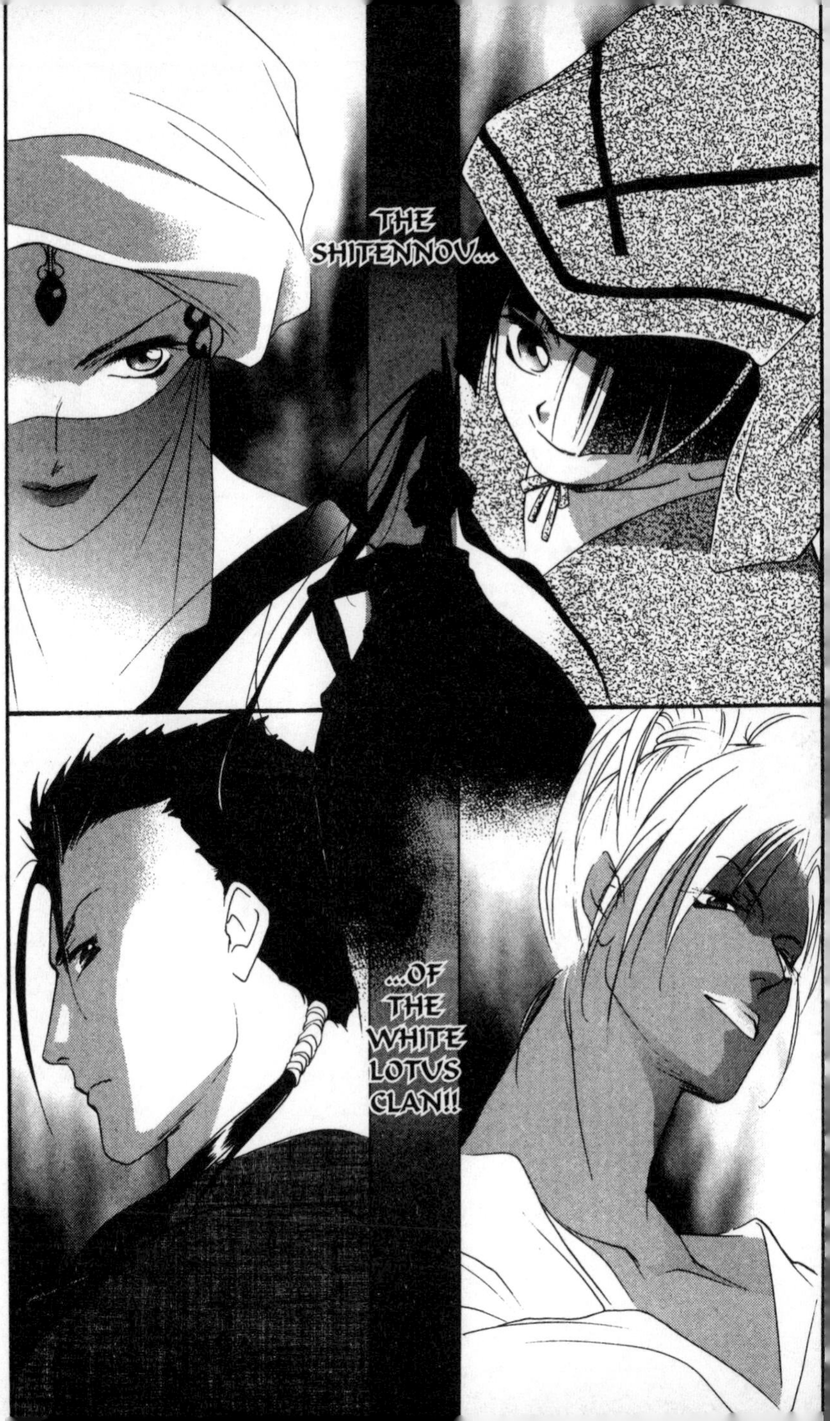
THE SHITENNOU...
...OF THE WHITE LOTUS CLAN!!

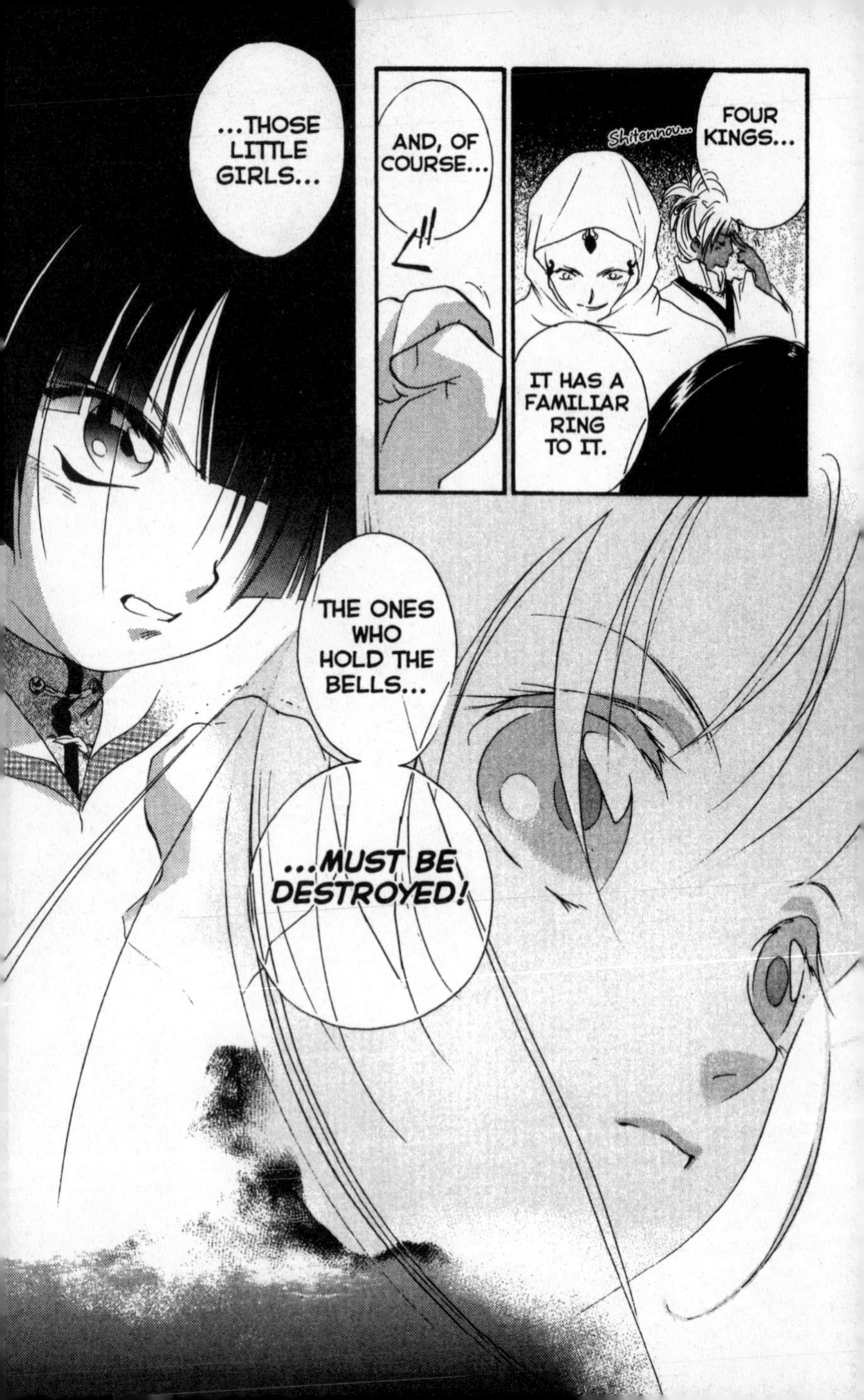
FOUR KINGS...
Shitennou...
IT HAS A FAMILIAR RING TO IT.
AND, OF COURSE...
...THOSE LITTLE GIRLS...
THE ONES WHO HOLD THE BELLS...
...MUST BE DESTROYED!

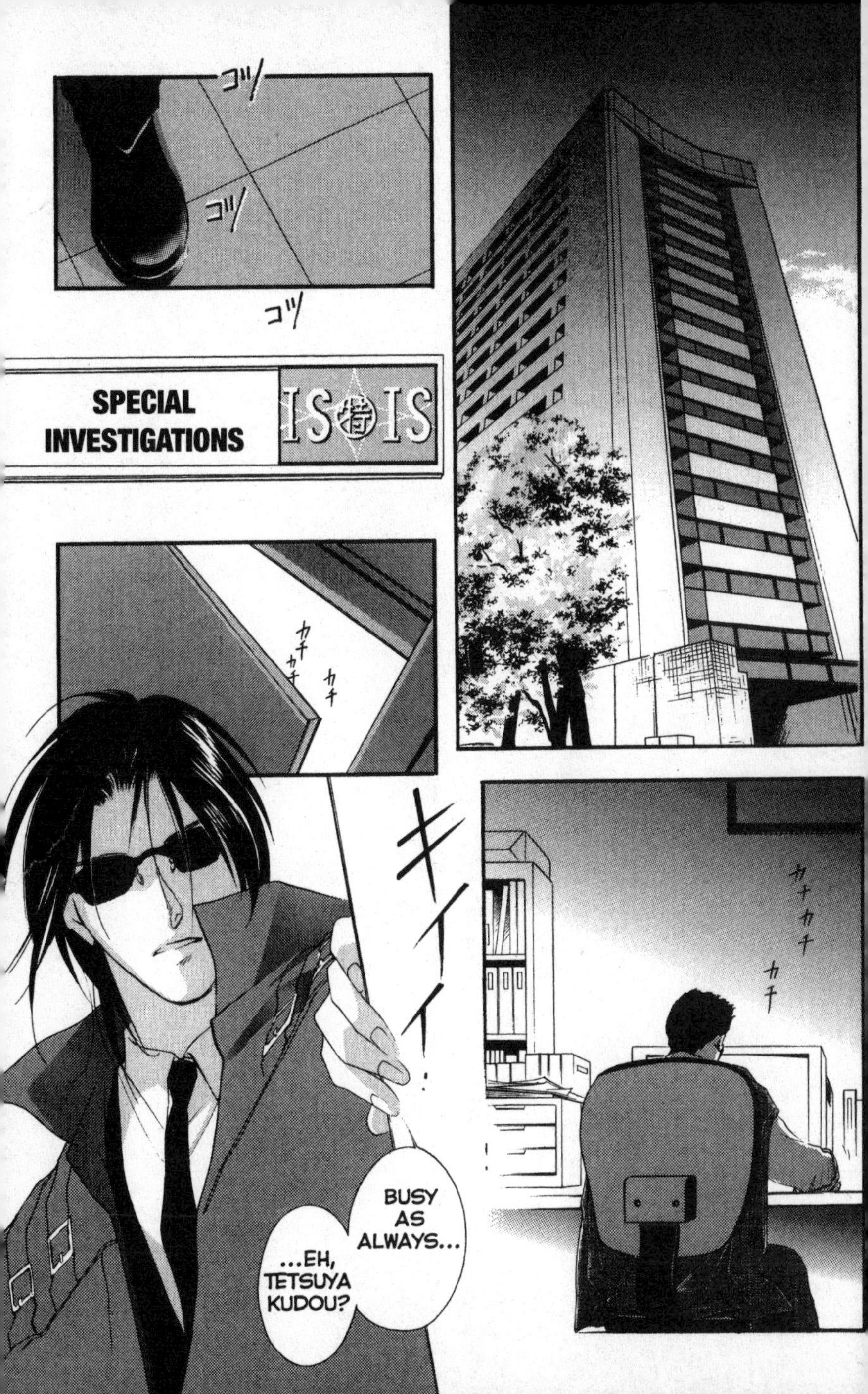
コツ
コツ
コツ
SPECIAL INVESTIGATIONS
カチ カチ カチ
カチ
カチカチ
カチ
キイイ!
BUSY AS ALWAYS...
...EH, TETSUYA KUDOU?

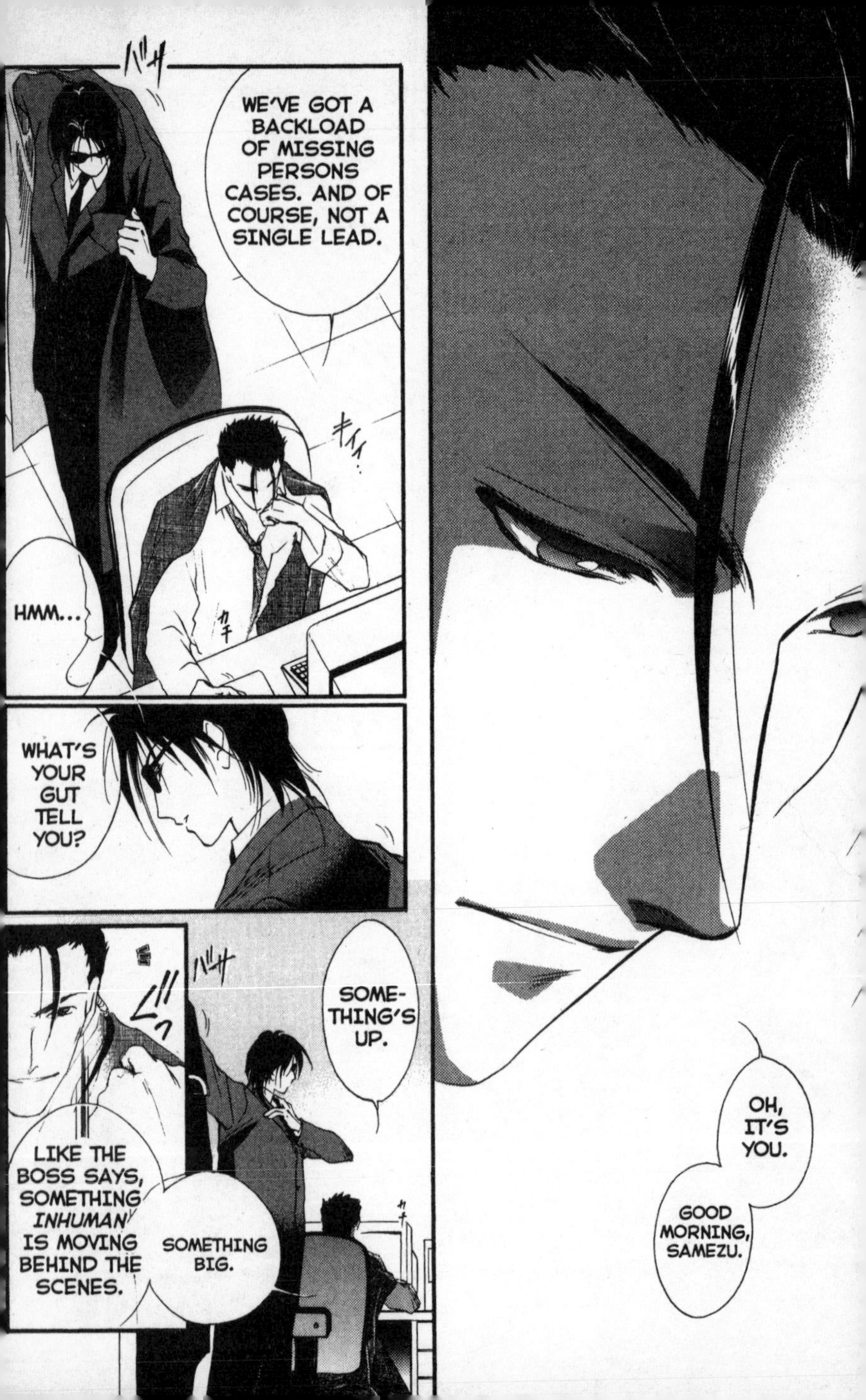
OH, IT'S YOU.
GOOD MORNING, SAMEZU.
WE'VE GOT A BACKLOAD OF MISSING PERSONS CASES. AND OF COURSE, NOT A SINGLE LEAD.
HMM...
WHAT'S YOUR GUT TELL YOU?
SOMETHING'S UP.
LIKE THE BOSS SAYS, SOMETHING *INHUMAN* IS MOVING BEHIND THE SCENES.
SOMETHING BIG.

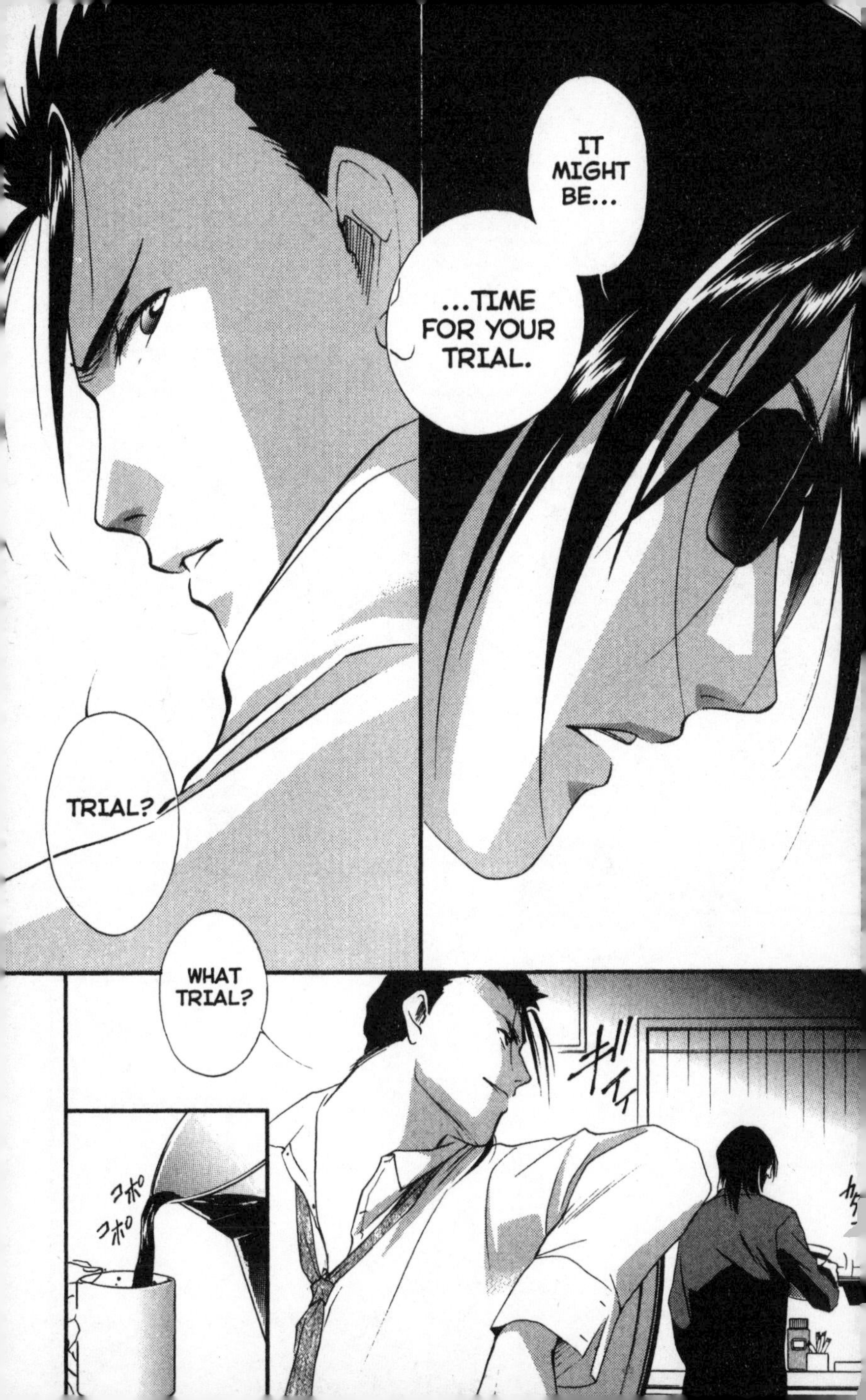
IT MIGHT BE...
...TIME FOR YOUR TRIAL.
TRIAL?
WHAT TRIAL?

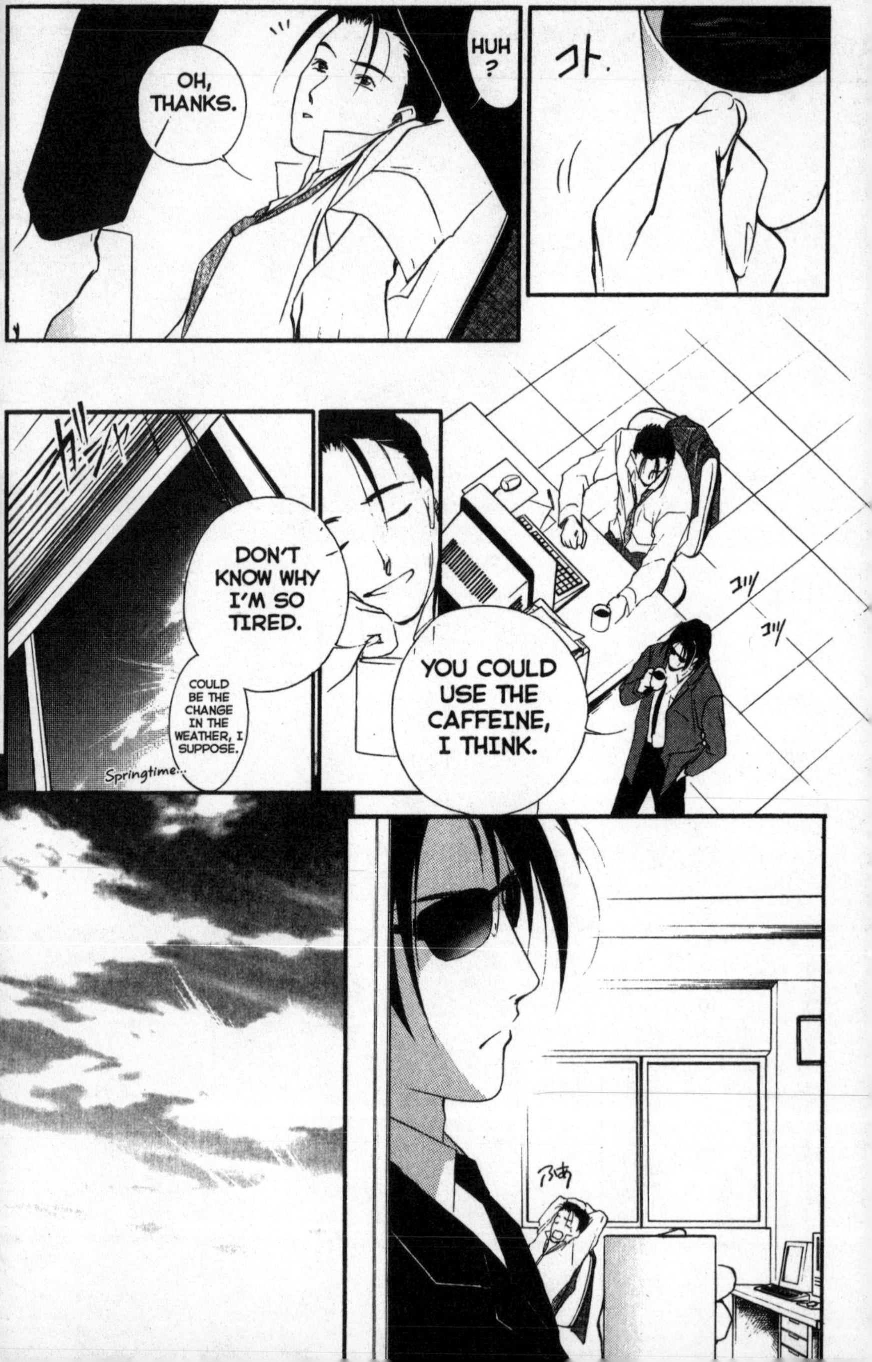
コト.
HUH?
OH, THANKS.
コツ
コツ
YOU COULD USE THE CAFFEINE, I THINK.
DON'T KNOW WHY I'M SO TIRED.
COULD BE THE CHANGE IN THE WEATHER, I SUPPOSE.
ガシャ
Springtime...
ふあ

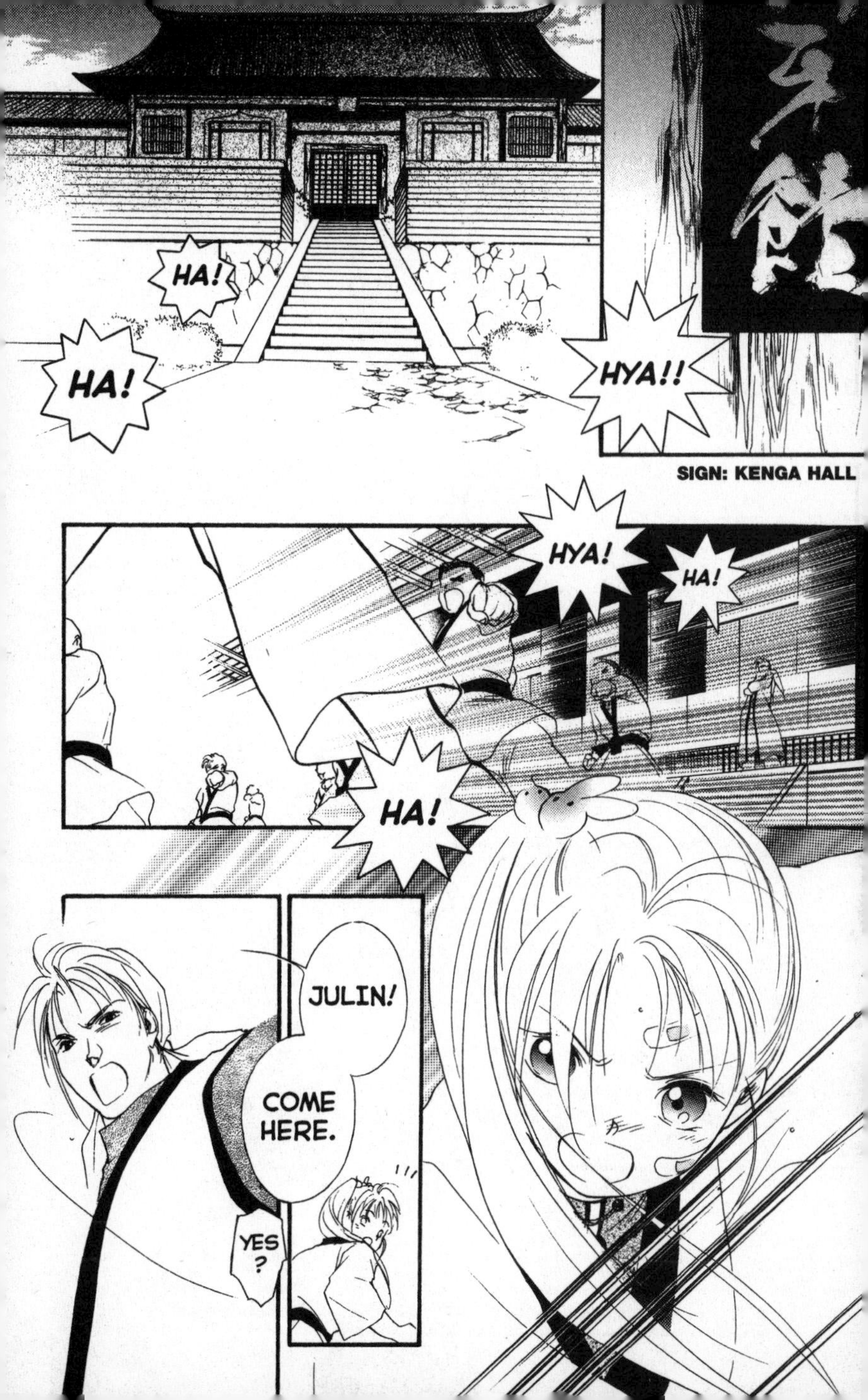
HYA!!
SIGN: KENGA HALL
HA!
HA!
HA!
HYA!
HA!
JULIN!
COME HERE.
YES?

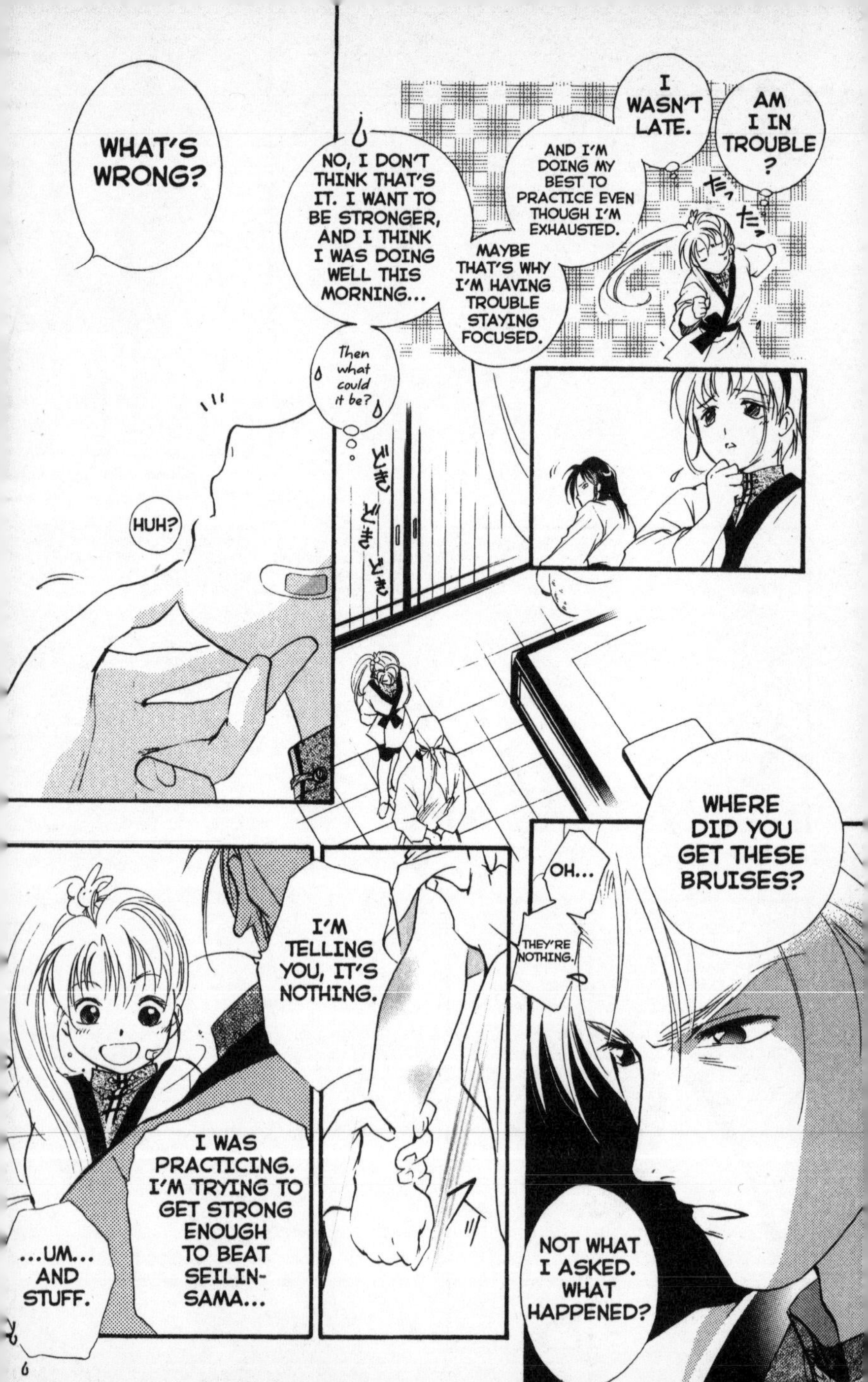
AM I IN TROUBLE?
I WASN'T LATE.
AND I'M DOING MY BEST TO PRACTICE EVEN THOUGH I'M EXHAUSTED.
MAYBE THAT'S WHY I'M HAVING TROUBLE STAYING FOCUSED.
NO, I DON'T THINK THAT'S IT. I WANT TO BE STRONGER, AND I THINK I WAS DOING WELL THIS MORNING...
Then what could it be?
WHAT'S WRONG?
HUH?
WHERE DID YOU GET THESE BRUISES?
OH...
THEY'RE NOTHING.
NOT WHAT I ASKED. WHAT HAPPENED?
I'M TELLING YOU, IT'S NOTHING.
I WAS PRACTICING. I'M TRYING TO GET STRONG ENOUGH TO BEAT SEILIN-SAMA...
...UM... AND STUFF.

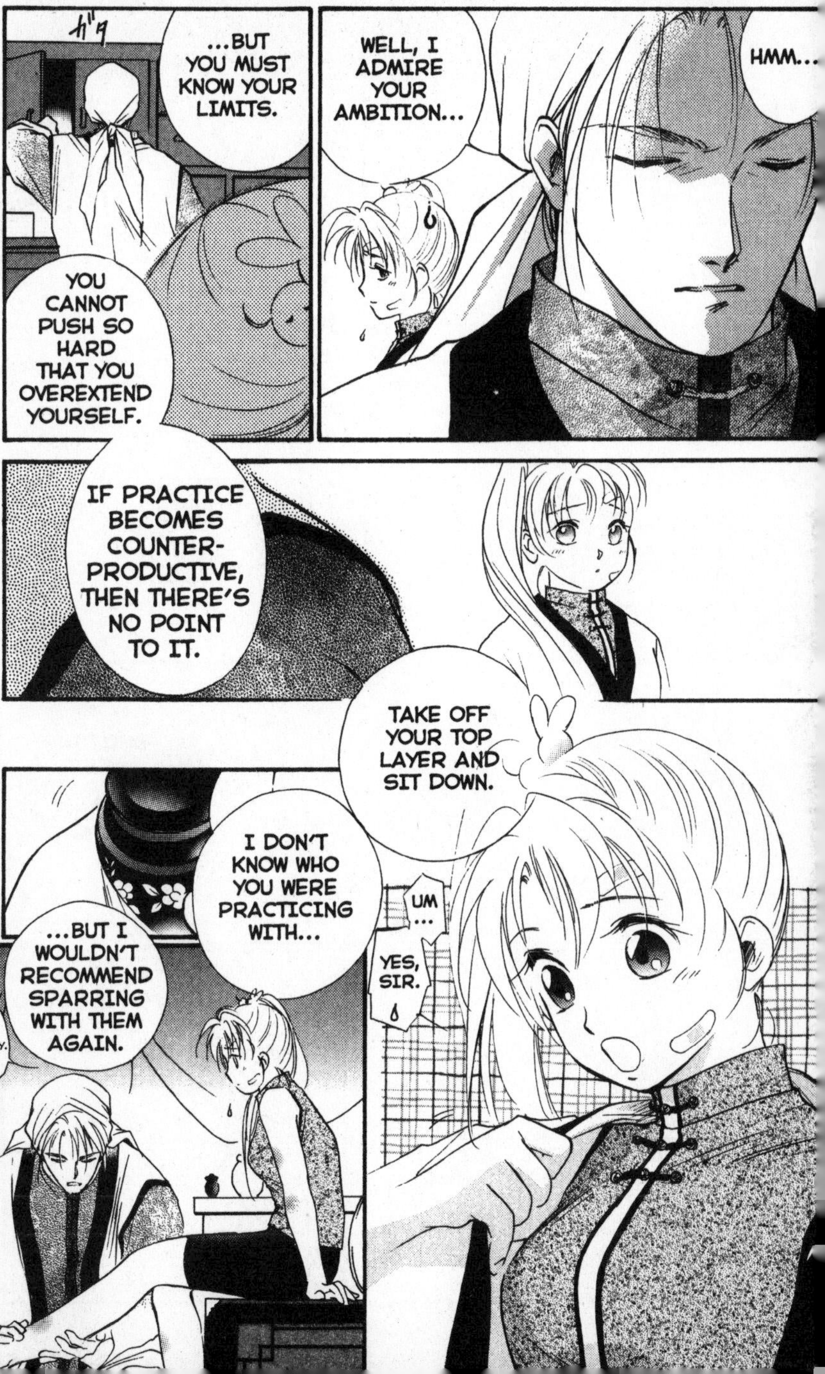
HMM...
WELL, I ADMIRE YOUR AMBITION...
ガタ
...BUT YOU MUST KNOW YOUR LIMITS.
YOU CANNOT PUSH SO HARD THAT YOU OVEREXTEND YOURSELF.
IF PRACTICE BECOMES COUNTER-PRODUCTIVE, THEN THERE'S NO POINT TO IT.
TAKE OFF YOUR TOP LAYER AND SIT DOWN.
UM...
YES, SIR.
I DON'T KNOW WHO YOU WERE PRACTICING WITH...
...BUT I WOULDN'T RECOMMEND SPARRING WITH THEM AGAIN.
SORRY.

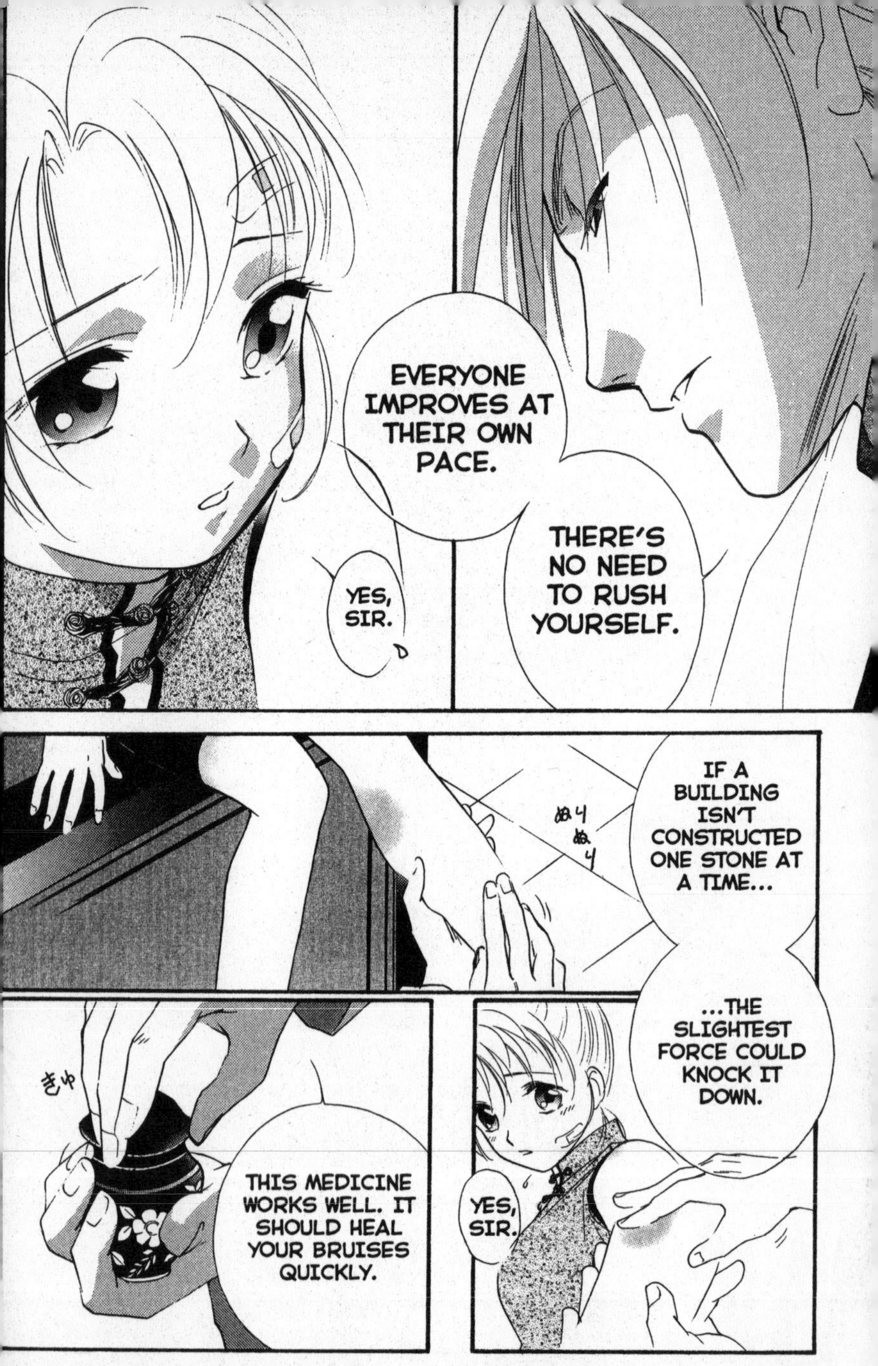
EVERYONE IMPROVES AT THEIR OWN PACE.
THERE'S NO NEED TO RUSH YOURSELF.
YES, SIR.
IF A BUILDING ISN'T CONSTRUCTED ONE STONE AT A TIME...
ぬりぬり
...THE SLIGHTEST FORCE COULD KNOCK IT DOWN.
YES, SIR.
きゅ
THIS MEDICINE WORKS WELL. IT SHOULD HEAL YOUR BRUISES QUICKLY.

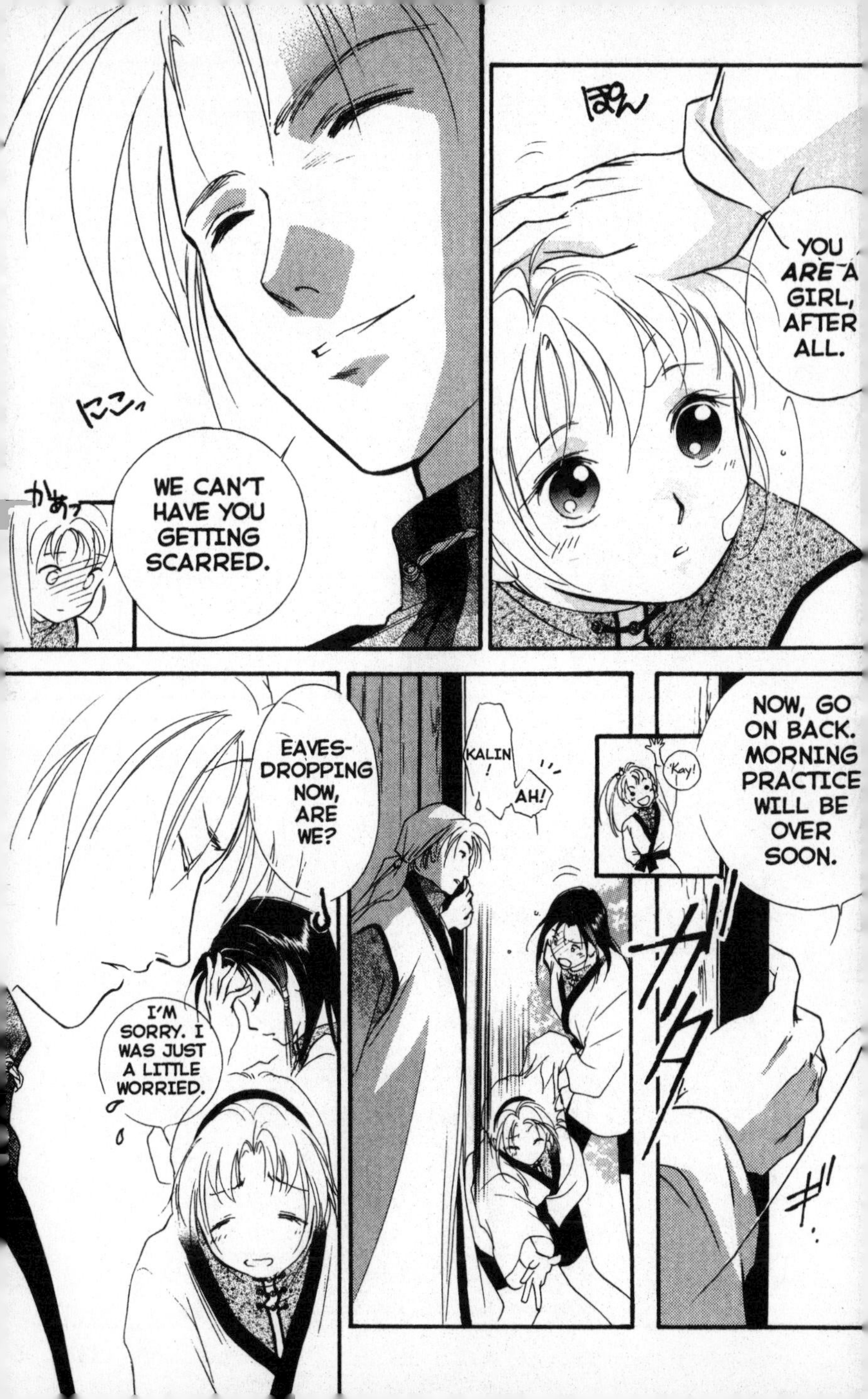

ぽん
YOU ARE A GIRL, AFTER ALL.
にこっ
WE CAN'T HAVE YOU GETTING SCARRED.
かぁっ
NOW, GO ON BACK. MORNING PRACTICE WILL BE OVER SOON.
'Kay!
KALIN!
AH!
EAVES-DROPPING NOW, ARE WE?
I'M SORRY. I WAS JUST A LITTLE WORRIED.

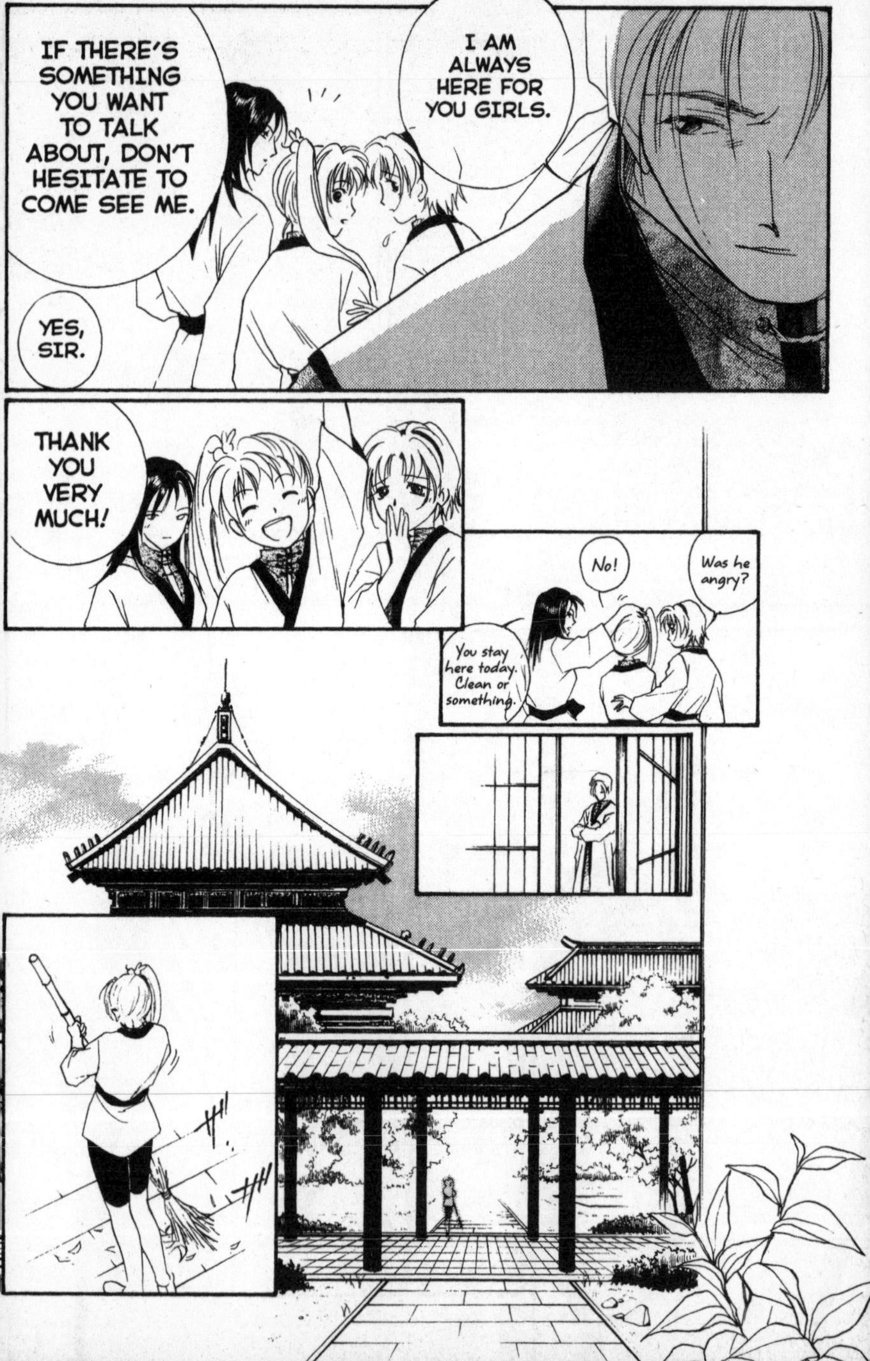
I AM ALWAYS HERE FOR YOU GIRLS.
IF THERE'S SOMETHING YOU WANT TO TALK ABOUT, DON'T HESITATE TO COME SEE ME.
YES, SIR.
THANK YOU VERY MUCH!
Was he angry?
No!
You stay here today. Clean or something.

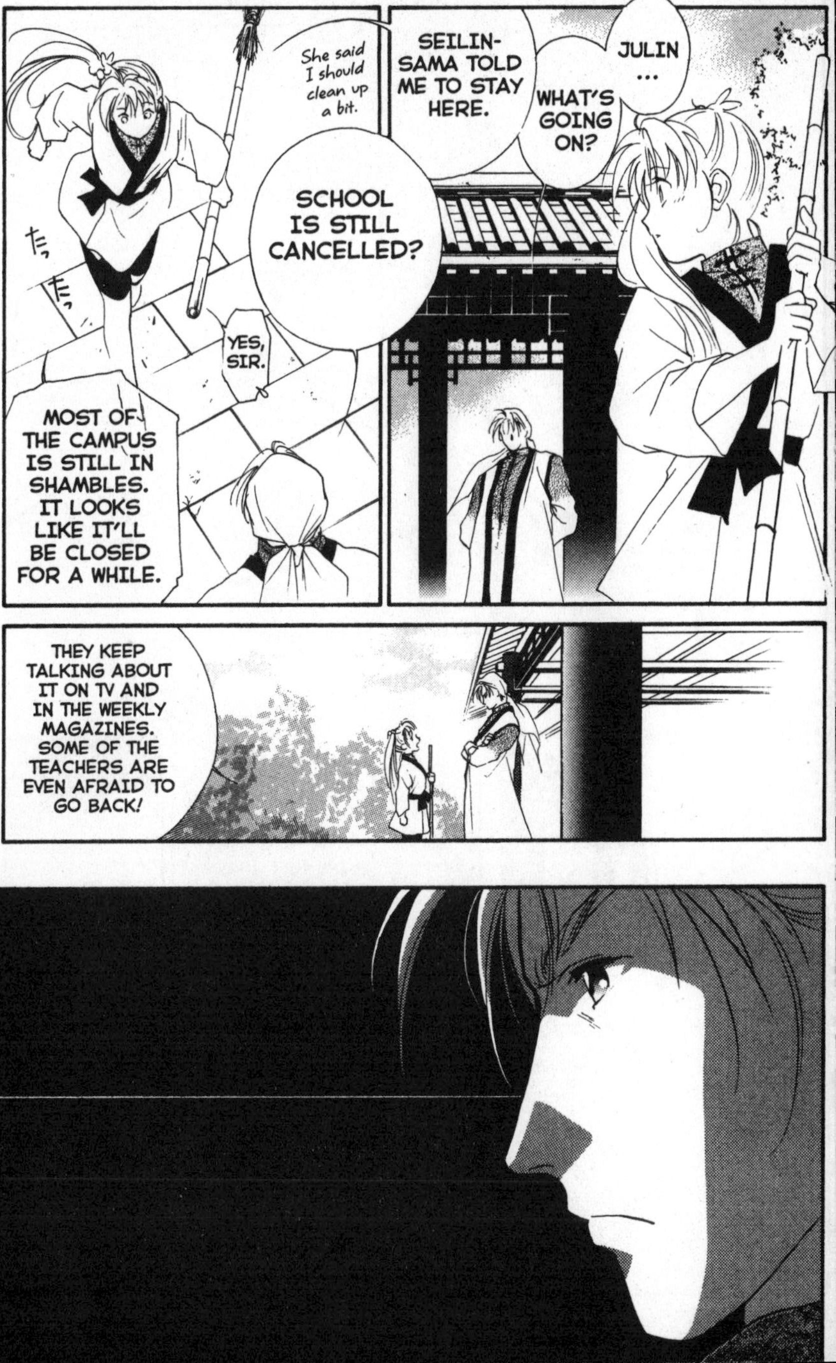
JULIN ...
WHAT'S GOING ON?
SEILIN-SAMA TOLD ME TO STAY HERE.
She said I should clean up a bit.
SCHOOL IS STILL CANCELLED?
YES, SIR.
MOST OF THE CAMPUS IS STILL IN SHAMBLES. IT LOOKS LIKE IT'LL BE CLOSED FOR A WHILE.
THEY KEEP TALKING ABOUT IT ON TV AND IN THE WEEKLY MAGAZINES. SOME OF THE TEACHERS ARE EVEN AFRAID TO GO BACK!

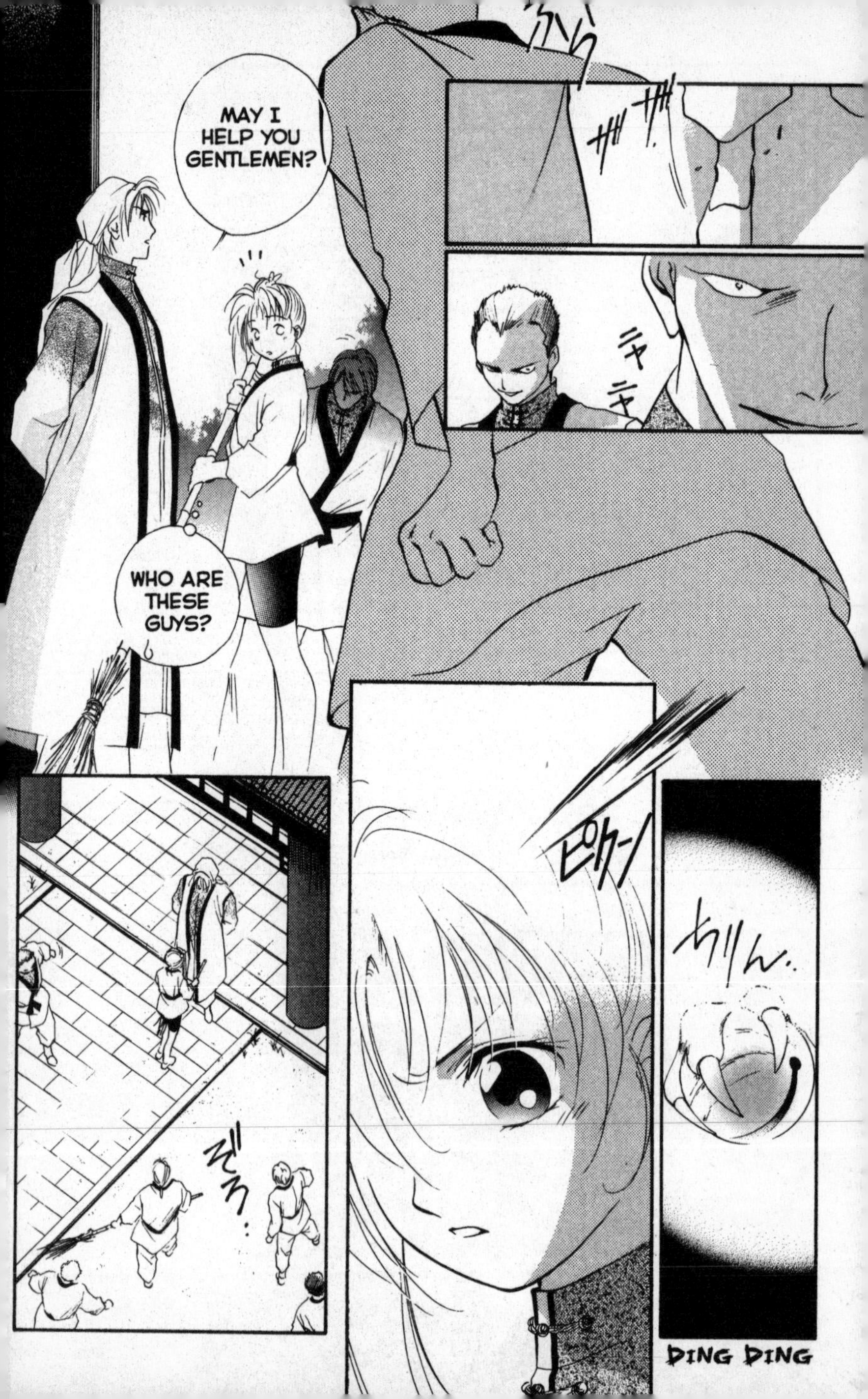
ニヤ
ニヤ
MAY I HELP YOU GENTLEMEN?
WHO ARE THESE GUYS?
DING DING

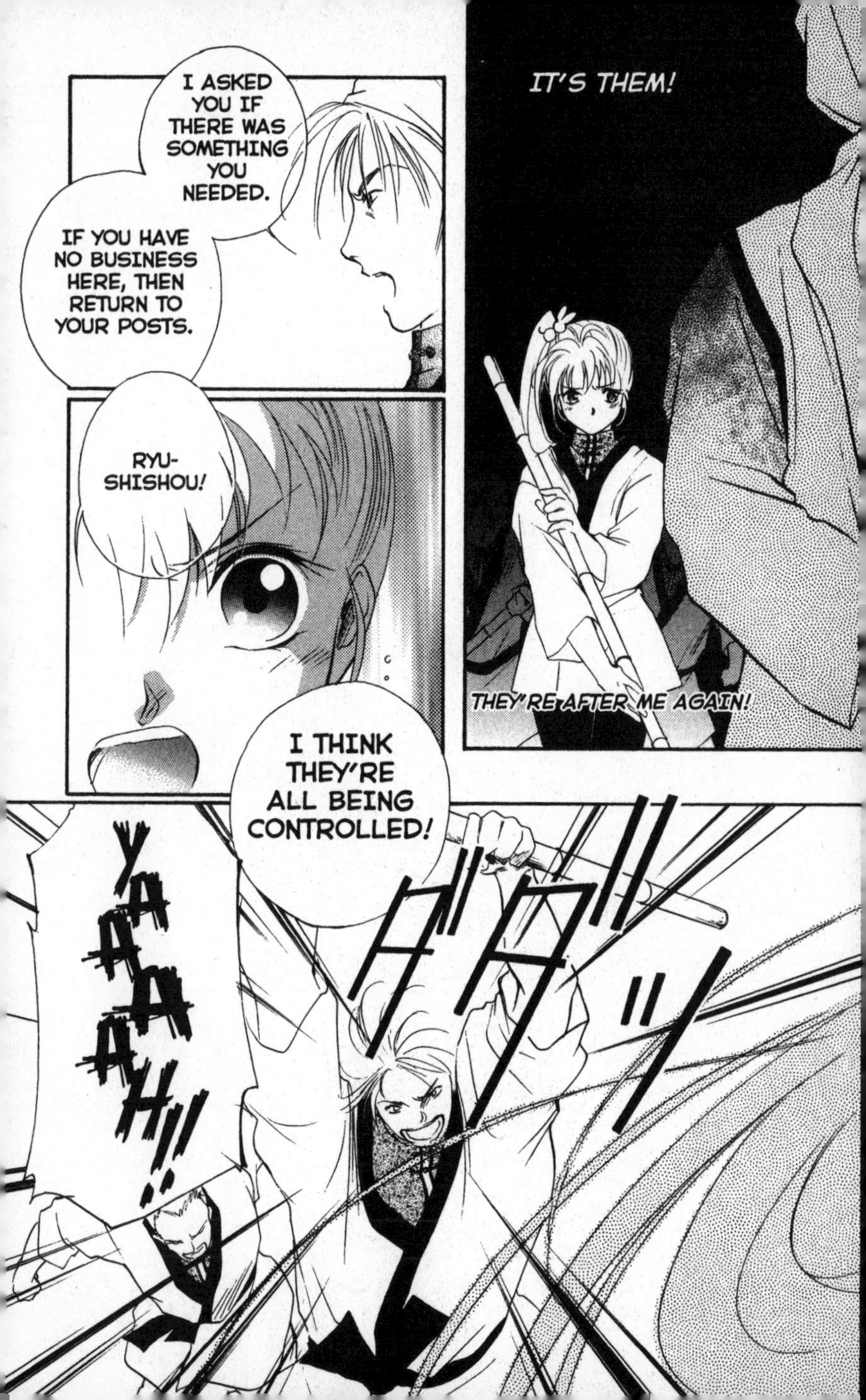

IT'S THEM!
THEY'RE AFTER ME AGAIN!
I ASKED YOU IF THERE WAS SOMETHING YOU NEEDED.
IF YOU HAVE NO BUSINESS HERE, THEN RETURN TO YOUR POSTS.
RYU-SHISHOU!
I THINK THEY'RE ALL BEING CONTROLLED!
ダダッ
YAAAAH!!

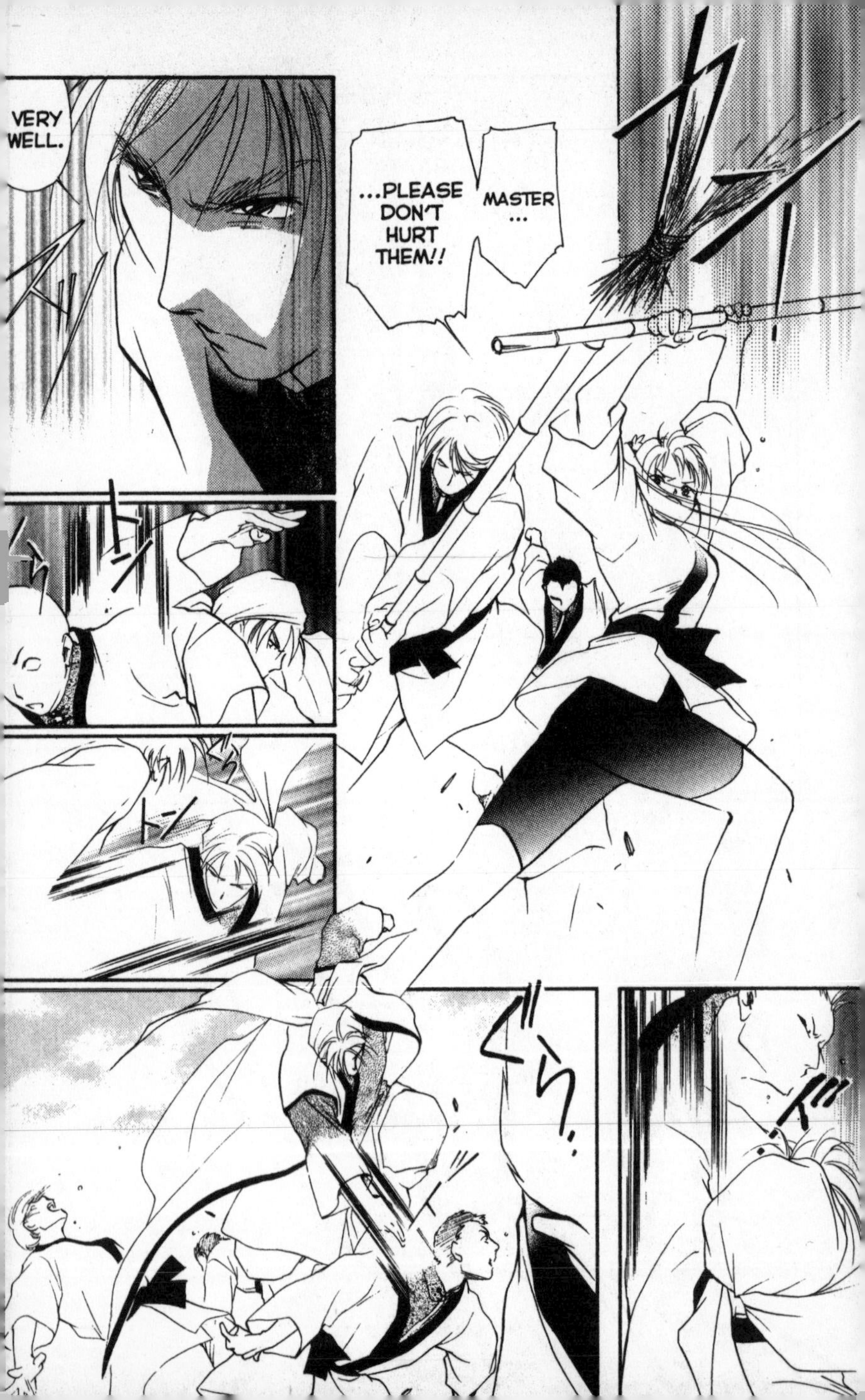
MASTER ...
...PLEASE DON'T HURT THEM!!
VERY WELL.

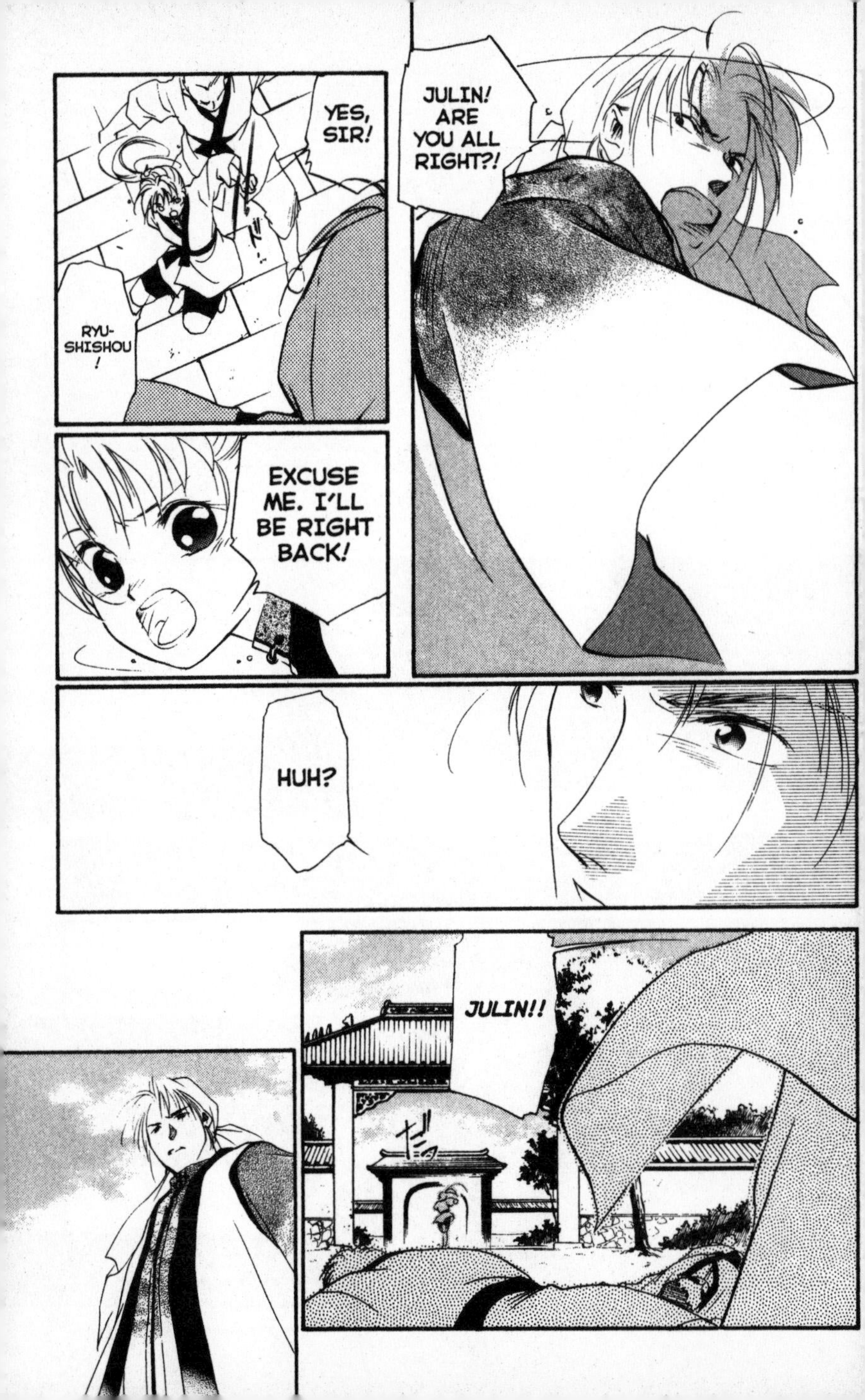
JULIN! ARE YOU ALL RIGHT?!
YES, SIR!
RYU-SHISHOU!
EXCUSE ME. I'LL BE RIGHT BACK!
HUH?
JULIN!!

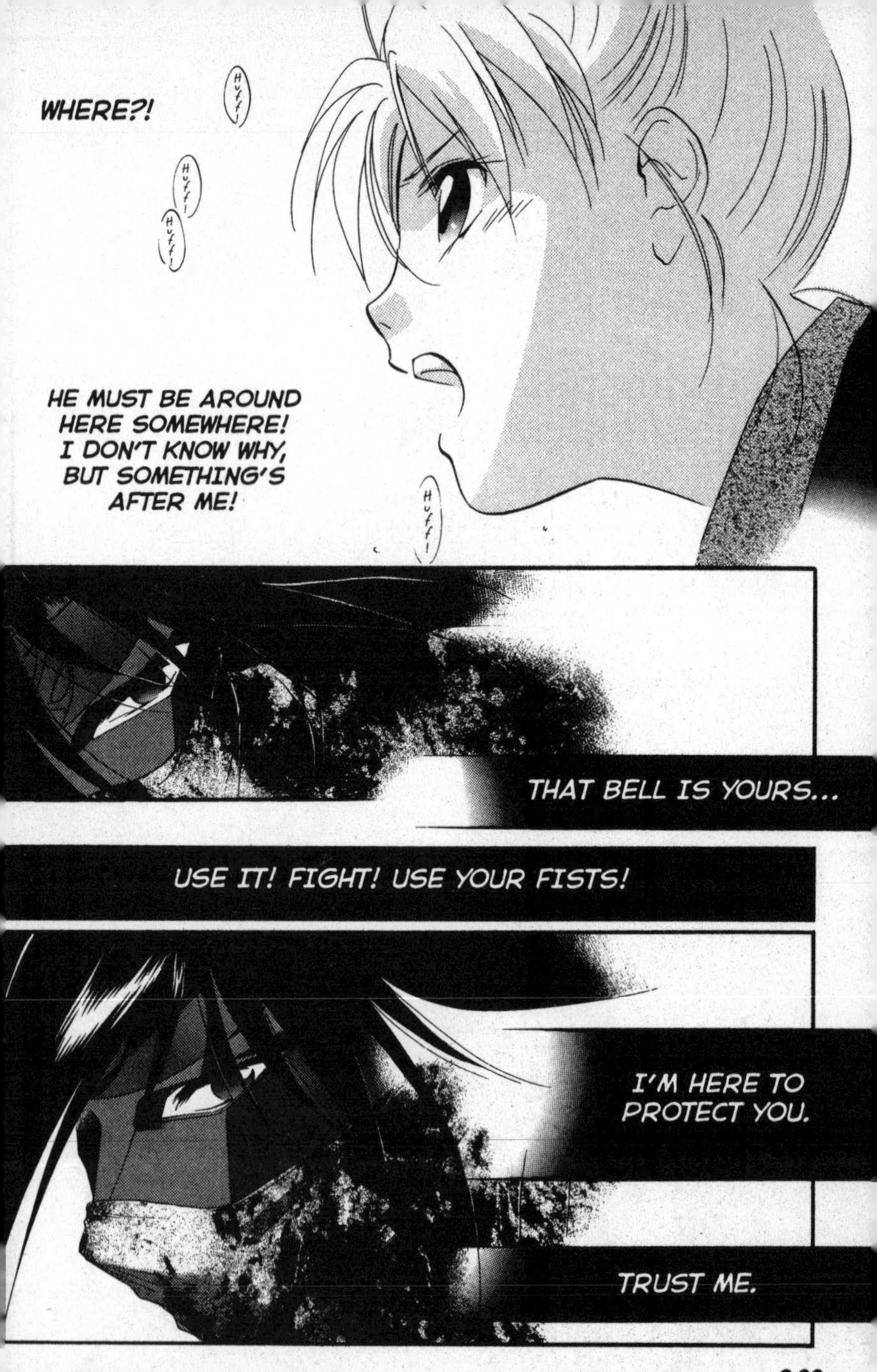
Huff!
WHERE?!
Huff!
Huff!
HE MUST BE AROUND HERE SOMEWHERE! I DON'T KNOW WHY, BUT SOMETHING'S AFTER ME!
Huff!
THAT BELL IS YOURS...
USE IT! FIGHT! USE YOUR FISTS!
I'M HERE TO PROTECT YOU.
TRUST ME.

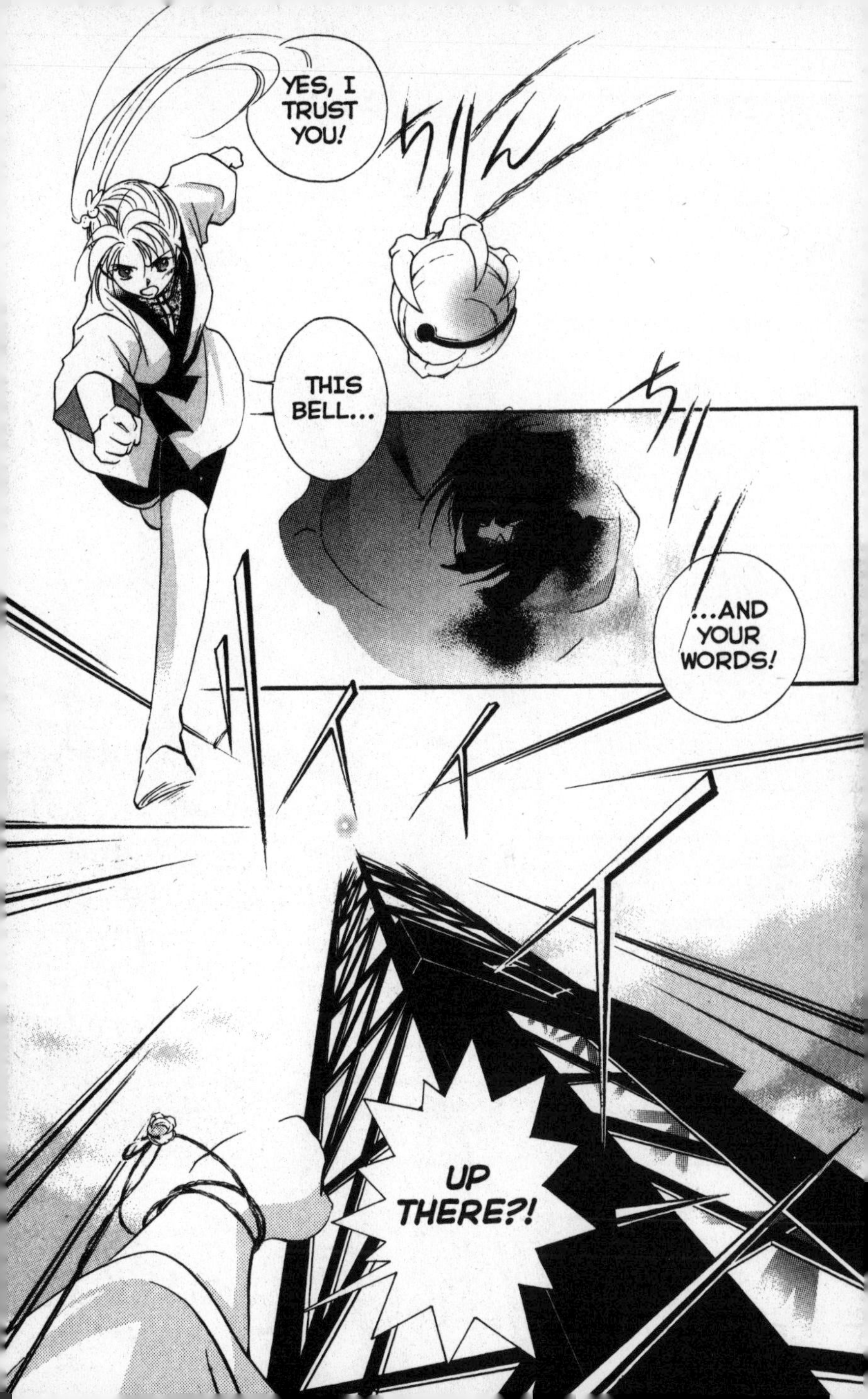
YES, I TRUST YOU!
ちりん
THIS BELL...
ちり
...AND YOUR WORDS!
UP THERE?!

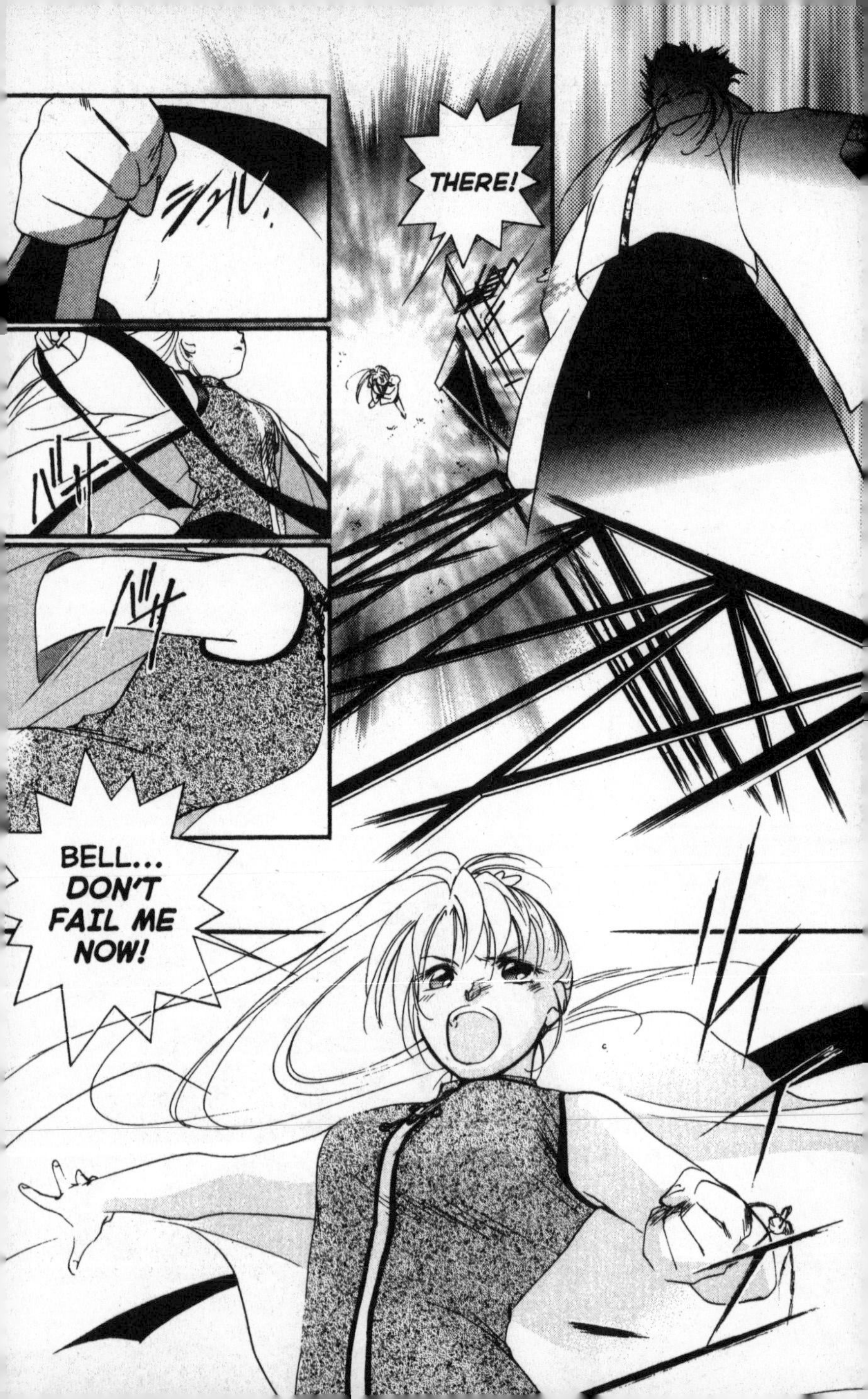
THERE!
BELL... DON'T FAIL ME NOW!

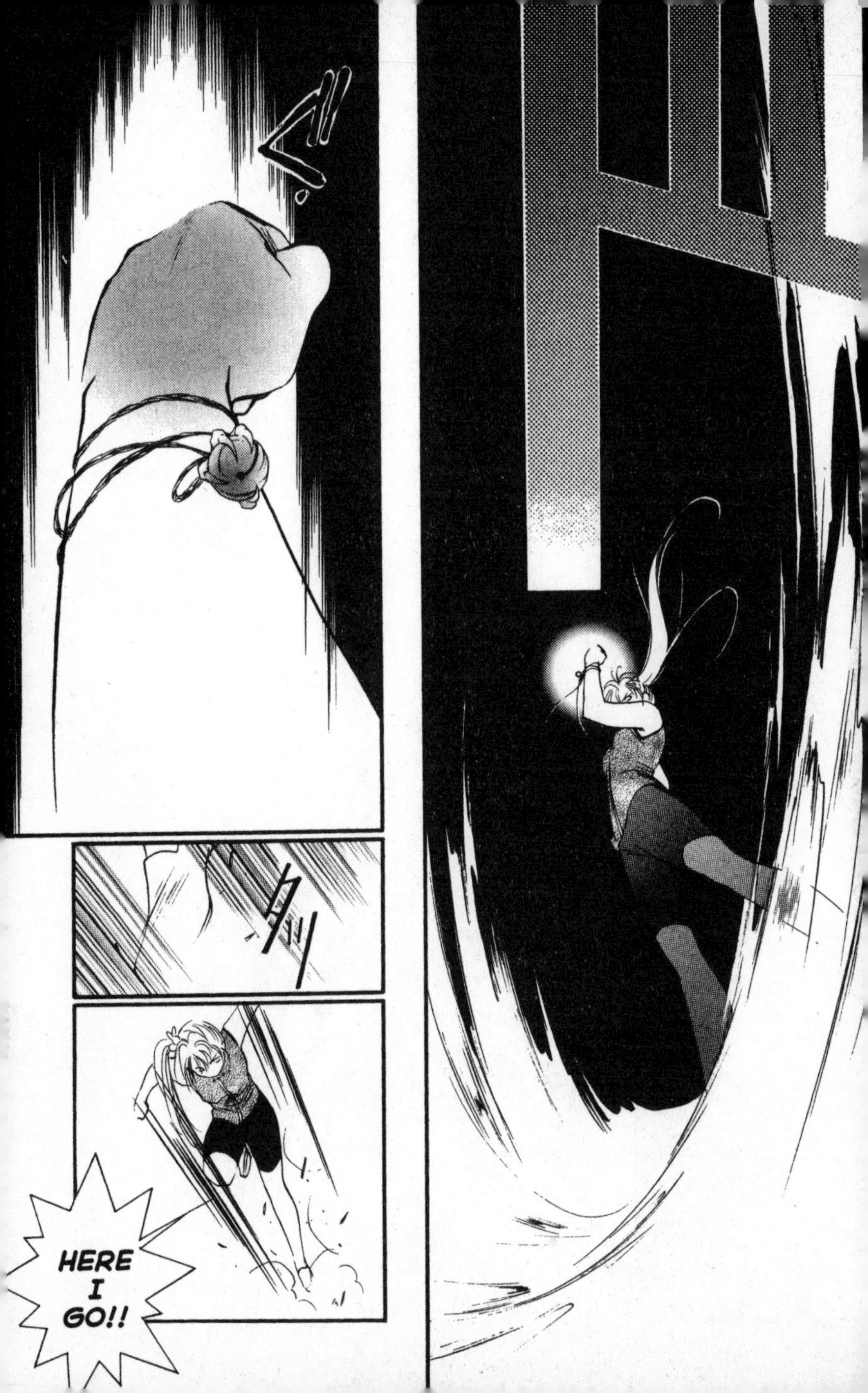
HERE I GO!!

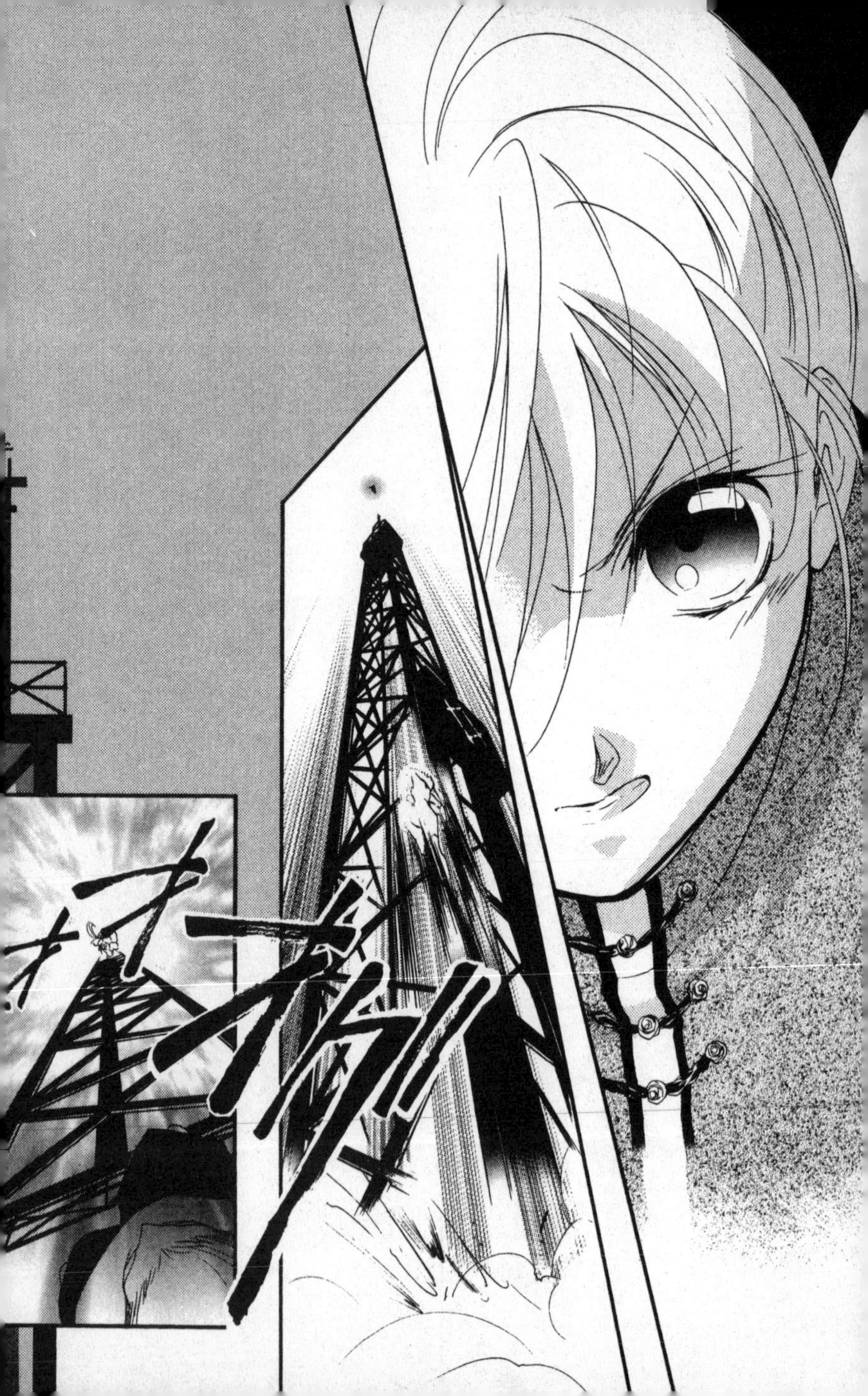

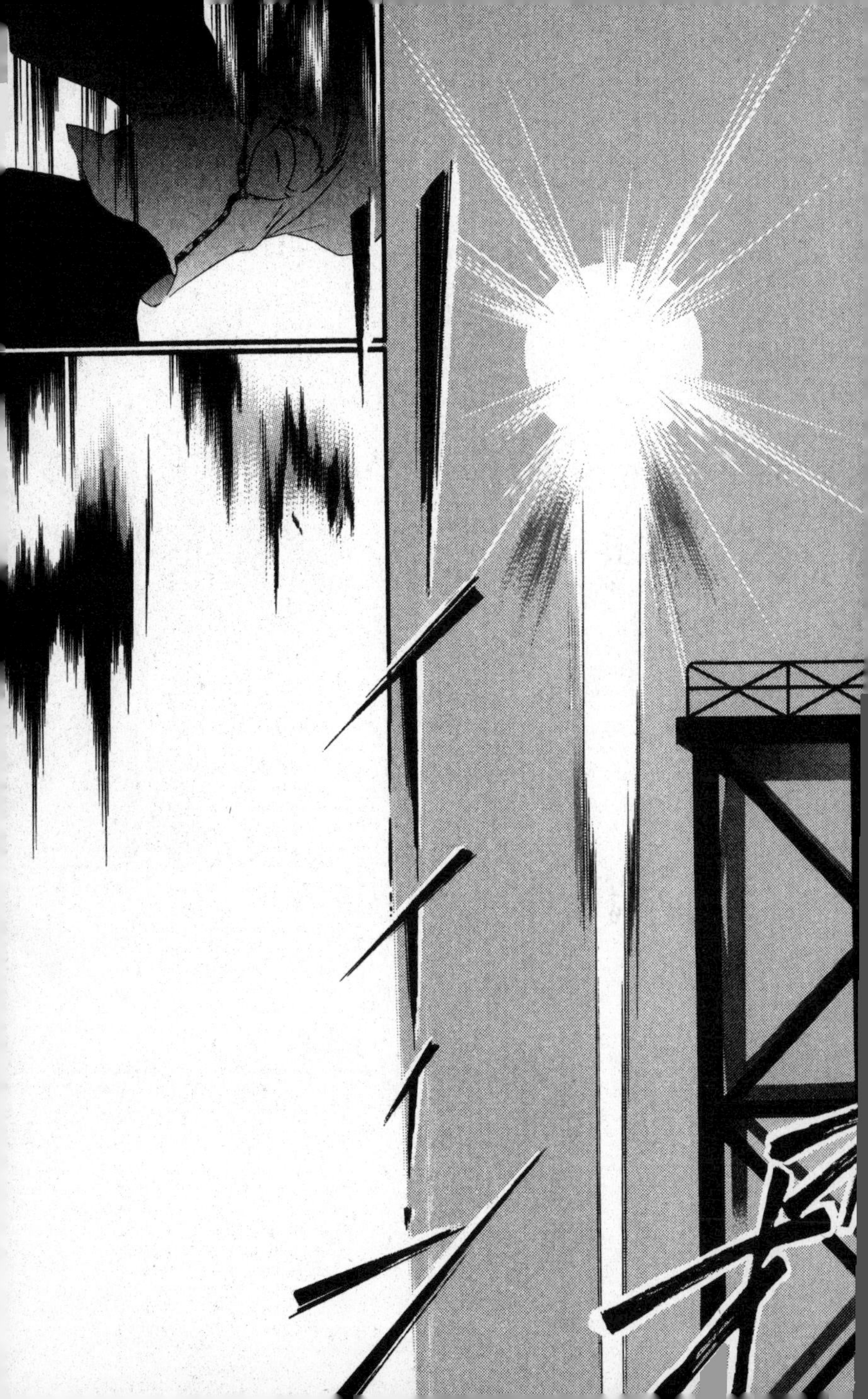

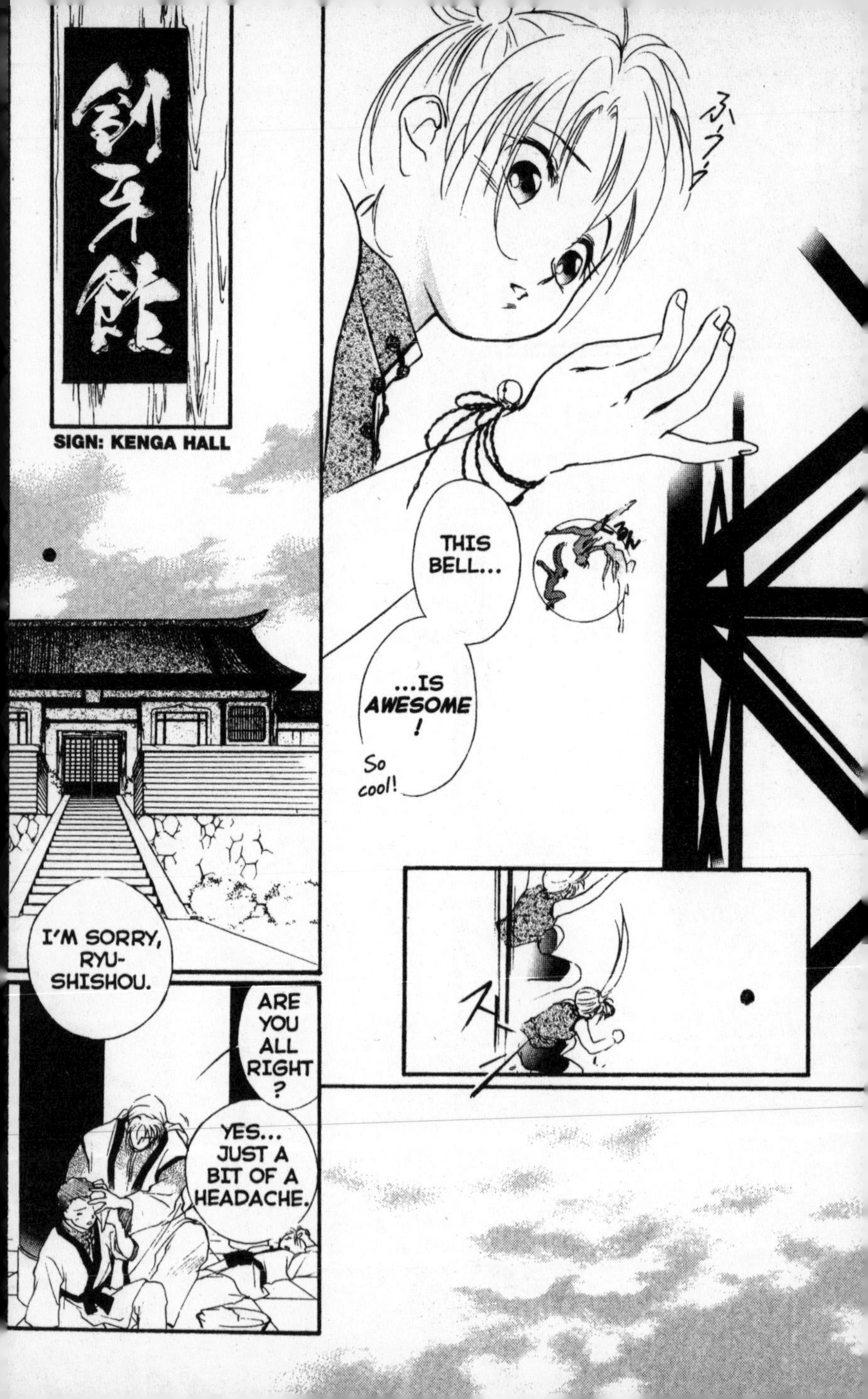

THIS BELL...
...IS AWESOME!
So cool!
SIGN: KENGA HALL
I'M SORRY, RYU-SHISHOU.
ARE YOU ALL RIGHT?
YES... JUST A BIT OF A HEADACHE.

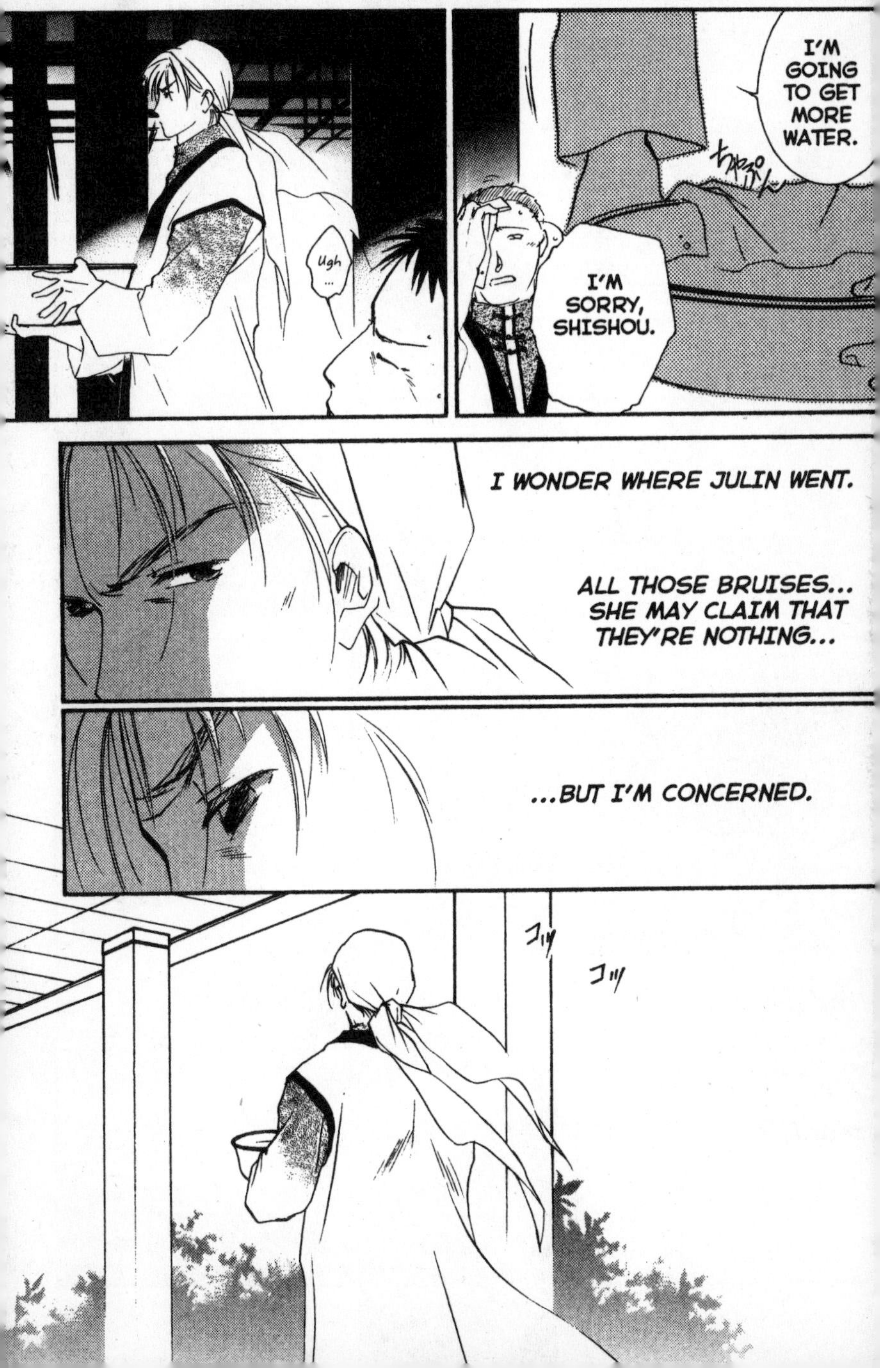
I'M GOING TO GET MORE WATER.
I'M SORRY, SHISHOU.
Ugh...
I WONDER WHERE JULIN WENT.
ALL THOSE BRUISES... SHE MAY CLAIM THAT THEY'RE NOTHING...
...BUT I'M CONCERNED.
コッ
コッ

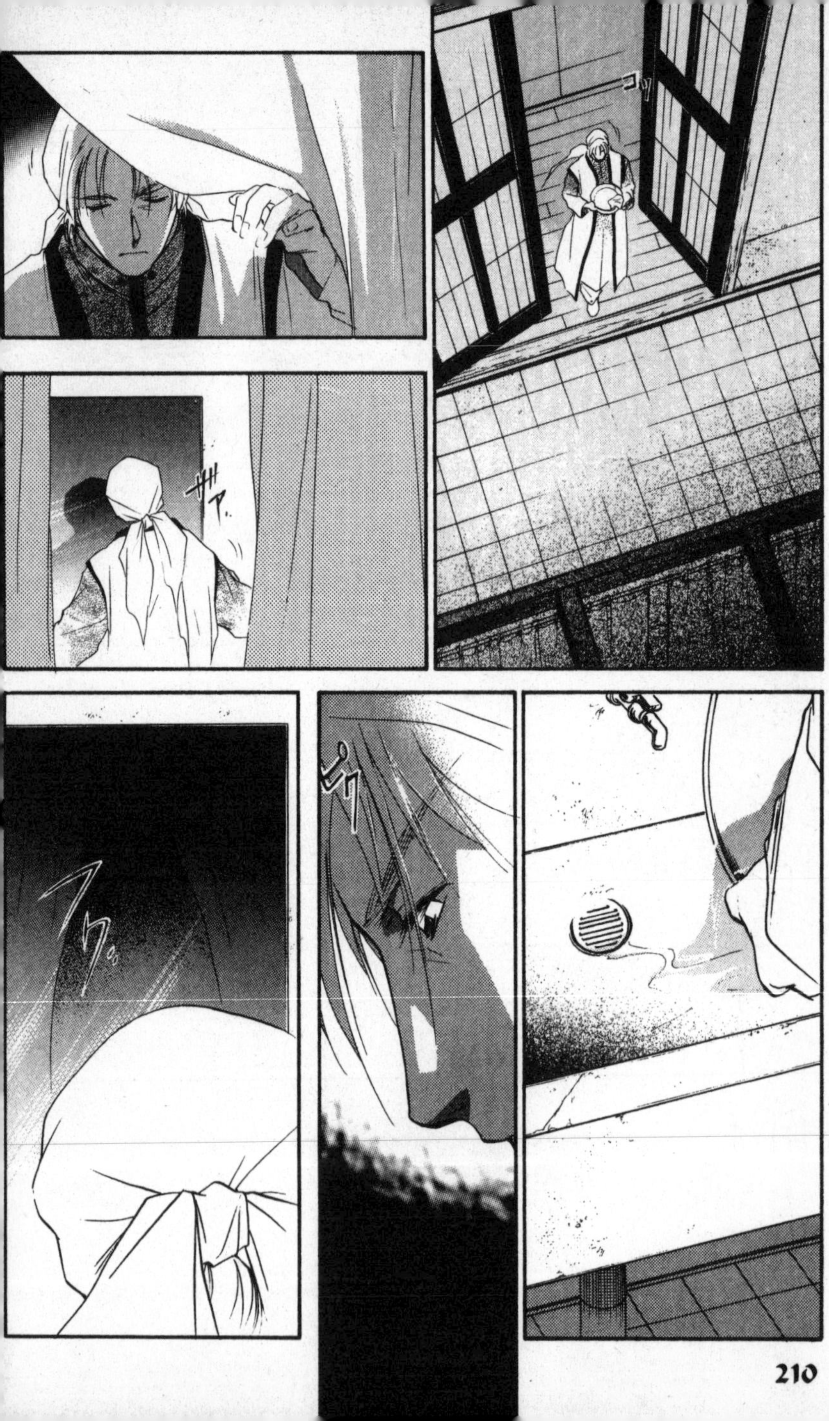
ザァ..
ピク

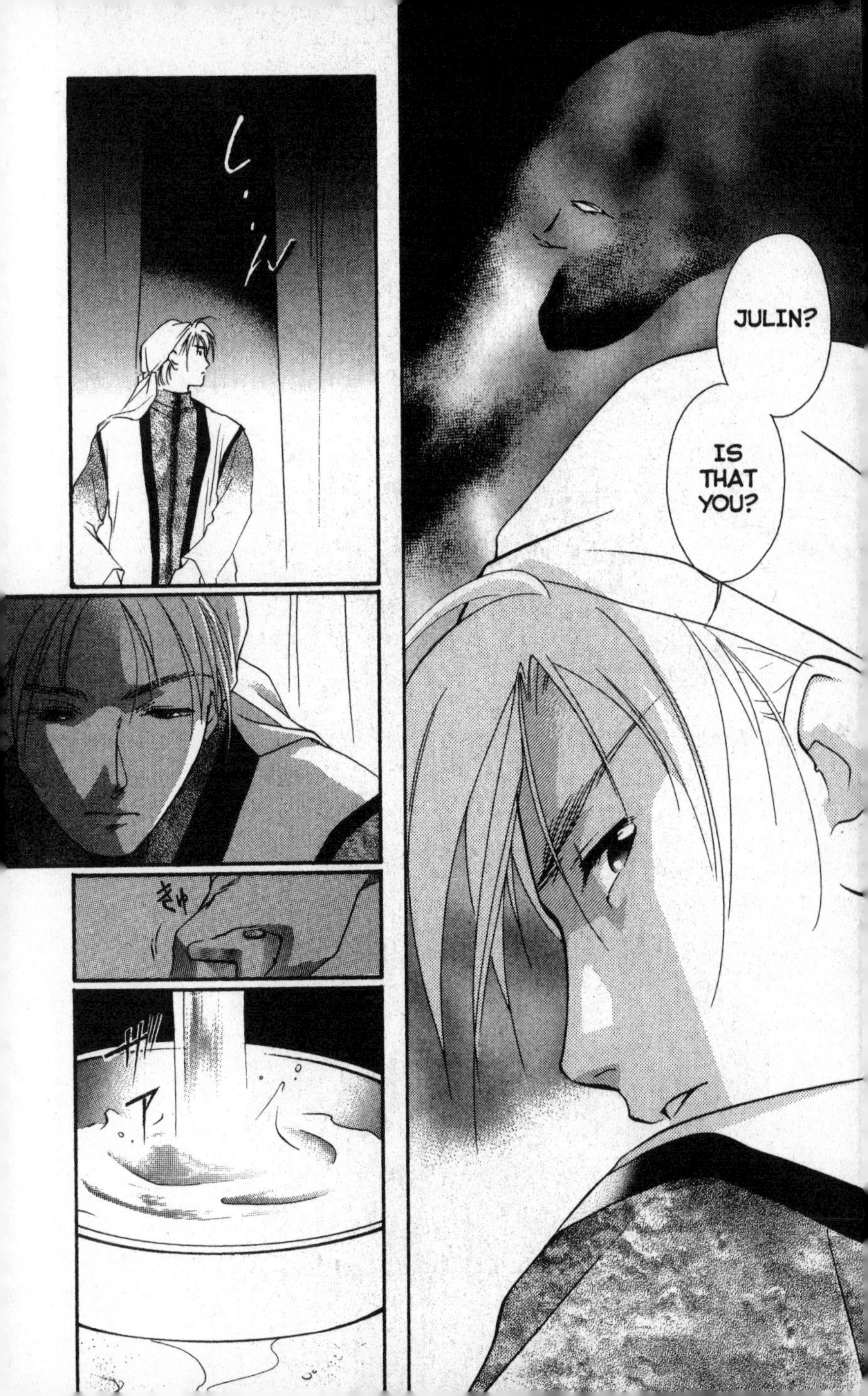
JULIN?
IS THAT YOU?
きゅ

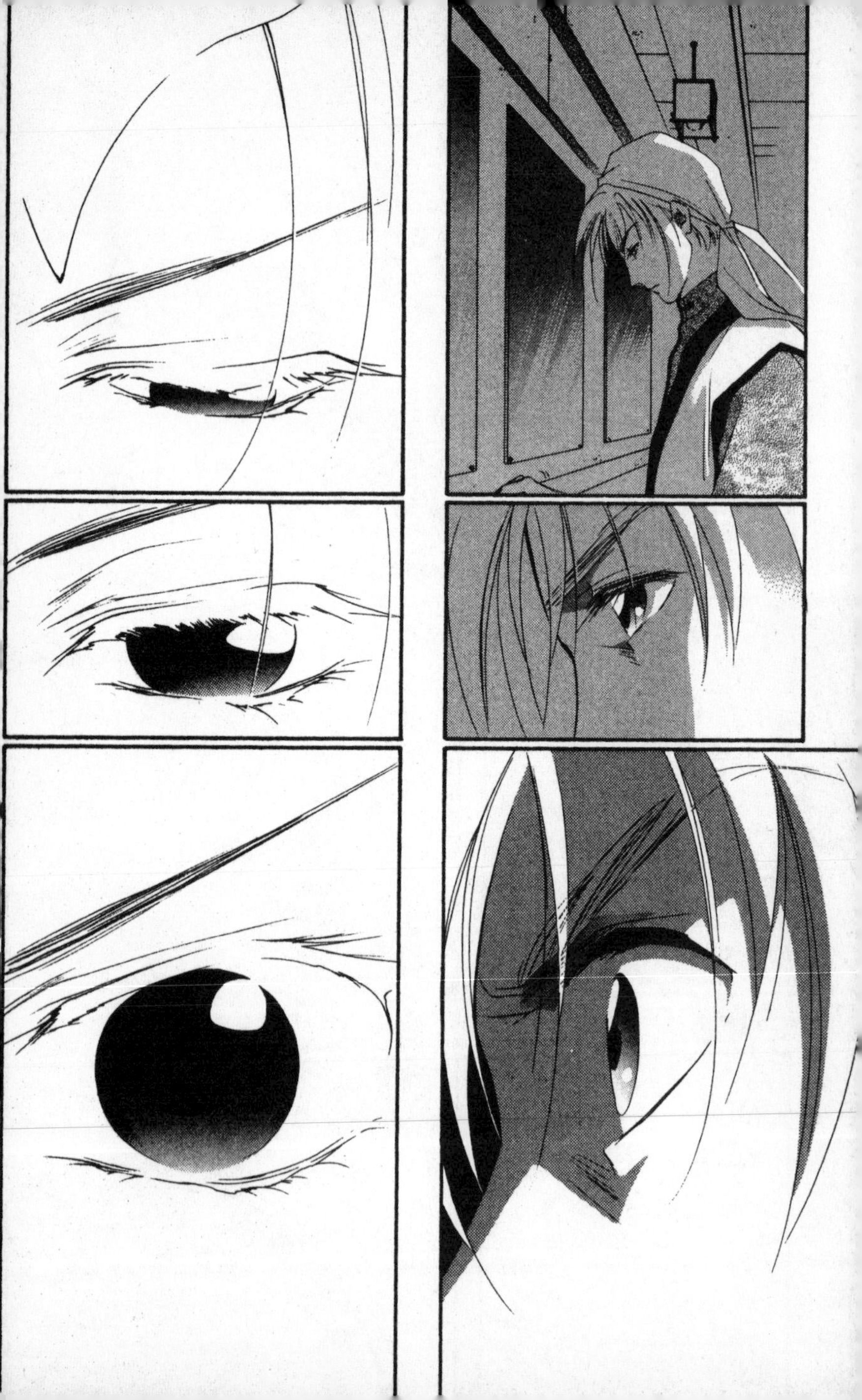

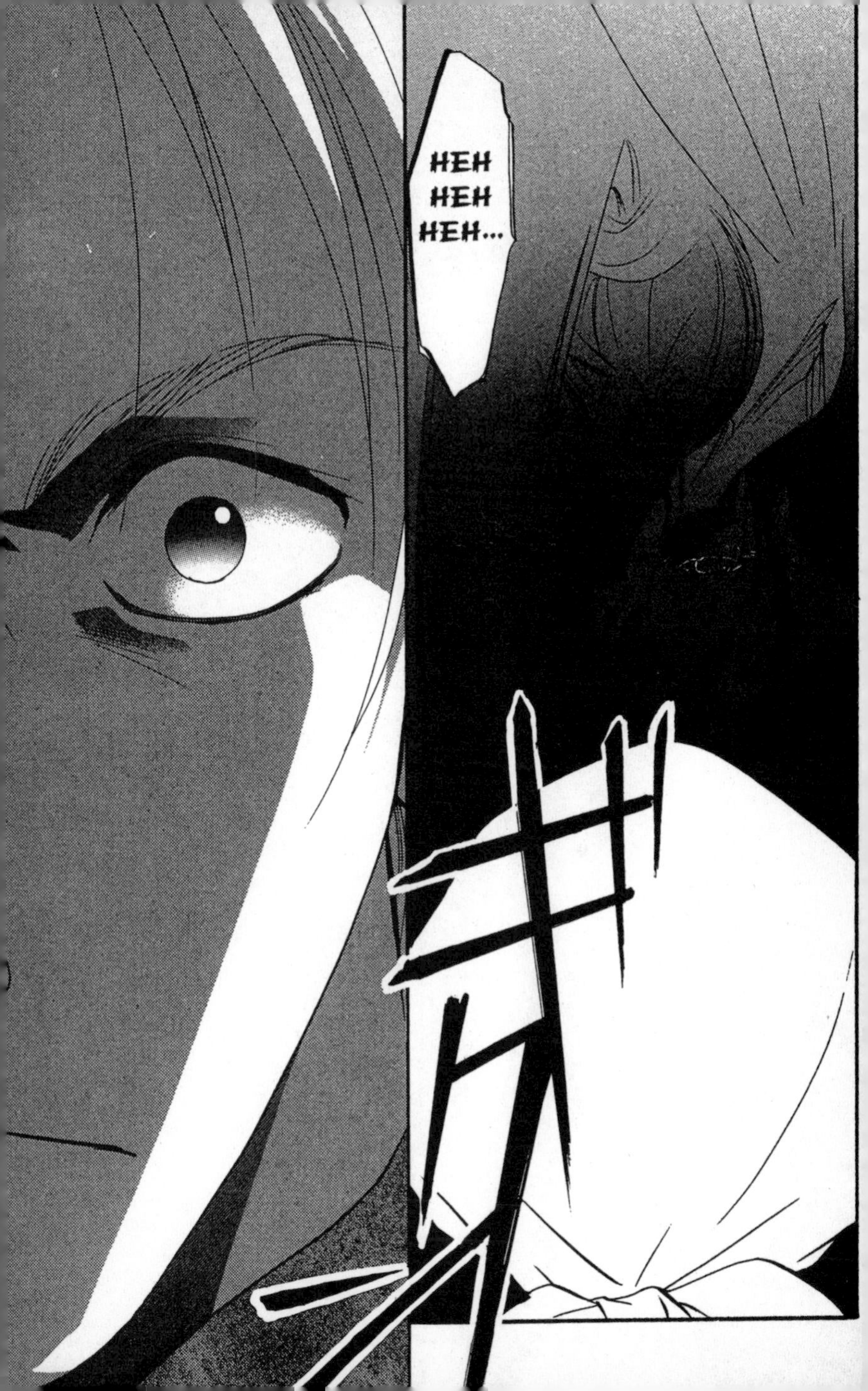
HEH HEH HEH...

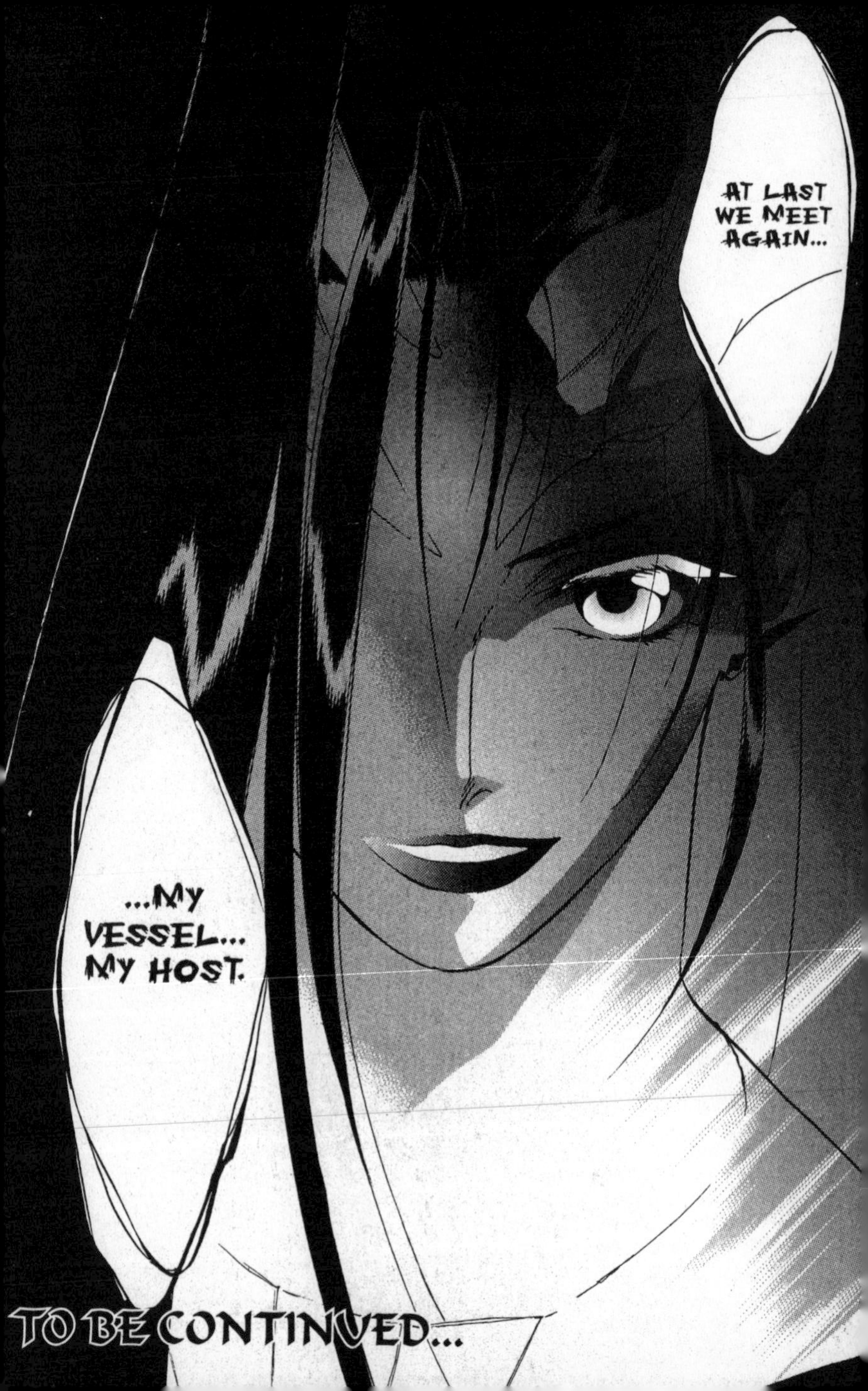
AT LAST WE MEET AGAIN...
...MY VESSEL... MY HOST.
TO BE CONTINUED...

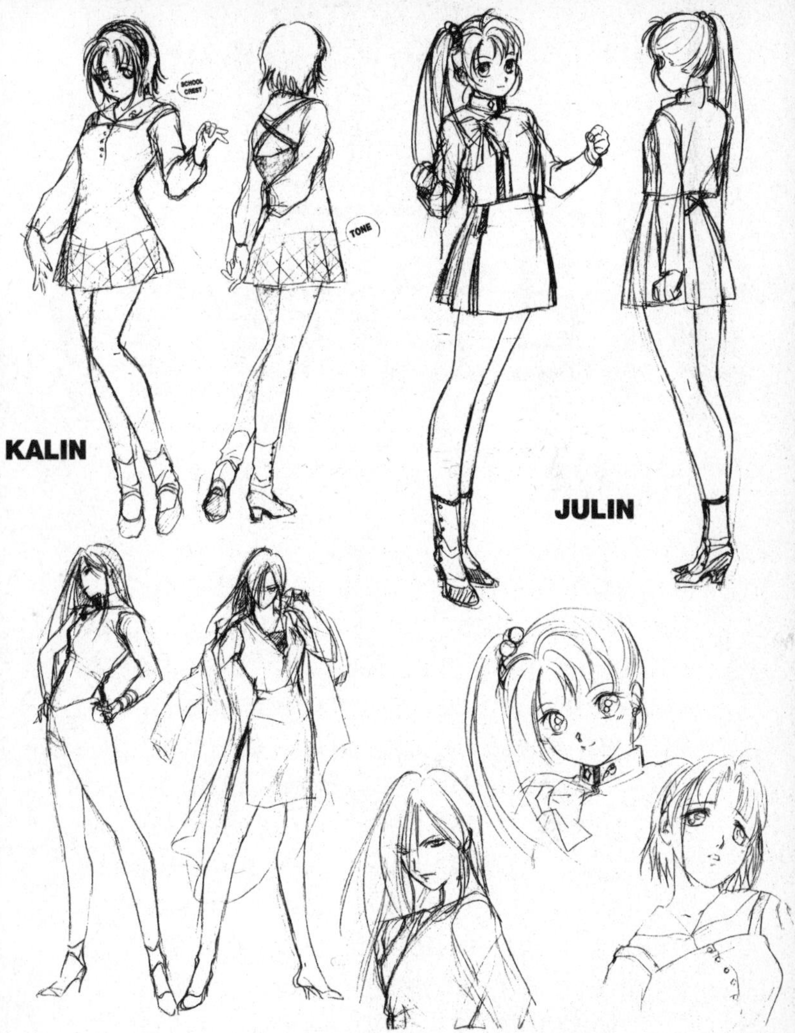
SCHOOL CREST
TONE
KALIN
JULIN

I based *Shaolin Sisters Reborn's* modern-day setting on Yokohama and Kobe. The ocean, the town, and the mountains... Since the three sisters are living normal, everyday lives, Julin and Kalin would be going to high school and Seilin would be in college. Here I've sketched them in school uniforms.

I tested the colors on the cover pages, and the director told me, "They look kind of like military uniforms." I thought it might be nice to have it look bold and have the top and bottom be dark colors. I mean, I made them black—but does it really look like they're in the military?

## In the Next Volume of...

# Shaolin Sisters Reborn

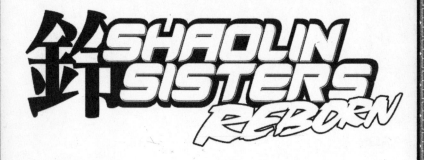

It is a dark time for humanity as one by one the White Lotus Four awaken and prepare for their master's revival. However, before Bai Wang can be resurrected, she'll need human energy—lots of it. Granted the power to absorb energy from the strongest of fighters, it will be up to the vile Shino to collect it. However, one man stands in his way: Drake. Will Julin's mysterious masked ally be able to stop Bai Wang's resurrection? Or is he merely putting off the inevitable? Find out as the saga of the Shaolin Sisters continues!

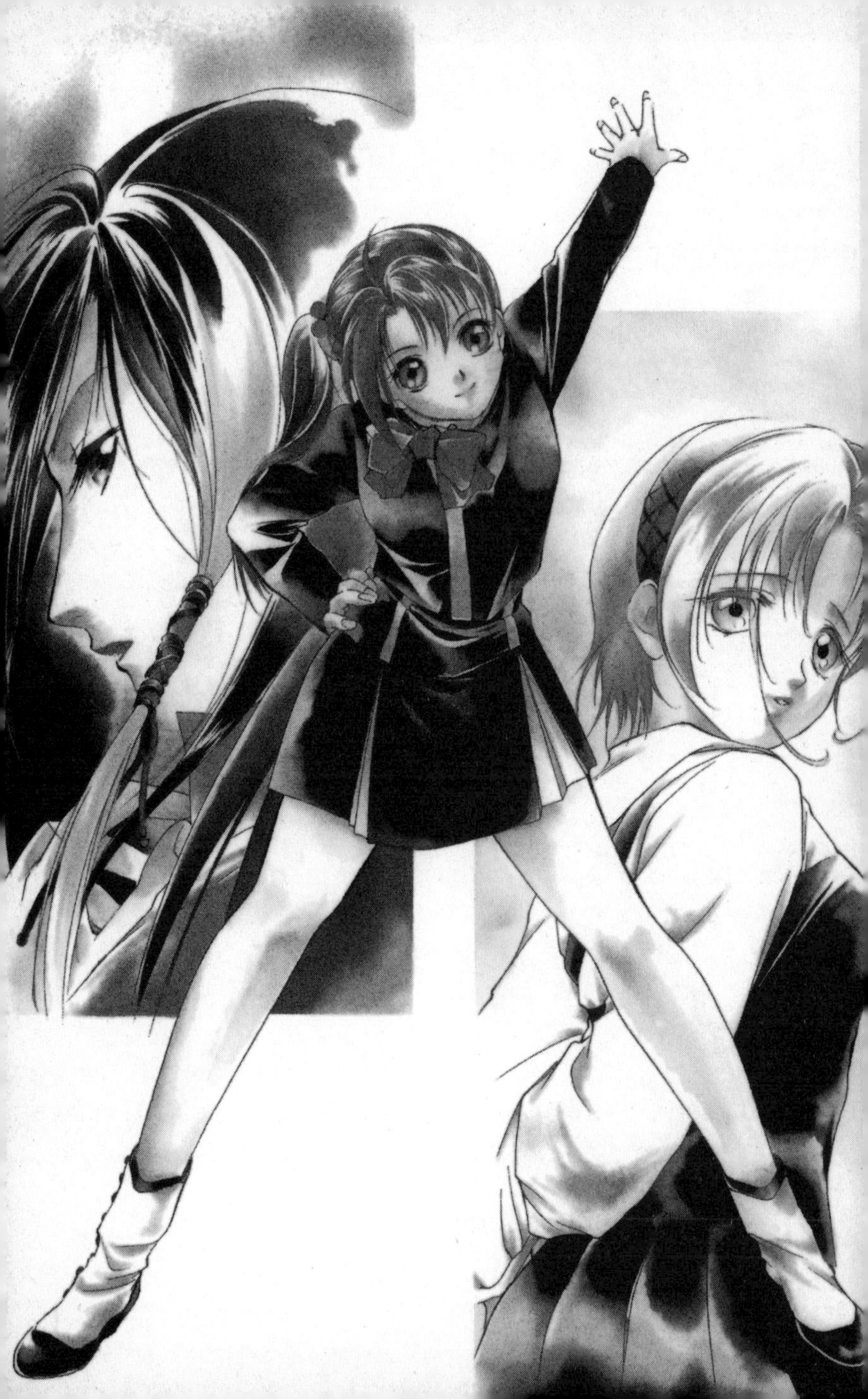

# TOKYOPOP SHOP

## WWW.TOKYOPOP.COM/SHOP

**HOT NEWS!**
Check out the
TOKYOPOP SHOP!
The world's best
collection of manga in
English is now available
online in one place!

## RG VEDA

## VISITOR

*Van Von Hunter*
and other hot
titles are available
at the store that
never closes!

# VAN VON HUNTER

- **LOOK FOR SPECIAL OFFERS**
- **PRE-ORDER UPCOMING RELEASES!**
- **COMPLETE YOUR COLLECTIONS**

## BLAZIN' BARRELS

Sting may look harmless and naïve, but he's really an excellent fighter and a wannabe bounty hunter in the futuristic Wild West. When he comes across a notice that advertises a reward for the criminal outfit named Gold Romany, he decides that capturing the all-girl gang of bad guys is his ticket to fame and fortune!

### MIN-SEO PARK HAS CREATED ONE WILD TUMBLEWEED TALE FILLED WITH ADVENTURE GALORE AND PLENTY OF SHOTGUN ACTION!

© MIN-SEO PARK, DAIWON C.I. Inc.

Y YOUTH AGE 10+

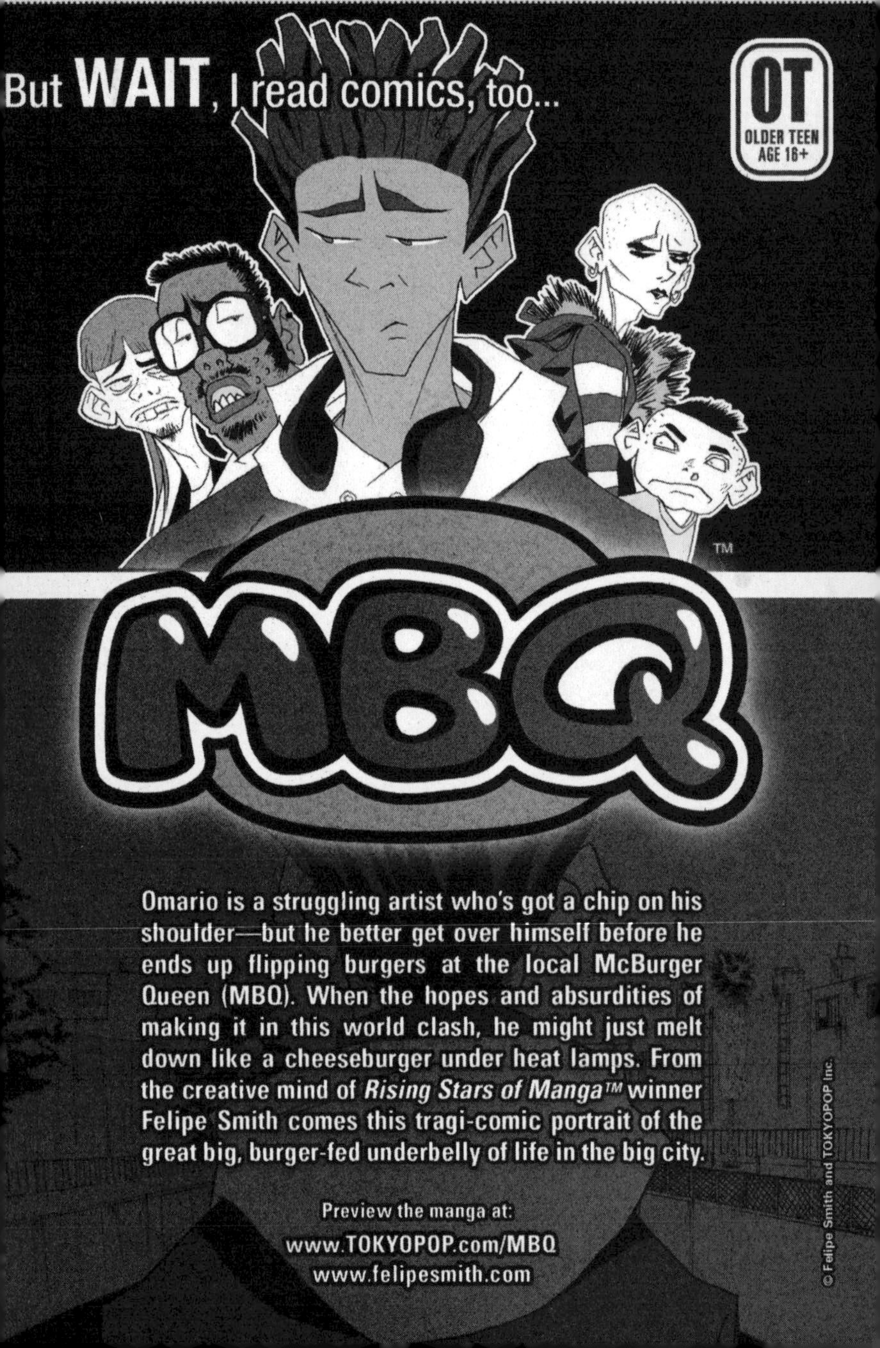
But WAIT, I read comics, too...
OT
OLDER TEEN
AGE 16+
TM
MBQ
Omario is a struggling artist who's got a chip on his shoulder—but he better get over himself before he ends up flipping burgers at the local McBurger Queen (MBQ). When the hopes and absurdities of making it in this world clash, he might just melt down like a cheeseburger under heat lamps. From the creative mind of *Rising Stars of Manga™* winner Felipe Smith comes this tragi-comic portrait of the great big, burger-fed underbelly of life in the big city.
Preview the manga at:
www.TOKYOPOP.com/MBQ
www.felipesmith.com
© Felipe Smith and TOKYOPOP Inc.

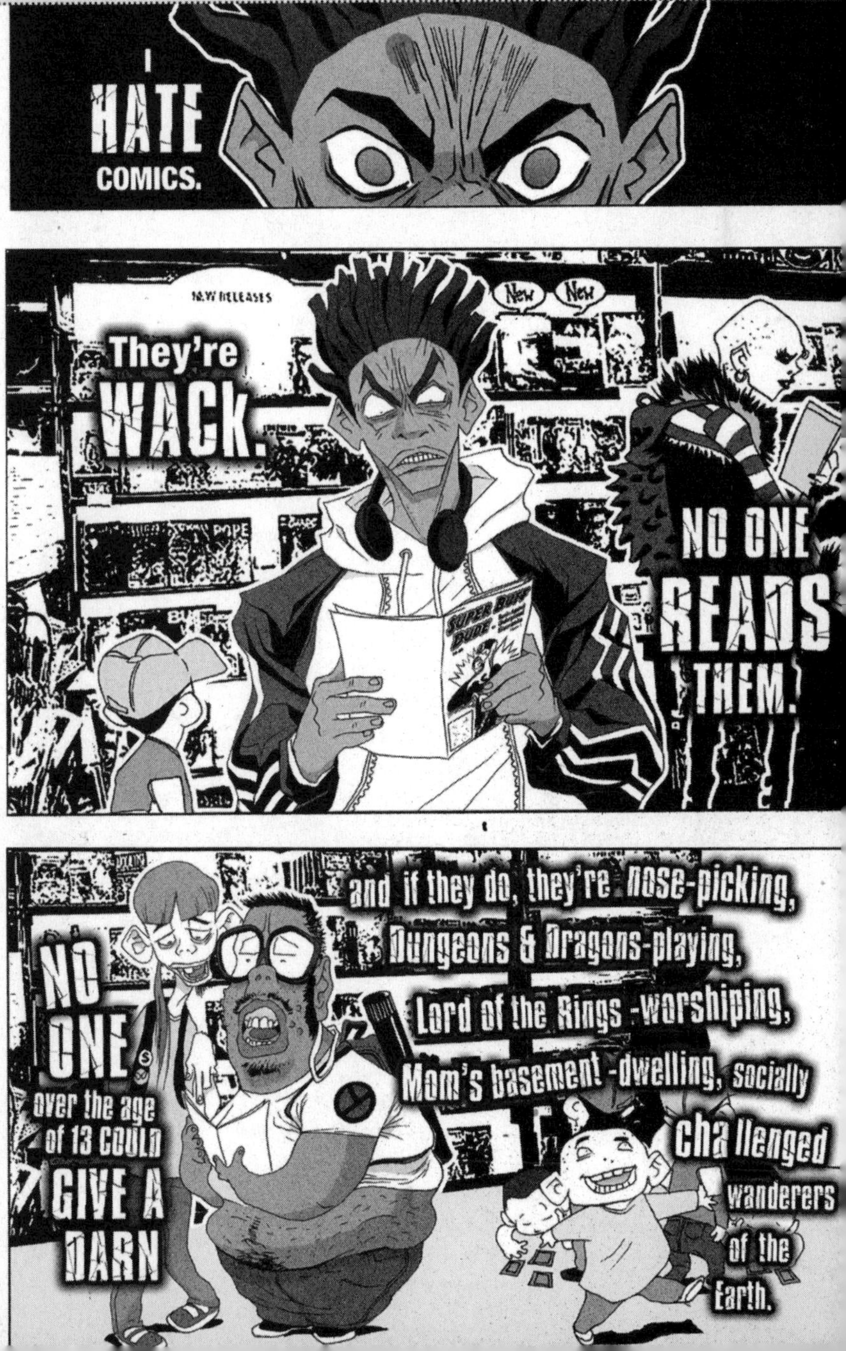
I
HATE
COMICS.
They're
WACK.
NO ONE
READS
THEM.
and if they do, they're nose-picking,
Dungeons & Dragons-playing,
Lord of the Rings -worshiping,
Mom's basement -dwelling, socially
challenged
wanderers
of the
Earth.
NO
ONE
over the age
of 13 COULD
GIVE A
DARN

# EDITORS' PICKS

TOKYOPOP MANGA SUPPLEMENT

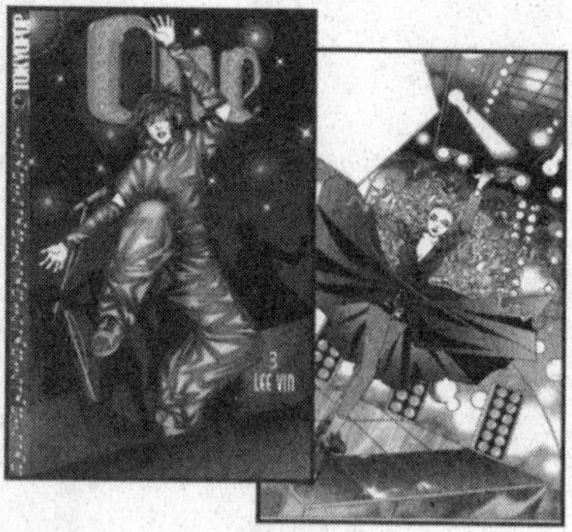
TOKYOPOP
3
LEE VIN

BY LEE VIN

## ONE

Like American Idol? Then you'll love *One*, an energetic manga that gives you a sneak peek into the pop music industry. Lee Vin, who also created *Crazy Love Story*, is an amazingly accomplished artist! The story centers on the boy band One, a powerhouse of good looks, hot moves, and raw talent. It also features Jenny You, a Britney-Avril hybrid who's shooting straight for the top. But fame always comes at a price—and their path to stardom is full of speed bumps and roadblocks. But no matter what happens, they keep on rockin'—and so does this manga!

~Julie Taylor, Sr. Editor

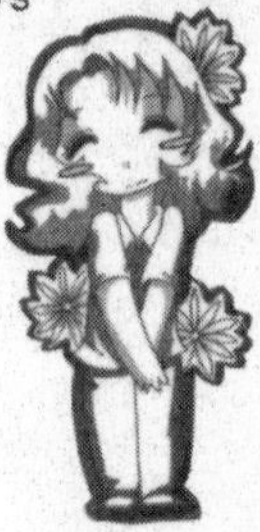

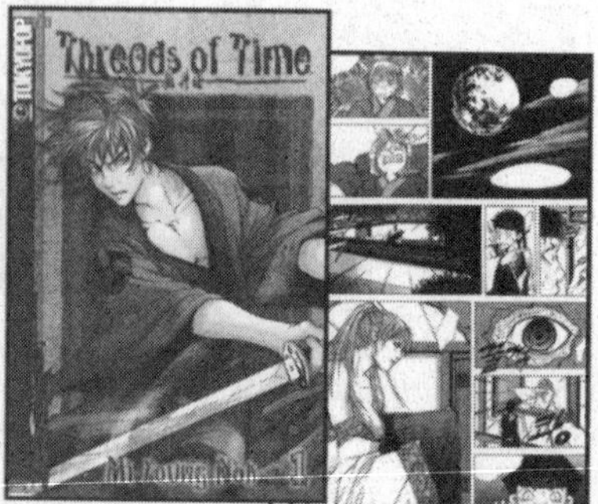
TOKYOPOP
Threads of Time

BY MI-YOUNG NOH

## THREADS OF TIME

The best thing about *Threads of Time* is its richly dramatic depiction of Korea's struggle to push back the Mongol Hordes in the 13th century. The plot focuses on a 20th century boy who ends up back in time. However, this science fiction conceit retreats to the background of this thrilling adventure in war-torn ancient Korea. Imagine a Korean general riding into battle with a battery of twelve men against two hundred Mongol warriors! Imagine back-stabbing politicians murdered in the clear of night. Imagine an entire village raped and slaughtered by Mongol hounds only to be avenged by a boy who just failed his high school science test.

~Luis Reyes, Editor

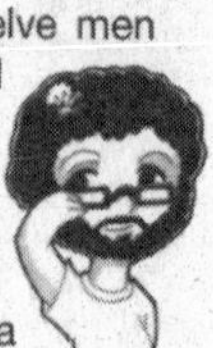